HARVARD ADVOCATE

CENTENNIAL

ANTHOLOGY

HARVARD ADVOCATE
CENTENNIAL
ANTHOLOGY

edited by Jonathan D. Culler

SCHENKMAN PUBLISHING CO., INC.
Cambridge, Massachusetts

Library of Congress Catalogue Card Number: 65–25588

PRINTED IN THE UNITED STATES OF AMERICA

ACKNOWLEDGMENTS

Thanks are due to all the authors who permitted us—some with considerable trepidation—to reprint their *Advocate* writings. In the preparation of the book many other debts have been incurred: Gerald Hillman, former president of the magazine, first conceived of the book and provided the impetus during its early stages. John Foster, Jamie Rosenthal, Richard Papper, Peter Jaszi, and other members of the *Advocate* board helped in the selection of material and the preparation of the book. Mr. Kimball Elkins of the Widener Library Archives helped us track down photographs and lost issues. Stuart Davis, president of the *Advocate*, offered indispensable criticism and suggestions at all stages, and Susan Evans of the Schenkman Publishing Company pulled all the loose ends together into a volume.

JDC

CREDITS

"Wedding Party" from *Exiles and Marriages* by Donald Hall, copyright 1950 by Donald Hall. Reprinted by permission of The Viking Press, Inc.

"Songs from a Picaresque Romance" by John Hollander, reprinted from *A Crackling of Thorns* by permission of The Yale University Press.

"The Wood-Weasel" by Marianne Moore, reprinted from her *Collected Poems* by permission of The Macmillan Company.

"Mrs. Alfred Uruguay," "Asides on the Oboe," "Of Bright and Blue Birds and the Gala Sun," and "Examination of the Hero in a Time of War," by Wallace Stevens, reprinted with the permission of the publisher, Alfred A. Knopf, Inc., from *The Collected Poems of Wallace Stevens*, copyright 1954.

The translation of "Roosters" by Boris Pasternak, copyright 1943, reprinted with the permission of Babette Deutsch.

Photographs of Theodore Roosevelt, Wallace Stevens, Conrad Aiken, E. E. Cummings, and Norman Mailer courtesy of Harvard Archives, Widener Library.

Photograph of T. S. Eliot from the Eliot Collection, Houghton Library.

LIST OF ILLUSTRATIONS

TABLE OF CONTENTS

THE LAST TWO DECADES: 1947–1966

Neo-Platonic love

INTRODUCTION

One hundred years ago, near midnight on May 10, 1866, two students crept through Harvard Yard tacking posters to the walls of the dormitories, University Hall, and even the President's house:

A New College Paper
for sale at Richardson's bookstore
Tomorrow

Meanwhile the paper's editor-in-chief, F. P. Stearns, had fallen asleep and "cared little whether I was suspended or not." The secrecy and sense of peril that surrounded this first issue of the *Advocate,* as the new paper was called, were not unwarranted, for the *Advocate* was successor to the *Collegian,* a lively fortnightly paper founded several months earlier, which had ventured a bit too far in attacking compulsory chapel and in alluding, without due respect, to certain venerable professors. The faculty had come to terms with the *Collegian* and its criticisms simply by forbidding its editors, C. S. Gage and W. G. Peckham, to publish another issue on pain of expulsion. Stearns had proposed the *Advocate* as a substitute, dispensing with his friends' services for their own safety. He enlisted the help of E. W. Fox who felt it intolerable that the students of Harvard College should not be able to express their views in print, and together they designed a paper to "advocate" the students' interests. Exulting in the uncertainty of their position, they adopted as mottoes "Dulce est periculum" and "Veritas nihil veretur"— "Danger is sweet," and "Truth fears nothing."

Actually the first issue of the *Advocate* proved less belligerent than its mottoes might suggest. The contents were innocuous enough: the mild suggestion that perhaps the faculty had been a bit hasty in banning the *Collegian,* together with a flippant allusion to the seven weighty objections which they had raised. "What we propose is to publish a paper in spite of the fate of our lamented predecessor and regardless of the seven lumps of wisdom."

The first issue was a great success and sold out by noon the next day. It only remained for the editors to wait until Monday when the faculty met and would determine the fate of the *Advocate.* Stearns spent the evening in his room.

A little after ten p.m. I heard rushing feet on the stairs and Peckham's vigorous knock on the door. With cool audacity he had interviewed the President himself on the way home from the faculty meeting. Dr. Hill had said that there had been some discussion concerning the *Advocate,* but that the faculty had finally decided to drop the question for the present and let the paper live and die on its own merits. "I have read it myself," he said, "and I liked it very well. There is one poem in it which is really excellent—'You Kissed Me in My Dreams' by a young lady of Cambridge—only it is perhaps a trifle too amorous."

The first dangers were past. There was a celebration in Gage's rooms to welcome the *Collegian's* editors back to respectability. The *Advocate* had won its first battle by a combination of good taste and good luck. Now it needed a purpose beyond survival.

❖   ❖   ❖

Like Dr. Hill, we value the *Advocate* more for the literature it has published than for its original polemics. But for the first few years it was primarily a bi-weekly newspaper. It reported football and baseball games, criticized college policy, printed staunchly traditional verses, and nipped slyly at the more venerable members of the faculty. From the first the tone was literary and refined; each piece tried to suggest a bold yet erudite author, and each was signed with a tasteful initial or latin pseudonym: "Loquax" or "Non Antiquus." Editorials were important. Compulsory chapel, the issue which had helped to give birth to the magazine, remained a favorite topic until chapel was finally made voluntary. There were editorials supporting an elective curriculum, proposing the admission of women to the college, attacking the university bookstore's monopoly, and castigating Walt Whitman's barbaric yawp: "nobody can force us to drink from the polluted bucket which a maniac has filled." There were other topics of current interest: "The Matthews pump has been without a handle for at least three weeks, and the southern part of the Yard is very much inconvenienced." When Wallace Stevens became President in 1900 he proposed that a fence be built around the yard.

Putting a fence around the Yard strikes us as being the easiest way of achieving order out of chaos. . . . The Yard would regain the hold on our imagination which it is gradually losing.

And he proposed a reform in cheers:

The present Harvard cheer, while it has an awesome voluminousness, is hardly the thing for contests which demand sharp, powerful cheers at crises. The present cheer, with its first three breath-consuming "Harvards" followed by nine enthusiastic "rahs," generally brings up with a gasp on the last "Harvard." It has to be coaxed; we need a cheer that would be irresistible.

He proposed simply "nine long 'Harvards.'" The *Advocate* has always been concerned with style.

Initially the *Advocate* was Harvard's only student publication, but in 1873 the Harvard *Crimson* was founded and the two papers vied for circulation and copy. At one time they nearly merged but the project was defeated by one vote—from the *Advocate* board, one is pleased to note. Not until the *Crimson* became a daily in 1884 did today's sharp distinction between the two journals begin to arise. And the cleavage in function—news, comments and *kitsch* to the *Crimson*, belles-lettres and "weighty" reviews to the *Advocate*—has resulted in sharp differences in tone: the newspaper is by turns cynical, fanatic, and awesomely professional, while the magazine has usually chosen to present its offerings through a dry and occasionally pompous editorial persona.

The *Advocate* came into its own as a literary magazine in the 1880's when it gave up its reportorial functions and welcomed to its pages a group of very literary undergraduates who were shortly to become famous. Edwin Arlington Robinson wrote poems for the *Advocate* which he later included in *The Children of the Night*. Other distinguished contributors included Albert Bushnell Hart, George Lyman Kittredge ("Kitty" to later generations of Harvard students), Charles Townshend Copeland, another of Harvard's great teachers, and the poets Witter Bynner and William Vaughan Moody. But the real Age of Giants came in the first decade of this century. At a time when Lowell and Longfellow still reigned in drawing rooms, T. S. Eliot, Wallace Stevens, and Conrad Aiken were developing in the *Advocate* some of the techniques that would revitalize English and American poetry in a few years.

The Eliot of the *Advocate*—largely unknown today, due to his reluctance to be republished—is a critic's delight, for with remarkable clarity his early lyrics show him developing into the poet of "Prufrock," the tired, slightly bored narrative voice capable of articulating only dried emotions. "Nocturne," published in 1909, is animated by Eliot's satiric transpositions of classical figures and scenes:

> Romeo, *grand sérieux*, to importune
> Guitar and hat in hand, beside the gate
> With Juliet, in the usual debate
> Of love, beneath the bored but courteous moon . . .

"Spleen," a slightly later effort, is even more of a warm-up exercise for "Prufrock."

> Sunday: this satisfied procession
> Of definitely Sunday faces;
> Bonnets, silk hats, and conscious graces
> In repetition that displaces
> Your mental self-possession
> By this unwarranted digression.
>
> Evening, lights, and tea,
> Children and cats in the alley;
> Dejection unable to rally
> Against this dull conspiracy.
>
> And Life, a little bald and grey,
> Waits, hat and gloves in hand,
> Languid, fastidious, and bland,
> Punctilious to tie and suit
> (Somewhat impatient of delay)
> On the doorstep of the Absolute.

All is here: the effete, "proper" diction, the deflating modifiers, the devices of pastiche and personification. What changed? Only the dramatization. Rather than describe "Life," Eliot went on to create J. Alfred Prufrock who would hesitatingly describe himself.

Wallace Stevens' case is different. He published almost nothing for twenty years after graduating from Harvard, and it is hard to relate the mature poet to the curious young man who published these uncompromisingly slight lyrics and short stories in the *Advocate* at the turn of the century. A diligent reader, indeed, might find in the *Advocate* writings patterns of thought that came to the surface later. The fence around Harvard Yard would "achieve order out of chaos" because the Yard would "regain the hold on our imagination which it is gradually losing." Later in poems like "The Idea of Order at Key West" and in his writings on poetry, this doctrine would emerge; the imagination would create order through poetry instead of fences. One can also compare the fluttering pigeons of "Street Songs" with those of "Sunday Morning:"

> At evening, casual flocks of pigeons make
> Ambiguous undulations as they sink,
> Downward to darkness, on extended wings.

In some ways, however, Stevens the insurance executive is more nearly typical of the *Advocate*'s personality. Longstanding financial problems—the magazine has never been subsidized or endowed on any regular basis—have compelled editors to think simultaneously in terms of both literary and economic values. Perhaps it was during his presidency that Stevens developed the dual sensibility that was to enable him to become both a vastly successful business executive and a major poet.

❖   ❖   ❖

As well as publishing a magazine the *Advocate* provided a gathering place for Cambridge literati, and from the earliest days there were parties, readings, and discussions in the sanctums of the various buildings which the magazine chose to call home—first in 19 Holworthy Hall; then, after years of wandering, on the top floor of the Freshman Union, and later, at 24 Holyoke Street, where the polished tankards hanging in rows gave the room the look of a Dutch kitchen; then at 40 Bow Street in a clean frame building near the site of today's *Lampoon* Castle; and finally at 21 South Street, where the Charles River used to run before its course was artificially shifted toward Brighton. At the old gatherings alumni like Teddy Roosevelt, Kittredge, and Copeland would drop in and talk far into the night.

There were formal reunions as well. The decennial celebration in 1876 put the then-prosperous magazine so far in debt to the Parker House Hotel that several later boards were forced to strive and skimp to pay for a party they never enjoyed. But the biggest gathering of alumni—both famous and obscure—came in 1916 at the anniversary dinner that marked the *Advocate's* first half-century. President Lowell of Harvard addressed more than one hundred graduate editors, and the students retaliated by presenting a mock faculty meeting with a slightly absurd Lowell presiding. Then an impersonator of Theodore Roosevelt arrived and the evening continued with the songs, mock speeches, and clumsy gaiety of reunions. The *Boston Evening Transcript* waxed eloquent over the event:

It would be difficult to find higher praise of the *Advocate's* birthday dinner than the testimony of the diners that it was a celebration worthy of the event. To launch a venture in the uncharted and rocky seas of the college periodical world, beset as they are with the dangers of a fickle student body and a fastidious faculty, and to see the same venture after fifty years still above water, still prevailing against an increasing competition, is an achievement in which every editor felt entitled to share.

BETWEEN THE WARS: 1916–1943

Despite the pressures of conscription and wartime shortages, the *Advocate* continued publication during the First World War—the only Harvard publication to do so. Even when the students in the college Military Training Corps were ordered to sever their connections with undergraduate papers, the *Advocate* persevered.

The only thing we are determined not to change is our literary standard. That this should be maintained, that there should be a sane continuity in the artistic life of the college, we feel to be a wartime duty. We feel, furthermore, that this duty devolves especially on the *Advocate*. She is the oldest of the college publications, she has kept the lamp burning in dark times before this, and fortune being willing, she shall be the last to die.

If, in its heroic defense of "sane continuity," the *Advocate* helped to make Harvard safe for poetry, she did very little with the opportunity during the next few years. Free verse, the *cause célèbre* of the literary world, meant whimsical formlessness and sordid realism to the *Advocate's* critics. "The undisguised unwholesomeness of the *new manner in poetry*," went a 1916 editorial, "we reject without more ado as unfit for human consumption." The modernist revolution was well underway, but not in Cambridge. The younger poets—Eliot, Pound, Cummings—

had fled to Europe, but by 1920 the *Dial* was publishing their work and providing American readers with alternatives to provincialism. The lines of dissension were being drawn in the *Advocate*'s spirited debates on free verse and throughout America. On one side was the *Dial*, which published "The Wasteland" in 1922 and awarded its annual prize during the next few years to Eliot, Marianne Moore, E. E. Cummings, William Carlos Williams, and Ezra Pound; on the other, the Pulitzer Prize committee, which relished Edwin Arlington Robinson's Arthurian romances and awarded him its prize three times in seven years.

Advocate poets, too, found themselves on the wrong side. Looking to Keats rather than Eliot, they engaged in what Robert Rockman called "sluggish excursions into beauty and truth."* Robert Hillyer's "The Question" is typical of the best poetry of this period. His Spenserian stanzas are polished and sonorous; his techniques are competent and quite conventional.

There were a few poets, though, at the beginning and end of this barren decade, who did not oppose modernism. In 1916 E. E. Cummings (see "The New Art," p. 101) gave *Advocate* readers something of a Cooks' tour through modern music, painting and poetry—particularly Imagist poetry, which he treats as the work of "sound painters" who "subordinate the meaning of words to the beauty of words themselves." His own undergraduate poetry, highly traditional and romantic though it is, makes some attempt to use words in a new way. In "Summer Silence" there are the phrases "sullen silver," "untranslated stars," "thirst-stricken" and "dumb-throated." Not quite the stuff of *Tulips and Chimneys*, but rarely had such attempts at verbal compression and linguistic novelty held any attraction at all for the undergraduate poet.

Malcolm Cowley, who sent back poems to the *Advocate* from his ambulance-duty in eastern France, is another who shows an awareness of possibilities: his "Theme with Variations" parodies and explores a variety of modern styles. He has written a poem four ways. A like control of language is evident in the sparse poignancy of "To a Dilettante Killed at Vimy."

After Cowley, then, ten barren years. It was not until 1930 that two undergraduate poets were able to create voices of their own out of the ferment and chaos of the period. James Agee and Robert Fitzgerald—

* *The Poetic Renaissance and Harvard: Studies in the Harvard Advocate, 1915–1930.* (Harvard Honors thesis, 1948).

two more different undergraduates can scarcely be imagined: Agee, the bard writing with Keatsian effusiveness; Fitzgerald, the craftsman working through a variety of forms and styles—sonnets, free verse, imagist poems centering on a classical allusion, a modernist poem on a locomotive. The violent aestheticism of Agee's poetry contrasts sharply with Fitzgerald's perfect control, his mastery of so many techniques, in "Sedes Ubi Fata Quietas." With Agee and Fitzgerald we are suddenly out of the desert. They are both able to use tradition to create something unique.

* * *

One reason that the *Advocate* had not excelled in poetry during the twenties was that its attention was turning outward; the magazine of precocious aestheticism became one of Harvard's links with national affairs and national public. Political consciousness—unspectacular as it may seem—came early, when in 1920 the editors requested campaign statements from both candidates for the Presidency, Harding and Cox. Cox produced a cheerfully irrelevant peroration on the subject of Honour, kissing all the political babies in sight, including soldiers, mothers, and college administrators. Harding's austere statement was a stylistic disaster:

Our need is now for less government and better government under those who are willing to gather and can command the best abilities of America to assist them in working out our problems and to prevent the results, so far as is possible, or injuries done to our American activities so grave that they may, unless averted, close the doors of American industries, paralyze the production of food, and turn American laborers into vain searching for employment.

In later articles Christian Herter analyzed the future of the Republican party; Henry Cabot Lodge, Jr. called for clear thinking on German reparations; Corliss Lamont pointed to the domination of Harvard by wealthy clubbies, creating a national furor; and T. S. Eliot wrote "The Problem of Education" especially for the *Advocate*. This temper continued in the 'thirties with Ezra Pound's vitriolic social criticism and Arthur M. Schlesinger, Jr.'s carefully reasoned articles on politics.

More symptomatic of the New Extroversion was the *Advocate's* penchant for making national headlines. At least a dozen times during the period between the wars the organization cashed in on the public's willingness to read about the exploits—serious and frivolous—of

Harvard students. In 1924 the magazine held a contest to find a suitable epithet for those who upheld the Eighteenth Amendment. Only shortly before, Harvard alumnus Delcever King had appealed for a damning title for the wets and from many entries had selected "scofflaw." With an irreverance for authority that was to become typical, the *Advocate* offered twenty-five dollars for an equally succinct smear on the "drys." A sixty-seven year old New York spinster, one of 3280 entrants from across the country, came up with "Spigot-Bigot," which finally won out over "cocktail flea," "Puritank," "cookie-pusher," and "dryrot." "Prohibition," Miss Welling told the *New York World*, "is what I call apron-strings. With it all identity, temperance, and will-power is lost." She donated her prize money to the Association Opposed to the Prohibition Amendment.

There were those who were not amused. Several alumni wrote the *Advocate* stern letters about breaking the law, and Amos R. Wells published a dismally unskilled poem in the *Christian Endeavor World* beginning

> So I'm a Spigot-Bigot because I uphold the law
> And because I'm trying to keep the young out of the
>   devil's maw

"I'm a Spigot-Bigot," he finally concluded, "and I glory in the name."

Parody issues were another means of catching the national eye, which they did with occasionally unexpected success. In 1924 a "Mirrors of Grub Street" issue included mock articles by GRG BRNRD SHW, RDYRD KPLNG, WLLM BTLR YTS, F. SCTT FTZGRLD, and others. The opening paragraphs of "A Personal Record" by JSPH CNRD read:

I had been sitting drowsily on the gunwale of my first ship, the Alba Longa, my feet hanging over into the pellucid water, my arms depending languidly from my shoulders, the point of my black beard urging its bristles into my hirsute chest, as my lungs palpitated with the hot steam which flowed through my nostrils. The obscure, half-slumber in which I had been indulging for an unpleasantly long, or an unpleasantly short time—one could not tell which from the dim memory of inestimable pulsations lingering in my consciousness —passed from me suddenly, vanished into the vapour which ascended about my face like the damp exhalation of a fen. I yawned vigorously, shook my hair, which clung in festoons from my forehead, an object at that time of my life both broad and flat. Awakened for the moment from my trance, I gazed at the humid expanse of water.

This issue was so successful that the following year the editors parodied the *Dial*. Prose by Oneway Waistcoat, poetry by O. O. Goings and Marianne Most, captured the magazine's *avant-garde* styles. And of course there was a piece by *Advocate* favorite, T. S. Tellatot, ending

> Ah! So soon? Come in next Sunday,
> China winks upon the shelves.
> Somewhere in the Bay of Fundy
> Twenty gardeners drown themselves.

A clever issue, but inopportune moment: these were the years when Cambridge Dogberries prowled through everything with sharpened blue pencils, looking for scraps of immorality. They had just banned an issue of the *Lampoon* because it contained a Manet nude winking and holding a cocktail glass. So, when the *Dial* parody appeared, police and postal clerks were alert for more dirt from Harvard. They found it—in a small line drawing of a couple embracing, entitled "Neo-Platonic Love." As the Boston *Post* so coyly put it, "there are no fashion hints in the drawing." "HARVARD ADVOCATE HELD UP," a banner headline announced. Copies were rushed to Washington for the verdict of the Postmaster General, but he spoiled the fun by affirming the *Advocate*'s purity.

Parodies of *Time, The Saturday Review, The Newer Republic,* and *The Atlantic Monthly,* though nearly as successful, were less notorious. In fact, the magazine was not banned again until 1935 when the Freshman issue was yanked off the stands by the police three weeks after it appeared. Assistant Attorney General Frank G. Volpe singled out two stories, "A Natural History" by James Laughlin IV and "Glittering Pie" by Henry Miller, as offensive, labelling them "obscene and degrading," and "crudely maudlin." His attack on college literature was widely reprinted.

It is about time that college authorities maintained a rigid supervision over the childish efforts of those embryonic authors (Miller was nearly fifty at the time) who seem to think it a mark of distinction to dish up dirt for the edification of other immature minds . . . This office must waste its time and the public funds considering the grotesque brainchildren of these college boys.

Generously, Mr. Volpe added "we don't want to send these earnest young writers, suffering from allusions of grandeur (sic), to jail. Their pitiful crime does not warrant such drastic action." Instead, he forced six editors, including President John J. Slocum '36, Pegasus John A. Strauss '36, and business manager Gerard Piel '37, to resign their posts.

The town-gown antagonism implicit in the District Attorney's remarks came to a head in 1938 when Cambridge City Councilman Mike Sullivan (a bolder prototype of today's Al Velucci who tried to have the intersection of Bow and Mount Auburn Streets named "Eli Yale Square") made public his demands that Harvard become a separate municipality. The City Council accepted his plea and passed a resolution requesting legislative action, while the *Lampoon,* the *Crimson,* and the *Advocate* shrewdly began jockeying for power in the emerging city. As the *Lampoon*'s storm-troopers goose-stepped down Massachusetts Avenue demanding a corridor to the Charles, someone kicked Sullivan from behind. Enraged, he called out the police, who drove back the crowd of thousands with tear gas. "GAS GUN GUARD OVER HARVARD" announced the headline in the *Herald* the following morning. Unwilling to submit to this reign of terror, the *Advocate* held a plebiscite to determine the true loyalties of the Harvard community. From their strategically located Bow Street headquarters they distributed ballots to all who wished to vote.

VOTE THE STRAIGHT TICKET!

1. Do you prefer separation from Cambridge?   -   -   ☐
2. Do you approve of kicking councilors? (Answer yes.)   ☐
3. If not, why not?   •   •   ▪   ▪   •   •   •   ☐
4. Are we an oppressed minority?   ▪   •   -   •   ☐
5. Should Radcliffe be included in the municipality?   ☐
6. Who would you nominate for Mayor?
7. *Tantaene animis caelestibus irae?*   -   ▪   •   •   ☐

Though the Dean's office rapidly closed the polls, it was evident that Ada Louise Comstock, President of Radcliffe, had won the mayoralty race. But she was never installed and Harvard's minorities remained oppressed.

Thwarted in their foray into politics, the editors concentrated on publishing a magazine and gained no less public notice, although from a different public. In 1938 and 1940 they brought out issues devoted to T. S. Eliot and Wallace Stevens, containing their undergraduate verse as well as critical articles from leading writers everywhere. These projects received recognition as nearly unique contributions to scholarship and criticism. The Seventy-Fifth Anniversary Issue, filled with contributions by Conrad Aiken, Wallace Stevens, William Carlos Williams, Djuna Barnes, Robert Hillyer, and Marianne Moore, was another testimony to the *Advocate*'s potential as a national literary magazine. It had come a long way since the days when it was Harvard's news and gossip sheet.

THE LAST TWO DECADES: 1947–1966

The War silenced the *Advocate* for nearly four years. By 1947, when the veterans had begun to drift back to school, it began to appear once more; but to revive the magazine after so long a lapse, the editors had to take stock and decide what kind of magazine would work at post-war Harvard. When they drew up a statement of purpose it became evident that there had been a break with the past. The *Advocate* faced new problems: bankruptcy and indifference. An editorial in the first issue compared the *Advocate*'s rebirth with its birth eighty years before when its main obstacle had been the wrath of the faculty. "Today, perhaps unfortunately, such unsophisticated obstacles no longer stand in the way of Harvard student publications. They have license to become great national forces if they like, or even to seek the new unifying principle of the world."

They had license to but didn't. The world remained disunited; and the editors tried instead to produce "a literary magazine in the broad sense of the word which excludes no subject but only the ill-considered and the badly written." The problem: to create a magazine of high quality that would sell. Formerly, when the *Advocate* had been a general college magazine and when the interests of the college had been more limited and provincial, it had been assured of its readers. Now it risked being ignored.

The stunts and headlines of the thirties were too crass for the serious *littérateurs* of the fifties, but the magazine could still gain national attention through special issues. The William Faulkner issue of 1951, now a collectors' item, contained critical articles by Alfred Kazin, Cleanth Brooks, Conrad Aiken, John Crowe Ransom, and Archibald MacLeish. The British Novelists issue of 1952 was another major critical achievement. And in 1961 the *Advocate* published a Robert Lowell issue, honoring the man whom, to its everlasting shame, it had rejected when he had been a freshman candidate for the literary board.

Most striking during these years, though, are not the special issues but the vitality and variety of undergraduate poetry. The magazine that had stayed Georgian ten years too late during the poetic ferment of the twenties was fully in stride with the poetic rebellion of the fifties against Eliot and the other modern poets who had become an establishment. Peter Viereck summed up the situation in "1912–1952: Full Cycle:"

> Must all successful rebels grow
> From toreador to Sacred Cow?
> What cults he slew, his cult begot.
> "In my beginning," said the Scot,
> "My end;" and aging eagles know
> That 1912 was long ago.
> Today the women come and go
> Talking of T. S. Eliot.

But attacks on this establishment were coming from all quarters. One group of *Advocate* poets, Kenneth Koch, Frank O'Hara, and John Ashberry, looked to the contemporary French poets for models of vigor and freedom. A few years later William Carlos Williams came to Harvard and challenged the preconceptions of *Advocate* poets. Attacking traditional prosody, he called on American writers to abandon regular forms and invent an American metric. When his *Collected Poems* appeared soon after, the *Advocate* reviewer called him "one of the very few adult poets who is communicating anything," and categorized him as a revolutionary "for whom the past and its traditions are anathema." But

Williams' challenge had been too much for some *Advocate* stalwarts who replied, appropriately enough, in rhymed couplets.

> It isn't my intention to eschew
> Rhythmic experiments just because they're new;
> But must we all adore the virtuosity
> Involved in tortured novelties of prosody?
> Let us not call traditional forms a crime
> Lest innovation be the thief of rime.

Williams later became the model for undergraduates like Robert Grenier, but for many *Advocate* writers the most exciting new poet was Robert Lowell. *Lord Weary's Castle* had been published and its intense personal energy had startled. Donald Hall writes, *"Lord Weary's Castle* came out just before I came to Harvard and when I arrived at the *Advocate* the argument still raged. The next event was the publication of *The Beautiful Changes,* and Lowell and Wilbur became the poles of energy and elegance on which the poetic world of the fifties turned."

To their followers—and they were legion, as the pages of this anthology show—Lowell and Wilbur *were* the poles of the poetic world. But to others they were mere "academic" poets. This dispute over "academic" and "non-academic" poetry, suggested by William Carlos Williams' remarks, began in earnest in the late fifties. Beat poetry had arrived. Allen Ginsberg's *Howl* swept the country as no other poem had. The challenge to Wilbur's kind of poetry seemed overwhelming. The challengers found support even in the *Advocate*'s tradition-laden pages. Robert Bly, editor of the magazine *The Fifties* came to Harvard and attacked "the prosody, insular and conservative in technique and statement, which clogs the quarterlies and little magazines." Anxious to keep itself out of that category, the *Advocate* ran the motto of Bly's magazine in bold-face capitals on the editorial page: "WE FEEL THAT MOST OF THE POETRY PUBLISHED NOW-A-DAYS IS OLD-FASHIONED." Bly's heroes were the non-academic Whitman, Hart Crane, and William Carlos Williams, as well as the Spanish poets Jiminez and Neruda. This was in 1953. By 1963 when Brother Antoninus came to read at Harvard, the "Beat poets" Ginsberg, Ferlinghetti, and Corso were established as prototypes of the non-academic poet. Academic versus beat, or in Antoninus' terms, "Apollonian" versus "Dionysian."

But the controversy seemed to be resolving itself. Asked where poetry was going, Antoninus paraphrased Robert Lowell: "It's in an in-between state, between the beats and the academics; everyone is fighting shy of the extremes and trying to come forth with a statement that will embody both the vigor of the beat and the structure of the academic."

Although it was the first magazine to publish Gregory Corso, the *Advocate* has not been a stronghold of beat poetry and has often sought the middle ground. *Advocate* contributions reflect Harvard—what is being taught and read. And so Robert Lowell reigns in the *Advocate* sanctum. Undergraduates have studied him and studied under him. A poem like Robert Dawson's "The Pigeon Roof" shows its lineage.

Robert Lowell, then. Also new criticism. One cannot overemphasize how deeply undergraduate poetry has been affected by the thorough-going changes in the teaching of poetry. When Reuben Brower brought his own brand of new criticism to Harvard, a revolution occurred. Students began to look at poems in terms of images, tone, narrative persona, ambiguity, and linguistic tension. Poems became technical constructs where the *words* mattered. Some English courses began to teach how to read and how words work, not what Shakespeare says. The impact of this kind of teaching on undergraduate poetry? A high degree of technical competence, great sophistication about forms and conventions, a delight in working closely with words and investing them with all the meaning they'll carry and some they won't. Both the complexity and crabbed obscurity of *Advocate* poetry come from changes in criticism and teaching.

*   *   *

If the fifties were a time of uncertainty and experimentation in poetry, they were, for the *Advocate* at least, a time of consolidation in prose. Writers like Sallie Bingham, Jonathan Kozol, Robert Cumming, and Nathaniel LaMar wrote highly proficient stories in preparation for that first novel which they would soon publish. Then, during the late fifties came the vogue of "The Harvard Square Sex Story," a genre confined to the pages of the *Advocate* and the bottom drawers of countless Harvard desks. Sallie Bingham's "Winter Term" is the prototype for many such stories, set in the reading room of Widener Library, in the Hayes-Bickford cafeteria, under the bushes on the Cambridge Common, and in rooms in Eliot House. For about two years these stories, replete with maudlin self-flagellation and disquisitions on the difficulties of love at the Puritans' own university, flooded into the *Advocate*. In 1959 William Bayer wrote "SEX: The Literary Breakthrough in Harvard Square." The new form was discussed in the pages of the *Advocate* as an established literary genre of some historical interest. It was even producing novels: Jonathan Kozol's *Fume of Poppies* and its less respectable successor, Leonie St. John's *Love With a Harvard Accent*. But by 1960 the trend seemed to be dying out. No longer did the familiar scenes and dialogue animate *Advocate* meetings where supercilious editors would read them to one another and sneer. Harvard writers had moved on to other concerns—to more verbal experimentation, to more serious attempts to create a new prose. Stories were beginning to sound like Kafka, Faulkner, or else John O'Hara. Somehow it had become unsophisticated to indulge in the kind of sincere self-examination and self-pity that had given these stories, and still gives them, such a ring of truth. The amateur writer was passing from the Harvard scene.

❊ ❊ ❊

What has happened to the *Advocate* during the past two decades? It is hard to say exactly. It is no longer the socially-exclusive club it once was—with the high initiation fees, the beer parties, the scurrilous plays presented annually in the privacy of the sanctum. Now even Radcliffe girls are members; the plays are only framed handbills on the walls; and beer parties have become cocktail parties where Cambridge *literati* of all ages gather to meet the famous and obscure. The result: a more literary and democratic, but occasionally equally snobbish organization. For several years, in fact, the magazine prided itself on its literary exclusiveness. The editors decided that there was no point in appealing to a stupid, uninterested public. It would be better to print a handsome, expensive flatback quarterly that a select few would buy. Advertising was ignored; unopened business mail collected. The literature in the magazine was superb, but printer's bills would soon have put the *Advocate* under. Something had to be done: the literary club had to yield to a magazine staff.

During the past few years the *Advocate* has begun to open its business mail and compete with other magazines. Circulation and advertising have increased tremendously. Writers like Robert Lowell, Norman

Mailer, Robert Frost, Adrienne Rich, I. A. Richards, John Hawkes, Allen Ginsberg, and Marianne Moore have been brought to Cambridge to give public readings. And now, in the centennial year, the trustees are working to create an endowment that will supplement the earnings of the magazine. Financial problems are becoming less pressing, but one problem remains.

The problem is the fragmentation of Harvard life. Writers have become more exclusively writers. They hole up in apartments working on that first novel. They slave over poems which they show only to a few friends. They take writing courses. They would like to write professionally. They come around to *Advocate* meetings occasionally, but their commitment to the magazine is smaller. They are not undergraduates working to put out a magazine so much as poets and novelists who will publish wherever their work is accepted.

This is a problem; but it is also the *Advocate*'s greatest strength. Never have undergraduate writers been so intense; never have they achieved such technical proficiency. Compare the poems of the last five years with Robinson's, Eliot's, and Stevens' early poems. Some readers may prefer the latters' *kind* of poetry, but they would still admit that their efforts are amateurish by comparison.

This new professionalism of undergraduates suggests two things. Harvard writers are not "undergraduate writers" but young writers speaking as individuals to the world at large. The *Advocate* must therefore make itself more than a college magazine, publish the best literature it can find, and efface the supposed distinction between "undergraduate" writer and "real" writer. It must continue to be a national magazine—national in scope if not in circulation. But the focus is still on Harvard writing. Proximity guarantees it; and the famous names that line the walls of the sanctum and fill the back issues on the shelves are witness to the possibilities latent in this kind of magazine. Given the frame of the past and the material of the present, the future looks very good.

JONATHAN D. CULLER

Advocate House
Cambridge
November, 1965

THE FIRST FIFTY YEARS:
1866–1916

THE FIRST DECADE

The Advocate *did not become a literary magazine until the 1880's. During the early years it
served primarily as a bi-weekly newspaper and
comment sheet, printing football and baseball
scores, editorials dealing with college problems,
letters to the editor, and occasional stories and
poems. Excerpts from these early issues capture
the flavor of late nineteenth-century Harvard:
the "presumptuous proposal" to publish literature in a college magazine, the manifesto from the
first issue of the* Advocate, *a proposal to admit
women to the college—for rather strange reasons, an attack on the University bookstore's monopoly, reviews of several popular books of the
period, an article proposing that "Crimson" be
made the school color, a vicious diatribe against
Walt Whitman, and an account of the first Har-
vard-Yale football game.*

COLLEGE LITERATURE

PERHAPS it was a little presumptuous for the editors of this paper, in their
prospectus, to propose to devote it in part to "College Literature"; for
that may seem a high-sounding name for the hasty articles that students
find time to write in the midst of their regular college duties. Yet it is
well known that there is much of such writing done here; and, whatever
its quality may be, it must be taken as the measure of students' literary
achievements.

Of all that has been written, far the greater part has consisted of lectures for societies, articles for society papers, and similar productions; and these efforts are mostly lost and forgotten. The materials which formed their framework, no doubt, have often been worked over, and subsequently used in preparing more elaborate works; but the originals have long since found their way to the waste-paper basket and the flames.

Still, many—though, we suspect, not always the best—productions from the pens of Harvard students have been published in the various periodicals which have preceded the "Collegian." In turning over the pages of the "Harvard Magazine," "Harvard Register," "Harvardiana," &c, it is easy to see the faults which mar these student compositions.

The first thing which strikes us is the very disproportionate amount of verse—very little of it, alas! deserves the name of poetry—which appears in these journals. A mania prevails among the contributors for torturing all sorts of subjects into such shapes as will allow them to be included in troches and iambics. There are, it is true, occasional poems which are really fine; many which are pretty or passable; but the larger portion of the verse is such trash as gods and men abhor,—a little better than the "Poet's Corner" in country newspapers, a little worse than similar effusions in the sensational "literary" periodicals.

When we come to plain prose, we find a decided improvement in the general merit of the articles, though there is still ample room for criticism. In the first place, the choice of subjects is often very injudicious. The writer has perhaps in the course of his reading met with some subject which is new, and for the time, very interesting to him; and he hurries to prepare an article upon it, without considering whether it is likely to be of general interest or not. Again: sometimes a similar ambition to that which leads so many to prefer doubtful rhyme and limping metre to sensible and straightforward prose causes others to be too aspiring in their selection of topics for discussion. Instead of contenting themselves with the abundant matters of common and immediate interest in college life, they are eager to mount to a loftier height, where they may engage in the philosophical discussion of moral, political, or aesthetic subjects,—subjects, it too often happens, which they do not well understand, and on which, at all events, they are hardly likely to throw any very brilliant light.

The selection of inappropriate topics and, still more, the universal want of experience among the writers, are the cause of the stilted and grandiloquent style which sometimes obtrudes itself. In fact, the style is not often free and natural, but, even in the best productions, is still too frequently a little too constrained and awkward.

One of the most prolific causes of bad writing here, as elsewhere, is carelessness. Many of the articles have evidently been hastily written, and not subjected to the revision of sober second thought. This leads to many slips and inaccuracies, and not unfrequently to worse blunders. The contributors of such articles should have heeded Horace's advice,—

> "exemplaria
> Nocturna versate manu, versate diurna,"—

till they had acquired, at least, the habit of writing correctly.

It is a trite but true remark that what we have denominated "College Literature" has little originality. This, however, we think, is scarcely a good reason for condemning it as useless. We must consider that it is the work of persons who are wholly engaged in learning from others, and who have not yet reached an age or, usually, acquired sufficient knowledge to be capable of very valuable independent thinking.

There is, after all, sometimes great merit in stating old truths in new words, though new ideas are more desirable; and students should be especially on their guard against making their own views merely reflections of those of some favorite authority.

We have purposely been critical in this article, not because we expect to avoid entirely all or any of the errors we have pointed out, but because we believe we can only begin to avoid them when we understand clearly what they are.

We hope, in some future number, to be able to show the other side of the question, and to point out some of the merits of the writings of which we have been speaking.

The Collegian
March 1866

OUR PAPER

THE "COLLEGIAN" was started two months ago as a Cambridge news-paper, intended to represent the views and opinions of Harvard students. Its prosperity was great; it had a long list of honorable subscribers, among both graduates and undergraduates and was favorably spoken of by the leading periodicals of Boston. Soon after the issue of its third number, the editors of the "Collegian" were summoned and informed that their publication must be discontinued. No direct reason was assigned for this unexpected step; and all attempts at conciliation and compromise on the part of the editors who offered to bind themselves to any restrictions whatever, were unavailing. Deterred from further pursuance of their undertaking by threat of a most severe college censure in case they continued it, the editors stopped their paper, and squared accounts with their subscribers. Impressed with a feeling that some such newspaper as was the "Collegian" is sorely needed here to express the wishes and opinions of the students, we propose to issue this, our present publication, as long as it is supported.

We do not make our attempt in any spirit of blind malignity to those who govern and instruct us, nor do we consider it mere school-boy senti-ment which animates this appeal to our right of free journalism. As boys, we were prejudiced against our masters; and there may be some of that instinct lingering about us still: but we believe ourselves, on this occasion, to be actuated by other and more liberal motives. It seems to us as if "leave to plead our own cause" had been asked for and refused. It is from no idle whim, nor in any spirit of unmeaning opposition, that we try to assert that we consider ourselves slighted by this relentless course of our rulers in overlooking our dearest wishes. The good order and correct discipline of the College is far more likely to be demoralized by one instance where all explanation of the disputed point has been refused, than it could be by many midnight revels in front of the Uni-versity. It is true that two or three articles in the "Collegian" contained indistinct allusions to those to whom we are rightfully expected to pay the highest deference, but such were hardly discernible to any save our-selves, and were not intended to be understood beyond the limits of a department or of a certain class. We admit that it may have been a mistake to have published such articles in the "Collegian," but we are positive that such a practice would have been entirely stopped as soon as it became known that they were a source of annoyance to their subjects. Harmless by-play the editors thought it, which no one need be offended at.

Here are four hundred young men, the greater number of whom have now passed that age at which the law prescribes that they shall become their own masters. All these have individual opinions, feelings, ideas, more or less, of their own. It would be absurd to attempt to gratify all their whims and tastes; yet, when a majority concur in claiming a right to this privilege or that privilege, we know there is some reason for it, which ought to be investigated. And we think that, if we are able to be responsible at all, we ought to be allowed a voice, or at least some expression of appeal, on the subject of those rules and customs here which determine so nearly our habits of thought and action throughout life. We confess that undergraduates are inexperienced, and, as compared with older heads, are ignorant enough of the realities of the world. "Yet he that wears the shoe alone knows where the shoe pinches." The scholarly senior, who knows well where the discipline of each day serves him as an assistance and a guide, also knows best of all where the chafing of his harness impedes free motion. "Times change, and men change with them." Is it expected that we should find suited to our best purposes those regulations which were framed for the government of our grand-fathers? If a change is to be allowed at any time, it is possible that one time may demand it as well as another.

We disclaim having received any assistance or co-operation in our project from the former editors of the "Collegian." Not even are they responsible for the original idea of our attempt. They were not alone in their belief that a newspaper of some sort was needed among the undergraduates, both for the purpose of expressing their sentiments to each other, and also their impressions of college matters to the world. We are not a small and insignificant minority, nor are the principles on which we act cherished within the breasts of a few proselytes. They have been for a long time echoed and re-echoed in college talk and society debates. We assure the public that our columns are open to all who desire to make fair, unbiased statement of their judgment on these subjects or on any others. Nothing abusive, nothing personally libelous, nothing which in the judgment of the editors would be likely to excite disobedience or disorder, will be received.

With this exposition of "our purposes," we intrust to the mercy of our readers the first number of the *Advocate*.

Frank P. Stearns
May, 1866

THE PROPRIETY OF ADMITTING WOMEN INTO OUR COLLEGE

THERE is one branch of reform that has not been touched on—a reform of paramount importance. I mean that advance upon our present state of civilization which will no longer exclude one-half of the human race from the walls of our college; which will no longer tolerate the barbarous idea that our sisters have not as good a right to a liberal education as ourselves.

Our sisters, who desire a collegiate education, cannot but feel disappointed to see us entering a first-class college, while they must put up with an Antioch or Oberlin. What a disgraceful sight!—an Eastern girl forced to leave her home in New England, so famous for its educational advantages, and seek the State of Ohio, as a place where she can enjoy even tolerable advantages! . . .

What a glorious era it will be for American civilization, when a brother and sister, after attending school together during their younger days, can finally be received under the classic shades of Harvard, hand in hand, and continue here together for four happy years! A blessed day, too, will it be for the morals of our College, when the young men have the restraining influence of women's society before them during their college course.

December, 1866

THE UNIVERSITY BOOKSTORE

A Case of Monopoly

WHAT is meant by a "monopoly in trade"? Is it not that one person has the exclusive privilege of selling, and that all the rest of the world who are going to buy are directly at his mercy, so far as their buying is a necessity? Hence, monopolies are always associated with despotism, and, in fact, can only be supported by some form of despotism. Wherever in the world they now exist, they exist as relics of barbarism, the very opposite of all that is free, enlightened, and democratic. Cain created the first monopoly when he slew Abel, and all others since then have been pretty much of the same order.

Have we a *despotism* in Harvard College?

Yes; for wherever and whenever men have control over the destinies of others a certain amount of despotism is sure to result, and for that very reason much that is despotic here is unavoidable under existing regulations. However, there are many instances where it might be avoided, and most certainly is not; and one such I intend to specify.

Sever & Francis, booksellers to the University, were, until within a year ago, a most decidedly privileged firm. They were expressly commissioned to sell books and stationery to the four hundred undergraduates, and many others in the Scientific and Law Schools. An arrangement of theirs with the College government—Faculty, Overseers, or whoever is responsible—provided that purchases at their store should be charged on the College term-bills, and thus the greatest of inducements, a convenience in money matters, made it for the interest of every student to buy of them. To cap the climax, they acted on no uncertainty, for they could always obtain information beforehand as to exactly what was wanted, and in exactly what amounts.

According to the original agreement, the University Bookstore was to have the opportunity and every advantage for selling books to the students, on condition that such sale was at the lowest or even lower than the market price. Now, it was notorious eighteen months ago, that nearly all text-books could be bought cheaper in Boston than at Sever & Francis'. A sharp-witted Junior one day discovered that blank-books, sold by Sever & Francis for *fifteen cents apiece*, could be readily bought in Boston for *one dollar a dozen*. He said to himself, "I am not rich; I work hard to get my education; and here I am constantly being cheated by this monopoly." So he started a petition. It went from the students to the Faculty, from the Faculty to the Board of Overseers, and ended nobody knows where. Next he started up Mr. Richardson in opposition to Sever & Francis. Mr. R. was very industrious and obliging, and from a small trade in March, 1866, by September of the same year he came to have a very large trade. More than half of all the undergraduates patronized him.

Fair play demands that Mr. Richardson should have an equal chance. No one has a right to dictate to the undergraduates of Harvard College where it is that they shall buy. They do *not* like the University Bookstore. They have good reasons for strongly disliking it. And is not a college education expensive enough in every other direction, without our paying extra blackmail into the pockets of two men who might obtain an honest living in any other part of the country? We demand it as our right, that monopolies be abolished, whether they appear in the form of bookstores, boarding-houses, or anything else; and we claim that Mr. Richardson, as our preferred employee, shall be allowed the same opportunities, the same privileges, and the same immunities, with which Messrs. Sever & Francis are now favored.

March, 1867

REVIEW: THE RING AND THE BOOK

by ROBERT BROWNING

WE HEARD that a new work by Robert Browning was to appear during the autumn. Ten or twelve years, so Rumor whispered, this great genius had been at work on some eighteen thousand lines of poetry. This work was to be his masterpiece: it was to surpass all his stirring lyrics, all his tender poems of love where harmony and melody abound, and finally all those wonderful dramatic poems where the smaller matters of perfect versification fell powerless before the intense dramatic action, as in the rush of a mighty cataract one loses sight and consideration of the minor beauties of vale and woodland. And here let us interrupt ourselves to reply to the nice rhetorician who measures Mr. Browning's poetry by the laws of ordinary writing. Admit that it has faults, who is able to judge them? His verse is sometimes defective, but such wonderful clothing for the idea as it is! He is sometimes obscure, says the rhetorician. O foolish man, study him as you study your well-regulated textbook, and you will find that this is not only a great genius, as you are forced to admit, but also a great artist.

Here we have his masterpiece. Will you trouble yourselves to examine this pearl, Messrs. Swine? This book is really not difficult to read. You need not be afraid that it will thrill your depths. The few who love Robert Browning unreservedly, as all must who read him with any care at all, will hail this greatest work of our greatest poet since Shakespeare; and some future reader, three hundred years hence, may write a treatise crediting it to Professor Bowen. In the mean time, since we cannot give any just outline of the plot of this wonderful book, and since we cannot do justice to its beauty by any quotation from it, we warn all readers of the ballads and lays and songs of Miss Ingelow and Miss Rossetti, also those who admire Lucy Larcom, together with the intelligent lady critics of Miss Anna Dickinson's "brave and noble book," and lastly that glorious company who are happy in the placid bleatings of the chaste Muse of Holland, to abstain from this book.

But to those young men whom this college is so liberally educating, we say that there are certain works which it becomes a duty to read. A college undergraduate who has reached the age of twenty, and knows nothing of Shakespeare, is a pretty poor example of the cultivation that American boys receive. The only author of real worth that is widely read here at Harvard is Thackeray; and our alarmingly large number of embryo Lord Steynes and Fokers and Warringtons and (worst of all) Pendennises, show what the effect has been.

The few students in Cambridge who appreciate the benefit that a certain amount of general reading can do them, should begin this book immediately.

January, 1869

REVIEW: FRANKENSTEIN

By MARY W. SHELLEY

MESSRS. SEVER AND FRANCIS deserve credit for publishing this work, since it has long been celebrated, while inaccessible to the curious reader on account of its rarity. But for the book itself we can say but little. It is intended to be frightful and impressive, as are generally accounts of goblins, djinns, vampires, and such pleasing beings. To us, however, it seems to have lapsed from the sublime to the ridiculous. We say this boldly, since the author is dead, and we cannot reasonably suppose that our remarks will hurt her feelings.

Frankenstein is a student, who, by tremendous application to the charming study of chemistry, becomes enabled to create a man. Wishing to "spread himself" on his work, he makes his fellow eight feet tall and large in proportion. When the work is done, Frankenstein is horrified to find he has made a monster. The monster naturally desires companionship, and requests his maker to create a female for a partner of his joys and sorrows. Frankenstein reflects that the consequences of so doing might be dangerous to the human race, and refuses. The monster enraged proceeds to slaughter all Frankenstein's relations and friends in the most bloodthirsty manner, and finally announces his intention of committing suicide after he has caused the death of his creator.

The principal moral to be derived by Harvard boys from this book is that dangerous proficiency in chemistry should be carefully avoided.

Stories like "Frankenstein" are, we think, either morbid or absurd. Probably the notoriety of this book arose from its author's being the daughter of Godwin and wife of Shelley, rather than from any merit of its own, as, with the exception of a few striking passages, its style is as flat as its plot is horrible and preposterous.

March, 1869

PRESIDENT ELIOT'S INAUGURAL ADDRESS (*excerpts*)

The System of Elective Studies

Only a few years ago, all students who graduated at this College passed through one uniform curriculum. Every man studied the same subjects in the same proportions, without regard to his natural bent or preference. The individual student had no choice either of subjects or teachers. This system is still the prevailing system among American colleges, and finds vigorous defenders. It has the merit of simplicity. So had the school methods of our grandfathers,—one primer, one catechism, one rod for all children. On the whole, a single common course of studies, tolerably well selected to meet the average needs, seems to most Americans a very proper and natural thing, even for grown men.

As a people, we do not apply to mental activities the principle of division of labor; and we have but a halting faith in special training for high professional employments. The vulgar conceit that a Yankee can turn his hand to anything we insensibly carry into high places, where it is preposterous and criminal. We are accustomed to seeing men leap from farm or shop to court-room or pulpit, and we half believe that common men can safely use the seven-league boots of genius. What amount of knowledge and experience do we habitually demand of our lawgivers? What special training do we ordinarily think necessary for our diplomatists? In great emergencies, indeed, the nation has known where to turn. Only after years of the bitterest experience did we come to believe the professional training of a soldier to be of value in war. This lack of faith in the prophecy of a natural bent, and in the value of a discipline concentrated upon a single object, amounts to a national danger.

In education, the individual traits of different men have not been sufficiently attended to. Through all the period of boyhood, the school studies should be representative; all the many fields of knowledge should be entered upon. But the young man of nineteen or twenty ought to know what he likes best and is most fit for. When the revelation of his own peculiar taste and capacity comes to a young man let him reverently give it welcome, thank God and take courage.

These principles are the justification of the system of elective studies which has been gradually developed in this College during the past twenty years. At present, the Freshmen year is the only one in which there is a fixed course prescribed for all. In the other three years, more than half the time allotted to study is filled with subjects chosen by each student from lists which comprise six studies in the Sophomore year, nine in the Junior year, and eleven in the Senior year.

The elective system fosters scholarship, because it gives free play to natural preferences and inborn aptitudes, makes possible enthusiasm for a chosen work, relieves the professor and the ardent disciple of the presence of a body of students who are compelled to an unwelcome task, and enlarges instruction by substituting many and various lessons given to small, lively classes, for a few lessons many times repeated to different sections of a numerous class. The College therefore proposes to persevere in its efforts to establish, improve, and extend the elective system.

Harvard College Not Exclusive

Harvard college has always attracted and still attracts students in all conditions of life. From the city trader or professional man, who may be careless how much his son spends at Cambridge, to the farmer or mechanic, who finds it a hard sacrifice to give his boy his time early enough to enable him to prepare for college,—all sorts and conditions of men have wished and still wish to send their sons hither. There are always scores of young men in this University who earn or borrow every dollar they spend here. Every year many young men enter this College without any resources whatever. If they prove themselves men of capacity and character, they never go away for lack of money. More than twenty thousand dollars a year are now devoted to aiding students of narrow means to compass their education, besides all the remitted fees and the numerous private benefactions. These latter are unfailing. Taken in connection with the proceeds of the funds applicable to the aid of poor students, they enable the Corporation to say that no good student need ever stay away from Cambridge, or leave college simply because he is poor. There is one uniform condition, however, on which help is given,—the recipient must be of promising ability and the best character. The community does not owe superior education to all children, but only to the *élite*,—to those who, having the capacity, prove by hard work that they have also the necessary perseverance and endurance. The process of preparing to enter college under the difficulties which poverty entails is just such a test of worthiness as is needed. At this moment there is no college in the country more eligible for a poor student than Harvard on the mere ground of economy.

Nevertheless, this College is deeply indebted to those who, bringing hither from refined homes good breeding, gentle tastes, and a manly delicacy, add to them openness and activity of mind, intellectual interests, and a sense of public duty. To lose altogether the presence of those who in early life have enjoyed the domestic and social advantages of wealth would be as great a blow to the College as to lose the sons of the poor. The interests of the College and the country are identical in this regard. The country suffers when the rich are ignorant and unrefined.

Harvard College is sometimes reproached with being aristocratic. If by aristocracy be meant a stupid and pretentious caste, founded on wealth and birth, and an affectation of European manners, no charge could be more preposterous: But there is an aristocracy to which the sons of Harvard have belonged, and let us hope will ever aspire to belong,—the aristocracy which excels in manly sports, carries off the honors and prizes of the learned professions, and bears itself with distinction in all fields of intellectual labor and combat; the aristocracy which in peace stands firmest for the public honor and renown, and in war rides first into the murderous thickets.

Women at Harvard

The attitude of the University in the prevailing discussions touching the education and fit employment of women demands brief explanation. America is the natural arena for these debates; for here the female sex has a better past and a better present than elsewhere. Americans, as a rule, hate disabilities of all sorts, whether religious, political, or social. Equality between the sexes, without privilege or oppression on either side, is the happy custom of American homes. While this great discussion is going on, it is the duty of the University to maintain a cautious and expectant policy. The Corporation will not receive women as students into the College proper, nor into any school whose discipline requires residence near the school. The difficulties involved in a common residence of hundreds of young men and women of immature character and marriageable age are very grave. The necessary police regulations are exceedingly burdensome. The Corporation are not influenced to this decision, however, by any crude notions about the innate capacities of women. The world knows next to nothing about the natural mental capacities of the female sex. Only after generations of civil freedom and social equality will it be possible to obtain the data necessary for an adequate discussion of woman's natural tendencies, tastes, and capabilities. Again, the Corporation do not find it necessary to entertain a confident opinion upon the fitness or unfitness of women for professional pursuits. It is not the business of the University to debate this mooted point. Practical, not theoretical, considerations determine the policy of the University.

October, 1869

COLLEGE PHRASES AND CUSTOMS

WHEN we think of all the expressions that we use continually, in college life, how many there are that must be perfectly unintelligible to any person other than the student. For instance: "I made a frightful rush to-day," and, again (perhaps more frequently), "I deaded in Latin to-day." A very valuable book has been published on this subject, entitled *College Words and Customs*, which gives not only a great number of phrases and slang expressions, but also quite a detailed account of some of the old customs at Harvard. A great number of these slang phrases are very familiar to us, such as,—"fizzle," "flunk," "squirt," "slump," "rag," "goody," "scout," &c. For students under the influence of vinous excitement, we find the following: over the bay, half-seas over, high, corned, shaved, jammed, damaged, snuffy, breezy, top-heavy, fuddled, swipey, slewed, cronk, battered, blowing, sawed, jug-steamed, tangle-legged, fogmatic, blue-eyed, a passenger in the Cape Ann stage, striped, faint, shot in the neck, bamboozled, and weak-jointed. A great many of the above expressions are (we regret to say) in very common use here; but "fogmatic" we consider to be an outburst of true genius. We hope that the inventor will accept our compliments, which we most sincerely offer him. The customs are too numerous to be given at full length; but, for the edification of the Freshman Class, we give the following: "No Freshman shall wear his hat in the College Yard except it rains, hails, or snows, he be on horseback, or hath both hands full." "When anybody knocks at a Freshman's door, he shall not ask who is there, but immediately open the door." "No Freshman shall call his classmate by the name of Freshman." "Freshmen are to find the rest of the scholars with bats, balls, and footballs." Imagine a member of the University Nine remarking to some disconsolate Freshman, "Now then, Freshy, come down with that new base-ball bat. We're rather out of bats just now." This would most certainly be a phase of college life which, to say the least, would not be "over and above" agreeable to the doting parents at home.

March, 1874

HARVARD'S COLOR

> " 'And when before your eyes I've set him,
> If you don't find him black I'll eat him,'
> He said; and full before their sight
> Produced the beast, and lo!—'twas white."

OUR friend with the chameleon could not have been more surprised and shocked at the change of color than were the old Harvard boating men to hear their proudly worn crimson called magenta, in 1866, by the newspapers: indignation was called forth from all quarters; but it was thought to be merely a newspaper mistake, that would be corrected. With the next year the same error was repeated, however; and all efforts at correction proved vain, and soon magenta was recognized as Harvard's color. At different times, attempts have been made by the boating men to get back to the true color, but so far without success. The present opportunity seems a good one to make a last final attempt. Union College puts in a claim for magenta. Let us see if it will not be well to let it go, and return to our true colors. What, then, are the facts about crimson and magenta? How did the colors originate, and how did they become confounded and changed?

The color came from the college boat crew in 1858. Before that, no particular color was recognized in any American college as pertaining thereto. Boating men were the only collegians who had occasion to sport a uniform; and, up to this time, the different clubs had each a different uniform, with no one general feature common to all. In races there was little worn that could show any special color. Up to 1858, the crews usually wore straw hats, or sometimes caps. But, in 1858, a handkerchief tied tightly around the head was used in practice, and proved a useful and sensible covering for the head. Just before the first race in that year in which the college crew was to row, it was decided to wear the handkerchiefs in the race; and, after some discussion, it was decided that the color should be blue. At no shop in Boston, however, could blue silk handkerchiefs of the right size be found, and six red ones were bought instead. The shade of red was very nearly a true crimson. It was called simply red, and was used for many years, and was the distinguishing uniform of the Harvard University Crew; and "red" was adopted from the crew as Harvard's color.

At that time, the little town or village of Magenta was unknown to fame. But, on the 9th of June, 1859, the famous battle near by was fought, and took its name from the village. Just afterwards the aniline dyes were discovered, and two shades took names from the battles of Magenta and Solferino. The color magenta is a flashy, purplish shade of red, which was greatly in vogue for a year or so in France, and thence imported with other fashions to America. It has now gone out of fashion, and is difficult to procure in consequence, and will soon be numbered with the fashions "which were." It would be rather singular if the only demand for the color should come from Harvard University. Much better let it drop, and take up again a name and a color which will always live on account of its beauty,—the noble crimson. Magenta is (like all the aniline colors) a loose color. It fades with sunlight, and will not stand soap and water. It is one of those sickly shades that is almost impossible to harmonize with any other color. Intrinsically, it has nothing to recommend it. How, then, did it come to be so successful a rival of the crimson?

When the war commenced, the boating spirit in Cambridge declined, but revived with the system of class crews in 1863. Each class then took a color for its crew, leaving red for the University. The class of 1866 chose magenta and white as its color, and, having a fine crew, brought its color into great prominence. In 1866, in the University race at Worcester, by mistake magenta handkerchiefs were used, that shade of red being then in common use; and, when the Harvard men arrived at Worcester to see the race, and inquired at the shops for red, they were obliged to take magenta or nothing, as that was the only shade of red obtainable. Finding this was the case, the University Crew, not wishing the colors to be confounded, took especial pains to have the color called "red" on the printed cards of the race, and not "magenta." The newspapers, however, were too much for them; and, ever since, "magenta" has been called Harvard's color by the papers, and later also by the students, in spite of repeated attempts by the boating men to set the colors right. Now every college in America has its distinctive color, and several have adopted shades of red. Some shade of that color would seem to belong to Harvard, as the general term "red" would interfere with others, and cause great confusion. "Magenta" has been used so long as the name of Harvard's color that some difficulty would be experienced at first in changing it. As the color, however, never was "magenta" really; and as the color "magenta" has nothing to recommend it; and as the color really was crimson, and crimson is a good name,—especially now that somebody else wants the color and the name,—would it not be a good thing in every way to give it up, and take back the handsomer, the truer, and the legitimate "crimson" in name and in deed?

April, 1875

FOOT BALL

THE YALE-HARVARD MATCH

THE first Foot-ball game ever played between Yale and Harvard took place in New Haven, on Hamilton Park, last Saturday afternoon.

About forty students accompanied the Harvard team on Friday, and nearly a hundred more arrived in New Haven Saturday morning, so that there was a large representation of the College at the match. Many of those who left Boston on the 9:30 train, Friday night, found Providence a convenient place for getting out to stretch themselves, and took the opportunity to expand their lungs by letting off a few rounds of "Rahs!" for Brown.

No one supposed that any members of that University were sufficiently owl-like in their habits to be up and in a railway station at that hour of the night, and great was the surprise amongst the Harvard men when their "Rahs!" were responded to by that single-jointed imitation of our cheer which the Brown men have affected of late. The two crowds coalesced, and united in a few jovial songs, and, when the time came for starting, cheers were exchanged once more, and our men left with the good wishes of their Brown friends for success.

Saturday morning was spent in visiting the colleges, boat-house, &c., and at two o'clock all started for the grounds where the match was to be played.

THE GAME

First Half Hour

Play was called at 2:45, Yale with kick-off. The ball was immediately carried in toward the Yale goal. It was kicked by Morse over the goal line, and, the Yale tenders failing to get it, Leeds rushed in and secured the first touch-down, which he followed up with a clean kick over the cross-line, securing the first goal for Harvard. Yale again took the kick-off, and drove the ball toward the Harvard goal, Thompson nearly getting a touch-down. He was stopped by the Harvard goal tenders, and the ball kicked back to the centre of the field. Here Seamans got it by a pass from Hall, and, dodging Thompson and the Yale tenders, kicked the second goal.

Yale opened again with the kick-off, and sent the ball up the middle of the field, where Thompson carried it in touch. In the rush for it, when it was thrown in, Keys was kicked in the wind, and the game was stopped for a couple of minutes.

Curtis, dodging the Yale rushers, carried it back to within twenty yards of their goal, and kicked it towards the goal, where it was stopped by Trumbull, who started with it toward the Harvard goal. He ran with great speed, but showed so little skill in dodging that he was soon stopped.

Harvard . . . 2 Goals; 1 Touch-down.
Yale . . . . . 0 Goals; 0 Touch-down.

Second Half Hour

Bacon led off with a long kick for Harvard. The ball was stopped by Thompson and sent back toward the middle.

Leeds, who kicked it just short of a goal, got a touch-down, which was ruled out on a claim of foul. Cushing secured a touch-down immediately afterwards by a kick of Towers, which hit the cross-line and just missed a goal.

This was followed directly by Wetherbee's getting the ball as soon as it was sent in, passing it to Thayer, who passed it to Blanchard, and the latter kicked a goal. Harvard again led off, and Cate, getting the ball, started for the Yale goal, but was stopped neatly by Elliot, who passed the ball to Trumbull. He got down as far as the middle of the field before he was stopped.

Harvard . . . 3 Goals; 3 Touch-downs.
Yale . . . . . 0 Goals; 0 Touch-downs.

Third Half Hour

Yale did her best playing in this half hour, the men backing each other up with much better success, dodging and running more than kicking.

Herrick got the ball from Baker, but was stopped by Thompson and Arnold, the former, by fine running, getting up toward the Harvard goal, when he was thrown, and falling on the ball, burst the wind out of it. It was blown up and thrown in the air by the referee, and Curtis got it after it touched the ground, and dodging two Yale men, who collided and knocked each other down, passed it to Blanchard, who secured a touch-down.

Bacon picked it up, and was chased by two Yale rushers, both of whom he threw heavily, shouldering them against each other, and followed his play up with a long kick. The fourth and last goal was won by Tower, who kicked it over by a pass from Leeds, the latter nearly getting a touch-down before the goal was kicked.

The last point won was a touch-down by Seamans, soon after which time was called at the end of the third half hour.

Harvard . . . 4 Goals; 4 Touch-downs.
Yale . . . . . 0 Goals; 0 Touch-downs.

The overwhelming defeat of Yale is to be attributed, in a great measure, to the comparative newness of the rules to them. They showed very little discipline on the field, the different players not seeming to know their positions, and above all, failing, in almost every instance, to back each other up properly. Our team were, on the average, heavier, and, of course, their experience, gained from former matches, gave them confidence and nerve. To Mr. Whiting the thanks of the College are due for the time and attention he has devoted to the team, in making preparations for the different matches this fall, and the care with which he has kept up their practice.

November, 1875

WALT WHITMAN

THE works of Walt Whitman have lately been very much reviewed in England, while in this, his native country, he has rarely been noticed. In America, through ignorance of all the characteristics of his works, the little value he possesses as a poet has been denied him; while in England, chiefly through ignorance of the American people, Mr. Whitman has been greatly overestimated.

He is spoken of in England as preeminently the poet of Democracy and of America, the first of Democracies; but we are not definitely told why. One English critic has gone so far as to style Whitman the "*sacer vates* to the growth of the American youth," implying, I think, that he is benefiting us and is well known to us.

We indignantly abjure Walt Whitman as a "*sacer vates*," or as a true representative of our national thoughts and feelings. Because he spreads American names over his pages, foreigners consider him as the long-looked for herald of Democracy! An excellent chance, forsooth, for any madman to be flatteringly belauded and crowned America's poet, by merely mumbling and writing down in broken-legged verse the names of his country's physical features, its fowls, brute kind, its institutions, and numerous occupations! Either we refuse to Mr. Whitman his claim to be the exponent of our national thoughts, ambitions, hopes, and progress, or we submit ourselves to be looked upon as a people whose marked characteristics are illiteracy, sensuality, clownishness, and an utter absence of delicacy in manners, thought, and feelings; in other words, as a people of Pariahs. This is a distasteful alternative, but I see no other. Englishmen and other foreigners have been eagerly looking for something decidedly original in American literature. Something abnormal was wanted, and at last is at hand: they have found a man of a nature less poetical than his pretensions would have us believe, but yet poetical; and, as his works show, possessed of a character the most eccentric and marvellous. Their joy at this discovery is boundless, and Americans cannot comprehend it. To us, such violent admiration of Whitman seems to be the sputtering of diseased minds; for their admiration of him extends to matter, the construction of which is opposed to every well-established rule of poetical form, and the vulgarity of which is revolting to the sense and distasteful to the intellect. There are times when Whitman is the poet; but at such happy times there is in him no more evidence of the influence of Democracy than in any other American poet.

But let us quote a few lines, which, chosen with a view to give true impressions, will show at once the worthlessness of his claims as a poet, and at the same time expose some of those literary monstrosities which his English and American friends admire. Our bard's admirers say that one of his most excellent poetical qualities is the faithful reflection of his character in his poems. If this is true, the following quotations tell a sorry story of his life, and will also help to explain his mysterious individuality, his governing motives, &c. He says he is—

"Turbulent, fleshy, and sensual, eating, drinking, and breeding," and not a "dainty, dolce affetuoso."

He takes a curious delight in repeating to his readers that he is sensual and lusty, without a greater fondness for the clean and respectable than for their opposites.

"No more modest than immodest."

"I am not the poet of goodness only—I do not decline to be the poet of
wickedness also."
"I am myself just as much evil as good, and my nation is. And I say
there is in fact no evil."

Whitman declares this repeatedly, as if he were afraid that some one
would deny to him those qualities which he asserts that he has. But his
glory, in so far as it depends on his sensuality, may rest safely; for in
his earlier works his declarations are supported by passages sufficiently
gross and indecent.

He tells us he is untranslatable; that when we think we have caught
his meaning,—presto! it vanishes. He thinks his accumulations of words
are:—

"Man's, woman's, child's, youth's, wife's, husband's, mother's, father's,
young man's, young woman's poems;
Head, neck, hair, ears, drop and tympan of the ears,
Eyes, eye-fringes," etc., etc., from "toe-joints" to "jaw-hinges,"
"O, I say now these are the soul."

To discuss such unmeaning trifles would be to insult the good sense
of the reader.

In his effusion headed "Salut au Monde," he applies to himself the
question, "What do you see, Walt Whitman?" and his reply is embrac-
ingly poetical, consisting of a bare list, not in rhyme, rhythm, or reason,
of every range of mountains, of every body of water, of every city,
noted in a comprehensive geography. And this, we are told, indicates
in him a vocabulary more fruitful than that possessed by Shakespeare.

Whitman is a materialist, and chants his belief thus:—

"Divine am I inside and out, and I make holy whatever I touch or am
touched from;
The scent of these arm-pits, sweeter than the aroma of prayer,
This head more than churches, bibles, and all the creeds."

It is not the subject of his poems, but its treatment, that we may justly complain of; and there is no one of his thousand and one poems, which exemplifies better than the preceding his disgusting taste.

He says if he worshipped any thing it would be his own body. Discussing one's duty to God makes our poet sick; so he would like to leave the society of those who do so discuss, and live with animals,—if they permitted it. He howls of the heavens, stars, moon, time, and space, leaping without difficulty from the infinite to the finite. Nothing too low or high but must bear the burden of his song. Whitman has no idea of delicacy, and supposes none in the reader. He penetrates our closets, accompanies us to the bath, pursues us through the day, passes the evening with us, sees us into bed, and then, unasked, jumps in with us. If we rebuff him, he reproaches us with "gossamer delicacy," taunts us with purism. Indeed, his sense of propriety is utterly dead.

In fine, then, we see nothing in Whitman, either in form of expression or in poetical nature, which does not grossly violate those standards by which the claims of the best of poets have been measured. Should we allow Whitman to embrace us, as he again and again says he wants to do, we should be erecting for ourselves a new standard of poetic thought and expression. His English admirers would carry Whitman in triumph over the muddy road which they have strewn with flowers torn from the tombs of the greatest poets. But we will not join them in their frenzied march. When, however, Whitman shall have given us noble thoughts or elevating ideals, he may be sure the youth of America will appreciate him; but nobody can force us to drink from the polluted bucket which a maniac has filled, and which English sensualism raises to our lips.

February, 1876

THEODORE ROOSEVELT

Class of 1880, (1858–1919)

Teddy's flamboyant sidewhiskers and jaunty pose set him off from his fellow editors in the Advocate *board photograph of 1880; his rise from treasurer of the magazine, to war hero, to President is too familiar to need repetition. His article on "Football at Harvard" reflects the interests of the* Advocate *in its early years; "Harvard and Preparedness" was printed on the eve of the First World War.*

FOOTBALL AT OTHER COLLEGES

THE FOOTBALL season has now fairly opened, and it is well to take a glance at what our rivals are doing. Yale has lost Thompson, who has twice turned the scale against us; but otherwise her team will probably be much the same as last year's, and there is plenty of good material from which to fill the vacancies. Captain Camp has already begun to put his men into regular training, running them in the gymnasium. Thirty men have been pledged to play against the team every afternoon, and games will probably be played with both Amherst and Trinity; so that there will be no danger of her men suffering from lack of practice. At present it hardly seems as if the team would be as good as last year's, but their playing is improving every day, and nothing but very hard work will enable our men to win the victory.

Princeton will undoubtedly have a good team, although the lower classes do not seem to possess very good material from which to choose; but it must be remembered that in Princeton, where there is no crew, all the best men go out on the football field, and work with a faithfulness not very common at Harvard.

At Cornell there has been some talk of organizing a team, but it is doubtful if it can be done this year. What Columbia will do, it is difficult to say. On the whole, the prospect should be by no means discouraging to us. We certainly have good teams to fight against; but there is plenty of excellent material in College, and our captain deserves most hearty praise, whatever be the result, for the pains he has taken, not only in keeping the men at work on the field, but in running them on the track every afternoon. What is most necessary is, that every man should realize the necessity of faithful and honest work, *every afternoon*. Last year we had good individual players, but they did not work together nearly as well as the Princeton team, and were not in as good condition as the Yale men. The football season is short; and while it does last, the men ought to work faithfully, if they expect to win back for Harvard the position she held three years ago.

October, 1879

HARVARD AND PREPAREDNESS

HARVARD ought to take the lead in every real movement for making our country stand as it should stand. Unfortunately prominent Harvard men sometimes take the lead the wrong way. This applies pre-eminently to all Harvard men who have had anything to do with the absurd and mischievous professional-pacifist or peace-at-any-price movements which have so thoroughly discredited this country during the past five years. These men are seeking to chinafy the country; and, so far as they have any influence, they are tending to chinafy Harvard too. The pacifist of this type stands on an exact level with the poltroon. His appropriate place is with the college sissy who disapproves of football or boxing because it is rough.

In all our history there have been few movements more detrimental to our people and no movement more essentially ignoble than the professional pacifist or peace-at-any-price movement which has reached its zenith during the past five years. This movement became part of our official governmental policy when five years ago the effort was made to adopt the all-inclusive arbitration treaties under which we covenanted to arbitrate questions of national honor and vital interest (specifically, this means questions such as the murder of American men, women and children on the high seas and the rape of American women, for instance). A couple of years ago we actually adopted certain ludicrous arbitration or commission-for-a-year's-investigation treaties which, when the proposal was made to reduce them to practice, were instantly repudiated by the very administration that had made them. Much harm has been done to America by crooked politicians and by crooked business men; but they have never done as much harm as these professional pacifists have sought to do and have partially succeeded in doing. They have weakened the moral fibre of our people. They have preached base and ignoble doctrines to this nation. For five years they have succeeded in tainting our foreign policy with mean hypocrisy.

I abhor wanton or unjust war. I believe with all my heart in peace, if peace can be obtained on terms compatible with self-respect. Even a necessary war I regard as a lamentable necessity. But it may be a necessity. It may be a necessity in order to save our bodies. It may be a necessity in order to save our souls. A high-minded man or woman does not regard death as the most dreadful of all things, because there are some things worse than death. A high-minded nation does not regard war as the most dreadful of all things, because there are some things worse than war.

Recently there have actually been political buttons circulated in this country with "safety first" as the motto upon them in the fancied interest of one of the party candidates for the Presidency next year. This is the motto which in practise is acted upon by the men on a sinking ship who jump into the lifeboats ahead of the women and children. Even these men, however, do not, when they get ashore, wear buttons to commemorate their feat.

This country needs to prepare itself materially against war. Even more it needs to prepare itself spiritually and morally, so that, if war must be accepted as the alternative to dishonor or unrighteousness, it shall be accepted with stern readiness to do any duty and incur any hazard that the times demand. It would be well if Harvard would establish as part of its curriculum an efficient system of thorough military training—not merely military drill, which is only a part of military training, and indeed a small part. I believe heartily in athletics; but from the physical

Theodore Roosevelt

and moral standpoint such a system of military training would be better for all the men in Harvard and would reach far more men than are now reached by athletics.

In addition, however, to such military training, and even if at present it proves impossible to get such military training, let Harvard men, graduates and undergraduates alike, start at once to practice and to preach that efficient morality which stands at the opposite pole from the milk-and-water doctrines of the professional pacifists. Remember that sentimentality is as directly the reverse of sentiment as bathos is of pathos. It is right and eminently necessary to be practical; it is right and eminently necessary to take care of our own fortunes, of our own bodies. Each man must do it individually; and the nation must do it in its corporate capacity, acting for all of us. But in addition, both men and nation must have the power of fealty to a lofty ideal. No man is worth his salt who is not ready at all times to risk his body, to risk his wellbeing, to risk his life, in a great cause. No nation has a right to a place in the world unless it has so trained its sons and daughters that they follow righteousness as the great goal. They must scorn to do injustice, and scorn to submit to injustice. They must endeavor steadily to make peace the handmaiden of righteousness, to secure both peace and righteousness. But they must stand ready, if the alternative is between peace and righteousness, unhesitatingly to face suffering and death in war rather than to submit to iniquity or dishonor.

December, 1915

EDWIN ARLINGTON ROBINSON

Attended Harvard 1891–93, (1869–1935)

Robinson left Harvard after only two years, but he had already developed a mature style and several of his Advocate *lyrics were later included in* The Children of the Night, *one of his best collections of poetry. He was constantly in financial difficulties until former* Advocate *editor Theodore Roosevelt gave him a job in the New York customs house. Recognition began to come with* The Man Against the Sky *(1916), and in 1921 his* Collected Poems *won the Pulitzer Prize. He won another Pulitzer Prize with the Arthurian trilogy,* Merlin, Lancelot, *and* Tristan, *completed in 1927.*

BALLADE OF THE WHITE SHIP

Down they went to the still, green water—
  The dim White Ship like a white bird lay;
Laughing at life and the world they sought her,
  And out they sailed on the silvering bay:
  The quick ship flew on her roystering way,
And the keen moon fired the light foam flying
  Up from the flood where the faint stars play,
And the bones of the brave in the wave are lying.

'Twas a king's gay son with a king's gay daughter,
  And full three hundred beside, they say,
Hurrying on to the lone, cold slaughter
  So soon to seize them and hide them for aye;
  But they danced and they drank and their souls grew gay,

Nor ever they knew of a ghoul's eye spying,
　　Their splendor a flickering phantom to stray
Where the bones of the brave in the wave are lying.

Through the mist of a drunken dream they brought her
　　(This wild white bird) for the sea-fiend's prey:
The ravenous reef in his hard clutch caught her
　　And whirled her down where the dead men stay—
　　A torturing silence of wan dismay;
The shrieks and curses of mad souls dying.
　　Then down they sank to slumber and sway
Where the bones of the brave in the wave are lying.

　　　　L'envoi

Prince, do you sleep 'mid the perishing clay
　　To the mournful dirge of the sea-birds' crying?
Or does blood still quicken and steel still slay—
　　Where the bones of the brave in the wave are lying?

October, 1891

VILLANELLE OF CHANGE

　　　　Since Persia fell at Marathon
　　　　　　The yellow years have gathered fast—
　　　　Long centuries have come and gone.

　　　　And yet (they say) the place will don
　　　　　　A phantom fury of the past,
　　　　Since Persia fell at Marathon;
　　　　And as of old, when Helicon
　　　　　　Trembled and swayed with rapture vast,—
　　　　Long centuries have come and gone—

Edwin Arlington Robinson 29

This ancient plain, when night comes on,
    Shakes in a phantom battle blast,
Since Persia fell at Marathon . . . .

With mouldering mists of Acheron
    Long have her skies been overcast,
Long centuries have come and gone;

The suns of other days have shone—
    The first has fallen to the last:
Since Persia fell at Marathon,
Long centuries have come and gone.

November, 1891

IN HARVARD 5

In Harvard 5 the deathless lore
That haunts old Avon's classic shore
    Wakens the long triumphant strain
    Of Pride and Passion, Mirth and Pain,
That fed the Poet's mind of yore.

Time's magic glass is turned once more
And back the sands of ages pour,
    While shades of mouldered monarchs reign
    In Harvard 5.

Thin spirits flutter through the door,
Quaint phantoms flit across the floor:
    Now Fancy marks the crimson stain
    Of Murder . . . and there falls again
The fateful gloom of Elsinore
    In Harvard 5.

December, 1891

SUPREMACY

There is a drear and lonely tract of Hell
    From all the common gloom removed afar:
    A flat, sad land where only shadows are,
Whose lorn estate no word of mine can tell.
I walked among the shades and knew them well:
    Men I had scorned upon Life's little star
    For churls and sluggards; and I knew the scar
Upon their brows of woe ineffable.

But as I moved triumphant on my way,
    Into the dark they vanished, one by one.
Then came an awful light, a blinding ray—
    As if a new creation were begun;
And with a swift, importunate dismay,
    I heard the dead men singing in the sun.

June, 1892

GEORGE LYMAN KITTREDGE

Class of 1892, (1860–1941)

"Kitty," as he was known by generations of Har-
vard students, was a Shakespearean scholar and
philologist who terrified his students with sharp
questions. President of the Advocate *while an*
undergraduate, he kept up his connections with
the magazine and was a frequent guest at parties
and discussions.

A TERRIBLE NIGHT

I HAD known him only a few weeks, and thought him a very jolly fellow.
He reciprocated my feelings, and we passed many pleasant hours in one
another's rooms, playing whist or discussing grave points in literature,
art, science, philosophy, and tennis. One night (I think it is extremely
doubtful—quite as doubtful, perhaps, as the championship problem—
if I ever forget that night)—one night in March we were sitting before
a blazing fire in his room, smoking and discussing the sonnet. The wind
howled outside like mad and the chapel choir, but within all was calm
save my new friend, who seemed strangely agitated. I wondered at this,
for I could see nothing in the subject of our discussion to rouse agita-
tion. Suddenly he sprang from his chair and with a sudden motion
locked and barred the door. I had never noticed before that there was
a bar, and was much surprised when I saw that it was arranged with a
spring-lock attachment. "Elton," I cried, "what under heaven are you
doing?" "Nothing, nothing, my dear fellow," and he laughed nervously,
"I only thought I heard Shakespeare's walk outside, coming to dun me
for my subscription to his sonnets, which I have never yet paid. Wait
a minute and I'll show you the book." I was not much reassured by this
reply, and watched Elton rather narrowly as he searched the bookcase

behind me, but I finally turned round again, as it took him a good while, and sat as before, facing the fire.

Perhaps I had been sitting thus thirty seconds, when I felt myself violently seized from behind, while a mocking laugh sounded in my ears. I was taken altogether at a disadvantage, and didn't quite know what was up, but soon came to the conclusion that Elton was trying to tie me to the chair. I don't mind telling you that I'm a pretty strong and agile fellow, my muscles having been well developed by constant base-ball practice. I'm on the Freshman Nine, you know. So I kicked and struggled desperately, but to no purpose. Elton's constant exercise at tennis had given him strength against which mine, though my sinew had been toughened in the way just mentioned, stood no chance. I soon found myself bound hand and foot to the heavy chair and locked in a room alone with a madman. For Elton was mad. There was no doubt of it. I think the presiding genius at the office was never madder, not even when a venturesome senior asked her recently for his mark in Forensics. "Faredale," said he, "I have you now. You are in my power. You have often conversed with me on the sonnet, little suspecting I am a poet. But a poet I am. I have sent my poems in to various college papers. They have never been accepted. I hired my goody to listen to my odes at ten dollars a line; she heard three lines and fled. I bribed my janitor. He heard six lines and went out, borrowing my umbrella. I persuaded Connors, and he seemed to stand it pretty well, but it was too much for his bull-dog. It killed him. I had to pay Connors heaven knows how much damages. But now I have you. Ha! ha! Just listen to my beautiful poems." And he produced a well-bound and well-thumbed MS. and began:—

"OWED TO THE OFFICE

"O dread abode of doubt and dreary woe!
O dreary, doubting woe, and dread abode!
Why dost thou tear, torment, and torture so
The trembling toiler of this thrice-told ode?
    Thou labyrinth of cave, thou cavy woe,
    Why dost thou torture and torment me so?"

While reading this frightful production, poor Elton gesticulated and gyrated as I had thought nothing on earth could make a man gesticulate and gyrate, always excepting Dr. James's spiral swing. As for me, I was *in articulo mortis*. But I held my breath. "Is it not glorious?" shrieked the madman. "Yes, indeed," assented I. "Then just listen to this," and on he went:—

"LINES TO THE TUBULAR VU

"God bless thee, good old Tubular! God save and send thee rest.
The errors of my judgment long since I have confessed.
I used to think it dreadful (when I was young and green)
To figure out your mysteries and make my blank out clean—
But standing on one foot
   At the bullention in U.
Has made me sigh for good old times
    When each student, rich or poor, bond or free, without re-
    gard to age or sex, could, by simply calling for it, obtain at
    no expense, a copy of that invaluable manual for students
    known as the Tubular Vu."

"How do you like that?" said Elton. I was fast growing weaker, but I managed to gasp out, "Lovely. The wild and luxuriant redundancy of the last line, the sort of harmony blossoming itself to death, reminds me of—" "No matter what it reminds you of," burst out the madman, "listen to this. It is a

"THRENODY

"Scarce can I think that he is dead.
Who's dead? A Senior, he
Slipped up on his degree;
   The mourners veil his head,
   He's dead. No doubt he's dead.
   Alas, why did he die?
    Who can tell?
   Dead he is, then let him lie,
    Toll the bell."

"The bell," laughed Elton, "is to be tolled five minutes. You have no more prayer-cuts. You will go to prayers or be put on special." "I shall die," I groaned. "No doubt," said he; "here is another. Something of a magical nature:—

xxx

"Three friends came forth out of the West,
Out of the East came they,
There came three friends out of the South,
And thus began their say—"

"Help! help!" I shrieked, able to bear no more. At my words the door was burst open, and two men rushed in. They seized Elton and secured him after a desperate struggle. It was the janitor and a friend, who, supposing Elton out, were going to drop in for a quiet smoke. They saved me, any way. Elton was sent to —— Asylum, where he got over his poetry, and has since become a useful member of the community.

June, 1881

George Lyman Kittredge 35

WALLACE STEVENS

Class of 1901, (1879–1955)

For two years Stevens contributed stories and poems to the Advocate, *but when he was elected President in 1900 it became his job to write editorials about cheers at football games, Memorial Hall, and other college issues. He continued to write poetry which was printed under the pseudonyms of R. Jerries and Carroll More. But after this prolific beginning he went to law school and into the insurance business, and for twenty years published practically nothing. In 1923 he broke silence with* Harmonium, *and by the time* Ideas of Order *(1936) and* The Man with the Blue Guitar *(1937) appeared he was established as a leading American poet. The* Advocate *brought out a special issue in his honor in 1940. In 1954 his* Collected Poems *won the Bollingen Prize for poetry.*

Wallace Stevens: the interacting veins of life between his early and later poems are an ever-continuing marvel to me. He seems to live in an unspoiled cosmos of his own, in which under surprises or alien pressure he is so constitutionally incapable of self-treachery that his poetry becomes for us a symbol of hope,—a kind of incorruptible Eleazar of the Apocrypha.

MARIANNE MOORE

SONNET

There shines the morning star! Through the forlorn
   And silent spaces of cold heaven's height
   Pours the bright radiance of his kingly light,
Swinging in revery before the morn.
The flush and fall of many tides have worn
   Upon the coasts beneath him, in their flight
   From sea to sea; yet ever on the night
His clear and splendid visage is upborne.

Like this he pondered on the world's first day,
   Sweet Eden's flowers heavy with the dew;
And so he led bold Jason on his way
      Sparkling forever in the galley's foam;
And still he shone most perfect in the blue,
      All bright and lovely on the hosts of Rome.

April, 1899

SONG

Ah yes! beyond these barren walls
   Two hearts shall in a garden meet,
And while the latest robin calls,
   Her lips to his shall be made sweet.

And out above these gloomy tow'rs
   The full moon tenderly shall rise
To cast its light upon the flow'rs,
   And find him looking in her eyes.

March, 1900

Wallace Stevens 37

OUTSIDE THE HOSPITAL

See the blind and the lame at play,
   There on the summer lawn—
She with her graceless eyes of clay,
   Quick as a frightened fawn,
Running and tripping into his way
   Whose legs are gone.

How shall she 'scape him, where shall she fly,
   She who never sees?
Now he is near her, now she is by—
   Into his arms she flees.
Hear her gay laughter, hear her light cry
   Among the trees.

"Princess, my captive." "Master, my king,"
   "Here is a garland bright."
"Red roses, I wonder, red with the Spring,
   Red with a reddish light?"
"Red roses, my princess, I ran to bring,
   And be your knight."

          March, 1900

STREET SONGS

I. THE PIGEONS

Over the houses and into the sky
   And into the dazzling light,
Long hosts of fluttering pigeons fly
   Out of the blackened night,

Over the houses and into the sky
   On glistening wings of white.

Over the city and into the blue
   From ledge and tower and dome,
They rise and turn and turn anew,
   And like fresh clouds they roam,
Over the city and into the blue
   And into their airy home.

II. THE BEGGAR

Yet in this morn there is a darkest night,
Where no feet dance or sweet birds ever rise
Where fancy is a thing that soothes—and lies,
And leads on with mirages of light.
I speak of her who sits within plain sight
Upon the steps of yon cathedral. Skies
Are naught to her; and life a lord that buys
And sells life, whether sad, or dark, or bright.

The carvings and beauty of the throne
Where she is sitting, she doth meanly use
To win you and appeal. All rag and bone
She asks with her dry, withered hand a dreg
Of the world's riches. If she doth abuse
The place, pass on. It is a place to beg.

III. STATUARY

The windy morn has set their feet to dancing—
   Young Dian and Apollo on the curb,
The pavement with their slender forms is glancing
   No clatter doth their gaiety disturb.

Wallace Stevens 39

No eyes are ever blind enough to shun them,
  Men wonder what their jubilance can be,
No passer-by but turns to look upon them—
  Then goes his way with all his fancy free.

IV. THE MINSTREL

The streets lead out into a mist
  Of daisies and of daffodils—
A world of green and amethyst,
  Of seas and of uplifted hills.

There bird-songs are not lost in eaves,
  Nor beaten down by cart and car,
But drifting sweetly through the leaves,
  They die upon the fields afar.

Nor is the wind a broken thing
  That faints within hot prison cells,
But rises on a silver wing
  From out among the heather bells.

April, 1900

NIGHT SONG

I stand upon the hills to-night
  And see the cold March moon
Rise upward with his silver light
  And make a gentle noon.

The fields are blowing with the breeze,
  The stars are in the sky,
There is a humming through the trees,
  And one cloud passes by.

I wonder if that is the sea,
   Rid of the sun's annoy,
That sings a song all bold and free,
   Of glory and of joy.

May, 1900

SONNET

Lo, even as I passed beside the booth
Of roses, and beheld them brightly twine
To damask heights, taking them as a sign
Of my own self still unconcerned with truth;
Even as I held up in hands uncouth
And drained with joy the golden-bodied wine,
Deeming it half-unworthy, half divine,
From out the sweet-rimmed goblet of my youth;

Even in that pure hour I heard the tone
Of grievous music stir in memory,
Telling me of the time already flown
From my first youth. It sounded like the rise
Of distant echo from dead melody,
Soft as a song heard far in Paradise.

May, 1900

QUATRAIN

He sought the music of the distant spheres
   By night, upon an empty plain, apart;
Nor knew they hid their singing all the years
   Within the keeping of his human heart.

June, 1900

Wallace Stevens 41

SONG

She loves me or loves me not,
    What care I?—
The depth of the fields is just as sweet,
    And sweet the sky.

She loves me or she loves me not,
    Is that to die?—
The green of the woods is just as fair,
    And fair the sky.

1901

OF BRIGHT & BLUE BIRDS & THE GALA SUN

Some things, niño, some things are like this,
That instantly and in themselves they are gay
And you and I are such things, O most miserable . . .

For a moment they are gay and are a part
Of an element, the exactest element for us,
In which we pronounce joy like a word of our own.

It is there, being imperfect, and with these things
And erudite in happiness, with nothing learned,
That we are joyously ourselves and we think

Without the labor of thought, in that element,
And we feel, in a way apart, for a moment, as if
There was a bright *scienza* outside of ourselves,

A gaiety that is being, not merely knowing,
The will to be and to be total in belief,
Provoking a laughter, an agreement, by surprise.

1940

MRS. ALFRED URUGUAY

So what said the others and the sun went down
And, in the brown blues of evening, the lady said,
In the donkey's ear, "I fear that elegance
Must struggle like the rest." She climbed until
The moonlight in her lap, mewing her velvet,
And her dress were one and she said, "I have said no
To everything, in order to get at myself.
I have wiped away moonlight like mud. Your innocent ear
And I, if I rode naked, are what remain."

The moonlight crumbled to degenerate forms,
While she approached the real, upon her mountain,
With lofty darkness. The donkey was there to ride,
To hold by the ear, even though it wished for a bell,
Wished faithfully for a falsifying bell.
Neither the moonlight could change it. And for her,
To be, regardless of velvet, could never be more
Than to be, she could never differently be,
Her no and no made yes impossible.

Who was it passed her there on a horse all will,
What figure of capable imagination?
Whose horse clattered on the road on which she rose,
As it descended, blind to her velvet and

The moonlight? Was it a rider intent on the sun,
A youth, a lover with phosphorescent hair,
Dressed poorly, arrogant of his streaming force,
Lost in an integration of the martyrs' bones,
Rushing from what was real; and capable?

The villages slept as the capable man went down,
Time swished on the village clocks and dreams were alive,
The enormous gongs gave edges to their sounds,
As the rider, no chevalere and poorly dressed,
Impatient of the bells and midnight forms,
Rode over the picket rocks, rode down the road,
And, capable, created in his mind,
Eventual victor, out of the martyrs' bones,
The ultimate elegance: the imagined land.

1940

ASIDES ON THE OBOE

The prologues are over. It is question, now,
Of final belief. So, say that final belief
Must be in a fiction. It is time to choose.

1

That obsolete fiction of the wide river in
An empty land; the gods that Boucher killed;
And the metal heroes that time granulates—
The philosophers' man alone still walks in dew,
Still by the sea-side mutters milky lines
Concerning an immaculate imagery.
If you say on the hautboy man is not enough

Can never stand as god, is ever wrong
In the end, however naked, tall, there is still
The impossible possible philosophers' man,
The man who has had the time to think enough,
The central man, the human globe, responsive
As a mirror with a voice, the man of glass,
Who in a million diamonds sums us up.

2

He is the transparence of the place in which
He is and in his poems we find peace.
He sets this peddler's pie and cries in summer,
The glass man, cold and numbered, dewily cries,
"Thou art not August unless I make thee so."
Clandestine steps upon imagined stairs
Climb through the night, because his cuckoos call.

One year, death and war prevented the jasmine scent
And the jasmine islands were bloody martyrdoms.
How was it then with the central man? Did we
Find peace? We found the sum of men. We found,
If we found the central evil, the central good.
We buried the fallen without jasmine crowns,
There was nothing he did not suffer, no; nor we.

It was not as if the jasmine ever returned.
But we and the diamond globe at last were one.
We had always been partly one. It was as we came
To see him, that we were wholly one, as we heard
Him chanting for those buried in their blood,
In the forests that had been jasmine, that we knew
The glass man, without external reference.

1940

Wallace Stevens 45

EXAMINATION OF THE HERO IN A TIME OF WAR

I

Force is my lot and not pink-clustered
Roma ni Avignon ni Leyden,
And cold, my element. Death is my
Master and, without light, I dwell. There
The snow hangs heavily on the rocks, brought
By a wind that seeks out shelter from snow. Thus
Each man spoke in winter. Yet each man spoke of
The brightness of arms, said Roma wasted
In its own dirt, said Avignon was
Peace in a time of peace, said Leyden
Was always the other mind. The brightness
Of arms, the will opposed to cold, fate
In its cavern, wings subtler than any mercy,
These were the psalters of their sibyls.

II

The God whom we serve is able to deliver
Us. Good chemistry, good common man, what
Of that angelic sword? Creature of
Ten times ten times dynamite, convulsive
Angel, convulsive shatterer, gun,
Click, click, the God whom we serve is able,
Still, still to deliver us, still magic,
Still moving yet motionless in smoke, still
One with us, the heaved-up noise, still
Captain, the man of skill, the expert
Leader, the creator of bursting color
And rainbow sortilege, the savage weapon
Against enemies, against the prester,
Presto, whose whispers prickle the spirit.

Wallace Stevens

III

They are sick of each old romance, returning;
Of each old revolving dance, the music
Like a euphony in a museum
Of euphonies, a skin from Nubia,
A helio-born. How strange the hero
To this accurate, exacting eye. Sight
Hangs heaven with flash drapery. Sight
Is a museum of things seen. Sight,
In war, observes each man profoundly.
Yes. But these sudden sublimations
Are to combat with his exaltations
Are to the unaccountable prophet or
What any fury to its noble centre.

IV

To grasp the hero, the eccentric
On a horse, in a plane, at the piano—
At the piano, scales, arpeggios
And chords, the morning exercises,
The afternoon's reading, the night's reflection,
That's how to produce a virtuoso.
The drill of a submarine. The voyage
Beyond the oyster-beds, indigo
Shadow, up the great sea and downward
And darkly beside the vulcanic
Sea-tower, sea-pinnacles, sea-mountain.
The signal... The sea-tower, shaken,
Sways slightly and the pinnacles frisson.
The mountain collapses. Chopiniana.

V

The common man is the common hero.
The common hero is the hero.

Imprimatur. But then there's common fortune,
Induced by what you will: the entrails
Of a cat, twelve dollars for the devil,
A kneeling woman, a moon's farewell;
And common fortune, induced by nothing,
Unwished for, chance, the merest riding
Of the wind, rain in a dry September,
The improvisations of the cuckoos
In a clock-shop ... Soldier, think, in the darkness,
Repeating your appointed paces
Between two neatly measured stations,
Of less neatly measured common-places.

VI

Unless we believe in the hero, what is there
To believe? Incisive what, the fellow
Of what good. Devise. Make him of mud,
For every day. In a civiler manner,
Devise, devise, and make him of winter's
Iciest core, a north star, central
In our oblivion, of summer's
Imagination, the golden rescue:
The bread and wine of the mind, permitted
In an ascetic room, its table
Red as a red table-cloth, its windows
West Indian, the extremest power
Living and being about us and being
Ours, like a familiar companion.

VII

Gazette Guerrière. A man might happen
To prefer *L'Observateur de la Paix*, since
The hero of the *Gazette* and the hero
Of *L'Observateur*, the classic hero

And the bourgeois, are different, much,
The classic changed. There have been many.
And there are many bourgeois heroes.
There are more heroes than marbles of them.
The marbles are pinchings of an idea,
Yet there is that idea behind the marbles,
The idea of things for public gardens,
Of men suited to public ferns ... The hero
Glides to his meeting like a lover
Mumbling a secret, passionate message.

VIII

The hero is not a person. The marbles
Of Xenophon, his epitaphs, should
Exhibit Xenophon, what he was, since
Neither his head nor horse nor knife nor
Legend were part of what he was, forms
Of a still-life, symbols, brown things to think of
In brown books. The marbles of what he was stand
Like a white abstraction only, a feeling
In a feeling mass, a blank emotion,
An anti-pathos, until we call it
Xenophon, its implement and actor.
Obscure Satanus, make a model
Of this element, this force. Transfer it
Into a barbarism as its image.

IX

If the hero is not a person, the emblem
Of him, even if Xenophon, seems
To stand taller than a person stands, has
A wider brow, large and less human
Eyes and bruted ears: the man-like body
Of a primitive. He walks with a defter

And lither stride. His arms are heavy
And his breast is greatness. All his speeches
Are prodigies in longer phrases.
His thoughts begotten at clear sources,
Apparently in air, fall from him
Like chantering from an abundant
Poet, as if he thought gladly, being
Compelled thereto by an innate music.

X

And if the phenomenon, magnified, is
Further magnified, sua voluntate,
Beyond his circumstance, projected
High, low, far, wide, against the distance,
In parades like several equipages,
Painted by mad-men, seen as magic,
Leafed out in adjectives as private
And peculiar and appropriate glory,
Even enthroned on rainbows in the sight
Of the fishes of the sea, the colored
Birds and people of this too voluminous
Air-earth—Can we live on dry descriptions,
Feel everything starving except the belly
And nourish ourselves on crumbs of whimsy?

XI

But a profane parade, the basso
Preludes a-rub, a-rub-rub, for him that
Led the emperor astray, the tom trumpets
Curling round the steeple and the people,
The elephants of sound, the tigers
In trombones roaring for the children,
Young boys resembling pastry, hip-hip,
Young men as vegetables, hip-hip,

Home and the fields give praise, hurrah, hip,
Hip, hip, hurrah. Eternal morning . . .
Flesh on the bones. The skeleton throwing
His crust away eats of this meat, drinks
Of this tabernacle, this communion,
Sleeps in the sun no thing recalling.

XII

It is not an image. It is a feeling.
There is no image of the hero.
There is a feeling as definition.
How could there be an image, an outline,
A design, a marble soiled by pigeons?
The hero is a feeling, a man seen
As if the eye was an emotion,
As if in seeing we saw our feeling
In the object seen and saved that mystic
Against the sight, the penetrating,
Pure eye. Instead of allegory,
We have and are the man, capable
Of his brave quickenings, the human
Accelerations that seem inhuman.

XIII

These letters of him for the little,
The imaginative, ghosts that dally
With life's salt upon their lips and savor
The taste of it, secrete within them
Too many references. The hero
Acts in reality, adds nothing
To what he does. He is the heroic
Actor and act but not divided.
It is a part of his conception,
That he be not conceived, being real.

Say that the hero is his nation,
In him made one, and in that saying
Destroy all references. This actor
Is anonymous and cannot help it.

XIV

A thousand crystals' chiming voices,
Like the shiddow-shaddow of lights revolving
To momentary ones, are blended,
In hymns, through irridescent changes,
Of the apprehending of the hero.
These hymns are like a stubborn brightness
Approaching in the dark approaches
Of time and place, becoming certain,
The organic centre of responses,
Naked of hindrance, a thousand crystals.
To meditate the highest man, not
The highest supposed in him and over,
Creates, in the blissfuller preceptions,
What unisons create in music.

XV

The highest man with nothing higher
Than himself, his self, the self that embraces
The self of the hero, the solar single,
Man-sun, man-moon, man-earth, man-ocean,
Makes poems on the syllable *fa* or
Jumps from the clouds or, from his window,
Sees the petty gildings on February . . .
The man-sun being hero rejects that
False empire . . . These are the works and pastimes
Of the highest self: he studies the paper
On the wall, the lemons on the table.
This is his day. With nothing lost, he

Arrives at the man-man as he wanted.
This is his night and meditation.

XVI

Each false thing ends. The bouquet of summer
Turns blue and on its empty table
It is stale and the water is discolored.
True autumn stands then in the doorway.
After the hero, the familiar
Man makes the hero artificial.
But was the summer false? The hero?
How did we come to think that autumn
Was the veritable season, that familiar
Man was the veritable man? So
Summer, jangling the savagest diamonds and
Dressed in its azure-doubled crimsons,
May truly bear its heroic fortunes
For the large, the solitary figure.

April, 1942

FRANKLIN DELANO ROOSEVELT

Class of 1904, (1882–1945)

FDR took charge of things even as an under-graduate. Not only was he elected permanent chairman of his class, he was President of the Harvard Crimson, and also contributed to the Advocate.

A NEWLY DISCOVERED FRAGMENT FROM A VOYAGE TO LILLIPUT

BUT STRANGER even than these nurseries for boys and girls past the nourishing age are the places where what the Lilliputians call "higher learning" is taught. Shortly after the fire in the Empress' wing of the palace, the Emperor, in order that I might not think him displeased with me, conferred upon me the degree of Doctor of Extinguishment, and commanded me to inspect one of these learned institutions which I have just mentioned. I found it situated in a pleasant marsh not far from the city of Axis—a town locally supposed to be the source and centre of all learning. The institution itself was called in the dialect a University, because, as I was told, it is the whole thing.

The earliest settlers of Lilliput founded this University soon after their arrival, chiefly for the purpose of a house of correction for the natives whom they found there. A few years later a worthy settler, dying, bequeathed a valuable set of printed notes to the institution which thereafter bore his noble name. Since then many life-like statues of him have arisen, all copied after an excellent sketch on the fly-leaf of a New England Primer, done of himself, by himself and for himself at the age of three and a half. His name also is frequently heard today, punctuated with sharp pleasure cries and given in chorus at a mystic sign from a six-inch giant who madly waves a cornucopia called in the language of the country megaphone. Owing, however, to a corruption of the name of the founder, the third letter, an r, is generally omitted by the inhabitants of Axis.

From a reformatory for the aborigines, the University has become the resort of thousands of Lilliputians, some even coming from the land of Blefuscu. Many of the inmates indeed come, not to study, but for the experience—"the finishing touch" which in many instances seemed to be indeed "the finishing touch." Some likewise go there for the sake only of exercise, but this practice has been lately discouraged because of a series of rules which it is said come down from Heaven, but which the Lilliputians to this day have been unable to interpret to their own satisfaction or that of anyone else. The University of the Big-Endians at Blefuscu is especially scornful of these rules, for they themselves have a rival set said to have been sent up to them by the Duskier God. The ill-feeling is further increased by the question of which can the better take exercise. The name of the Big-Endians itself is due to the swelling pride which these take in their victories in pushing a lima-bean through the ranks of the Lilliputians. On the other hand these latter, at the University I visited, because of a superior skill in killing fleas in mid-hop with a bow and arrow, claim to be the whole shooting-match.

In contests of needle threading, addition and subtraction, and reading aloud, the Little-Endians have also proved their mental superiority by victories for many moons. The needle-threading competition is especially thrilling, and the rapidity with which they passed the invisible thread through the invisible needle appeared to me quite out of sight. The enthusiasm at these contests is remarkable, very different I am told from what it was several moons ago. The din of the male students could be heard for many feet, while the co-educational members from the Sadstiff Annex signified their approval by "yum-yums" long and ponderous. I was told that the men who barked the loudest, and the lady students who yummed with greatest energy were as a rule the most liked in the University but that often in later life they did not come to high positions, probably because this form of strenuousness is not the best training to pass the great State rope dancing examinations.

The former custom of chorus singing at these matches is being superseded by hymns of praise sung alternately by a solo male and such a high female.

At the end of the contest the two umpires render diabolically opposite decisions, and the final result is announced many moons later by a partial Board of Arbitration.

Finally as a climax the two Universities rise as one man and sing their anthems. That of the Big-Endians started with the

> "See such a mighty tail behind
> And such a face before."

In the meantime my friends, starting at the same time in a deliciously different key sent heavenward their song—a beautiful diatribe composed of a sunset sonnet, a joke, and a communication, all taken from their leading University publications.

Such is the institution of highest learning among the noblest race in Lilliput—an institution which I would my own dear country would imitate.

On my return from Axis to the Capital I received another mark of the Emperor's favor.

[Here the manuscript stops.]

February, 1903

VAN WYCK BROOKS

Class of 1908, (1886–1963)

Brooks wrote poetry, short stories, and essays for the Advocate, *and was elected President in his senior year. After graduation he went into journalism, but soon returned to the academic world as a literary historian. In a series of books—* America's Coming of Age, The Flowering of New England, New England: Indian Summer, *and* The Confident Years—*he wrote an intellectual history of New England which provided a generation of American critics and readers with an approach to their own literature.*

THE POET WHO DIES YOUNG

"Il se trouve en un mot, dans les trois quarts des hommes, comme un poète qui meurt jeune, tandis que l'homme survit."

SAINTE-BEUVE.

ONCE a Frenchwoman wrote in her journal: "I have given up writing poetry because I have recognized that God does not ask it of me." There appears to be in most lives this moment, consciously or unconsciously a sacrifice, when the trees and the flowers once for all make their final demand upon us and we give them their final answer—either to become henceforth impersonal objects for which we have no time and for which we can allow none of that softening affection which undermines the necessary hardness of practical life, or else to stamp us with the seal of dreaming, and to make us forever unfit and scoffed at, dwellers in hidden worlds. It is this question that marks the effectual soul. There are many who drift through life too blind to recognize the question, too weak to answer it, and who shall say that even these have lived in vain?

But there is the mighty soul that answers yes, and there is the mighty soul that answers no.

When we are children we are forever weaving fancies about imaginary things: our soldiers and sailors, our cannibals, or it may be our policemen, our coachmen, ideal projections of what we ourselves desire to be, bear no relation to the reality of these forms of occupation, except as the spiritual essence of them, perhaps, brought down from other worlds. We desire to be sailors so that we may fly in swift galleys over unknown seas, and to be coachmen so that we may drive glorified horses for ever and ever, with the chariot of Aurora behind us.

But there comes a moment when Tom or Harry lets out the secret of his profession. Tom had a broken-down mare, and he had to earn his living—so he went into the "livery" business: and Harry was old Mrs. Leary the washerwoman's son, who ran away to sea and comes back with coarse hands and coarser words.

So then the question comes. For a moment we compare Tom with those wonderful horses and Harry with those wonderful galleys, and in the sober instant we feel, bitterly, that never again can there be an illusion or a charm. And we set about to make of ourselves lawyers and engineers.

The greatest untruth in all the world is that you have not time for so and so. The greatest fallacy in all the world is that your duty leads you into material ways that leave no room for beautiful things. A glimpse at pictures now and then, a poem to read three times a day, a walk at sunset along the brookside—who shall rob the practical man of these?

Too often we let the poet die away and amuse ourselves with grosser joys, that fasten themselves upon us and push out the delicate significance of solitude and charm. The whole world is against us, trying to make us like other men,—jealous of other worlds. Every instant of solitude that we allow ourselves is in opposition to the combined forces of the universe. Even if your hair has been gray now for twenty years, there is some far-away closet, some mouldering chest, where the yellow leaves of our old notebook are measured off into equal lines beginning with capital letters. The moon meant a great deal more in those days than it will ever mean again. What a poet you were! There was no object in the universe that was not haloed with a thousand sentiments. Do not imagine that you are free of them yet. "That Shakespeare," cries Colonel Bath, "was a fine fellow! He was a very pretty poet indeed."

What criticism that is from an old man who had outlived his poet in so many other ways—how much more naïve, more trenchant, more stimulating than to have said, Shakespeare was a great poet; he was familiar with all sides of human nature, very profound, very tender. "A fine fellow," "a very pretty poet indeed"—there is the heart of the matter, there is a poet's critique. A child will never inform you of the things that all men know in the words that all men use,—not a child, nor a poet.

The truth is that we deliberately acquire our ungraceful ways in an effort to be manly. Where the child is charmingly shy, the man is awkwardly bashful; where the child is fresh in his comments, the man cultivates long words and well-tried phrases to get along with other men. O wise generation, to advance your own pettiness, your own stateliness, how you despise the poet in yourself, how you would blush to be thought naïve, and would not for the world be heard to say anything natural! Very well you have understood the gospel of the Anglo-Saxon race: "When a man has learned to trust to his impressions, he had best be knocked on the head." An excellent law, most useful for rapid transit through this world of ours.

But before, and after, and above this world? I can give you no pithy word to match this stagnant and useful prudentiality. Throw open your shutters to the green grass glittering with dew, each blade turned whitish in the gentle breeze, with here and there a pale rose clover topping its rounded leaves,—to the twitter of early robins, busy among the longer blades: and with the faint scents of the morning quivering in your nostrils, behold the great rich sun throwing splendor across the maples by the road.

November, 1907

THE REST OF THE CIRCLE

Even in our undergraduate days at Palermo, Caracciolo was the type of a modern degenerate. To such a degree did he carry his excesses, that he was shunned like a leper by the students of even a Sicilian university. And, indeed, toward the end of our second year, they led to his expulsion. We were drawn together from the first by certain marked traits of mind which we had in common and which made me, in spite of his revolting nature, the ardent disciple of his intellect. To justify myself, I merely refer you to his *Purple Sunflowers,* in which all the lurid fascination of that singular man becomes as vivid as in life.

It was characteristic of him that his whole intellect should have been enslaved by that fantastic treatise *De Psychis Veritate;* and especially, I believe, his whole subsequent life was a morbid pondering upon the single *theory of curves.* Shöpenkreg's argument is somewhat thus:

Every mind, unknown to itself, formulates an ideal series of curves —a combination peculiarly its own, and differing from the combination of every other mind. Affection between two minds is simply a similarity of combinations. I like you more or less if your curves more or less coincide with mine. If I dislike you, the opposite is true. We have more than one instance in history of where two systems have exactly coincided, but these occasions have all been marked by memorable results. The wonders of Heaven and Hell were revealed to Dante after he had seen his Beatrice. Too recent for comment is the hideous death of the poet Citore, exhausted in the search for that chance face once seen in a crowd, which he has immortalized in his *Soul among Bodies.*

Caracciolo and I were by chance reunited during the seventh winter after his expulsion. I met him in Rome where he was engaged upon his famous *Breath of the Catacombs.* At that time his mind was riddled with loathsome fancies, his body half-decomposed with the effects of too often visualizing them. But once more I fell a prey to his fascinating personality. Together we planned a Neapolitan April, and by the middle of that month were installed in an ancient and spacious villa on the slopes of Casamicciola.

I recollect the lofty *salon* in which until long after midnight we lost ourselves in conversation. The flickering candles between us hardly penetrated to its vast and shadowy corners. The massive and graceful furniture grew perceptibly smaller by perspective, and at an immense height overhead, the ceiling was boldly ornamented with frescoes of a free though decadent splendor.

"And so," said I, "you argue that every one has his complementary soul?"

"Yes," he answered, "you will remember how my essay on Oscar Wilde proves him beyond question to be the remainder of Praxiteles, whose *Delian Memnon* is absolutely unique in conception, but coincides exactly with the *Charmides* of Wilde."

"But how," I asked, "do you connect this with personal likes and dislikes?"

"Precisely thus," he replied. "Every man likes himself more than anyone else. When he likes someone else, it is because that person's curve-system resembles his own and thus approaches the remainder of his actual self. You may remember that symbolic line in Browning:

'On the earth the broken arcs; in the heaven the perfect round.'

"Let me carry the symbol into prose. Every soul is, as it were, part of an ideal circle, an arc perhaps approaching the whole circumference, perhaps no more than a few degrees. When two curve-systems combine, it will be found that they complete each other also, and out of the *two* 'broken arcs' form the *one* 'perfect round.' Browning's 'heaven' is thus the meeting of complementary souls. Symbols become almost mechanical when we try to reduce such spiritual ideas to terms of the mind."

"But," I broke in, "how would one be aware of his astonishing good luck if he should find out this other soul?"

"Recognition at first sight, and then would come whatever more love a man could call up beyond the already vast amount bestowed upon his own person: in fact the moment would be supreme—Dante's was, but no one could answer for the consequences."

"But still no place for morality?" I asked.

"Certainly, and this is the most singular phase. A man's own greatness determines the size of his arc. Socrates would have been so much of a circle that his complementary soul would hardly exist at all. Still to use our diagram, a soul of three hundred and fifty degrees leaves only ten for its complement."

My sense of humor stole in. "What a lot of degrees it will take some day to fill you and me up," said I blowing out the candles.

We were about with the first signals of morning, watching the uncertain light pierce each corner where little patches of the night still lay, and fall flaming upon every white turret and crumbling wall half-hidden in the verdure. Behind us the mountains rose up with immense firmness against a sky very clear and now filled with a gray and deepening reflection.

For certain aesthetic reasons divorced as far as might be from any religious motive, we had set out for the sunrise mass, not long in finding ourselves before the ancient and decayed portal of San Niccolo. One corner of the church was still enshadowed, and there, now fully filled with the mystical and passionate genius of the mass, we knelt down facing the darkness.

How long my eyes were shut, my mind answering the appeal of the organ, I cannot say. When at last I looked up, it was to find Caracciolo beside me straining forward over his prayer-stool, his lips purple, his cheeks ashen, his breath coming in quick, audible jerks, his eyes wide with horror, disappointment,—and love.

I looked forward. A ray of the early sun had fallen through the red window, illuminating that portion of the wall which had before been in darkness. There, hanging against a pillar and framed in black, I recognized what I could not doubt to be the true portrait of the Saviour of Men—a long, mystical face sloping off into void, quite bodiless, and concentrating in white, bloodless, upturned eyes; beneath them a drawn mouth within a beard half lost in gathering mist.

Then I heard Caracciolo's broken words: "It *was* true, it *was* true! Christ—and I, the rest of the circle!"

November, 1905

T. S. ELIOT

Class of 1910, (1888–1965)

"My earliest recollection of our sixty-year-old hero is of a singularly attractive, tall and rather dapper young man, who reeled out of the door of the Lampoon *on a spring evening, and, catching sight of me, threw his arms about me . . ." wrote Conrad Aiken in* T. S. Eliot, a Symposium, *in 1958. The young Eliot soon abandoned the* Lampoon's *frivolities and gravitated to the more austere headquarters of the* Advocate, *where he was secretary on the board of 1910. He was class poet at Harvard, and after submitting a doctoral thesis on F. C. Bradley (but failing to complete the requirements) and clerking in a London bank, he rose gradually to literary prominence. These eight undergraduate poems, published in the* Advocate *from 1907 to 1910, have never been reprinted in an anthology of his work. The article "The Problem of Education," also uncollected, was written especially for the* Advocate *in 1934.*

SONG

When we came across the hill
   No leaves were fallen from the trees;
   The gentle fingers of the breeze
Had torn no quivering cobweb down.

The hedgerow bloomed with flowers still
No withered petals lay beneath;
But the wild roses in your wreath
Were faded, and the leaves were brown.

May, 1907

SONG

If space and time, as sages say,
Are things that cannot be,
The fly that lives a single day
Has lived as long as we.
But let us live while yet we may,
While love and life are free,
For time is time, and runs away,
Though sages disagree.

The flowers I sent thee when the dew
Was trembling on the vine
Were withered ere the wild bee flew
To suck the eglantine.
But let us haste to pluck anew
Nor mourn to see them pine,
And though the flowers of life be few
Yet let them be divine.

June, 1907

BEFORE MORNING

While all the East was weaving red with gray,
The flowers at the window turned toward dawn,
Petal on petal, waiting for the day,
Fresh flowers, withered flowers, flowers of dawn.

64   *T. S. Eliot*

This morning's flowers and flowers of yesterday
Their fragrance drifts across the room at dawn.
Fragrance of bloom and fragrance of decay,
Fresh flowers, withered flowers, flowers of dawn.

November, 1908

CIRCE'S PALACE

Around her fountain which flows
With the voice of men in pain,
Are flowers that no man knows.
Their petals are fanged and red
With hideous streak and stain;
They sprang from the limbs of the dead.—
We shall not come here again.

Panthers rise from their lairs
In the forest which thickens below,
Along the garden stairs
The sluggish python lies;
The peacocks walk, stately and slow,
And they look at us with eyes
Of men whom we knew long ago.

November, 1908

SONG

The moonflower opens to the moth,
    The mist crawls in from the sea;
A great white bird, a snowy owl,
    Slips from the alder tree.

Whiter the flowers, Love, you hold,
  Than the white mist on the sea;
Have you no brighter tropic flowers
  With scarlet life, for me?

January, 1909

ON A PORTRAIT

Among a crowd of tenuous dreams, unknown
To us of restless brain and weary feet,
Forever hurrying, up and down the street,
She stands at evening in the room alone.

Not like a tranquil goddess carved of stone
But evanescent, as if one should meet
A pensive lamia in some wood-retreat,
An immaterial fancy of one's own.

No meditations glad or ominous
Disturb her lips, or move the slender hands;
Her dark eyes keep their secrets hid from us,
Beyond the circle of our thought she stands.

The parrot on his bar, a silent spy,
Regards her with a patient curious eye.

January, 1909

NOCTURNE

Romeo, *grand serieux,* to importune
Guitar and hat in hand, beside the gate
With Juliet, in the usual debate
Of love, beneath a bored but courteous moon;

66   *T. S. Eliot*

The conversation failing, strikes some tune
Banal, and out of pity for their fate
Behind the wall I have some servant wait,
Stab, and the lady sinks into a swoon.

Blood looks effective on the moonlit ground—
The hero smiles; in my best mode oblique
Rolls toward the moon a frenzied eye profound,
(No need of "Love forever?"—"Love next week?")
While female readers all in tears are drowned:—
"The perfect climax all true lovers seek!"

November, 1909

HUMORESQUE

After J. Laforgue
One of my marionettes is dead,
Though not yet tired of the game—
But weak in body as in head,
(A jumping-jack has such a frame),

But this deceased marionette
I rather liked: a common face,
(The kind of face that we forget)
Pinched in a comic, dull grimace;

Half bullying, half imploring air,
Mouth twisted to the latest tune;
His who-the-devil-are-you stare;
Translated, maybe, to the moon.

With Limbo's other useless things
Haranguing spectres, set him there;
"The snappiest fashion since last spring's
"The newest style on Earth, I swear.

T. S. Eliot 67

"Why don't you people get some class?
(Feebly contemptuous of nose),
"Your damned thin moonlight, worse than gas—
"Now in New York"—and so it goes.

Logic a marionette's, all wrong
Of premises; yet in some star
A hero!—Where would he belong?
But, even at that, what mask *bizzarre!*

January, 1910

SPLEEN

Sunday; this satisfied procession
Of definitely Sunday faces;
Bonnets, silk hats, and conscious graces
In repetition that displaces
Your mental self-possession
By this unwarranted digression.

Evening, lights and tea'.
Children and cats in the alley;
Dejection unable to rally
Against this dull conspiracy.

And Life, a little bald and gray,
Waits, hats and gloves in hand,
Languid, fastidious, and bland,
Punctilious to tie and suit
(Somewhat impatient of delay)
    On the doorstep of the Absolute.

January, 1910

THE PROBLEM OF EDUCATION

AT THE present time I am not very much interested in the only subject which I am supposed to be qualified to write about: that is, one kind of literary criticism. I am not very much interested in literature, except dramatic literature; and I am largely interested in subjects which I do not yet know very much about: theology, politics, economics, and education. I am moved at the moment to say something on the last of these subjects; so, if my comments appear very scrappy, I can only say that it is hard to start one's own education over again when one is in the forties. I have had some practical experience of education; first, having been educated myself, and in my opinion very badly. Second, I have taught boys of all ages in English schools; I was once an assistant in the Philosophy Department at Harvard; I have conducted Adult Education classes, and I have lectured at Cambridge in England and Cambridge in Massachusetts. I mention these facts because they are what might be considered credentials. But I do not feel that I have learned very much except to appreciate the magnitude of the educational problem. A great many men have taught for many more years than I, and yet are no more qualified to make any general statements about education. Indeed, most of the people engaged in educating seem to have very little conception of the general problem of education for a race and a nation, or of what purpose in a general scheme their own work is serving. They are merely Ford operatives. As for the big executives of education, I suspect that many of them have their minds filled with unexamined assumptions. Yet after feeding and clothing and housing people, the problem of how they should be educated is the most important you have, and perhaps the most difficult. Wherever you begin, you are led on to everything else. The problem of education leads you out to every other, and every other problem leads you back to education.

If what I am concerned about were merely the local problem, the question of what kind of education we ought to have in England, or in America, I should feel certainly that I am too ignorant to have the right to say anything. But I do not consider that there is one problem of education in America and another in England. However different the present systems may appear, I am sure that fundamentally we have one problem, at least in all English speaking countries, and that the things which alarm or depress me in America are equally present and alarming or depressing in England. English education is changing just as American education is changing: with only the trifling difference that the former seems to be going to the devil rather more slowly. The provincial universities, in any case, have much the same problem as the state universities of America: what sort of an education to give when the population to be educated includes almost everybody.

The chief persisting advantages of Oxford and Cambridge over American universities are (1) theological (2) economic.

I cannot attempt to demonstrate here that education, as the finest training of the finest minds, in contrast to the general education of everybody or the special technical training of persons to fill definite social needs, cannot afford to be separated from religion. But I am certain that the theological background—however far back it may be—is the only one that can provide the idea of order and unity needed for education. And I believe that if education is not rearranged by people with some definite social philosophy and some notion of the true vocation of man, the only education to be had will be in seminaries and colleges run by Jesuits. There is a good one in St. Louis, Mo. Incidentally, the only two men I know who have had what seemed to me hopeful theories of education and put them into practice, are Father Herbert Kelly of the Society of the Sacred Mission in Nottinghamshire, and Canon Iddings Bell of Providence, Rhode Island. I have no first-hand acquaintance with Canon Bell's frustrated attempts at St. Stephen's College, Annandale; and Father Kelly's system was designed for theological students; but I know of no other ventures in higher education of equal interest to these.

The leading American universities were, of course, originally directed by clergy of definite denominations. They now suffer from the dreadful blight of non-sectarianism, which means substituting a vague Christianity which the modern mind despises, for a precise Christianity which it may hate but must respect. Oxford and Cambridge are to a large extent atheist, but they remain in structure and ceremony foundations belonging to the Church of England. They may lose religion altogether, in time, but they are hardly likely to become non-sectarian; one feels, in their precincts, the sharp division of clerical and anti-clerical which is beneficial to both.

The American universities struck me, in contrast to Oxford and Cambridge, appallingly centralised in administration. That however is not the economic advantage of the latter universities that I have in mind. The English colleges own property; and much of their property is still that kind of property which is the least ignoble to possess: land. The ownership of land in England by individuals is now discouraged by Estate Duties, but ownership of land by colleges is still tolerated. The riches of the Oxford and Cambridge colleges do not, for the most part, consist in shares or debentures of fluctuating or doubtful value. Consequently the two older universities of England are on the whole independent of millionaires. Neither are their methods easily pliable to the theories of any one powerful administrator, like the late President Eliot. A Vice-Chancellor, or the Head of a House, does not have to spend much of his time begging for endowments; nor would he have unlimited control over their use when received. In fact, the two older English universities are not quite so dependent upon an industrial aristocracy as the American: they sprang from and flourished in conditions older than capitalism, and they can perhaps survive it.

When I have mentioned these advantages, and that fact that a classical education, although no longer imposed, is still regarded as normal, I have stated what seem to me the essentials. The other advantages of Oxford and Cambridge are in comparison trivial or irrelevant. I should not care to see American universities imitating Oxford and Cambridge, even to the worm-holes in the system.

Of course there are many details which might be examined. But whom do you want to educate? The answer will depend upon your conception of a good society; and so will the sort of education you want to give. The answers depend upon your notion of the place of man in the world, of the relation of a supernatural order, if any, to the natural; they depend upon our answers to all the questions which we tacitly agree not to raise, when we discuss educational matters. You may have a notion of the understanding of certain things as valuable in itself, so that you want a few people in every generation to be educated to understand and value and preserve them. Or you may have a notion of the kind of society you want, and concentrate upon whatever seems to subserve the interests of that society. Or you may have a vague notion that a university "education" confers a social degree, and proceed to overrun the country with gentlemen. Instead we assume at the same time that education is for those individuals who are fine enough to deserve it, that it is for the upper classes, that it is to make everybody a member of the upper classes, that everybody is entitled to the same education, that education is something to give one an advantage over the uneducated, and that education is going to make it possible to get a good job, according to whatever be our notion of goodness in jobs. But once you start to think about education you must go on thinking about your whole social system, and about politics and economics and theology. At any rate I am glad to think that all these subjects in which I am uneducated but interested are fundamentally related.

September, 1934

FROM THE T. S. ELIOT ISSUE, 1938

THE New Englander is a useful symbol, to which one is permitted to attribute a perennial and almost sensual enjoyment of starch and morality. Mr. Eliot has been refined and colored by an environment in which experience is necessarily circumlocution. As a tireless Calvinist, he has formulated Catholic plays and harried his pagan English public with godliness. Otherwise, he has devoured aesthetic criteria and actuality from the Symbolists and compatible areas of the arduous European tradition. Turbulence of experience, adroitness of sensibility, and artistry of presentation are fused in the terrifying solution.

A bias so complicated, snooty and immaterial—happily, psychologically tortured—is desperately precious. Its current worms against our flooding modernity. Form and finesse are its hallowed properties. These had to be protracted even among the empty shells, form for form's sake, before they flowered as something better than sensitivity, something heavily selfish—creation and faith. Mr. Eliot and another unautochthonous New Englander, Miss Marianne Moore, are the last creatures of the savage sophistication. Obviously, they are unparalleled in world literature; but Mr. Eliot, religiously oppressed from the beginning, has gone much farther. They are the last creatures, probably, because antithetical to this massive and mannerless democracy which has dedicated its institutions of learning to a populous pragmatism.

ROBERT LOWELL

I DON'T know what there is (any longer) to say about Eliot. His prodigious reputation is a great difficulty.

While that sort of thing: more or less complete acceptance of it, helps to create the poetry of any poet, it also helps to destroy it.

Occasionally I pick up Eliot's poems and read them, eliminating from my mind all thought of his standing. It is like having an opportunity to see, in an out of the way place, a painting that has made a great stir: for example, it is like having a Giotto in what is called a breakfast nook.

Reading Eliot out of the pew, so to speak, goes on keeping one young. He remains an upright ascetic in a world that has grown exceedingly floppy and is growing floppier.

WALLACE STEVENS

THOUGH he ultimately succumbed to the new conditions, T. S. Eliot was one of the very few who have succeeded in carrying the revivifying influence of the best of American letters into the atmosphere of English literary tradition. His great strength has been his ability and willingness to take world poetry as his criterion in seeking a judgment of excellence. But to do this in face of the terrible isolation which it breeds was more than he could stand under the primary conditions. From the first his lilting talent won us all, intrigued the ear and forced a music upon us as seductive as any popular tune. But craving a wider range and a surer base for his development, Eliot had to leave a semi-savage environment for a safer, more amenable, more cultured one. He might not otherwise have survived. There, in England, he did survive, much to his credit, mollified, if beaten about in such a way as to be almost unrecognizable, as the man who left America twenty years ago with his bundle of arrows gripped in one hand. His earlier poems, especially his Preludes and a few of the slighter pieces, seem best today. He has persistently used a right-side-up language now beautifully modeled, trimmed and dressed to his purpose. In this, in his command of the means of expression, he is a master. If he has fallen off in other respects he will be thoroughly able to defend himself against his detractors with the ablest of arguments.

WILLIAM CARLOS WILLIAMS

T. S. ELIOT, '10,
AN ADVOCATE FRIENDSHIP

ON THIS occasion when mother *Advocate* gives accolade to T. S. Eliot she celebrates the first occasion when one of her sons has acquired international renown before reaching middle-age, not only as a poet, dramatist and critic, but as the spokesman of intellectual youth on both sides of the Atlantic.

My assignment is to present Eliot as an *Advocate* editor. Because the privilege of contacts with a choice personality befell me. I find myself reviving memories of an *Advocate* friendship instead of the casual relations of editorial activities. In doing so, however, I realize that I raise hopes of a vivid personal portrait such as that undergraduate friendship justifies; whereas I find myself facing a problem which Eliot, the literary critic, has often encountered.

To look back over more than a quarter of a century and try to recapture a personality from a remote and limited period, especially of one who was then as shy and reticent as he is probably still, is a difficult task. This is not to say that the necessarily brief friendship was not intimate and rewarding, nor that Eliot was wholly different as an undergraduate from the personality which he has since revealed in his poems, plays and critical opinions. Let me say, however, that while he was then no less concerned with literature than he is today, to regard the undergraduate writer as one who was even then conscious of literary destiny among his fellow editors of the *Advocate* is to do him an injustice.

Small wonder that in retrospect those episodes, conversations and ideas of our undergraduate days become hopelessly kaleidoscopic. What we were like then and what we wanted to do and become are things which elude us who are now armed with experience and chastened by realities. Having to readjust our lives after two major crises like a world war and a world depression, the poets of our troubled generation seem to be "world-losers and world-forsakers."

Thus the ambitions and desires of our youth have long since made their quaint compacts with Necessity. In our twenty-fifth anniversary class report Eliot told us of his lean years in England as a school teacher on a pittance with a dinner thrown in, and as a bank clerk with a free

T. S. Eliot

tea at four o'clock. Was it irony that led the poet to add that he liked banking? Recalling his sensitive nature, and the inspissated gloom of a London bank interior, that rather sounds like the sort of humor that was permitted in the last carriage of a funeral procession in the Cambridge of our day!

I am also aware that such glimpses and memories as survive precariously today remind us that our personalities at that period of our lives did not have so much finality in them as they pretended to. Withal, there is the temptation to rationalize in our endeavor to overcome what James Huneker somewhere called "the pathos of distance."

II

It was in the old *Advocate* sanctum under the eaves of the Harvard Union that I first met Eliot. As I was the first to be elected from our class, I was able to watch the other 1910 candidates. Eliot was the most promising of these, and as he was the next to be elected we began a friendship based upon such literary tastes and enthusiasms as we shared or induced each other to share.

But Eliot's *Advocate* days were numbered. In his sophomore year he decided to complete his course in three years and take a master's degree. Thereafter the sanctum saw less of him; his comments in a minuscular hand on the contributions of candidates soon ceased along with his own. Only now and then did he come to initiations and punch nights to expand, in the midst of our hilarity, into his quiet, subtle humor; and we saw as little of him at the Stylus Club and the Signet Society. As president, during the first half of our final year, I made a desperate effort to get editorials from him, but by then he was working harder than ever in the Graduate School. To his classmates and the *Advocate* board he became a recluse, and I used to run him to earth in his room.

But he was not lost to undergraduate life. He was always ready to lay his book aside and fill his pipe. With his analytical mind his curiosity was insatiable as to the meanings and motives in the literary and social currents of our day. He was always the commentator, never the gusty talker, and seemed to cultivate even then a scholarly detachment. And there was a lot to talk about, for the university was then peculiarly, and perhaps for the last time, a kind of national clearing-house, a laboratory, such as would delight the pedagogues of today. As the Ph.D. degree had just become a pedagogical fetish, the university attracted a host of aspirants for doctors' and masters' degrees from all over the country, and that microcosm, Harvard College, with its elective system of study, exposed us undergraduates to a variety of stimulating contacts and experiences. I like to account for Eliot's flair for eclectic scholarship, which is revealed in his poems and which is perhaps their outstanding characteristic, by recalling the intellectual excitements in this competitive atmosphere which the swarm of graduate students from small and large colleges created in our class-rooms, for we rubbed shoulders with them in undergraduate as well as graduate courses. In that experience Harvard to us seemed truly a university.

I have no doubt that in Eliot's case all this was a vivid, formative influence, as indeed it was in the lives of all our generation at Harvard during those last years of the elective system. If the College seemed to us to lose its identity in this almost alien, as it were cosmopolitan, atmosphere, at least it had more of the atmosphere and fellowship of the medieval university than Harvard's cloistered undergraduates today enjoy in those replicas of Oxford and Cambridge on the banks of the Charles.

What if certain graduate courses received us undergraduates with sublime toleration, even reluctance? Our barbarian airs and graces saved those courses from the heavy-witted Teutonism with which the Ph.D. aspirants tried to flavor them. Our professors were more amused than flattered by the atmosphere of *lèse-majesté* with which these earnest souls surrounded them, and in turn doubtless appreciated our undergraduate anticlimaxes. How often during a lecture was the absurdly rapt attention of those grinds disturbed, if not shocked, when someone of our group, after a riotous evening in Boston or Cambridge, would begin to nod and finally pass into unabashed slumber? It was Professor William James who, during a lecture, upset a post-graduate questioner with, "What is mind? No matter! What is matter? Never mind!"

The unfailing punctuality of these strangers within our gates irked instead of reproached us; we sometimes wondered if that exemplary phalanx had left the class room since the last lecture. And yet, we had all the breaks. None of the graduate grinds was ever late because, running to a lecture, he had almost bumped into Henry James at the corner of Linden and Massachusetts, and knocked off his hard, high-low-crowned English hat which resembled a Regency coachman's, and picked it up with breathless apologies, and then politely waited upon a sentence which had a beginning and a middle, but which tailed off unfinished in a despairing smile. If any of them had had this experience, it should have furnished him with a doctor's thesis on that distinguished novelist's style, since appropriate subjects for theses were always uppermost in their minds.

And if during lectures these greasy grinds had their laugh when they selectively poised their pens over their notebooks while we industriously plied ours like "pickers-up of unconsidered trifles," it is a surprising amount of information that we managed to pick up. We learned to swim by going beyond our depth. But we had our innings when those post-graduates from the sticks appeared in the *Advocate* sanctum to submit contributions which, when published, were proudly sent back to their home town and *alma mater.*

III

So much for the intra-mural influences of Eliot's day. The result was, for one of his precocious mind, a healthy sophistication, which is quite another thing from the sophistry which, a lecturer told us, Bacon ascribed to the medieval university. And since Eliot wrote some of his early poems during his last two years of college, it is worth our while to ask why they were not published until 1925 by that professional world of letters to which we aspired. The answer is that the New York world of editors and publishers reminded the young writer that the cautionary Victorian advice of being seen and not heard was still in force.

I recall the sensation caused in the *Advocate* sanctum when the *Literary Digest* wrote asking for samples of *Advocate* poets which he wanted for a survey of American undergraduate verse. Of the samples submitted, needless to say, none of Eliot's was used by the *Digest* editor.

Today young writers, even those in college, are cultivated and encouraged by editors and publishers to submit their work. Not so in our day. As yet the young writer, especially the poet, was not supposed to have anything worth saying. Of course there were certain publishers who would gladly publish your poems at your own expense, and the custom was more common than is known. The late Edwin Arlington Robinson, whom I came to know in New York, told me that his first book, "Captain Craig," was subsidized. And when I met Eliot's English contemporary Rupert Brooke in New York, still unknown in 1913, he told me that he had paid for the publication of his first book of poems in London.

In the light of these conditions and influences, within and without Harvard in our day, it is not surprising that the writers of 1910 have been, like Eliot, rebels, though not all have remained so. For that world we faced three years before the World War was a smug, somnolent world: as yet the word Armageddon was only used by divinity students to scarify their first congregations. It will sound like rationalization to say that, although we entered college soon after the century opened, by the time we left we found, or rather sensed, an atmosphere of *fin-de-siècle*, even of disillusion, in the literary and political world. The note is evident in our classmate Walter Lippmann's first three books. Reading once more Eliot's essay "For Lancelot Andrewes" I have wondered in what mood he first discovered this stanza of Dryden's which he quotes in that study:

> All, all of a piece throughout!
> Thy Chase had a Beast in View;
> Thy Wars brought nothing about;
> Thy lovers were all untrue.
> 'Tis well an Old Age is out,
> And time to begin a New.

As regards *belles lettres*, the field was dominated and monopolized by a coterie of pundits, a sort of superannuated, mutual admiration circle. Their prestige might have been said to rest upon an axiom "that which is new is not true, and that which is true is not new." Some occupied academic chairs of literature and others were editors. The magazines always found room for their long colorless odes which we characterized as "spindaric." There were, however, notable exceptions, two of whom were sons of Mother Advocate. One was that inspired poet and teacher, Professor George Woodberry '77, of Columbia, whose poems appeared too seldom, and the other was one of the founders and during its best years the editor of the original *Life*, Edwin S. Martin '77, who welcomed us to his pages. He was a modern survival of Chaucer's "verray parfit gentil knight." His son was our classmate.

These were formative influences for Eliot and his generation of writers. Almost too late in college we heard of the literary revolt abroad, which in time found American supporters like the poets Amy Lowell, John Gould Fletcher of the *Harvard Monthly* and the *Advocate*'s Conrad Aiken. And let me proudly add that it was in our *Advocate* that Ezra Pound's first book of verse was reviewed, with Eliot and myself among his admirers. It was Eliot who first told me of the Vers Libre movement, of the work of Paul Fort and Francis Jammes; and he was to go over to the Sorbonne for study and to assess these literary influences which, stifled by the War, were to end in the literary and artistic nonsense that was appropriately termed Dada.

Meanwhile Eliot had found what he wanted in Paris and returned to Harvard for his Ph.D. study. I can testify to the fact that he had now already begun to shape his own technique of verse form and style, for, after leaving Cambridge to become a cub reporter on the *New York World*, I kept up a correspondence with him, and he sent me copies of these early poems, among which I recall the "Preludes," "Cousin Nancy," "The Boston Evening Transcript" and "Aunt Helen." There may have been others which have not since been published, and I regret that another Harvard man to whom I showed them never returned them. The point is that these poems waited until 1925 for publication, and it is surprising to find that even those of the post-war period do not as yet begin to date; each character seems to have its note of universality.

Those who bring against Eliot the charge of a wilful or perverse obscurantism should remember that these poems crystallize the suppressed ideas, emotions, aspirations of a period of catastrophe, when the experiences of our stratified world, the world of Aunt Helen Slingsby and the Lady of the Portrait, were destined for Limbo. It is not only that some medium was necessary for a distillation of these crowded, complex and inarticulate moods and experiences, but that Armageddon liquidated that world. By what miracle could a conventional or traditional frame-work contain and adequately convey their significance?

Thus it seems as if Eliot set himself the task of assessing, with his fastidious sincerity and scholarship, the myriad contacts and experiences of a transitional epoch. There was so much to record of this Human Comedy whose characters with their moods, attitudes and whispers were destined to create international crises, that Eliot's elliptical mode of expression alone could celebrate. Even the Boston of our day was less "a state of mind" than a world of characters, some of whom we met in the portraits of Sargent's exhibition of 1908 in Copley Hall. In depicting this scene Eliot seems to have borrowed from the canon of classical Chinese painting, where linear perspective is modified by the tone values and shading of atmospheric perspective. It is futile to classify him as a symbolist, an imagist, an impressionist or a surrealist, since all these things are the concern of the modern creative artist. The poet, moreover, often found himself assuming the roles of biographer and historian. Incidentally, it is not surprising that Eliot has shared in the silly stricture which Oscar Wilde passed on Browning—of using poetry as a medium for writing prose.

While Eliot's meticulous classification of fugitive types, situations and motives may seem like rummaging in an intellectual attic among outworn emotions and ideas, certainly these things also have their tears and laughter. And so his types, his characters, are never ludicrous; they become prototypes instead of caricatures. J. Alfred Prufrock, Sweeney and his landlady Mrs. Turner, Aunt Helen Slingsby and the Lady of the Portrait, all have their dignity and their lawful occasions. If they seem like memories of our dead lives, that quality makes them the stuff of literature. And if Eliot's poetry sometimes suggests an atmosphere of *fin-de-siècle*, that is because of the curious time-lag which seems to haunt our tardy American reactions to the social, spiritual, intellectual, and economic currents of the Europe towards which we so reluctantly and ruefully turn for orientation, and which by sacrifice of our lives and treasure we were to help to save in 1917.

When the young and untried writer faces the compromise which he must make with the professional world, by a self-preservative instinct he chooses a milieu in which that compromise is not likely to be threatened with spiritual and literary extinction. Thus it was natural that, when his academic apprenticeship was over, Eliot should prefer to take his chances at making a living in London. As writers the idea had come to us in college when we discussed Ezra Pound's case. Pound, like Eliot, was a gifted poet and scholar. After teaching for a brief period in Pennsylvania, he had gone to London for literary recognition, and his first poems, which reached us here in 1908, were published there. In the fall of 1913 I decided to exchange the journalism of New York for that of London, and Eliot came to see me off when I sailed on this forlorn hope from Boston. Thus the idea of London must have been in his mind during those last years in Cambridge when he was beginning to write with professional ambitions.

Before he left, however, I used to descend on him at his summer home in East Gloucester on my way to Maine. There I saw him in a quiet, charming family circle of parents and sisters, whose affectionate understanding of his arduous scholarship and his untried gifts must have been an inspiration for him in those lean years he later faced in a foreign land. He used to take me sailing in his catboat, and he could handle the sail with the best in Gloucester harbor.

Although I lost touch with him when he finally went abroad, it is sad to relate that this friendship died when it should have been revived. A guilty conscience compels me to admit that I did not see him while I was in London in the months before and after the Armistice. And if those months were not propitious, I failed again to see him while I was working in London as a newspaper correspondent during 1924-26, and once more when I passed through to Constantinople in 1927 as special correspondent of the *New York Times*. Our only excuse for such seemingly perverse omissions is that the world is too much with us in earning our living. But, like so many poets, Eliot remained in that cold British world until it gave him his first recognition, and repaid it by becoming its citizen.

W. G. Tinckom-Fernandez

JOHN REED

Class of 1910, (1887–1920)

*A classmate of T. S. Eliot's, the boisterous Reed
had already made a name for himself while his
more sedate friend was still a London bank clerk.
Only a week after graduation he became a murder suspect; he was clapped in irons aboard a
cattle-boat headed for Europe after his travelling
companion lost interest in the trip, leapt into
Boston harbor and swam home, leaving Reed
holding "evidence" which upset the captain of
the vessel.*

   *His subsequent career was no less colorful.
During the Mexican Civil War he proved an outstanding war correspondent and was sent to Europe during World War I. He was in Russia when
the Bolshevik Revolution broke out and wrote*
Ten Days that Shook the World, *probably the
finest first-hand account of that revolution.
Meanwhile he had become a Communist himself
and after the war helped to found the American
Communist Party. He died in Moscow in 1920
and is the only American to be buried in Red
Square.*

THE WEST

Gulls to their home on the aged rock
   Wheeling athwart the spray,
Thrill of the wind from the isles of Ind
   In the heart of the dying day.

Dreams in the depths of the solemn pines
    Ancient before our birth,
Hearing the speech of the plains that reach
    To the ends of the happy earth.

Out of the years that have passed away
    Out of the days to be,
Night brings the pang of the salt air's tang
    And the call of the West to me.

June, 1908

THE SEA-GULL

Wet with the stinging spray he skims the deep,
A livid gleam of life, and scans afar
Where the great breakers pound across the bar,
Beneath the headlands where his nestlings sleep.
Above the light the keeper sees him sweep
From fog to fog, and vanish like a star
Down where the unknown ocean monsters are,
And hears his mournful crying on the steep.

And when on winter days he rises high
Against the squall, and swift on-coming night,
And bares his gleaming armor to the fight,
Then are the sailors startled by his cry;
Darting spear-like athwart the dark'ning main
To ride the helmet of the hurricane.

October, 1908

John Reed 83

CONRAD AIKEN

Class of 1911, (1889–   )

Aiken was prolific in his contributions to the Ad-vocate and became President of the magazine in his senior year. Three years later he published his first volume of poems. Called before the draft board, he claimed he was exempt from military service since as a poet he was engaged in an es-sential industry. The draft board gave in to so spirited a defense and let him pursue the occu-pation which was to bring him the Pulitzer Prize in 1929, the National Book Award in 1954 and the Bollingen Prize for poetry in 1956.

FRANCOIS VILLON

How bitter cold it is! It *looked* like snow—
    I hear the wolf-wind now; wolf-wind, d' I say?
    Aye, hear the host a-snoring! Fire's gray
With ashes. Hey, you drunkard! Stir your—No;—
He must not wake. I turn my pockets, so—
    And—am I startled? nothing, nothing falls,
    No laugh of silver mocks me from these walls
So desolate, so bare. Well, here I go
To mill a verse. Ha ha! It's Christmas time!
I want a hollied verse, a berried rhyme—

O sleepy, sleepy eyes! Will verses keep?
    Aye, think of roast-fowl, then,—Lights! Christmas spread!
    Ah, what a vision! (*Smiles—nods low his head*)
O! Verse, d' I say? Aye—(*murmuring, falls asleep*).

January, 1908

LE PENSEUR

I made a statue; out of formless marble
I fashioned him to image in my brain
With smooth, white muscles, cunningly, and brow
Unluminous with mind. I made him sit,—
This thing uncouth,—and wrestle with his thoughts;
And then I dreamed I heard him stir, and cry,—
Baffled and hopeless in his quest for truth,—
"Why do you hew me out of the marble, Man?
Surely I did not cry to you in sleep—
For I have lain long aedolons in chains
And whimpered not, nor sorrowed in my soul;
And I have slept a deep and peaceful sleep.
And yet there comes an alien god to me,
Some meddling god, who seeth with his soul,
And speaks to me, and bids me stir; in dreams
I feel his presence near me, strange and strong,
And know him for a Messenger of Pain.
His fiery hands burn through the snows of sleep,
He tortures me to restlessness; his brain
Afar off knows me, pictures me, conceives
My power of limb and powerlessness of thought.
My eyelids, sealed for centuries in stone,
Feel now his icy chisel, and unclose
To rims of fire, inquisitorial Light.
The world breaks on me like a stormy sea
And crushes me,—before one breath is drawn,
Before my head is raised from fume of dreams,
Or heavy limbs unchained from lethargies.
Unhappy spirit who created me!
Play me a sweeter song than this you learned
To charm me out of marble, and to wake
My dreaming ears; the sunlit world is sweet,
And it is sweet to crush with careless hands,
To break, to snare, to kill, to overcome,—
But oh, my soul is filled with weariness.

Conrad Aiken 85

Play me a sweeter song, oh mighty god!
Of Lotus flowers, forgetfulness, and peace—
Bring back my thousand thoughts, my vagrant dreams,
Where they have wandered in the search for truth,—
Yea, I am sick of questioning the stars.
So play to me that I may be enthralled,
And pause, and dream, and close my eyes, and sleep
Once more the sleep of marble; lose once more
The world and thee and all unhappiness.
Play me a song such as the headland hears
Softly about its feet, in break of seas
Enchanting it to dreams; dim surge and fall;
Till, like the headland, I may lose the world,
Hearing the song grow fainter at my feet."

February, 1910

LE REVEUR

Bring me the chisel! Hot is the impulse now,—
One fiery stroke will work a miracle,
Yea, like a magic, change this shaggy brute
Into a god! Ho, boy—thou heartfree elf!—
Bring me the chisel, where it lies and gleams
There by the grindstone; yea, and I will smite
Such master-stroke as never Phidias smote
Among his Parian marbles: feel such bliss
As God once gloried in, when out of dust
He fused a beautiful man and laughed to see!
O thou dull brutish shape of marble! Clod,
Spiritless clod of manhood, pitiful thing
Who knowest nothing of heaven or of song:
Base crawling thing, blinker upon the sun,
Whose happiest pleasure is to count the stars

As one counts bees, with pointing finger, so!
(*Bring me the chisel, quick, thou lazy boy!*
Thinkest thou noon is all eternity?)
Thou thoughtless killer of all soft things that live
In sunlight, thou whose hairy hands are red
With blood of birds and animals thou hast slain:
One sharp ecstatic torture of my steel
Driven by all my soul and thou art changed
To something beautiful; a light will shine
From those wide eyes where dullard cruelty
Basks like a serpent now; and in thy face
Will shine a new intelligence of heaven,
A love of stars, a glory in the sun.
Already with that master stroke I thrill;
Already do I feel my nostrils flare
In ecstasy of sensuous bliss,—I know
Already how my breath will sear my lips,
My tongue go dry, my hand go tremulous
With frenzied happiness! And thou shalt stand,
Upright and strong and beautiful and pure,
Looking beyond me to the sea and sky
Which through the doorway gleam, and lo the sun,
Falling upon thee slantwise out of heaven,
Will fire thy face to splendor. Warm and soft,
Who knows but it will open thee thy lips
And give thee power of hymn to praise the world
Wherein thou livest; loosen in thy breast
The prisoner song which lodges there in gloom,
That song which came from heaven to sleep in thee.
Thinkest thou life so fruitless, O thou clod?
Under my chisel dost thou writhe and burn
In anguish, like a sleeper stirred from dreams?
For thee is everything so profitless,
And life so filled with pain? And art so weary
Of feeling with dull fingers after truth?
Nay, look not at me with so hard an eye!
Dream not of snarling at me! I am strong
To make or mar thee with a touch, a breath,—

To lift thee out of sorrow with a song
Or charm thee slowly into endless sleep
With some smooth euthanasia.—Ho, thou boy!
This brute hath glowered at me long; bring here
My chisel, where it sparkles in the grass.
Unto the genial sun will I unfold
His spirit, till it gulps like thirsty flower
That cordial golden wine; till it becomes
Drunk and reeling with utter happiness;
O, I will make him luminous with soul,
This starless creature pale with dreams of stars. . . .
What if it pain him, or he long to sleep?
Hot is the impulse, now—bring me the chisel!

June, 1910

VAUDEVILLE

I. THE LEADER

Each time the sign flashed 'Hayes and Mayne'
His frantic heart began to beat.
A fiery music laced his brain.
And through his veins her golden feet
Danced and glistened, danced and turned,
Pirouetted without a sound;
Up and down his blood they burned;
Glided and winked and swished around;
Until he longed to drop his bow,
And break his torturing violin,
And dance with her who witched him so
In a moonlight carnival of sin.
Her partner was a fool, and blind;
He smiled and smiled, and did not guess;
He skipped and hopped with vacant mind
Beside that fiery loveliness,—

Held out his hand for her to take,
And grinned, like a sawdust mannikin. . . .
Sometimes he thought his heart would break;
Sometimes he thought his violin
Would crack to pieces, rather than play
That everlasting idiot tune. . . .
But then he thought of nights in May,
And moonlight seaside nights in June,
And how they'd walk along the sands,
And laugh a little, and hear the sea,
And feel strange magic, touching hands,
And kiss, and shiver . . . . and there would be
Eternities like this. . . . But then
She ran to the wings, and turned, and screamed,
And waved her hand . . . . And once again
The whole thing like a nightmare seemed. . . .
The music changed, the curtains rose,
Two acrobats, in yellow tights,
One with an artificial nose,
Signalled into the wings for lights;
And coldly, above a falling flame
That lately set his pulses wild,
Freezing memory once more came
Of crippled wife and crying child.

II. FRONT ROW

Day after day she came, day after day
She sat in the front row, fixing her eyes upon him,
And never spoke to him, and never smiled.
Like one in a spell she watched his fingers moving
On the little silver levers, watched his lips,
And how he moistened them before he played;
The blue eyes, slowly gliding across the music,—
The lamplit music; and how, when he was tired,
He sighed, and rested his oboe on his knee.
The people on the stage meant nothing to her:

She'd seen them all before, perhaps, remembered
All that they said and did. They came and went
Silent as thought:
The fair-haired girl who played the violin,
Smiling a fixed and foolish smile; the clowns
Who lifted horrible faces into the spotlight
And sang so out of tune; the screaming monkeys;
The dwarfs, the trapeze artists, the bottle-jugglers;
And the young men who played pianos blindfold. . . .
Pictures upon the white screen flashed and faded,
The music changed, the spotlight cast new shadows
Sharply against the drop; and still, unseeing,
Never lifting her eyes, never applauding,
And only faintly smiling at some old joke,
She sat and stared. So near she was to him,
That sometimes, lifting her dress to cross her knees,
Her slipper brushed his elbow, and he'd turn
And peer at her, one instant, above his glasses,—
Still blowing a tune; and edge his chair away . . . .

What was it like, that unknown world of hers,
Those sinister streets in which no lamps were lighted,
And no doors ever opened, and no voice heard?

May, 1916

LIGHTS AND SNOW

I

The girl in the room beneath
Before going to bed
Strums softly on a mandolin
The three simple tunes she knows.
How inadequate they are to tell what her heart feels!
When she has finished them several times
She strums the strings softly with her fingernails
And smiles, and thinks, happily, of many things.

II

I stood for a long while before the shop window
Looking at the blue butterflies embroidered on tawny silk.
The building was a tower before me,
Time was loud behind me,
Sun went over the housetops and dusty trees,
And there they were, glistening, brilliant, motionless,
Stitched in a golden sky
By yellow patient fingers long since turned to dust.

III

The first bell is silver.
And, breathing darkness, I think only of the long scythe of time.
The second bell is crimson,
And I think of a holiday night, with rockets
Furrowing the sky with red and a soft shatter of stars.
The third bell is saffron and slow,
And I behold a long sunset over the sea
With wall on wall of castled clouds and glittering balustrades.
The fourth bell is the color of bronze,
I walk by a frozen lake in the dun light of dusk:
Muffled crackings run in the ice,
The trees creak, the birds fly.
The fifth bell is a cold clear azure,
Delicately tinged with green:
One golden star hangs melting in it,
And towards this, sleepily, I go.
The sixth bell is as if a tiny pebble
Had been dropped into a deep sea far above me . . .
Rings of sound ebb slowly into the silence.

IV

On the day when my uncle and I drove to the cemetery
Rain rattled on the roof of the carriage

And talking constrainedly of this and that
We refrained from looking at the child's coffin on the seat before us.
When we reached the cemetery
We found that the thin snow on the grass
Was already half transparent with rain,
And boards had been laid upon it
So that we might walk without wetting our feet.

V

When I was a boy, and saw bright rows of icicles
In many lengths along a wall,
I was disappointed to find
That I could not play music upon them.

VI

This girl gave her heart to me,
And this, and this.
This one looked at me as if she loved me,
And silently walked away.
This one I saw once and loved, and saw her never again.

Shall I count them for you upon my fingers?
Or like a priest solemnly sliding beads?
Or pretend they are roses, pale pink, yellow and white,
And arrange them for you in a wide bowl
To be set in sunlight?
See how nicely it sounds as I count them for you—
'This girl gave her heart to me
And this, and this!' . . .

And nevertheless my heart breaks when I think of them,
When I think their names,
And how, like leaves, they have changed and blown

And will lie at last pitifully forgotten
Under the snow.

VII

The music of the morning is red and warm;
Snow lies against the walls;
And on the sloping roof, in the yellow sunlight,
Pigeons huddle against the wind. . .
The music of the evening is attenuated and thin—
The moon seen through a wave by a mermaid—
The crying of a single violin. . . .

Far down there, far down where the river turns to the west,
The delicate lights begin to twinkle
On the dusky arches of the bridge;
In the green sky a long cloud,
A smouldering wave of smoky crimson,
Breaks on the freezing wind; and above it, unabashed,
Remote, untouched, fierily palpitant,
Sings the first frosty star.

January, 1919

IMPROMPTU FROM "SENLIN"

Death himself in the rain . . . death himself . . .
Death in the savage sunlight . . . skeletal death . . .
I hear the clack of his feet,
Clearly on stones, softly in dust,
Speeding among the trees with whistling breath,
Whirling the leaves, tossing his hands from waves . . .
Listen! the immortal footsteps beat and beat! . . .

Death himself in the grass, death himself,
Gyrating invisibly in the sun

Conrad Aiken 93

Scattering grass-blades, whipping the wind,
Tearing at boughs with malignant laughter . . .
On the long echoing air I hear him run!

Death himself in the dusk, gathering lilacs,
Breaking a white-fleshed bough,
Strewing the purple spikes on a cobwebbed lawn,
Dancing, dancing,
Drunk with excess, the long red sun-rays glancing
On flourishing arms, skipping with hideous knees,
Cavorting his grotesque ecstasies . . .
I do not see him, but I see the lilacs fall,
I hear the scrape of his hands against the wall,
The leaves are tossed and tremble where he plunges among them,
And silence falls, and I hear the sound of his breath,
Sharp and whistling, the rhythm of death.

It is evening: the lights on a long street balance and sway.
In the purple ether they swing and silently sing,
The street is a gossamer swung in space
And death himself in the wind comes dancing along it
And the lights, like raindrops, fall and tremble and swing. . . .

Hurry, spider, and spread your glistening web,
For death approaches!
Hurry, rose, and open your heart to the bee
For death approaches!
Maiden, let down your hair for the hands of your lover,
Comb it with moonlight and wreathe it with leaves,
For death approaches! . . .

Death, colossal in stars, minute in the sand-grain,
Death himself in the rain, death himself,
Drawing the rain about him like a garment of jewels . . .
I hear the sound of his feet
On the stairs of the wind, in the sun,
In the forests of the sea . . .
Listen! the immortal footsteps beat and beat.

November, 1918

NUIT BLANCHE

Red and green neon lights, the jazz hysteria,
for all-night movie and all-night cafeteria;
you feed all night in one and sleep in the other,
and dream that a strip-tease queen was your sweetheart's mother.

A nickel for a coffee-half, a dime for a seat,
the blonds and the guns are streamlined and complete;
streamlined, dreamlined, with wide open cactus spaces
between the four-foot teeth in the ten-foot faces.

Hot trumpets and hot trombones for a soft-shoe shuffle—
sailors, bring in your tattoos, park your duffel.
There's a green-tailed blue-eyed mermaid stinging my shoulder,
And I've got to pass out before I'm a minute older.

Sawdust, spittoons, no smoking, please excuse—
afloat or ashore we mind our p's and q's.
Longhorn stand back, shorthorn stand close, is all
the circular eye makes out on the circular wall.

And still the red neon lights go round and round,
the red mouth opens and drinks with never a sound;
red on the Square, red on the jingling Palace,
where all night long you rumbaed and drank with Alice—

red on the tattoo artist's sign, that shakes
anchors and flags together, ships and snakes,
roses, and a pink Venus, on a shell,
la la, all dancing fast in a neon hell—

while round and round the red beads wink, and faster
empty and open, pour and fill, disaster:
the red mouth opens and drinks, opens and winks,
drinks down the hotel wall, the drugstore, drinks

Conrad Aiken 95

the Square, the statue, the bright red roofs of cabs,
and the cleaning-women, who arise with pails and swabs;
then stains the dawn, who, over the subway station,
steals in with sandals grey, and no elation.

April, 1942

Conrad Aiken

E. E. Cummings

E. E. CUMMINGS

Class of 1915, (1894–1963)

*Cummings' undergraduate poetry bears little re-
semblance to his later work. As an undergraduate
he was aware of the avant-garde, as his essay
"The New Art" shows, but he did not develop the
style which made him "the typesetter's nightmare" until his years in exile in Paris after the
war. His first book,* The Enormous Room *(1922)
was based on his experiences as a prisoner of war.
It was soon followed by* Tulips *and* Chimneys,
XLI Poems, *and* &, *the collections of poems for
which he is best known.*

OF NICOLETTE

Dreaming in marble all the palace lay,
Like some colossal ghost-flower, born by night,
Blossoming in white towers to the moon;
Soft sighed the passionate darkness to the tune
Of tiny troubadours, and, phantom-white,
Dumb-blooming boughs let fall their glorious snows,
And the unearthly sweetness of a rose
Swam upward from the moonlit dews of May.

A Winged Passion woke, and one by one
There fell upon the night like angels' tears
The syllables of that ethereal prayer.
And as an opening lily, milky-fair,
When from her couch of poppy petals peers

The sleepy morning, gently draws apart
Its curtains to reveal the golden heart,
With beads of dew made jewels by the sun,

So one fair, shining tower, which, like a glass,
Turned light to flame, and blazed with silver fire,
Unclosing, gave the moon a nymph-like face,
A form whose snowy symmetry of grace
Haunted the limbs as music haunts the lyre,
A creature of white hands, who, letting fall
A thread of lustre from the opened wall,
Glided, a drop of radiance, to the grass.

Shunning the sudden moonbeams' treacherous snare,
She sought the harboring dark, and, catching up
Her delicate silk,—all white, with shining feet,
Went forth into the dew. Right wildly beat
Her heart at every kiss of daisy-cup,
And from her cheek the beauteous courage went
At every bough that reverently bent
To touch the yellow wonder of her hair.

March, 1913

SUNSET

Great carnal mountains crouching in the cloud
That marrieth the young earth with a ring,
Yet still its thoughts builds heavenward, whence spring
Wee villages of vapor, sunset-proud.—
And to the meanest door hastes one pure-browed
White-fingered star, a little, childish thing,
The busy needle of her light to bring,
And stitch, and stitch, upon the dead day's shroud.

Poises the sun upon his west, a spark
Superlative,—and dives beneath the world;
From the day's fillets Night shakes out her locks;
List! One pure trembling drop of cadence purled—
"Summer!"—a meek thrush whispers to the dark.
Hark! the cold ripple sneering on the rocks!

March, 1913

SUMMER SILENCE

(SPENSERIAN STANZA)

Eruptive lightnings flutter to and fro
Above the heights of immemorial hills;
Thirst-stricken air, dumb-throated, in its woe
Limply down-sagging, its limp body spills
Upon the earth. A panting silence fills
The empty vault of Night with shimmering bars
Of sullen silver, where the lake distils
Its misered bounty.—Hark! No whisper mars
The utter silence of the untranslated stars.

March, 1913

BALLADE

The white night roared with a huge north-wind,
And he sat before his thundering flame,
    Quaffing holly-crowned wine.
"Say me, who is she, and whence came
The snow-white maid with the hair of Inde?
    For I will have her mine!"

"She was crouched in snow by the threshold, lord,
And we took her in (for the storm is loud),
   But who, we may not know.
For, poorly-clad, she is strangely proud,
And will not sit at the servants' board,
   But saith she comes of the snow."

"She shall sit by me," he sware amain;
"Go, ere another ash-stick chars,
   Ask of her whom she loves."
"We ask her, lord, and she saith, 'The stars.'"
And he sware, "I will kiss with kisses twain
   Those cheeks which are two white doves."

The wind had tucked in bed her earth,
And tiptoed over valley and hill,
   Humming a slumber-croon;
And all the shining night lay still,
And the rude trees dropped their hollow mirth;
   Silently came the moon.

He rose from the table, red with wine;
He put one hand against the wall,
   Swaying as he did stand;
Three steps took he in the breathless hall,
Said, "You shall love me, for you are mine."
   And touched her with his hand.

White stretched the north-land, white the south . . .
She was gone like a spark from the ash that chars;
   And "After her!" he sware . . .
They found the maid. And her eyes were stars,
A starry smile was upon her mouth,
   And the snow-flowers in her hair.

April, 1913

THE NEW ART

THE NEW art has many branches,—painting, sculpture, architecture, the stage, literature, and music. In each of these there is a clearly discernible evolution from models; in none is there any trace of that abnormality, or incoherence, which the casual critic is fond of making the subject of tirades against the new order.

It is my purpose to sketch briefly the parallel developments of the New Art in painting, sculpture, music, and literature.

I.

Anyone who takes Art seriously, who understands the development of technique in the last half century, accepts Cézanne and Matisse as he accepts Manet and Monet. But this brings us to the turning point where contemporary criticism becomes, for the most part, rampant abuse, and where prejudice utters its storm of condemnation. I refer to that peculiar phase of modern art called indiscriminately, "Cubism," and "Futurism."

The name Cubism, properly applied, relates to the work of a small group of ultra-modern painters and sculptors who use design to express their personal reaction to the subject, i.e.—what this subject "means" to them,—and who further take this design from geometry. By using an edge in place of a curve a unique tactual value is obtained.

Futurism is a glorification of personality. Every so-called "Futurist" has his own hobby; and there are almost as many kinds of painting as artists. For instance, one painter takes as his subject sounds, another colors. A third goes back to old techniques; a fourth sees life through a magnifying glass; a fifth imposes an environment upon his subject proper, obtaining very startling effects; a sixth concerns himself purely with motion,—in connection with which it is interesting to note the Japanese painters' wholly unrealistic rendering of the force of a river.

The painter Matisse has been called the greatest exponent of Cubist sculpture. At the 1912 exhibition the puzzled crowd in front of Brancusi's "Mlle. Pogany" was only rivalled by that which swarmed about the painting called "Nude Descending a Staircase." "Mlle. Pogany" consists of a more or less egg-shaped head with an unmistakable nose, and a

E. E. Cummings 101

sinuous suggestion of arms curving upward to the face. There is no differentiation in modelling affording even a hint of hands; in other words, the flow of line and volume is continuous. But what strikes the spectator at first glance, and focusses the attention throughout, is the enormous inscribed ovals, which everyone recognizes as the artist's conception of the subject's eyes. In the triumph of line for line's sake over realism we note in Brancusi's art the development of the basic principles of impression.

II.

Just as in the case of painting, it is a French school which brought new life to music; but at the same time, Germany has the honor of producing one of the greatest originators and masters of realism, Richard Strauss.

The modern French school of music finds its inspiration in the personal influence of César Franck. Debussy, Ravel and Satie all owe much to this great Belgian, who (like Maeterlinck and Verhaeren), was essentially a man of their own artistic nationality.

It is safe to say that there will always be somebody who still refuses to accept modernism in music, quoting in his defense the sovereign innovator, Beethoven! On a par with the sensation produced by the painting and sculpture of the Futurist variety was the excitement which the music of Strauss and Debussy first produced upon audiences. At present, Debussy threatens to become at any moment vulgarly common; while Strauss is fatuous in his clarity beside Schönberg; who, with Stravinsky, is the only god left by the public for the worship of the esthetes.

Erik Satie is, in many respects, the most interesting of all modern composers. Nearly a quarter of a century ago he was writing what is now considered modern music. The most striking aspect of Satie's art is the truly extraordinary sense of humor which prompts one of his subjects, the "sea cucumber," to console himself philosophically for his lack of tobacco.

The "Five Orchestral Pieces" of Arnold Schönberg continue to be the leading sensation of the present day musical world. Their composer occupies a position in many respects similar to that of the author of the "Nude Descending a Staircase." I do not in the least mean to ridicule

Schönberg;—no lawlessness could ever have produced such compositions as his, which resemble bristling forests contorted by irresistible winds. His work is always the expression of something mysteriously terrible,—which is probably why Boston laughed.

I have purposely left until the last the greatest theorist of modern music,—Scriabin. Logically, he belongs beside Stravinsky, as leader of the Russian school. But it is by means of Scriabin that we may most readily pass from music to literature, through the medium of what has been called "sense-transference," as exemplified by the color music of the "Prometheus."

This "Poem of Fire" is the consummation of Scriabin's genius. To quote the Transcript: "At the first performance, by the Russian Symphony Society, on March 20, for the first time in history a composer used a chromatic color score in combination with orchestration. . . . At the beginning of the orchestration, a gauze rectangle in about the position of a picture suspended on the back wall became animated by flowing and blending colors. These colors were played by a 'color-organ' or 'chromola,' having a keyboard with fifteen keys, and following a written score."

III.

The suggestion of an analogy between color and music leads us naturally to the last branch of the New Art,—to wit, literature. Only the most extreme cases will be discussed, such as have important bearing upon the very latest conceptions of artistic expression.

I will quote three contemporary authors to illustrate different phases and different degrees of the literary parallel to sound painting—in a rather faint hope that the first two may prepare the way for an appreciation of the third. First Amy Lowell's "Grotesque" affords a clear illustration of development from the ordinary to the abnormal.

> "Why do the lilies goggle their tongues at me
> When I pluck them;
> And writhe and twist,
> And strangle themselves against my fingers,
> So that I can hardly weave the garland
> For your hair?

Why do they shriek your name
And spit at me
When I would cluster them?
Must I kill them
To make them lie still,
And send you a wreathe of lolling corpses
To turn putrid and soft
On your forehead
While you dance?"

In this interesting poem we seem to discern something beyond the conventional. The lilies are made to express hatred by the employment of grotesque images. But there is nothing original in the pathetic fallacy. No one quarrels with Tennyson's lines

"There has fallen a splendid tear
From the passion-flower at the gate"—

Let us proceed further,—only noting in the last three lines that brutality which is typical of the New Art,—and consider the following poem by the same author:

"THE LETTER"

"Little cramped words scrawling all over the paper
Like draggled fly's legs,
What can you tell of the flaring moon
Through the oak leaves?
Or of an uncurtained window, and the bare floor
Spattered with moonlight?
Your silly quirks and twists have nothing in them
Of blossoming hawthorns,
And this paper is chill, crisp, smooth, virgin of loveliness
Beneath my hand.
I am tired, Beloved, of chafing my heart against
The want of you;
Of squeezing it into little ink drops,
And posting it.

And I scald alone, here under the fire
Of the great moon."

This poem is superb of its kind. I know of no image in all realistic writing which can approach the absolute vividness of the first two lines. The metaphor of the chafed heart is worthy of any poet; but its fanciful development would have been impossible in any literature except this ultra-modern.

I shall now quote from a sonnet by my second author, Donald Evans:

"Her voice was fleet-limbed and immaculate,
And like peach blossoms blown across the wind
Her white words made the hour seem cool and kind,
Hung with soft dawns that danced a shadow fête.
A silken silence crept up from the South,
The flutes were hushed that mimed the orange moon,
And down the willow stream my sighs were strewn,
While I knelt to the corners of her mouth."

In the figure "Her voice was fleet-limbed," and the phrase "white words," we have a sought-for literary parallel to the work of the "sound painters." It is interesting to compare Dante's expressions of a precisely similar nature, occurring in the first and fifth cantos, respectively, of the Inferno—"dove il Sol tace," and "in loco d'ogni luce muto."

From Donald Evans to Gertrude Stein is a natural step,—up or down, and one which I had hoped the first two might enable us to take in security. Gertrude Stein subordinates the meaning of words to the beauty of the words themselves. Her art is the logic of literary sound painting carried to its extreme. While we must admit that it is logic, must we admit that it is art?

Having prepared the way, so far as it is possible, for a just appreciation, I now do my best to quote from the book "Tender Buttons," as follows:

(1) A sound.
Elephant beaten with candy and little pops and
    chews all bolts and reckless, reckless rats,
    this is this.

(2) Salad Dressing and an Artichoke.
    Please pale hot, please cover rose, please acre in
        the red stranger, please butter all the beef-
        steak with regular feel faces.
(3) Suppose an Eyes

.   .   .   .

    Go red, go red, laugh white.
    Suppose a collapse is rubbed purr, is rubbed
        purget.
    Little sales ladies, little sales ladies
    Little saddles of mutton.
    Little sales of leather and such beautiful, beau-
        tiful, beautiful beautiful.

The book from which these selections are drawn is unquestionably
a proof of great imagination on the part of the authoress, as anyone
who tries to imitate her work will discover for himself. Here we see
traces of realism, similar to those which made the "Nude Descending a
Staircase" so baffling. As far as these "Tender Buttons" are concerned,
the sum and substance of criticism is impossible. The unparalleled
familiarity of the medium precludes its use for the purpose of esthetic
effect. And here, in their logical conclusion, impressionistic tendencies
are reduced to absurdity.

The question now arises, how much of all this is really Art?

The answer is: we do not know. The great men of the future will most
certainly profit by the experimentation of the present period. An insight
into the unbroken chain of artistic development during the last half
century disproves the theory that modernism is without foundation;
rather we are concerned with a natural unfolding of sound tendencies.
That the conclusion is, in a particular case, absurdity, does not in any
way impair the value of the experiment, so long as we are dealing with
sincere effort. The New Art, maligned though it may be by fakirs and
fanatics, will appear in its essential spirit to the unprejudiced critic as
a courageous and genuine exploration of untrodden ways.

June, 1915

BETWEEN THE WARS:
1917–1943

ROBERT HILLYER

Class of 1917, (1895–1961)

Robert Hillyer's first book of poems, Sonnets and
Other Lyrics *was published while he was still an
undergraduate. He later published more than a
dozen volumes of poetry. His* Collected Verse
*(1933) won the Pulitzer Prize. Hillyer was Boyl-
ston Professor of Rhetoric at Harvard from 1937–
45.*

THE QUESTION

Now the sick earth revives, and in the sun
The wet soil gives a fragrance to the air;
The days of many colors are begun,
And early promises of meadows fair
With starry petals, and of trees now bare
Soon to be lyric with the trilling choir,
And lovely with new leaves, spread everywhere
A subtle flame that sets the heart on fire
With thoughts of other springs and dreams of new desire.

The mind will never dwell within the present,
It weeps for vanished years or hopes for new;
This morn of wakened warmth, so calm, so pleasant,
So gaily gemmed with diadems of dew,
When buds swell on the bough and robins woo
Their loves with notes bell-like and crystal-clear,
The spirit stirs from sleep, yet wonders, too,
Whence comes the hint of sorrow or of fear
Making it move disquiet within its narrow sphere.

This flash of sun, this flight of wings in riot,
This festival of sound, of sight, of smell,

Wakes in the spirit a profound disquiet,
And greeting seems the foreword of farewell.
Budding like all the world, the soul would swell
Out of its withering mortality;
Flower immortal, burst from its heavy shell,
Fly far with love beyond the world and sea,
Out of the grasp of change, from time and twilight free.

Could the unknowing gods, waked in compassion,
Eternalize the splendour of this hour,
And from the world's frail garlands strongly fashion
An ageless paradise, celestial bower,
Where our long-sundered souls could rise in power
To complete the fulfillment of their dream,
And never know again that dreams devour
Petals and light, bird-note and woodland theme,
And floods of young desire, bright as a silver stream,

Should we be happy, thou and I together,
Lying in love eternally in spring,
Watching the buds unfold that shall not wither,
Hearing the birds calling and answering,
When the leaves stir and all the meadows ring?
Smelling the rich earth steaming in the sun,
Feeling between caresses the light wing
Of the wind whose fragrant flight is never done,—
Should we be happy then? happy, adorèd One?

But no, here in this fragile flesh abides
The secret of an infinite delight,
Hidden in dying beauty there resides
Something undying, something that takes its flight
When the dust turns to dust, and day to night,
And spring to fall, whose joys in love redeem
Eternally, life's changes and death's blight,
Even as these pale, tender petals seem
A glimpse of infinite beauty, flashed in a passing dream.

April, 1917

MALCOLM COWLEY

Class of 1919, (1898–   )

President of the Advocate *while an undergraduate, Cowley was associate editor of* The New Republic *from 1929–1944. He was in close contact with most of the important American writers of the period and later edited anthologies of Hemingway, Faulkner, and F. Scott Fitzgerald. Since 1948 he has been literary advisor to the Viking Press and has served several terms as president of The National Institute of Arts and Letters. His published work includes translations of Paul Valéry's* Variety *and Gide's* Imaginary Interviews, *as well as* Blue Juanita, Exiles' Return, The Dry Season, *and* The Literary Situation.

A THEME WITH VARIATIONS

I.

As Written by Miss Edna St. Vincent Millay on Her Typewriter.

My thoughts had festered in the heat
Three months; I could not do a thing.
The pavement boiled beneath my feet
Three months; I could not even sing
And wondered what the fall would bring.

But yesterday at dusk, the lost
North wind sprang up after a rain,
And when I woke, I saw the frost
Had patterned lacework on the pane,
And on my lips were songs again.

II.

As It Appeared in 'The Pagan.'

Three months summer held me like malaria.
A fever drove me up and down the streets;
Underfoot the pavement
Was soft and viscous with heat.
About garbage cans flies came into being
And buzzed their enjoyment of the world
And died.
Children played about like flies
And died.
I fled to the wild places
But there in the solitude my thoughts festered
And to forget their foulness
I fled among people.
Yesterday.
A wind sprang up after a rain
And this morning there was a delicate tracery of frost on the window.
I have been praising the beauty of men all day.
I am a god in a new creation.

III.

With Apologies to Mr. William Carlos Williams.

> I wish I could pass out
> lie with my toes towards the daisies
> it must be cool even now
> down there.
> > Next autumn
> there'll be wind, frost,
> biting rain.
> > I'll be peppy.
> August is like last night's
> Stale Pilsener.

IV.

*As Rendered by a Member of the Spectric School
with Appropriate Overtones.*

Crawling infinities of atoms. Death. Sweat and the livid perfume of surheated asphalt. Thing unmentionable floating down sewers. All humanity is floating down a sewer into the cleansing sea.

A Brahmin once, performing his ninth pilgrimage to the waters of the sacred Ganges, observed a maize field drying up in the sun. "May the seven seas and the thirteen rivers of Paradise shed their healing moisture on that field." And the sun beat down, and the maize turned from yellow to brown, and the people starved. But that winter came the rains, and all those that survived blessed the words of the prophet.

My soul is a larva, a fat grub that feeds on flies.

Crack ... crack ... crack. The leaves are snapping off in the frost and falling one by one. On my window is the forest of Arden.

A young man in a silk hat runs down the street like a little boy. Someone asks him why, but he only stares. Paradise looms behind swinging doors.

The wind is my breath and the sea is my spittle. I shall overthrow a hundred Brahmas and gods greater than Vishnu shall I raise up.

April, 1918

TO A DILETTANTE KILLED AT VIMY

Years of small sorrows and of small endeavor;
Years of great plans, and mental cowardice;
And we that hoped they would not last forever:—
That's all. To cut the whole thing short, came this.

Malcolm Cowley 111

And yet the petty muddle you made of it;
The pose; the brave dreams foundered in a sea
Of idle talk, now seem to us resolved
Into clean metal by catastrophe.

February, 1918

NANTASKET

Denise, the manicure, strolls on beside
Her lover, who is working on the Street.
They talk in broken words, and watch the tide
Come sedulously licking at their feet.

This is her Day. Her glances go a-roving
Among the bathers, searching every feature.
This place, she thinks, is made for pleasant loving
And not uncomfortably close to nature.

And now Society comes marching by,
Young Kuppenheimer gods in bathing suits
And flappers with their bonnets stuck awry:—
Sand filters into patent leather boots;

The sun is scorching painted cheeks; the sea
Growls at the littered beach complainingly.

November, 1919

Malcolm Cowley 113

JOHN MASON BROWN

Class of 1923, (1900–   )

Brown wrote dramatic criticism while at Harvard and went on to become drama critic for Theater Arts Monthly, The New York Evening Post, *and* The Saturday Review. *Since 1955 he has been editor-at-large for* The Saturday Review. *His published work includes* The Modern Theater in Revolt *(1929),* Upstage—The American Theater in Profile *(1930),* The Art of Playgoing *(1936),* Two on the Aisle *(1938), and* Dramatis Personae *(1936).*

GREASE-PAINT AND PURITANS

PHILIP BARRY's "You And I" has just opened in New York. It is a Harvard Prize Play, and being such it quite properly elicited from a prominent dramatic critic there an announcement in his columns, with "whatever that may mean" as a legitimate query. He was puzzled. Why a prize-play and why from Harvard? Moreover he was busy. A dramatic critic leads a hard life. He must go to the theatre three or more times a week, and write intelligently about what he sees for the morrow's paper. And to do that he must keep abreast of the times. No wonder, then, that this particular critic was puzzled, and annoyed. What was this "upstart crow" from New England? He certainly was not alone in wondering what Harvard had to do with the theatre, and why a prize play. Hearsay and tradition have it that Calvinistic Cambridge with its frigid creed would never have had a weakness for the tinsel and corruption of the theatre. But history may at times be at odds with hearsay and whispered tradition. Harvard in a modest way has had long dealings with the theatre.

As early as 1665 there is a record of amateurs being summoned to court for presenting a play in the Colonies. Even then the conflict! Even then the amateur was doing the unusual thing! But that is not Harvard. Harvard's first claims to dramatic distinction can be traced to 1690 when the first play written by an American was staged in Cambridge by those lantern-jawed, and stern Puritan ancestors. It was Benjamin Colman's "Gustavus Vasa," and was performed just sixty-two years before the coming of Lewis Hallam's first professional English company of note to New York, Philadelphia, and Williamsburg.

Needless to say, between that pioneer performance and the productions of the 47 Workshop and the Dramatic Club of today, has come no unbroken record of theatrical performances. The tradition for open-mindedness and liberality has, however, in most cases, been observed. The reactions against the theatre were all-inclusive in those early days. They seem utterly preposterous to most of us today, but the colleges naturally felt them and were affected by them. Laws against theatrical performances became current in many of the colonies, including Massachusetts. To the defense of drama came John Gardner in a speech delivered before the Massachusetts House of Representatives in 1792. With that admirable rationality of the legendary Puritan, he remarked that "the illiberal, unmanly, and despotical act which now prohibits theatrical exhibitions among us, to me, Sir, appears to be the brutal, monstrous, spawn of a sour, envious, morose, malignant, and truly benighted superstition." Even so mild a rebuke did not change the administrative attitude of American colleges to the theatre. As late as 1824, President Dwight of Yale could say in an "Essay on the Theatre" that "to indulge a taste for playgoing means nothing more or less than the loss of that most valuable treasure, the immortal soul."

It is not in the dead record of early plays, nor even in those justly dead compositions—amusing as literary curios and comments on the tastes of our much-praised forebears—that we are interested. It may be worth mentioning that Royall Tyler's "The Contrast" (1787), the second native play professionally produced in this country, came from a Harvard graduate and was advertised as "written by a citizen of the United States." That same astonishment, when an American writes a good play, is observable even today. And if the colleges, and among them Harvard, had not given some dramatic training, our billboards might still read in that manner. To understand fully what the colleges have done in America is to appreciate the difficulties that lay in the path of officially recognizing the theatre and the drama, particularly in practice, as parts of a college's equipment. Tradition and polite scruples have always damned the theatre to the layman. Newspaper scandals have had their hand. Actors and actresses have become famous overnight by commercialized eccentricities as mild as milkbath habits or as wild as human thought can imagine. Certainly for the colleges to fly in the face of such misconceptions was no easy thing. And Harvard had its part in the revolt.

Professor Baker was one of the first to teach the history of dramatic literature in this country. He was also the first to give courses in play-construction. Inspired by the success that attended the Abbey Theatre adventure in Dublin, he set out to establish a play-writing course, and by 1907 was giving his now famous English 47, at Harvard and Radcliffe. It was not until 1912, that the 47 Workshop, which produces plays written in the courses at the two colleges, was founded, giving to dramatic workers a chance to experiment and test before an audience. Before that time the Dramatic Club had produced the original plays. But after that, with a student company and stage force, the student plays were produced under Professor Baker's direction. The process involved the happy custom of making the audience cooperate by writing criticisms of the plays and thus giving to the authors a chance to study their plays in relation to an audience. Mr. Baker has tried "in the light of historical practice merely to distinguish the permanent from the impermanent in technique." In the classroom, "by showing the inexperienced dramatist how experienced dramatists have solved problems similar to his own, to shorten his time of apprenticeship," he has given to the embryo dramatist the same "instruction in art granted the architect, the sculptor, the painter, and the musician." All this in its way has given answer to the critic's query of "why a prize play" and "why from Harvard?"

Such work and the work of other teachers of the drama, won for the doers the title of "St. Pauls of the drama," from Henry Arthur Jones. Professor Brander Matthews at Columbia, Professor Phelps at Yale, Professor Kochs at the University of North Carolina, and Professor Dickenson at Wisconsin are a few of the more prominent men who are actively teaching drama in this country now. The list could be extended to include almost every state university or college. And the remarkable thing is that we have been much quicker to take the feared, despised, and condemned trappings of the theatre under academic wings than has England. The work here has been going on for twenty years and more. In fact dramatic instruction has become almost a platitude with us, and for that reason obscured the struggle and enlightenment that brought it into being. Within the last two years, the first chair of dramatic literature in an English university was given to Granville Barker at the University of Liverpool.

Out of the instruction given at Harvard, and out of Harvard have come some few men and women who have created a slight stir in theatrical circles, even in New York, and perhaps, elsewhere. Among the earlier or pre-Workshop dramatists was William Vaughn Moody, who is known by many for "The Great Divide" (1906) and the "Faith Healer," both significant plays, that had their essence in native problems, and that have had their effect on what has followed them. Percy MacKaye—whose "Sappho" was written and acted when he was in undergraduate Cambridge, and performed with the help of Wellesley—was another. To him the civic masque and community drama of this country owe something, the recognition due the leader. His "Caliban" (1916) and "The Scarecrow" (1908) are perhaps not forgotten. Still another of these earlier dramatic writers was Edward Knobloch, who gained attention by his picaresque "Kismet" (1911) and followed it with the technically interesting "Milestones" (1912) written in collaboration with Arnold Bennett. From Radcliffe at that time came Josephine Preston Peabody, whose "Marlowe" (1901) opened the Agassiz Theatre, Radcliffe, and whose "The Piper" won the first prize, among the fifteen hundred manuscripts submitted, as the best play with which to open the Memorial Theatre at Stratford.

In the actual literary output of the Workshop dramatists who have received dramatic instruction here, an admirable catholicity of subject and treatment shows that no definite school or stamp has been arbitrarily established. Free rein has been granted to the embryo dramatists. The list includes some names of interest. Edward Sheldon's is among the earliest. In 1908 he wrote "Salvation Nell" while still an undergraduate, and in 1909 had the pleasure of seeing "The Nigger" produced at the ill-fated New Theatre in New York. "Romance" (1914), played for eight years by Doris Keane, here and abroad, his adaptations of "The Jest" (1919) and "The Czarina" (1922) are still fresh in our memories. Perhaps Eugene O'Neill, master of phrase and character, leader in both realistic and expressionistic schools of play-writing, equally adept in the short and long play, and three times winner of the Pulitzer Prize for the best American play of the year, may be pointed to with pride. He harks back to no European tradition. He writes without artistic forebears. After a year at Princeton and several years at sea, he came to the Workshop (1914–1915). There is a noticeable change in his work after that year, a mellowing, an improvement. "Bound East of Cardiff" was written while he was here, and it is different from the O'Neill of "Fog" and "Thirst." "Beyond the Horizon" (1920), "The Straw" (1922) and "Anna Christie" (1921)—examples of his realistic writing,—and "The Emperor Jones" (1920) and "The Hairy Ape" (1922)—examples of his expressionistic tendencies—are too well-known to warrant comment.

The New York critic wanted to know "why a prize play?" He had forgotten in his rush and worry that John Craig and Oliver Morosco had both offered production and $500 to the best play written in the 47 courses during a year. Craig started the competitions, Morosco followed him, and now Richard Herndon is conducting them. They have been of unquestionable value in giving impetus to dramatic composition at Harvard, and some of them have not yet faded from memory. Frederick Ballard's "Believe Me, Xantippe" (1915), and Cleaves Kinkead's "Common Clay" (1916) were among the Craig plays. Rachel Butler's "Mama's Affair" (1920) was probably the best-known of the Morosco winners.

Among the long plays of Workshop origin or by graduates of English 47 are Edward Massey's "Plots and Playwrights" (1915), which won a considerable following when given by the Washington Square Players, Frederick L. Day's "Makers of Light," produced last spring at the Neighborhood Playhouse, Hubert Osborne's "Shore Leave" and "Rita Coventry," and Lewis Beach's "The Square Peg," all of the present season.

The one-act play has also been studied at Cambridge. "The Clod" of Lewis Beach, "Will O' The Wisp" (1916) and "The Playroom" (1915) of Doris Halman, "Torches" of Kenneth Raisbeck, "The Hard Heart" of Mark Kister, are fine contributions not unknown to the Little Theatres and amateur stages. So, too, are "Three Pills in a Bottle" (1917) of Rachel Lyman Field, "The Florist Shop" (1915) of Winifred Hawkridge, and "Two Crooks and a Lady" (1917) of Eugene Pillot. Impetus to the short play has been given by production within the Workshop and the published volumes of Harvard Dramatic Club and 47 Workshop Plays.

Play-writing has not been the only way in which Puritan Harvard has touched the theatre. Along with it go the other arts of the theatre. And the critic mentioned above must have been tired indeed when he forgot that Robert Edmond Jones and Lee Simonson studied here. Jones, whose settings for "The Jest," "Hamlet," "Macbeth," and "The Hairy Ape" have merited no little attention, was once an instructor in Fine Arts here, before he studied under Reinhardt and designed his set for Granville Barker's production of "The Man Who Married a Dumb Wife." Simonson, first with the Washington Square Players and now with the Theatre Guild, has done notable work as scenic artist in "He Who Gets Slapped," "Back to Methuselah," "R.U.R.," and "Peer Gynt."

In a modest way, too, founders of Little Theatres and teachers of the drama have come from Harvard. These men have brought to communities far from the pulse of a New York theatrical season, the best that the theatre has to offer in the form of either local productions or lectures. Among them are Sam Hume and Irving Pichel at the University of California, Louise Burleigh in Richmond, Frederick Kochs at the University of North Carolina, and Samuel Eliot at Smith.

Papers and publications have often turned to the Harvard-bred for dramatic critics. Needless to say, the critic first mentioned was not from Harvard, but there are other critics who are read. In New York one finds Walter Prichard Eaton, John Corbin of the "Times," Kenneth Macgowan, whose "Continental Stagecraft" and "The Theatre of Tomorrow," written with Jones, are fascinating annals of the newer methods in the theatre; Hiram K. Moderwell, whose "The Theatre of Today" was significant as first catching hold of the new movement, and phrasing the reaction against photographic realism to "inscenierung"; Robert C. Benchley, a master of the lighter critical vein, and Heywood Broun. It is interesting in passing to note that in 1911 Benchley was on the Executive Committee of the Dramatic Club, when Macgowan was President, and R. E. Jones was an honorary member. In Boston, H. T. Parker, noted musical and dramatic critic, of the "Transcript," came from Harvard.

Among the actors, Walter Hampden is most important. The tradition that demanded that actors and actresses first appear as Cio-Cio-San's present from Pinkerton or a truly little Eva is passing. Yearly more and more college graduates are turning to the theatre. Among New York producers, Winthrop Ames—who once directed a Pudding show—is prominent. Theresa Helburn and Maurice Wertheim, who have been courageous in their management of the Theatre Guild, have studied in Cambridge, as did Agnes Morgan of the Neighborhood Playhouse.

So much for those who have gone in the past. The record is not one of which one should be ashamed, branching out as it does into all the departments of the theatre, and including an electrical artist and specialist such as Munroe Pevear. And there are still signs of dramatic activity in Cambridge. Here is the 47 Workshop with its six annual productions. Here is the Dramatic Club producing notable foreign plays for the first time in this country, and the Cercle Français, performing distinguished French pieces. Here, also, is the Circulo Español. In the lighter field of musical comedy there is the Hasty Pudding and the Pi Eta. The last two have theatres, small and private, but for the housing of the production of the first three organizations, cramped Agassiz, beamed Brattle Hall, or echoing Jordan Hall serve as temporary shelters.

Perhaps, after all is said, the critic who was perplexed by the announcement of a Harvard Prize Play, who wondered why Harvard in connection with the theatre, and why a prize play, was tired and overworked. Perhaps, in his daily rush he had not the chance to trace college alliances in men of the theatre. To give a list of Harvard and Radcliffe graduates, prominent in the theatre, is not to claim that Harvard or Radcliffe endowed them with their talents. It is to explain the length and importance of that list, in the light of the laboratory work done at colleges, where a chance for dramatic expression, experimentation, and practice has been given. It is to realize the importance of a college's admission of the theatre and the drama as legitimate parts of an education. And even a weary dramatic critic, who has to write wisely of what he sees in the course of a season's play-going, might find such a background helpful and significant.

March, 1923

HENRY CABOT LODGE, JR.

Class of 1924, (1902–   )

After graduating from Harvard, Lodge worked on the Boston Evening Transcript *and the* New York Herald Tribune *before going into politics. He has been United States Senator from Massachusetts, Representative to the United Nations, Republican nominee for Vice-President, and Ambassador to South Vietnam.*

POLITICAL SENTIMENTALISTS

ROLAND W. BOYDEN first sprang into the limelight in November, 1922, as a result of the reparations plan which he advanced when he had no right officially to do so. Since then there has been a lot of argument and a lot of confusion as to what we should do with him. Should we recall him? Should we establish him as official representative?

The very fact that the case is so simple probably accounts for its having been so confused. This article will try to show the real facts in the Boyden case. The case is worth treating because the ignorance of the college on Roland W. Boyden is typical of its ignorance on most political subjects. This article plans to present the facts of the case and then digress on the value of facts and the need of them in Harvard College today. A certain type of Harvard man, in so far as we can generalize, often feels he can see the truth without knowing the facts; he is sometimes inclined to sniff at facts as too material. The result often is that even in a case like that of Roland W. Boyden, he becomes confused and reaches absurd conclusions.

There have been complicated arguments pro and con, but Mr.

Boyden's status in Europe is really perfectly simple. He is a personal agent of the President. The President is, of course, exclusively charged with all negotiations dealing with foreign relations, and has the right to appoint personal agents to represent him. The reason for this is obvious; the President cannot carry on all his foreign negotiations himself. Thus Mr. Boyden is sitting at the Reparations Commission having no vote, taking no official part in the proceedings and merely observing and reporting to the President the transactions vital to the best interests of the United States. The President has the absolute right to appoint anyone he pleases to carry on negotiations for him and represent him, and this power has always been exercised by the President from the beginning of the Government. There is thus nothing abnormal, nothing revolutionary about Mr. Boyden's being over there and his position has ample precedent. Here are some of the better known precedents.

There was a very famous case when Mr. Fillmore sent Mr. Ambrose Dudley Mann to report on the situation in Austria at the close of the Korsute revolution about 1848. This led to a controversy with the Austrian Government and Mr. Webster wrote an historic dispatch to Baron Hulsemann replying to his objections, not to the official character of Mr. Mann, but as to what he was supposed to have reported.

President Wilson also used personal agents on a very large scale. Colonel House was the best known among them, but when he made the Treaty of Versailles, although he was there himself, Mr. Lansing, Mr. White and General Bliss were all representatives and agents of the President.

It was the same when we made the Treaty of Paris with Spain; President McKinley appointed three Senators, the Secretary of State, and Mr. Whitelaw Reid, a private citizen. They were all his agents and representatives.

At the Disarmament Conference in Washington last year, the four delegates, Secretary Hughes, Senator Underwood, Mr. Root and Senator Lodge were the President's representatives and personal agents in making the treaties.

These are some of the precedents in Mr. Boyden's case that show that his position is perfectly legal.

The history of the case is short and equally simple. Mr. Boyden was appointed by President Wilson to succeed Mr. Rathbone, appointed in December, 1919, as his representative in order to keep him informed as to what was being done by the Reparations Commission. He was not a member of the Commission; he had no right to vote, but was merely an observer, and was there through the courtesy, of course, of the powers who had signed the Treaty of Versailles. He went out with Mr. Wilson and was reappointed in May, 1921, with his staff, by President Harding.

It is a very important thing to have an informant as to the activities of the Reparations Commission where the vital interests of this country are often concerned. But this informant should not go beyond his function, he should say nothing which might be misunderstood as being official. Unfortunately Mr. Boyden has taken action in cases where he cannot separate himself in the popular mind from the United States government. He has been unwise and has unintentionally misrepresented the United States in proposing a reparations plan, which, personal though it was, might have caused serious misunderstanding. His error is best shown by the official statement issued by the Department of State on January 16, 1923, parts of which are quoted below.

"It appears that on November 13th Mr. Boyden had been requested by one or more members of the Reparations Commission to draft, as a purely *personal* suggestion, a proposed letter to be sent by the Reparations Commission to the German Government on lines he had informally indicated. This Mr. Boyden did in the memorandum in question which he gave as a draft to one of the members of the Reparations Commission."

". . . This memorandum was prepared and submitted by Mr. Boyden as a *personal* matter and without consultation with the Department. When its text was subsequently received by the Department, it was not regarded as a plan for the settlement of reparations or as requiring any action whatever on the part of the Department. Rather it was deemed to be a *personal* memorandum, which Mr. Boyden had already submitted to one of the members of the Commission, of a general nature and which merely emphasized some of the fundamental considerations which were deemed to be pertinent to the situation in a large way." There is no basis for treating the general suggesting of Mr. Boyden as a reparations plan."

(The italics are my own.)

From this it may be seen how unofficially Mr. Boyden's statements are regarded by the Department of State. This plan which he drafted, although he himself said it was purely personal, was taken very seriously by some European nations. The French Foreign Office immediately asked whether Secretary Hughes was proposing a reparations plan and the Department of State had to issue statements denying that any plan had been officially proposed.

Mr. Boyden should never have drawn up that plan. If he had to draw one up, he should never have made it public because, purely personal though it is, it makes for serious misunderstanding. There is Mr. Boyden's mistake and there is where he exceeded the duties of his office.

Mr. Boyden now knows the result of action of that sort. He probably realizes that a breach of tact can in certain cases be as serious as a breach of duty. Mr. Boyden is a good lawyer of high standing in Boston. He has discharged his duties intelligently and well but he has been unwise in proposing his personal reparations plan. In the event of another mistake of that sort his recall should be immediate.

The misunderstanding and theorizing which has been going on in a small way about Roland W. Boyden is going on on a much larger scale about other political questions which are not nearly so easy to explain. The tendency here in college has been to neglect fact and to cater to the sentimental side of our natures. It is my belief that this state of mind is extremely prevalent; that the larger part of this college is imbued with a false altruism; and that most political questions are looked at from a false angle.

Roland W. Boyden naturally suggests to me the question of our general foreign policy. I am therefore going to advance some arguments in support of some of the phases of our foreign policy. The subject is, of course, too vast to give even a slight consideration to in an article of this scope. I am therefore not trying to prove points so much as to make some of us think about politics along a different line. It has become a foregone conclusion with so many people that the foreign policy of the Administration is thoroughly bad, that, without deliberately taking the defence of the Administration, I shall merely point out the other side of the question, and show that the Administration is not so spineless as some would think. I shall finally make a plea for clear thinking, more along the lines of tangible fact than along those of vague theory.

How many of us have heard the following sort of conversation when our foreign policy is talked of? To how many does this seem familiar? I am quoting from the words of an acquaintance—a man who won his

"H" in football, who has held class office and whom I consider thoroughly representative of the undergraduate attitude. This is what he says: "We ought to go and put Europe on her feet; we ought to step in and lend a hand. What did we do in the war? Nothing. What did Europe do? Saved us from being wiped out by Germany. All the money is in this country; we ought to go in and help. Let's cancel the debt; let's help European industry and lower the tariff. We ought to put Europe on her feet." And so it goes; we ought to "cooperate," we ought to step in and fix things up. This is surely a typical cross-section of a widely shared idea. How many there are who utter a fervent "My God" when they look at the paper and see what our action is with regard to Europe! How many there are who say "Wanted—a foreign policy," when, deploring the conduct of our government, they wonder what can be done!

Let us therefore see just what can be done and just what the Government *can* do before we criticize too harshly.

Many of us mistake loose thinking for altruism; and many of us are willing to substitute phrases for facts. It is only too natural; we are young, we have no property, no immediate responsibility toward our community. Imbued with an idealism which is the privilege of our irresponsible youth, we can well afford to say lightly "Cancel the debt," or "Give Armenia five billion dollars"—we can say this so long as it is not we but the bulk of the American people who are footing the bill. From this angle our collegiate altruism shows up under a rather different light. Yet in spite of this apparently caustic view, I believe I do not exaggerate when I say that the large majority of the country and certainly of Congress want just what our college idealists are searching for.

We all want to put Europe on her feet. Of course we do. We should all like to see her industry prosper and her production increase. We all —at least those of us who have any human feeling—deplore the chaotic condition of Europe. But it is just because it is so chaotic that we should think not only twice but many times, before we take any rash step.

There is one type of college visionary who raves eloquently about Europe's self sacrifice, deplores our "inaction" and ends by cursing the Republican party, the Administration and often the Government itself. When asked what he thinks ought to be done, he usually answers one of three things, viz: "America should go in" or "The Government ought to cancel the Allied Debt" or "We ought to lower the tariff."

Perhaps there are more answers to this question but these are the most common.

Let us take up these answers in order, not trying so much absolutely to disprove them as to show their weaker points.

When our college visionary says "America should go in," he immediately ranks himself with many great minds. Those who advocate "America's going in" are legion. I should like to have "America go in" after one question has been satisfactorily answered. That one question is "How?" *How* is America going to "go in"? *How* is she going to act once she is "in"? *How* is she going to apply her great forces most effectively? How . . . but there are innumerable "hows" to be applied. And no statesman can answer this question, and you, my friend can't answer it, and none of us can—much as we'd all like to. Some have answered it for temporary conditions, and Europe's condition is such that any kind of a permanent answer is out of the question. Europe is in a state of flux, everchanging and undependable. Were we to "go in," it is my opinion, and I am using the phrase in its broadest possible sense, we should go on the most gigantic wild goose chase the World has ever known, involving the risk of leaving Europe even worse off than she is now and risking the money and lives of our own people. So much for the please "America should go in."

The question "How?" usually calls forth the next topic in this discussion, namely "The Government should cancel the Allied Debt." This is a very current belief in collegiate circles. Preposterous as it is even to touch on so vast a subject in an article of this sort, there are two main objections to cancelling the debt which are worth stating. In the first place the Government has no right to cancel the Allied Debt. The Government is the trustee and executor of the people's property and of its welfare. The Government is a business concern and it must be run on the most business-like basis possible, for the millions of people whose interests it administers. There can be no sentiment in business and there should be even less sentiment in our Government. The Allied Debt was incurred legally and with entire understanding by each of the parties involved, and our Government has no more right to cancel the debt than the trustee of a private sum of money would have in spending it on charities which he personally happened to think deserving. Just as the trustee of an individual's money has no right to give it away, however worthy the cause of the gift may seem to him, even so the Government, the trustee to us all, has no right to deprive us of our due.

The second objection to cancelling the Allied Debt is that it is one of the surest ways to encourage war. As soon as a nation realizes that it can invade and make war on another nation and have fighting expenses paid by some other party who will never hold it accountable,— as soon as this happens, Bedlam will break loose and any thought of peace can speedily be relegated to the limbo of oblivion.

And now comes the tariff. The tariff which has never wholly pleased anybody and never will; the tariff which will always be the great American topic of conversation. Thoroughly and completely to defend the tariff, or equally thoroughly to condemn it are things which I will not attempt. I have not read all the schedules and all of the several hundred amendments and cannot feel justified in giving any opinion. I do not know enough. I shall merely state that the protective tariff has not made for a decrease in imports from Europe. By passing this bill, we have not built a wall around ourselves, we have not stifled budding European industry, and we have not done Europe any harm.

These are a few of the erroneous conceptions under which many of us here in college are now laboring. Characteristic of our ignorance of fact, of our lack of experience and of our fondness for a well-turned phrase, many of us swallow the mouth-filling words of our more garrulous sentimentalists only soon to become bloated with flaccid theory. Facts speedily go out of the question and revolutionary changes are vehemently supported. This sort of thing is often said: "So it isn't right for the Government to cancel the debt! Very well then, let's change the Government, but let's do something." Yes, let us do something, most heartily, let us do something and the very best way is first to look around and see just *exactly* what we can do.

My discussion of these tremendous and *really* important points has been most cursory; my opportunities for information and for knowledge are too limited to have this more than the merest outline. I have not tried to prove my points so much as merely to show the other side of a question on which the majority of the college has a curiously one-sided attitude.

Let us use as few theories, as few concepts and as few phrases as possible. Let us have a minimum of wild thinking; let us have facts.

March, 1923

Henry Cabot Lodge, Jr.   127

CORLISS LAMONT

Class of 1924, (1902–   )

Lamont studied at Columbia and Oxford after graduating from Harvard. From 1932 till 1954 he was director of the American Civil Liberties Union. He has been very active as a speaker and has written numerous books and articles on philosophy, Russian civilization, and various political and social issues. Among his works are The Illusion of Immortality *(1935),* You Might Like Socialism: A Way of Life for Modern Man *(1939),* The Peoples of the Soviet Union *(1946),* Humanism as a Philosophy *(1949), and* The Independent Mind *(1952).*

IDEAS FOR IRRECONCILABLES

THE FORMATION this spring of a college division of the League of Nations Non-Partisan Association has been one of the most hopeful occurrences of the year in college circles. The Division was spontaneously started by college undergraduates who themselves originated the idea and later brought it before the Association's executives for ratification. The very fact that this Division has been organized should be encouraging to all thinking persons, because it shows that college students are beginning to stir from their apathy towards American politics, and towards foreign affairs, which are now inseparably linked up with our country's life. Even the most vehement irreconcilable must admit that an organization which tends to break down student indifference towards politics has some value. And, though the arousing of undergraduate opinion along general political lines is not the College Division's chief purpose, it is a most important consideration. For pro-

Leaguers the formation of the Division is reassuring, because it proves that there is a strong sentiment towards the United States entering the League among the most intelligent and enlightened group of young people in the country.

The aims of the College Division can best be explained by first outlining the principles and purposes of the Non-Partisan Association itself. In simple terms, the Association is a group of men and women of different party affiliations who are seeking to cultivate "such a public opinion as will induce the present administration, or if not this, the next one, to enter the League of Nations" either with or without reservations. The Association has already organized committees in every state, plans to do the same in every congressional district in the Union, and purposes to secure the insertion in both the Republican and Democratic party platforms in 1924, of a plank favoring entrance of the United States into the League. It is also an object of the Association to secure approval by the members of the Senate of President Harding's World Court recommendation.

Most emphatically the Association does not accept the statement that the Republican majority in 1920 meant repudiation of the League by the voters of the country. As Samuel Colcord, a Republican, points out in "The Great Deception," the League was, by a natural confusion of ideas associated in the minds of a great mass of voters with other parts of the Treaty of Versailles, which were particularly offensive to the foreign element. This confusion sent many votes to the Republican ranks. To my mind, "anti-Wilsonism" and the natural reaction following the war played almost as important parts in the election as any other one thing. Then, also, it must be taken into consideration that millions voted for Mr. Harding, following the advice of Taft, Hughes, Hoover, Root, and the rest of the "31," who predicted that with the Republicans in power the United States would enter the League. In this group were included that large body of voters who went Republican, not because of hostility towards joining the League at all, but on account of opposition to going in without adequate safeguards. Finally there were those reservationists, who, though realizing in spite of the "31" that a Republican administration would shelve the League, voted for Mr. Harding rather than to give their approval to the nation's entering without suitable reservations. With these facts in mind it is difficult to see how any fair-minded observer can say: "The League is a dead issue; it was settled in 1920." Suppose there had been a clear-cut issue between the irreconcilables and the reservationists aided by the non-reservationists. Suppose that the issue had been entering the League with the Lodge reservations or not at all. Would the people have rebuked the Senator from Massachusetts? Certainly not; for there is every reason to believe that a majority of the voters in 1920, all other issues disregarded, would have declared themselves in favor of this country's entering the League *with reservations.*

At the present time it seems plausible to go on the assumption that everyone who is not an irreconcilable is for this League either with or without reservations, and that very few who desire reservations wish to go beyond the Lodge proposals of 1919. The Association aims to unite all those who are not irreconcilables and all who can be won over from the irreconcilables. When such a combination has been effected, it will, I believe, be plain to the administration in power that the irreconcilable element is in the minority. There can be little doubt, however, that the country as a whole is against the United States joining the League *without reservations*; and that no administration within the next decade can bring about our entrance without reservations, unless there is an almost unbelievable reversal of popular feeling.

The part the 618 colleges and professional schools of the country can play in the carrying out of the purposes outlined above is a great one. If the colleges line up solidly in favor of the United States entering the League, the effects will be far-reaching. The very fact that the colleges are behind the movement will, of course, carry weight throughout the country just as the united appeal of labor or any other group of public opinion would be influential. This will be a direct effect. The indirect effects will perhaps be more important. In 1924, practically all students now in college above the present Freshman Class will be old enough to vote; by 1928 four more college classes will have become eligible. Knowledge of this will cause party headquarters to look up sharply, not only because of the votes these students will cast, but on account of the influence they will exert on other voters in their communities and various fields of activity.

Although the Division is essentially an undergraduate affair, no opportunity will be lost in enlisting the support of the members of the faculty and the graduate schools. In fact, in the branch recently established at Harvard the graduate schools are represented by two members on the Executive Council, while three faculty members are serving in an advisory capacity. The further technical details of the scheme I do not intend to discuss here, inasmuch as they have already been announced elsewhere.

I have not the space in this article to go deeply into the arguments for and against the United States entering the League. Nor is that the purpose of this essay. Rather than trying to prove conclusively any specific points, let me make a few self-evident observations.

The great tragedy of 1919 and 1920 was that the League question became the plaything of party politics. It never had a fair showing in the United States, misinterpreted and misrepresented by the politicians as it was. But this is 1923; and my plea is for all citizens of all parties to join now in repairing the mistakes of the past, whether Lodge or Wilson or both were in the wrong. Let the President, who as a Senator voted for the League with reservations in 1919, and the Republicans and Democrats of the Senate, a great many of whom did the same, reconsider, and if they want reservations, make them—but go in! That the League will accept reservations from this country there can be little question. For instance, let us study what Lord Robert Cecil said recently in regard to Article X: "Article X is an ill-drawn article and I never cared much for it. In practice it is doubtful if it could ever be brought into operation. Doubtless when the United States decides to enter the League, it will ask, reasonably and properly, that the article should either be struck out or redrafted, so as to make its real purpose unmistakable, and I do not imagine that there will be any serious opposition to that being done." But even with the Article X bogy eliminated and the "six votes to one" bogy answered in full by the President in his World Court defense, the irreconcilables can read into the League covenant numerous other objections which I am unable to include here.

Supporters of the League in this coutry have often been called impractical idealists. Let me simply call attention here to the present plight of the farmers in the Middle West. Why are they suffering so? The hard-headed business men of the country, to whom reasoning in facts is more familiar than to most of us, say that the primary cause is the lack of foreign markets. I can illustrate my point no better than by quoting from Mr. Bernard M. Baruch's address on "Agricultural Finance." He says in conclusion: "I affirm that there is nothing in the world that affects your credit so much as the shrinking of foreign markets for your products. There is nothing to which you can give your attention that is of greater moment to you in a practical way than the creation of the international relations that are a precedent to a re-establishment of those markets. I do not speak of our moral responsibility in the matter, nor of the great opportunity that America has to lead a stricken world into a finer and better order of things—an opportunity toward which the noble thoughts of all men urge them, though I do think this consideration the most compelling of all.... Rather, I dwell merely upon what enlightened selfishness or even just plain greedy selfishness demands—the necessity of keeping open and enlarging an ever-increasing market for the products of your hands and minds."

Of course there are those who wish to see the United States enter the League, not merely because such a step will aid our country materially, but also because it will help Europe and the world in general, because it will further the interests of world peace, because it will make this country greater in the eyes of its own and other peoples. Such sentiments may indeed be termed idealism, but combined as they are with common sense and practicability they express a kind of idealism of which we should be most proud. Impracticable idealism I decry; and it is just that sort of idealism, which I believe the bitter-enders uphold. They demand a perfect League, a perfect Treaty, and they will never obtain either. Of course the League has its grave faults, but what human document of its kind has not? I call it impracticable idealism of the plainest sort to oppose the United States' joining the League or the World Court, because these organizations are imperfect. Yet that is a fundamental part of the irreconcilables' doctrine. (Their other cry, for out-of-date "isolationism" based on an utter disregard of fact, is not worthy to be discussed.) And yet they have the effrontery—they who have grown morbidly sentimental over sentimentalism—to call their opponents political sentimentalists or impractical idealists.

It does not seem probable that these pages will be read by those whom I wish the most to reach. They are sitting back in contentment timorously meditating—if they meditate at all—on worn-out common-places,—certainly least of all things on politics. This is not Harvard indifference. It is the same throughout all the colleges of the country. Most of the students will live prosperous lives as bankers, lawyers, doctors, or what not. A courageous few will enter politics to struggle in an uphill battle against the sort of loose, timid, or wilfully perverted thinking that we see now on every hand in our government. I repeat the well-known statement that more college men must enter politics and that those who do not go in must, from the outside, take a keener interest. This must be if the United States is to attain the greatness of which it is capable. That is for the future. Even for the present every college student has a direct opportunity to use his influence in politics, to help make this America a greater nation at home and abroad—the opportunity of fighting, preferably but not necessarily as a member of the Non-Partisan Association, for the entrance of the United States into the League of Nations.

June, 1923

DUDLEY FITTS

Class of 1925 (1903–   )

An editor of the Advocate *while at Harvard, Fitts is now chairman of the English Department at Andover and still devotes much of his time to literary activities. He has published several volumes of poetry and since 1961 has been the editor of The Yale Series of Younger Poets. He is perhaps best known for his translations from French, Spanish and Greek, especially* Poems from the Greek Anthology, *and Aristophanes'* Lysistrata, The Frogs, *and* The Birds.

TRANSLATION IN SONNET FORM

> *I diss'n: "Lo palvro catto della vuostra quéra xia*
> *Hat relitto chesta vista." et jò diss', "In pace sía!"*
>
> CARMEN DÈ MARIÂ CALVULÂ

They said to me: "Your Aunt Priscilla's cat
　Is dead"; and I responded *"Requiem!"*
　They said: "By evil chance your Uncle Lem
Has caught the mumps." I sighed and said "That's that!"
They said: "Whilst dining in the Automat
　A misplaced bean cut off your Cousin Em."
　I dropped a silent tear and answered them:
"As God wills, be it done; Amen; *fiat!*"

They said: "Your house has burned down to the ground;
Your bank account has been attached"; no sound
    Of dole greeted this news with dolor rife.
They said: "Mary has bobbed her hair"; the cord
Of my endurance snapped; I cried "O Lord,
    It is enough—now take away my life."

March, 1925

ALLERSEELEN

> '. . . *sed signifer sanctus Michael*
> *repraesentet eas in lucem sanctam . . .'*
>
> MISSA DEFUNCTORUM.

'May every faithful soul, O Lord, find rest
In thee henceforth for all eternity:
May Michael the great Captain guide its quest
Unto the light!' Our prayers falter and die
Before the altar-flame that rising thrills
And trembles in the chill November air;
But even as they cease, along the hills
A radiance ever stronger and more fair,
And all-suffusing splendour surges high,
As morning moves the rose-stained clouds among.
The weary night of tears and prayer is done . . .
Up from the East, across the gale-swept sky
With thundering tread and full-choired triumph-song
The shining hosts pass onward toward the sun.

S. TERESIAE

January, 1924

JOHN FINLEY, JR.

Class of 1925, (1904–   )

Finley has been Master of Eliot House at Harvard for over three decades and has left his mark on generations of Harvard students. President of the Advocate *while an undergraduate, he has gone on to become Eliot Professor of Greek and has published* Thucydides *(1942) and* Pindar and Aeschylus *(1955) as well as* Thalia, A Masque in Verse.

LOGIC, OR THE EVANGELICAL VENTRILOQUIST

JAMES TUCKER sat on the steps of his brownstone house, looking at the street and otherwise diverting himself while he waited for the newsboy who presently arrived. The newsboy went off about his delivery, and James opened the paper. When he saw what he looked for, he smiled knowingly, folded the paper, and whistling, walked inside where he sat down at a desk facing a class room. Here he made things ready for the pupils he expected, practicing ventriloquistic conversation with the empty seats, so that the room was full of different voices. After a while a bright and spirited-looking young man, evidently an eager pupil, came in and found James supporting a lonely but speciously dual argument about religion with an imagined party in the back corner seat. Naturally surprised, he asked,

"Are you Mr. James Tucker who advertised for pupils in this morning's paper?"

"Yes," replied James. And other voices in the room added confidently, "Yes, yes. By all means."

The pupil went on with gathering amazement, "And is this the School of Practical Evangelism that I read of in the paper?"

"Yes," said James again and confirmed himself ventriloqually, saying, "Yes, yes," and "Dear sir, be assured."

"Are you sure this is your advertisement," the pupil protested in an obvious but cheerful impotence. "Look at it. See." He showed James the second page of the paper where stood the sign in large letters.

> Mr. James Tucker announces a school of
> Practical Evangelism
> to help serious-minded young men to
> Usefulness in Religion.
> Will help young or old in matters of
> Domestic or Social Inspiration.
> Come early   Chance for few only.
> 69 Mt. Auburn Street.

"Yes, I assure you this is mine," said James firmly. "Rather catching, don't you think so?"

"Very," said the pupil with feeling. "But what's it about?"

"I'll tell you," said James motioning him into a seat. "I have come to the conclusion that the only way to be efficient about serious matters is to go at them lightly. And in this school I teach how to be efficiently volatile, mercurially practical, how to turn people to a bright life, how to breathe romance and a bewitching mystery into the daily tedium."

"But that is not religion," said the pupil.

"Oh, yes, it is," replied James. "Anything that shows unexpected lights of the spirit is religion. Now please listen. You believe that having life more abundantly is a good part of Christianity, don't you?"

"Yes."

"Well, if you believe that, why don't you go about doing it sensibly? You think doubtless that the soul is a very serious and important thing. And just for that, you insist on being grave about it. There are enough people to do that, in fact, a lot too many. That's why people in the churches are mostly so stupid, because their preachers make them reverent where they ought to be amused." The young man began to protest and James with a soothing spread of his hands pursued his theme warmly. "Reverence is a nice thing, but too much is blighting. Come with me."

By this time the young man's actions closely resembled somnambulism.

He put on his hat and followed James out of the house like a man in a spell. The two walked along the street which shined in the sun of early spring, and James, who felt particularly sprightly, hummed and rose on his toes as he stepped. Once he stopped, picked up a kitten that was playing on the street, and handed it gravely to a passer-by who looked bored. But the pupil did not mark this as particularly amazing, since he was bewildered. Not long after, the two reached the lecture hall of the prominent college in that town and went in. A philosophy lecture was going on.

"Now watch," whispered James. "Philosophy is a serious and important thing but the students are asleep or heavily assentive which is the same thing. The lecturer should be more lively. I shall help him, as you shall learn to in my school."

The lecturer was moving in sober progress to his dull conclusion. "Berkeley," he was saying, "postulated a solely mental existence of external phenomena. Sense impression . . ."

". . . Was nothing to him. Whee!" cried James the ventriloquist in a voice that emerged from the center of the class, yards from him. The lecturer stopped, students sat up, tired eyes opened, and a fortuitous breeze blew open a window, like Zeus thundering on the right.

"I'll try it once more," James whispered again, "and the class will have spirit enough for a week or so to go on profitably."

"Sir," he pursued in yet another voice, "I don't see how all minds see the same thing, when they are all so different. If one person is not looking at a mountain, some one else is. But if the mountain exists in the first man's mind alone, the second man might see an elephant or three-ringed circus instead. People differ about what they like to imagine. But I may be stupid. You know I think I like April better than any other month."

The voice expired after its last sentimental confidence, and the class went on, like an old automobile repainted. Through that week and the next the students were attentive and the lecturer cogent and sprightly, since all expected some new outburst. They put some pleasant value to life then, like the children of Israel in the desert, since miracles were as likely as not to happen any time. James and the pupil went home.

"Perhaps by now you see what I wish to do," James said out of a long silence as they walked.

"Perhaps so, I am not sure," the pupil answered.

John Finley, Jr.   139

"I am the prophet of trifles, the evangelist of the commonplace, the rescuer from listlessness. Boredom is a worse menace than sin, and exuberance must be the daily savior. Here is the way to be useful in the world. Do not set out to be serious. You say you are religious-minded. If you become a clergyman, you will wear a professional sombreness and most of your usefulness will be lost. You will save old ladies' souls, but theirs would be saved anyway. Do not let the people know you are saving them, and you might do it. I know a way. You may learn to pass a life of greater service and most vital utility beginning as a street-car conductor."

"What!" cried the pupil in a sharp voice.

"As a street-car conductor. By the way what is your name."

"Francis Smith. I'm a cousin of yours as a matter of fact."

"Oh, so you are. Fine. Come with me."

They entered the brownstone house by the steps where James had sat that morning waiting for the paper. A sign announcing the school swung plaintively over the door as a spring wind danced in the street.

"I'll wait out here and see if I can get things straight," said Francis sitting down.

"All right. Don't run away. I'll only be a minute," James replied, diving into the house. The pupil sat with his head in his hands, trying to find a rational order in the events of the morning, the ventriloqual conversations, the incident of the kitten, the inspirating of the philosopher, and James's running talk, like prolix footnotes to a classic text. It was an excusably confusing matter, Francis confessed to himself.

"We're off," James said suddenly, emerging again from the house dressed like a street-car conductor.

"You certainly are," sighed Francis, thinking that this was a little too much of a good thing. "Where are you going with that outfit?"

"To my new job where you can watch me and learn practical philanthropy. I shall be conductor of the last car on a train to pass Park Street in about twenty minutes. You can get on there. Cheerio. Don't be careless and miss the car." And James went off arranging some papers in the inside band of his hat in his best street-car-conductor manner.

An half-hour later the distracted Francis boarded the car at Park Street, having composed his countenance but not his mind in the peaceful interim of James's absence. He noticed right off with sinking horror that all eyes were on James who was at the moment closing the car door with the proud jesture of a perfect conductor, and thought, "He's done it now. Why did I come?"

The train started forward with laborious grinding, and James stepped from the platform to the center of the car. No one in the car looked dully at the advertisements but all turned sparkling eyes on James. One old lady could scarcely contain herself for delight at finding something pleasant in the subway. She chuckled to herself and with her elbow nudged her neighbor, an Italian workman, who smiled now and softened his woody face with such a grin as was never before seen in the subway.

"Playa some more widda mouth organ," he urged hoarsely.

"Oh, do!" cried the old lady clapping her hands and rocking a little on her seat in senile rapture.

"Not now," replied James, "for we are coming out to look at the beautiful, though artificial, basin of the Charles River and see what Aeschylus (Greek author living from about 510 to 440 B.C. in Athens—a useful fact to remember) called the 'unnumbered laughter of the waves,' referring as you will understand to the sun sparkling on each ripple. I assure you that this is a very beautiful thought. I shall now execute a dance accompanying myself on the mouth organ." The whole car cheered and laughed, apparently convulsed by the idea that anybody should attempt relieving the torment of the subway. But the enlarging black hole at the end of the bridge swallowed the train, and James said, "Pardon me a minute. We shall have to let off the people at Kendall. For myself, I don't like that neighborhood, but doubtless some do. In fact, if you press me, I think it is one of the worst places I have ever seen. I urge the people who don't know whether to get off here or at Central to ride on to Central, where things are much livelier. Kendall! Kendall. Change upstairs for other places. Be sure to change if you get out. Any place is preferable." The train stopped but no one got off. The Italian forgot, and a weak-minded person was intimidated to ride on to Central. James then did his dance, recited "Once more unto the breach, dear friends," receiving great applause by his rendering of the passage "o'erhang and jutty his confounded base, swilled by the wild and wasteful ocean," yodeled, and would have done a card trick but was interrupted by the train stopping at Central. Here he walked to the door and shook hands with people that got off, leaving them to go in a radiance that illuminated their lives for the rest of the month. The old

John Finley, Jr. 141

lady and the Italian continued on to Harvard. They never recovered fully from the spasm of their ecstasy. People thought the old lady crazy since she was so garrulous of James. And that was an unpleasant consequence, though one of no great importance, because in strict fact she was crazy, and concealment was increasingly difficult at her time of life. In other respects, James's benevolent vaudeville accomplished only good. For days after you could see people smiling to themselves with a furtive idiocy all over Cambridge. And when people make fools of themselves by innocent happiness the millennium is nearly come.

After a little while James and Francis walked out to the bank of the river that ran near the car barns, the one very jaunty in the spring air, the other yet lost in whirling reflections. For a space they proceeded in silence, though James whistled every now and then and kicked at the gravel.

"Don't you see now what it all is?" said James suddenly.

"Yes, I see perfectly well," said Francis, "that you wish to help people by amusing them and making life pleasant in an informal way. But if you can do this so well, why don't you do something serious and worth while instead of wasting time with your idiotic school?"

"Oh, dear," sighed James, "I thought you might see. But people never do. My dear young man, you are the victim of an inverted education, the useless product of a college that teaches usefulness in trifles alone and forgets important present things. Neither the college nor you recognize the facts. Your wish to help is touching and deserves a better success. You see, you all think that the world is run by very grave processes like legal transactions, and political steps, and put your education into the service of these. But you must see that your assumption is wrong. People have had politics and law for centuries, and nobody now finds life a bit more animating than it was at the start. It is clear to me that the things you call important are not important at all. They are the trifles and should engage the attention of trifling men. The really important things are those that we face daily. A subway ride, for instance, is much more vital than a crisis, a great transaction, and things like that, because people spend more time in the subway than they do in crises. To be interested in crises, which never or rarely occur, and to be bored in the subway seems idiocy to me. So a college which teaches you to be successful in the crisis but a failure at amusing yourself in the subway is wrong, and you, I am very sorry to say, must be wrong too."

"Pitiful," said Francis, shaking his head. But James would not be blocked and went on.

"You ask me why I have my school. It is to bring the most intelligent young men into the most important places. A college trains them assiduously for the trifles of law and business. But I shall disclose to them the great future of being radio announcers, street-car conductors, head waiters, clerks in stores, floor walkers, and policemen, persons whom we meet in our tedious daily activity. I, for instance, never see a steel magnate, and don't care if he is a great and interesting man. But I do see policemen all the time and should be relieved if they were sprightly minded persons. Wordsworth is right. Children are much more correct in their ambitions than grownups. They see the realities of life. Here take this and save your soul." James threw him a copy of Greenough and Hersey's *Principles of Ventriloquism*. The two by this time had reached the house again and entered it, James yet talking, his eyes bright with the dull glint of conviction.

"But I don't want this book," Francis protested helplessly.

"Of course you do," said the implacable James. "To know it is as important as philosophy. Remember this morning. Without my ventriloquisms, the lecturer could never have made his pupils listen. Which then is the more necessary, philosophy or ventriloquism? Besides it is useful to entertain girls, children, and oneself in dull moments. Hello! Here's grandfather. What's he doing here?"

"Good morning, James," said the old gentleman standing sternly with his cane in the doorway. "I thought we could trust you now without a guardian. I sent your cousin Francis here this morning when he came in from the West. From what he says you are not less unbalanced than before. It is a trial to me, James, to have a deranged grandson."

"Oh, grandpa, don't go into that again," said James, and turning to Francis he explained, "I had a little wind organ with a beautiful *vox humana*. Now the only place I feel musical is in the shower bath. So I made a rubber covering for the organ and put it there. Grandpa thought I was crazy and had me watched."

"Surely, that was the act of a deranged person," the old man said. "And here now you are at your ventriloquism, and your senseless stunts in trolley cars. I must call in your guardian," and he turned to motion a man outside.

Here James in desperation turned to the respected Francis and risking everything on that young man's good word, cried "I was logical before, I am logical now. There was no point in having an organ if you could not play it where you wanted to. There is no point in having life if you cannot be amused by it as it passes. I do the reasonable thing to make people happy. That is not being crazy, is it?"

"Yes," said Francis.

January, 1925

JAMES GOULD COZZENS

Class of 1926, (1903–   )

Cozzens had already sold work to The Atlantic Monthly *by the time he came to Harvard; he dropped out of college during his sophomore year to devote himself entirely to his literary career. Since then he has published more than ten novels. He won the Pulitzer Prize in 1949 for* Guard of Honor. *His most recent works are* By Love Possessed *(1957) and* Children and Others *(1964).*

THE PASSING

Always at evening, I shall pause and turn;
Look down the years; mark in the lambent light
The grass-choked paths, the wood ways deep with fern,
Of the untrodden way to that blue height,
On whose bold verge one may draw rein and scan
The warm, small valleys where the white road ran.
There my strange Archer, fled from his last fight,
Still broods on his red horse, like a warrior from Camlan.

Once as a whirl-wind he would raid my heart.
His furious hoof-beats woke the expectant dusk,
And in my camp the glittering shields would start
While the gold bound trumpet carved from ivory tusk,
Exulting, cried the combat. Loud I laughed
With stern delight to hear his singing shaft—
Of our rich fights, lingers a brittle husk,
An empty goblet, once to a proud victory quaffed.

His two lean greyhounds, still as clouds at dawn,
Fret on the leash. The red horse throws its mane.
Gone are my gilded arms, my legions gone.
The scarlet faded, trophies old with stain.
And this the triumph; Romance overthrown,
No graven Vincimus on stately stone,
But weak, sad disbelief and wan old pain
And the strange Archer, bowed, on the far hills, alone.

January, 1923

REMEMBER THE ROSE

THE afternoon sunlight fell in shafts between the elms; hollyhocks along the brick wall stood like trophies and standards of August, bathed in golden glory. Above, the hills were settling into cool shadows and heights of sunny trees. A sky like unrippled blue silk came down to them and steep white clouds appeared with slow, adventurous intent along the crest.

There were cedars in one corner. The grass, a thick green tapestry reaching down from the wall by the road, hesitated, and gave way to warm, needle-soft openness about them; there was a faint perfume of cedars in the sun. A tea table was set here in the shadows with the tremble of breeze-stirred linen, the sheen of silver, and the fineness of pale porcelain.

Mrs. Bakewell, a contrast in her black silk and snowy hair, looked half smiling at a friend who had finished tea. The friend was a boy. He regarded abstracted the cigarette between his fingers and its slim straight column of smoke. You noticed first that he had that casual tan which comes from mornings on the links and the blaze of the tennis court. Afterwards you saw his hair was the color of old gold.

He broke the intimate silence at last, rousing himself and smiling a little; "I was in town this morning," he said "I managed to get hold of that old book of Monsieur Hardy's." He produced a dingy volume from his pocket and laid it on the table beside her. "I thought you'd like it," he said.

"How very nice of you, Blair!" Mrs. Bakewell's smile carried you back to the days when she had been Nancy English and Joseph Ames had done her in oils, astounding the old Philadelphia Academy and making his own reputation. She looked at the battered gold lettering: *Un Fainéant dans la Roseraie*.

"I looked to see if this was the one in which he told about his work on the Damask roses," remarked the boy, "it's got a whole chapter on the Amanda Patenotte."

"It's been out of print for thirty years at least," Mrs. Bakewell turned the pages thoughtfully. "The love of roses, except for fanatics like you and me, died even longer ago. This had five editions in its day, and now it can't be bought."

Blair dropped the cigarette in the ash tray on his chair arm.

"Aren't the Duchess of Southerlands blooming yet, Mrs. Bakewell?"

"Oh, Blair, they are. I almost forgot. Shall we go and look at them?"

He arose and drew the chair away. Still bearing the book she led him through the round arch where the brick was lost under the green of the ramblers. It opened into a second walled garden with spacious gravel paths radiating from the steps and stone work of a sun dial in the center. They went down to the glossy leaved bed where the fresh buds of the Duchess of Southerlands had broken gently into crimson.

"It's really a triumph to have them blooming now," said Mrs. Bakewell, "it's because I pruned them so hard this spring. Thomas protested a great deal, but he found he couldn't do anything with me. He is really a good gardener in the sense that he keeps the paths so neat, but he will not learn about roses. I shall never forget his chagrin when he came that morning to tell me they had budded after all."

She and Blair passed down to the dial. The stone was softly grey and graceful, the old bronze clear cut for all the long exposure, the rain and snow.

"I've always meant to look at that inscription," said Blair, bending before the metal plate set in the side. He read aloud the fine swash-letter script; 'Remember the Rose, how it doth fall.'

"Yes," smiled Mrs. Bakewell, "that dial was set up by my father and he had those lines put on it. A rebuke to youth, he called them. I can remember him so well on summer evenings walking the paths here in a yellow linen suit with a long cigar that trailed a delicious aroma, holding my brother's hand on one side and mine on the other. He would walk about and look at the roses and grumble over his problem of the moment—Verdier had sent him cuttings of his Souvenir de Malmaison, I remember one year, and he was trying to make them grow, refused to believe they were dead long after they really were—he would always end his stroll before the dial and read the words solemnly,—'Lines to take note of . . .' he would say, and thump off leaving us there to look at them. My brother used to make little parodies and father would be annoyed when we came out of the garden squealing with laughter."

They walked down toward the back. Those were the Phaloes, dusky over a faint flush of rose. So would Cleopatra's cheek have been, thought Blair. The Eugenie Jovins were like tinted foam. What could one call the Barbots? Blair thought of Watteau's fawns in a painted park.

Here were Eliza Sauvages, yellow like aged silk, and as thin and fine.

"You know," he said after a moment, "one can't say much of anything. I hate people who whisper 'ah, beautiful!' at everything from roses to Walter Pater."

"Some people can't say anything else, and they do mean it."

"I should think if they meant it they could say something else. They've spoiled a good word."

He paused among the musk roses. The Princess of Nassaus were in bud, golden.

"They are very white when they open," said Mrs. Bakewell, "it's like magic."

Beyond were the Eponines, true Persian roses, white as milk; Eponines, the slow drift of whose petals wise Omar hoped would soothe him in his grave. They stood in the gate presently.

"Such roses!" said Blair at last. "It's a dream, it really doesn't exist at all. You step through this gate into a dream garden which vanishes when your back is turned."

"Yes, but it always comes back, when, like Peter Ibbetson, you dream true."

After he had left and a dusk was settling on the garden, dulling the rambling lines of the old white house, Mrs. Bakewell sat in the candle light at her desk waiting for dinner to be announced. She penned a fine script in a black bound book.

'My sixty-ninth birthday,' she wrote, 'I had a delightful tea with Blair and we looked at the roses afterwards. He and I, are I think, the last of the rosiéristes. . . .'

Her eye wandered to the book he had brought and from there the albums in the bottom of the book cases.

When Parke entered to tell Mrs. Bakewell dinner was served, he found her looking at the pages of faded letters; good wishes, congratulations and advice, written long ago by Vibert and Laffay and Hardy; the notes in the great Rivers' angular characters, the neat little lines from old Wood. Mr. English had known them all.

"Blair," said Mrs. Bakewell one afternoon as they left the garden, "would you care to come over for dinner Thursday night? My niece Millicent is going to spend a few weeks with me, and I would like very much to have you meet her."

"I'd love to," said Blair.

He rode John Halifax down to the village to get the mail the next afternoon. The train was in, dark and compact along the open gravel platforms. He saw Mrs. Bakewell's carriage with the team of chestnuts waiting. John Halifax objected to trains, and pawing the air refused to go nearer. A girl appeared, laughing, followed by Mrs. Bakewell's man carrying bags. The train gathered strength with a tremendous burst of steam and iron roar, John Halifax backed away with desperate vigor, Mrs. Bakewell's carriage turned about. Blair went over to the post office steps and swung out of the saddle. As he lit a cigarette he saw the carriage disappear up the long maple arch of the road.

On the evening Blair was to come to dinner Millicent English had appeared in Mrs. Bakewell's rooms clad in heavenly blue over laid with silver, accepted Mrs. Bakewell's admiration with a happy smile, and gone downstairs. Mrs. Bakewell still stood by a window looking out over the gardens in the gathering twilight. The sound of Millicent at the piano reached her faintly and seemed to bring with it years very long ago. Late afternoons were perhaps more golden then, or better, a gold more soft. A certain magnificence had given way to cool efficiency; you saw it in the summer dusk, you saw it—Mrs. Bakewell half smiled—in Millicent's dress. She thought of the flowing gowns of those days, the billows and gorgeous mounds of lovely cloth. The evening clothes of today had none of the leisurely grace.

The pace of life had quickened. Men no longer wore such beautiful linen; their gloves and hats, the cut of their clothes, had sacrificed pleasant dignity and beauty. She thought of her husband with his curling mustachios, his graceful capes, the glitter of quiet gold, the cambrics no longer made, the rich folds of black satin. Such things had been relegated to a past which seemed now subtly better bred.

Her attention was taken by the appearance of Millicent and Blair strolling on the garden path. She saw thoughtfully the white of his shirt front, the cigarette in his hand. A gauze veil Millicent had slipped about her shoulders detached itself a little and floated after her in the light breeze. Across the sounds of summer evening her laugh came low and clear. Mrs. Bakewell turned away, went out of the room and down the wide cool stairs pensively.

The sound of horses hoofs died away on the road beyond the wall. The long shadows had sunk the tea table in coolness and quiet, and Mrs. Bakewell sat alone.

I'm glad they like each other so much, she thought. Blair and Millicent were always together, riding, or playing tennis, or paddling on the river. Only yesterday Millicent had brought home an armful of water lilies, wanly fragrant. There had been a dance or two in the village, dead dances, Blair had said, but they went none the less, laughing, and came back quite late still laughing.

Young people did things differently now, Millicent would come down in boyish riding clothes, flit into the breakfast room where the morning coolness yet remained, urge Parke to hurry and be out on horseback to ride away with Blair into the nine o'clock shadows, under breezy elms, up sunny slopes, untold miles into the summer country before she appeared dusty and breathless, late for lunch.

They had left now to ride over the hill road and see the sunset. Up there the long fields were yellow with golden rod; cardinal flowers and gentians grew in the hollows about the brooks, the asters, blue beneath the dust, thronged along the road. So Millicent said.

She had told Blair when they had finished tea a little while before that the Moirés were blooming at last. Once, she thought a little wistfully, he would have wanted to see them. Millicent had got up and gone toward the stables and he had followed, unreluctant.

It was late in September when Millicent left. The next afternoon Blair came in. He was very hurried.

"Thank you," he said. "I can't stay to tea, I've got lots of packing to do to get back to the University tomorrow."

"I'm sorry you're going, I haven't seen you at all lately, Blair; you and Millicent were so busy."

"She's very nice."

Mrs. Bakewell walked to the gate with him.

"The roses will soon be gone," she said.

"There will be more roses next spring," said Blair, and he smiled and turned down into the glory of the afternoon sunlight.

June, 1923

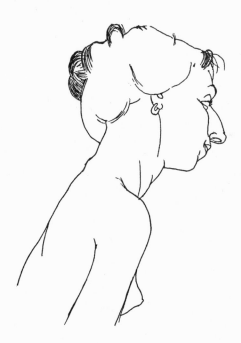

JAMES R. AGEE

Class of 1932, (1909–1955)

Agee was President of the Advocate *as an undergraduate. His first book of poems,* Permit Me
Voyage, *won the Yale Younger Poets Award in
1934. He also wrote* Let Us Now Praise Famous
Men *(1941) and* A Death in the Family *(1957)
as well as television and motion picture scripts.
From 1942–1948 he was movie critic for* Time
and The Nation." *The most recent collections of
his work are* Agee on Film *(1958) and Letters of*
James Agee to Father Flye *(1962).*

SONNET

Death never swoops us round with sudden black.
No Gothic grin greets our affrighted groans.
Our flesh alone cries out, upon his rack,
Of snapping cartilage and splintering bones.
Secret and happy as a summer dawn
Blooms and releases its reluctant light
Full blown along the dusk, our souls are drawn
Beneath the vast and unrelenting night.

Even now, a serpent swells my living skull:
Its thirsty tongue, struck barbèd through my brain,
Sucks all the cherished beauty dry and dull
As dust: and faint and failing is the pain.
I murdered joy, that your love might abide:
A precious skeleton lies at my side.

June, 1930

THE POETS' VALEDICTION

We, with our eyes impaled of fire,
We, with our flesh suffused of flame,
Our lips made purple with desire,
And our hearts dark with hooded shame:

Once in a young and evil hour
Ran foul of Beauty on the air
And since that time are in her power
To her delight and our despair;

Whence forth through all her weird ways
And devious incarnations, we
Have sought, whom guileless things amaze
With labyrinthine falsity,

That essence which is Beauty's life
Clothed in a myriad disguise
Which keenest thought nor shrewdest knife
Most swiftly urged may ever surprise.

When we were nearest her deceit
And she imperilled of her power
With windy grass she bound our feet
Or in a bright malignant shower

Involved our passage, and when these
Delusions served but to refresh,
In new dissemblance of dis-ease
She spun herself a gown of flesh:

Wherein she strolled athwart our way
Young, and irrationally wise,
And swift accomplished our dismay
With furious and gentle eyes.

James R. Agee 153

Some time, as thoughtless as the air,
Remorseless and regardless quite
Of lost and further seeking, there
By love deceived and love's delight

We lingered in the simple joy
And operation of our lust;
Which that sweet texture did destroy
And sharply ravel toward the dust.

Then rose the mind in his despair
To kind obscene philosophy:
Superior to such repair
Love died of unsimplicity.

Half sure of finding, surer of
Solaceous ease if she were sped,
Rifling all various looms of love
We set corruption on each thread.

She was denatured out of flesh,
And was departed out of love,
And urged no summer wind to thresh
Music from no harmonious grove,

But from all bygone semblances
Which now were vulnerable of proof,
And every proof the heart assays
And soon destroys, she held aloof.

All these old seemings were become
Our properties, who exercised
Our wit and knowledge of their sum
And that familiar sum despised.

Out of that wealth which we despise
We fashioned various hymns to be
Sung in her worship, which, being lies,
Fractions of false totality,

As well we knew, whenever sung
Did but contaminate her name:
Men's praise and her own silence flung
Throughout our hearts the midnight's shame.

In self-despisal and despair
Alone and unobserv-ed each
Knelt and addressed to her a prayer
In broken undevis-ed speech:

And saw the hills resolve to their
Essential and primeval fire,
The shaken seas on air the air
Athwart ethereal space expire,

While through demolishment and smoke
And all creation set awry
Loud the ambiguous thunder spoke
Articulate along the sky

The lightnings wrote what none might read
The imperious patterned stars revolved
Their influence round the changing seed,
Despite which seed and stars dissolved.

The mad oracular din was quelled
All elemental stuffs unjointed
And all molecular mists dispelled
And all sure substance disappointed,

And down that spaceless disarray
Where now we waited undistressed
Where night concentralized with day
Beauty her Self made manifest.

Of that high Presence who shall prate,
Who from the black disanimate flame
And quiet whence all things emanate
Declared her multiplicit name?

Silent we knelt and silent she
With never a need for any word
Proclaimed those verities which we
May find no speech for, who have heard,

While still we knelt, from out that space
Of holy nothingness exhaled
All things to their appointed place
And we to earth, whom speech has failed

Truly to make what we perceive
Identical with what we see:
Those guileful things which now amaze
With labyrinthine verity.

To the old quest we've fallen heir
Once more and to the ancient pain
And sick desire, who could not bear
For long the sight without the stain.

Wherefore with eyes impaled of fire
And with our flesh suffused of flame,
Our lips made lurid with desire
And our dark hearts destroyed by shame,

Silent henceforth we march toward
That silence which is Beauty's soul:
Be our oblivious reward
That some man tell of Beauty whole.

April, 1933

A WALK BEFORE MASS

HE AWOKE at a little after four, and knew it was upon him again. It was
scarcely daylight, and rain was dropping out of a bare sky. He watched

blades of water delicately overlap and riffle down the pane. Mary was sleeping with her head thrown back, her mouth gently flared. For quite a while he lay staring at her, glancing up occasionally at the rain, trying to think it out.

Once more it had become unbearable, quite unbearable. He had gone through all this once before, so thoroughly, so pitilessly, that he had thought, "Nothing can ever hurt me again."

"From the many-venomed earth . . .

. . . .

Mithridates, he died old."

He'd always trusted Housman, and yet—here he was again, caught in the same inexorable cogs of pain. The first inoculation, then, had failed to "take." Yes, that was it: he had to be roused from the years of tundra-like discontent; his soul had to go on the table once more.

For over a week now, he had known. That was the really queer part of it; for a week he'd known, and gone ahead just as before. It had made no apparent difference. Indeed, he had been so foolish as to smile, silently quoting those silly verses of Housman's. Even the night before, the same unperturbed level of unhappiness had closed above him. Something profounder than a dream had moved toward this awakening.

He looked at his watch. Nearly five. He'd better try to get another hour of sleep, before they got up for Mass. "They?" He turned his head and looked at her for a long while as she slept. Could he ever again kneel at her side and take God into his body? How had he ever been able to, since first he had known it? How could he lie there beside her a moment longer?

And yet he did lie there, thumbs gnawing into palms; lay staring down upon the sleeping head. In the brief months of happiness after their marriage he had often looked thus upon her and had thought, "It is like looking into a mirror." He remembered that now, and as he gazed more intently he saw dark floodgates spread like wings in his soul.

He pressed his knuckles into his eye-sockets, and tried desperately to pray. He couldn't make up his mind what he was to pray for. There was so much. It was so utterly beyond remedy.

He must pray for Mary . . .

God . . . O God, deliver my wife out of her iniquity . . . God keep her, make her pure. . . .

Blessed is the fruit of thy womb, Jesus . . . .

Blessed is the fruit of thy womb. Impossible . . . Blessed . . . Jerome . . . .

He must go to Jerome.

He got up, and tiptoed into the next room. Kneeling beside his son, he raised his palms and tried to pray. He looked at the window; water panelled it like a bird's wing, and beyond was blank sky.

God . . . God . . . God!

Only when the child awoke did he realize he had spoken aloud. Jerome looked up at him, smiling, and he said. "Get up son. We must go for a walk."

The boy said nothing, but got up sleepily and began to dress. If Mary had made such a demand . . . or anyone except him. He sat on the edge of the bed, exulting in the quiet, the comprehending obedience.

Jerome stood puzzled over a complication of buttons. He drew him between his knees, finished dressing him. He held him for a moment, looking at him, then pushed the hair back from his forehead warm with sleep, and whispered, "Wait for me downstairs."

Quickly and silently he dressed, stopped at the door to look once more at his wife. Mary was sleeping with her head thrown back, her mouth gently flared. Vaguely he glanced at the mirror. It held only the rain-washed window. He shut the door quietly and stole down into the hall. They put on their coats and walked into the rain.

The street stretched downward like a hard cone. He took Jerome by the hand and they walked down the hill.

He walked heavily at first, dragging his feet through the filmy water. It seemed impossible to straighten his back and to hold his head where it belonged. In a despairing way he was still trying to think it out and to pray. As they came to the end of the pavement the country wind sowed rain into his eyes, and immediately he knew what had moved down his sleep in depths beneath dreaming.

Such a rain as this had fallen through that other dawn—just such a streaming silent mesh, drawn like a tent over all the sky and all his soul.

His shoulders straightened, and his head fell back upon them.

Before them stretched an expanse of spongy grass, belted by the river. On that other morning, he remembered, he had walked down here, alone, that time:

He had walked across the meadow and down to the river's edge; had stood beneath an elm; that elm at the bend. Alone. Jerome: He'd scarcely realized Jerome's existence then; Jerome was a baby. Only a few months old. Naturally, he hadn't given him a thought. Too little, almost, to be considered human . . . anything above, say, a helpless——

What was he dodging? What was his mind scurrying from on so many soft feet? What was there, hidden, that he could not——that he refused to remember?

Face it, admit it; confess it. Yet was it a thing to confess? He had scarcely thought it, certainly . . .

> I came down to the river, trying to puzzle it out, I couldn't bear to live with her any longer. And yet I knew I couldn't leave her. Jerome held us together, I thought, as if we were tied in a sack, I thought . . . I thought: If only *he* had never been born . . . or were out of the way . .

Well . . . He'd admitted it now had confessed it to himself. He must confess it, now, to God, must——

But, was it a thing worth confessing? There had been no definite thought; the words had merely trailed across his soul, scarcely leaving a trace. It wasn't as if he had planned to kill his son. As if he hated him.

Hate Jerome! The child was all his heart and all his life. It was he who had made the whole thing bearable; no empty inoculation of pain. See how he had turned to him this morning, when God Himself gave him no help!

He looked down to the boy at his side as they kicked their way through the drenched grass. And he had thought, once, to . . . had wished his death. As dreadful, that, as murder. As wholly a mortal sin.

The elm was near at hand. He said to himself: "I will take him to the place where I thought it, and there I'll tell him about it and beg his forgiveness. Then we shall go to Confession and to Mass.

He took long steps, heedless of the sodden mounds and hollows in the earth. Jerome trotted after him, dragging at his hand. Breathless, they stopped beneath the elm.

After his haste his mind was broken and clattering. He put an arm around his son, and they leaned back against the tree. Above and below the bend the river stretched like a bolt of silk. Just at their feet the water roughened, but the rain quickly molded it into the smooth-skinned current. Rainpocks slid quietly down the surface.

He looked down at Jerome, and tried to begin.

"My dear, my beloved son . . ." he said . . . then caught him up and bruised the thin body against his own and with all his strength hurled him into the water.

The circles broke like bells against the bank, and smoothed away into the rain. For a few seconds he stood motionless, arms above his head, flayed eyes fixed on the water.

Suddenly he clenched his fist and so struck himself upon the temple that he had to lean against the elm.

December, 1929

THE SILVER SHEET

GOD'S MAN, A Novel in Woodcuts.
  Lynd Ward.

It would be interesting to estimate the influence of the movies upon recent literature. This influence is a perhaps subconscious absorption of the movie idiom which makes a marked difference in the writer's manner of dealing with his subject. This is evident, for instance, in the recent writing of younger poets, whose work betrays an intensified sense of form and of organic motion, and a somewhat diluted feeling for color.

However that may be, such a book as *God's Man* could certainly never have existed, but for the movies. The author tells his story in woodcuts, using not a single word. His technique is traceably that of such advanced film directors as Murnau (whom he most closely parallels), Von Stroheim, Lang, and Von Sternberg. The close-up, the flashback, even (by means of successive pictures) the truck shot, as well as innumerable lesser tricks, are used in telling the story. Every woodcut is, of course, made with an eye to the best possible pictorial effect—as are all of the better movies. The compositions are those invariably sought by a good director, rather than by a more conventional artist. There are innumerable angle-shots, shots of massed shadows, symbolic against a white background, shots which show neither situation nor character, but substitute some suggestive miniature, such as a landscape or a hand. In sequence, the cuts are splendidly timed. Ward has an extremely good sense of movie rhythm; he knows just when to use a close-up, when a panoramic shot; he understands the gradual plastic flow of a series of pictures to a climax.

According to his lights and the demands of his story, he handles his situations pretty well, though in this he is rather behind the directors mentioned above. A half-dozen or so of his close-ups are excellent character studies. I particularly liked those of the Patron, the Artist, The Masked Man, the Wife, and the Haunting Whore. But on the whole he is most successful when the story requires symbolic rather than human presentation. He deals somewhat better with nature than with the city, although there are a few notably fine city pictures—as, on the cathedral steps.

Reversing the ordinary method of reviewers, I have first discussed the technique, because the story is so very bad. In view of the worthiness of the book, from one point of view, I think it best to say little more about the story. Suffice it to say that it is Allegorical, but that even if you can stomach Allegories, this one will probably be too much for you. It's all about Art, and Sacred and Profane Love, and Life, and Death.

Strangely enough, this ham narrative is ideally suited to the author's chosen medium. (This was true, too, of Murnau's "Sinrise", which pictorially was one of the best movies ever made). In fact, the author has done such a fine job with his pictures as to make the book rather a tour de force; and his story is so immoderately bad as possibly to make a laughing-stock of the novel. Neither of these facts encourages further work of the sort. We may possibly hope for development abroad, where Masereel and a few German artists have produced several such books.

April, 1930

ROBERT FITZGERALD

Class of 1933, (1910–   )

A member of the Advocate *while at Harvard, Fitzgerald went on to work for* The New York Herald Tribune *and* Time. *Later, he taught at Sarah Lawrence and Princeton and in 1965 was appointed Boylston Professor of Rhetoric at Harvard. His own poetry is collected in* Poems *(1935),* A Wreath for the Sea *(1943), and* In the Rose of Time *(1956), but he is also known for his translations of* The Odyssey *and* Sophocles' Oedipus at Colonus.

SYMPHONY ENDED

Say by what hale reverberance of music
Our lands lie borderless, unplumbed our main.
Jade time and crystal in a wrist-watch tick
Mental division to the falling grain,
And from the fire-thin sweet channeling
Which is our love and labyrinth of time,
Never ascends the distanceless pure wing
Drawn out of night in the undreamed to climb.
Never. O men and women of the world,
Hard shackled to the rock and the mind's blood
Ruinous, drink comfort from those lands
Whereto he only comes whose song is furled
White into silence, who has seen and stood
And taken to his lips the beggar's hands.

November, 1932

SONG FOR SEPTEMBER

Respect the dreams of old men, said the cricket,
Summer behind the song, the streams falling
Ledge to ledge in the mountains where clouds come.

Attend the old men who wander, said the cricket.
Daylight and evening in the air grown cold
Time thins, leaving our will to wind and whispers.
The bells are swallowed gently underground.

Because in time the birds will leave this country
Waning south, not to appear again
Because light is a mad thing
And love falters without music

Because we walk in gardens among grasses
Touching the garments of the wind that passes
Dimming our eyes.

Give benches to the old men, said the cricket,
Listening by cool ways to the world that dies
Fainter than seas drawn off from mist and stone.

The rain that speaks at night is the prayer's answer.
What are dry phantoms to the old men
Lying at night alone?

They are not here whose gestures we have known:
Their hands in the dusk, the frail hair in the sun.

December, 1932

SEDES UBI FATA QUIETAS

Descend in wispy evening, walking down from
Plato's golden dome, and crossing, frailly

Robert Fitzgerald 163

Light windy quiet places, benches, leaves
To Tremont Street and traffic, among pigeons
(White needle of evening) walking down
Through cries and marvels, terminals, the dark
Singing

"Time is a cubist tune the dusk remembers,
Lake of dim planets. From the foundered sun
Islands recede, the sheeted oceans run,
Narcotic splendor in the firmament
For mountaineers, whose guts and lungs are spent
Against the Andes or the Matterhorn.
Thermopylae the Greeks mourn:
Their chariots spin the hours. Cool
Stars rise on Hymettus. Flutes in the wind.
The relics of the slain are thinned,
And over Asia in the wings of noon
Dark engines dwarf a continent . . . Here, now
This city, city, violet crowned, where night's
Wild winsome stallions brood, this coil of sea . . ."

Descend now in the evening's charity
From tea-cups and the mild light in the hall, referring
Nothing to nothing, whispering, walking down
From one year to the next, a smile, a dream.

November, 1932

LEDA

Drift like the cold moon, sorrowful
Thy path as hers, O swan
That in the night stream silently
Takest thy shadow on.

It is the dream's shape and the voices
Stiller than thought: O queen
Of the chill lands and dark waters
Thou art not lonely seen.

November, 1932

LOCOMOTIVE

The train moves grudging, fumes, the slowly driving
Iron on splendid iron, glare of the pit,
Strains forward, glooms, and lengthens under the diving
Smoke of the light-limbed limited lickety-split.

November, 1932

PARK AVENUE

Between dinner and death the crowds shadow the loom of steel.
Engines dwell among the races; the tragic phrase
Falls soundless in the tune and tremble of them.
Spun beyond the sign of the virgin and bloomed with light
The globe leans into spring.
The daughter from the dead land returns.
Between the edges of her thighs desire and cruelty
Make their twin temples, whereof the columns sunder
In the reverberations of time past and to come.
A pestilence among us gives us life.
Sparks shot to the cylinders explode softly
Sheathing speed in sleep.

December, 1932

Robert Fitzgerald 165

EZRA POUND

(1885–   )

Pound came out of an Idaho mining town to re-fashion modern poetry, to discover and encourage young poets like Robert Frost and T. S. Eliot, to promote the study of Provencal, Italian, and Chinese literature, and to support 'social credit' economics and Mussolini. A few of his published works are Personae *and The* Cantos, *collections of poetry;* The Spirit of Romance, Polite Essays, *and* Make it New, *literary essays;* The ABC's of Reading *and* The ABC's of Economics, *didactic works; and the* Money Pamphlets *and* Jefferson and/or Mussolini, *essays in economics and politics. Pound has been awarded the Bollingen Prize for poetry and sports a magnificent beard.*

CANTO XXXVIII

> . . . . *il duol che sopra Senna*
> *induce, falseggiando la moneta.*
> PARADISO XIX, 118

An' that year Metevsky went over to America del Sud
(and the pope's manners were so like Mr. Joyce's—
got that way in the Vatican, weren't like that before)
Marconi knelt in the ancient manner like Jimmy Walker sayin' his prayers.
His Holiness expressed a polite curiosity

                     as to how His Excellency had chased those
electric shakes through the a'mosphere,

                                   Lucrezia.
Wanted a rabbit's foot,

                     and he, Metevsky said to the one side
(three children, five abortions and died of the last)

he said: the other boys got more munitions
(thus cigar-makers whose work is highly repetitive can perform the
necessary operations almost automatically and at the same time listen
to readers who are hired for the purpose of providing mental entertainment while they work: Dexter Kimball 1929.)
Don't buy until you can get ours.
And he went over the border

                                   and he said to the other side:
The *other* side has more munitions. Don't buy

                                        until you can get ours.
And Akers made a large profit and imported gold into England.
Thus increasing gold imports.

                           The gentle reader has heard this before.
And that year Mr. Whitney
Said how useful short sellin' was,

                           We suppose he meant to the brokers
And no one called him a liar.
And two Afghans came to Geneva
To see if they cd. get some guns cheap,
As they heard about someone's disarming.
And the secretary of the something
Made some money from oil wells
(In the name of God the Most Glorious Mr. D'Arcy is empowered to
scratch through the sub-soil of Persia until fifty years from this date . . .)
Mr. Mellon went over to England
and that year Mr. Wilson had prostatitis
And there was talk of a new Messiah
(that must have been a bit sooner)
And Her Ladyship cut down Jenny's allowance
Because of that Agot Oswich
And that year (that wd. be 20 or 18 years sooner)
They began to kill 'em by millions
Because of a louse in Berlin

                           and a greasy ———— in Austria
By name François Giuseppe.
"Will there be war?" "No, Miss Wi'let,
"On account of bizschniz relations."

                     Said the soap and bones dealer in May 1914

Ezra Pound   167

And Mr. Gandhi thought:

if we don't buy any cotton

And at the same time don't buy any guns . . .
Monsieur Untel was not found at the Jockey Club (Paris)
. . . . but was, later, found in Japan
And so and so had shares in Mitsui.
　"The wood (walnut) will always be wanted for gunstocks"
And they put up a watch factory outside Muscou
And the watches kept time . . . Italian marshes
been waiting since Tiberius' time . . .
"Marry" said Beebe, "how the fish do live in the sea"
Rivera, the Spanish dictator, dictated that the
Infante was physically unfit to inherit . . .

gothic type still used in Vienna

because the old folks are used to that type.

And Schlossmann

suggested that I stay there in Vienna
As stool-pigeon against the Anschluss

Because the Ausstrians needed a Buddha

(Seay, brother, I leev et tuh yew!)
The white man who made the tempest in Baluba
Der im Baluba das Gewitter gemacht hat . . .

they spell words with a drum beat

"The country is overbrained" said the hungarian nobleman
in 1923. Kosouth (Ku' shoot) used, I understand
To sit in a café—all done by conversation—
It was all done by conversation,

possibly because one repeats the point when
conversing

"Vienna contains a mixture of races."

wd. I stay and be Bhudd-ha—

"They are accustomed to having an Emperor.
　They must have
Something to worship. (1927)
But their humour about losing the Tyrol?
Their humour is not quite so broad.
The ragged arab spoke with Frobenius and told him
The names of 3000 plants.

                         Bruhl found some languages full of detail
—words that half mimic action; but
analysis is beyond them, a white dog is
not, let us say, a dog like a black dog.
Do not happen, Romeo and Juliet . . . unhappily
I have lost the cutting but apparently
such things do still happen, he
suicided outside her door while
the family were preparing her funeral,
                         and she knew that this was the case.
Green, black, december . . . Said Mr. Blodgett:
"Sewing machines will never come into general use.
"I have of course never said that the cash is constant (Douglas) and in
fact the population (Britain 1914) was left with 800 millions of "*deposits*"
after all the cash had been drawn, and
these deposits were satisfied by the

                         printing of treasury notes.
A factory
has also another aspect, which we call the financial aspect
It gives people the power to buy (wages, dividends which are power
to buy) but it is also the cause of prices
or values, financial, I mean financial values
It pays workers, and pays *for* material.
What it pays in wages and dividends
stays fluid, as power to buy, and this power is less,
per forza, is less
than the total payments made by the factory
(as wages, dividends AND payments for raw material)
and all, that is the whole, that is the total
of these is added into the total of prices
caused by that factory, any damn factory
and there is and must be therefore a clog
and the power to purchase can never
(under the present system) catch up with prices at large,
                         and the light became so bright and so blindin'
in this layer of paradise
                         that the mind of man was bewildered.
Said Herr Krupp (1842): guns are a merchandise

I approach them from the industrial end
I approach them from the technical side
'47 orders from Paris and Egypt . . .

                       orders from the Crimea
Order of Pietro il Grande,
               and a Command in the Legion of Honour . . .
500 to St. Petersburg and 300 to Napoleon Barbiche
from Creusot. At Sadowa
                      Austria had some Krupp cannon
                      Prussia had some Krupp cannon.
"The Emperor" ('68) is deeply in'erested in yr. catalogue
and in yr. services to humanity"
              (signed) Leboeuf
who was a relative of Monsieur Schneider
1900 fifty thousand operai
            53 thousand cannon, about half for his country,
Bohlen und Halbach.
     Herr Schneider of Creusot
Eugene, Adolf and Alfred "more money from guns than from tractiles"
Eugene was sent to the deputies;
          (Saone et Loire) to the Deputies, minister—
Later rose to be minister,
             "guns coming from anywhere,
but appropriations from the Chamber of Parliaments"
In 1874 recd. license for free exportation
Adopted by 22 nations
1855–1900 produced ten thousand cannon
to 1914, 34 thousand
one half of them sent out of the country
always in the chamber of deputies, always a conservative,
Schools, churches, 'orspitals fer the workin' man
Sand piles fer the children
Opposite the Palace of the Schneiders
             Arose the monument to Herr Henri
Chantiers de la Gironde, Bank of the Paris Union
The franco-japanese bank
         François de Wendel, Robert Protot
To friends and enemies of tomorrow

"the most powerful union is doubtless

that of the Comité des Forges"
"And God take your living!" said Hawkwood
15 million: Journal des Débats
30 million paid to Le Temps
Eleven for the Echo de Paris
Polloks on Schneider patents
Our bank has bought us
        a lot of shares in Mitsui
Who arm 50 divisions, who keep up the Japanese army
and they are destined to have a large future
"faire passer ces affaires
        avant ceux de la nation."

February, 1934

A PROBLEM OF (SPECIFICALLY) STYLE

*The Sage of Rapallo Discusses Among Other Things
the Nature of Religion*

EVEN THE death of the last survivors of the clogging and war-causing
generation that preceded us, will not bring a new and illumined era
unless at least the élite of ours or (that being unlikely) the next, make
some effort to understand the function of language, and to understand
why a tolerance for slipshod expression in whatever department of writing gradually leads to chaos, munitions-profiteers, the maintenance of
wholly unnecessary misery, omnipresent obfuscation of mind, and a
progressive rottenness of spirit.

Mr. Eliot in advocating a species of Christianity has, so far as I am
aware, neglected to define religion. His readers are befogged as to
whether he wants a return to the Christian Church (as it was in the
year Sixteen Hundred in Chiswick) or whether he wants us to turn
religious, or in what order.

There *is* a distinct difference in Anschauung between men who believe that the world needs religion and those who believe it needs some particular brand or flavour of religion.

Among professionals, that is, men who get their board and keep by religion, it is today almost impossible to find any professional competence in theology. I have yet to find a professor or religious writer who has bothered to formulate a definition of "religion" before touting his own particular brand. George Washington, refusing to be cornered and driven into profession of belief in an undefined something or other, commended the "beneficent influence of the Christian Religion."

Given an effect, even the most agnostic and merely logical mind will admit a cause.

Given the necessity of volition, the freest thinker might admit the necessity or advisability of a direction of that volition.

Given an increasing awareness that there exists circumvolving us a vast criminal class that never infringes any "law" on the statute books or breaks an enforceable police regulation, the more perceptive tend in some cases to believe in the usefulness of a "general disposition," you might even say they incline toward a belief in the *need* of a general disposition, toward the Whole, the cosmos, and even toward the consciousness inherent in that cosmos.

No man is aware of that consciousness save by way of his own, but believing in a great telephone central or not, or in minor centrals or not, no scientist can deny at least fragmentary portions of consciousness which have a sum, a totality, whether or no they have coherent inter-organization.

The minute a man takes into consideration the totality of this universe, or the sum of this consciousness, he has, whether he wants it or not, a religion. And some phase of that consciousness in his *theos:* whether coherent or non-coherent, labile, intermittent or whatever.

And into his thought and action there enters a component influence affecting, in all degrees from the infinitestimal up to 100%, his volition, and his specific acts or the general tone of his action.

Religion in humanist terms would be valuable in the degree in which it directed a man toward the welfare of humanity (judged not necessarily in mere terms of eating, but also in terms of mental condition, peace of mind, mental vitality).

Granting that mankind may need a religion; that, in concrete instances, many men will—so long as they lack one—do nothing that is of the faintest use or of the faintest possible interest, I should have to have some evidence that the given professional had reason for touting his own particular brand in preference to any three dozen others; and such evidence would have to come to me, either from a greater efficiency in good action or a greater mental clarity and honesty as displayed in his manifest thought. Thought to be manifest would have to be so, either by verbal expression or by demonstration in some other sensible medium.

A manifest funking of straight thought or honest action in any specific field falling under one's examination, would obviously throw out the fakers, i.e., it would obviously bring any brand of religion into disrepute with thoughtful observers, whether this applied to an individual exponent or to an "organization."

The Medieval Church in its wisdom placed excessive sloth among sins. In no field has the sloth of our time been more foul and oppressive than in the search for clear terminology. In no field have the English-speaking nations been more damned than in failing to dissociate ideas.

In all fields this muddiness is so great that any field serves as repulsive example; and among all morasses the economic morass is the dankest.

Experts representing their nations in international congresses are no better than timorous instructors holding their jobs on sufferance and fearing for the good of their offspring.

Lacking a religion or a decent ethical base, there is no reason why Bug'ush and Co. shouldn't be content in creating confusion. Lacking an ethical basis there is no argument against the perpetual (as I see it) infamy or dragging discussion continually onto the unessential, and continually away from the search after truth and knowledge.

If scientists are not always free from a personal vanity, we have at least proof that in the laboratories a great number of men do search after biological and chemical knowledge without being continually led off into personal bickerings and petty struggles for precedence. Medical science does and a number of medical scientists do set an example, however, many fools may have on dramatic occasions tried to obstruct a medical hero.

In no science can truth go forward when men are more anxious to show up another man's minor error, or to prove his failure of fool-proof formulation, than to use his perception of truth (however fragmentary) for a greater perception and for the formulation of valid equations.

We were, manifestly, drug up analphabetic in economics. We are manifestly surrounded by an ignorance of economic history which sheds infamy on every college and university and shows up the whole congeries of economic professors as apes with the rarest possible exception.

September, 1935

HENRY MILLER

(1891–   )

Henry Miller grew up in the 14th ward of Brooklyn and attended City College for two months. After a trip to the West he returned to New York and worked in a tailor shop, a cement factory, and a Greenwich Village speak-easy. In 1924 he resolved to devote all his energy to writing and four years later he moved to Europe where his best known books, The Tropic of Cancer, Black Spring, *and* The Tropic of Capricorn, *were written. During the war he returned to the United States, and he now lives in the Big Sur area of California, where he wrote* The Big Sur and the Oranges of Hieronymous Bosch. *"The Most Lovely Inanimate Object in Existence," reprinted below, first appeared in the* Advocate, *but was later published as a part of* The Air-Conditioned Nightmare. *"Glittering Pie" caused the banning of an issue of the* Advocate *in 1935.*

GLITTERING PIE

DEAR FRED:

I will probably take the Champlain, the boat I arrived on, because it is French and because it leaves a day earlier than necessary. I will bring the stockings for Maggy—and anything else I can think of. Don't know yet about going to the Villa Seurat, but Hotel des Terrasses suits me down to the ground—because it's 13th Arondissement and no ecologues. Make sure my bike is there. I am going to use it! And where is my phono? I am bringing back some of the famous jazz hits, the crooning, swooning lullabys sung by the guys without—. (The popular favorite is: "I Believe in Miracles!" How American! Well—, I'll explain all this in detail when I see you, and have a fine bottle of wine handy, a mellow one, a costly one. Here nothing but California vintages, or dago red, which is vile stuff. One must "alkalize" every day. . . . I'll explain that too, later.)

So, Joey, what are we going to do for a living, hein? Search me! But I feel that we're going to live just the same. Anyway, I come. . . . The Jew who published my notes on N. Y. C. in that revolutionary Dance Program got back at me by entitling it: "I came, I saw, *I fled.*" The expatriates are anathema to the Americans, particularly to the Communists. I have made myself heartily disliked everywhere, except among the dumb Gentiles who live in the suburbs and guzzle it over the weekends. With those blokes I sing, dance, whistle, make merry the whole night long. I have nothing in common with them aside from the desire to enjoy myself. To know how to enjoy oneself is something unknown here. Usually it consists in making a loud noise. At Manhasset one night Emil and I did the cakewalk so strenuously that Emil dislocated —— —. It was a marvellous night in which we drank ourselves sober. Towards the end I sat down and, striking every wrong note on the piano, I played as only Paderewski himself could play, *if he were drunk.* I broke a few keys and every nail on my fingers. Went to bed with a Mexican hat three feet broad. It lay on my stomach like a huge sunflower. In the morning I found myself in the child's bedroom and beside me a little typewriter made of hard rubber which I couldn't write on, drunk as I was. I also found a rosary and crucifix awarded by the Society of the Miraculous Medal, Germantown, Pa. It was *"indulgenced for a Happy Death and the Way of the Cross."*

I have had a lot of funny experiences, but few gay ones. When I get back to Paris I shall remember the evenings spent sitting on couches in studios with everybody talking pompously and callously about social-economic conditions—with cruel lapses of Proust and Cocteau. (To talk of Proust or Joyce today in America is to be quite up to the minute! Some one will ask you blandly—"What is all this crap about *Surrealisme?* What *is* it? Whereupon I usually explain that *Surrealisme* is when you —— your friend's beer and he drinks it by mistake.)

Met William Carlos Williams the other night and had a rousing time with him at Hiler's place. Holty arrived with two dopey brother-in-laws, one of whom played the piano. Everybody crocked, including Lisette. Just before all hands passed out some one yelled—"all art is local"— which precipitated a riot. After that nothing is clear. Hiler sits in his drawers with legs crossed, and plays "Believe it Beloved," another hit of the season. The janitor comes and raises hell—he was an aviator for Mussolini. Then come the Dockstadter Sisters who write for the pulps. After that Monsieur Bruine who has been in America 39 years and looks exactly like a Frenchman. He is in love with a dizzy blonde from the Vanities. Unfortunately she got so drunk that she puked all over him while sitting on his lap. He's cured of her now.

I mention these little details because without them the American scene is not complete. Everywhere it is drunkenness and vomiting, or breaking of windows and smashing heads. Twice recently I narrowly missed being cracked over the head. People walk the streets at night lit up and looking for trouble. They come on you unexpectedly and invite you to fight—for the fun of it! It must be the climate—*and the machine*. The machines are driving them screwy. Nothing is done by hand any more. Even the doors open magically: as you approach the door you step on a treadle and the door springs open for you. It's hallucinating. And then there are the patent medicines. Ex-lax for constipation—everybody has constipation!—and Alka-Seltzer for hangovers. Everybody wakes up with a headache. For breakfast it's a Bromo-Seltzer—with orange juice and toasted corn muffins, of course. To start the day right you must *alkalize*. It says so in all the subway trains. High-pressure talks, quick action, money down, mortgaged to the eyes, prosperity around the corner (it's always around the corner!), don't worry, keep smiling, believe it beloved, etc. etc.

The songs are marvellous, especially as to words. They betray the incurable melancholy and optimism of the American race. I wish I were a foreigner and getting it from scratch. A good one just now is: "The Object of my Affection can change my Complexion. . . ." I'll bring this along too.

At the burlesk Sunday afternoon I heard Gypsy Rose Lee sing "Give Me a Lei!" She had a Hawaiian lei in her hand and she was telling how it felt to get a good lei, how even mother would be grateful for a lei once in a while. She said she'd take a lei on the piano, or on the floor. An old-fashioned lei, too, if needs be. The funny part of it is the house was almost empty. After the first half-hour every one gets up nonchalantly and moves down front to the good seats. The strippers talk to their customers as they do their stunt. The *coup de grace* comes when, after having divested themselves of every stitch of clothing, there is left only a spangled girdle with a fig leaf dangling in front—sometimes a little monkey beard, which is quite ravishing. As they draw towards the wings they stick their bottoms out and slip the girdle off. Sometimes they darken the stage and give a belly dance in radium paint. It's good to see the belly button glowing like a glow worm, or like a bright half-dollar. It's better still to see them — — —, — — — — — — — —. Then there is the loud speaker through which some idiotic jake roars: "Give the little ladies a hand please!" Or else—"now, ladies and gentlemen, we are going to present you that most charming personality fresh from Hollywood—Miss Chlorine Duval of the Casino de Paris." Said Chlorine Duval is generally streamlined, with the face of an angel and a thin squeaky voice that barely carries across the footlights. When she opens her trap you see that she is a half-wit; when she dances you see that she is a nymphomaniac; when you go to bed with her you see that she is syphilitic.

Last night I went to the Hollywood Restaurant, one of those colossal cabaret entertainments that cost a dollar and a half, sans vin, sans pourboires. Cold sober you watch a string of dazzling ponies, fifty or more, the finest wenches in the land and empty as a cracked peanut shell. The place is like a huge dance hall, thousands of people eating at once, guzzling it, socking it away. Most of them stone sober and their eyes jumping out of their sockets. Most of them middle-aged, bald, addle-pated. They come to hear "torch songs" sung by middle-aged sirens. Sophie Tucker, the principal event of the evening, sings about a fairy whom she married by mistake. When she says "Nuts to you!" he answers—"Oh swish!" She is very fat now, Sophie, and has blue veins relieved by 36 carat rocks. She is advertised as "the last of the hot mommers." America isn't breeding any more of this variety. The new ones are perfect—tall, long-waisted, full-busted and rattle-headed. They all sing through the microphone, though one could hear just as well without it. There is a deafening roar which, without any wine under your belt, makes you sick and dizzy. They all know how to shout. They love it. They develop whiskey voices—hard, sour, brassy. It goes well with the baby face, the automatic gestures, the broken-hearted lullabys.

A colossal show that must cost a fortune and yet leaves you absolutely unmoved—despite the fine busts I mentioned a while back. I do honestly believe that a poor skinny, misshapen French woman with just a ounce of personality would stop the show. She would have what the Americans are always talking about but never achieve. She would have *it*. America is minus *it*. *You* think maybe I'm sour on my own country, but so help me God, that's what's the matter with America—*IT*. "They" and "it" go together—follow me?

And now, Joey, I'm going to tell you a little more about my lonely nights in New York, how I walk up and down Broadway, turning in and out of the side streets, looking into windows and doorways, wondering always when the miracle will happen, and if. And nothing ever happens. The other night I dropped into a lunch counter, a cheesy looking joint on West 45th Street, across the way from the Blue Grotto. A good setting for "The Killers." I met some pretty tough eggs, all dressed immaculately, all sallow complexioned and bushy eyebrowed. Faces like sunken craters. The eyes mad and piercing, eyes that pierce right through you and appraise you as so much horse meat. There were a few whores from Sixth Avenue together with some of the most astonishingly beautiful chorus girls I ever laid eyes on. One of these sat next to me. She was so beautiful, so lovely, so fresh, so virginal, so outrageously Palm Olive in every respect that I was ashamed to look her straight in the eye. I looked only at her gloves which were porous and made of fine silk. She had long hair, loose-flowing tresses which hung down almost to her waist. She sat on the high stool and ordered a tiny little sandwich and a container of coffee which she took to her room to nibble at with great delicacy. All the yegg men seemed to know her; they greeted her familiarly but respectfully. She could be "Miss America, 1935." She was a dream, I'm telling you. I looked at her furtively through the mirror. I couldn't imagine any one — — — — — — — —. I couldn't imagine her hoofing it either. I couldn't imagine her eating a big juicy steak with mushrooms and onions. I couldn't imagine her having a private life. I can only imagine her posing for a magazine cover, standing perpetually in her Palm Olive skin and never perspiring. I like the gangsters best. These boys go everywhere and by aeroplane and streamlined platinum, lighter than air, air-conditioned trains. They are the only ones in America who are enjoying life, while it lasts. I envy them. I like the shirts they wear, and the bright ties, and flashy hair-cuts. They come fresh from the laundry and kill in their best clothes.

The opposite to this is the suburban life. Manhasset, for instance. The idea is—how to kill the weekend. Those who don't play bridge invent other forms of amusement, such as the peep-show. They like to get undressed and dance over the week-ends. To change wives. They don't know what to do with themselves after a hard week at the office. *Donc,* the car, the whiskey bottle, some strange—, an artist if possible. (I, for example, made a hit because "I was so unconventional." Sometimes, when you are regarded as being so unconventional, it is embarrassing to be obliged to refuse — — — — — — your host's wife, let us say, size 59 and round as a tub. Larry's wife, for example, is a miniature hippopotamus who gets jealous if you dance with any of the good-looking wenches. She goes off and sulks.)

And now let me tell you what one brilliant man in the suburbs thought of last week-end to regale us. When we were all good and crocked he got out an old talking record of the Prince of Wales. We had to listen to that high and mighty potentate (then about nineteen years of age) tell us what the *idealllll* of the Englishman was. I don't have to tell you, Joey, that it was our old friend "fair play." An Englishman never *twists* you. It went on for three records—it must have been a golden jubilee or something. In the midst of it I got hysterical and began to laugh. I laughed and laughed and laughed. Everybody began to laugh, even the host, who, I discovered later, was highly insulted. No sir, an Englishman never *twists* you! He just falls asleep on you. . . .

September, 1935

THE MOST LOVELY INANIMATE OBJECT IN EXISTENCE

When I walk the streets of this city in which I was born and raised* I ask myself what am I doing here? What life is there for me in the midst of this stagnation? I look in the shop windows and they are filled with objects which I have no desire to own. I look at the activity of

* New York

my nine million neighbors and I see it as a kind of insanity. I go to a bar for a quiet drink and a bit of enjoyable conversation and I find myself surrounded by brutes and imbeciles. I go to a cinema for relaxation and I am bored to tears. I pick up a newspaper and it is full of sensational lies, slander, gossip. In the subway I see a George Grosz parade of human caricatures. If I visit the office of a public official I have the impression that I am dealing with Al Capone's thugs and bandits. If I go to the public library the books I would like to read are not there; if I go to the art museum the pictures I would like to see are in the cellar; if I go to the concert hall the music I would like to hear is not on the program. . . .

I speak now of the great metropolis, the cosmopolis of America. What the other cities of America lack is an infinitude beyond description or enumeration. Beyond the pale of a dozen barren centers of culture lies the wasteland, a territory so vast, so sterile, so utterly meaningless from the standpoint of human values, that the mind is appalled, the heart stopped, the tongue speechless. Only what is non-human in this "wild, wide land of mysteries" speaks of grandeur, nobility, dignity, splendor and sublimity. In the great Salt Lake of Utah there is one living creature, they say, which has found the means of surviving, and that is the shrimp. The contemporary native American leads a life homologous to that of the shrimp in the great Salt Lake. We do not know how or why he survives in a world which is turning to salt. He does not melt down with love, as Vivekananda says the Sattvikas do. The salt doll does not melt in the ocean of love; instead it turns the ocean itself into a lake of salt.

Coronado seeking the Seven Cities of Cibola found them not. No white man has found on this continent what he came in search of. The dreams of the acquisitive whites are like endless journeys through petrified forests. On the River of Mercy they were borne to their graves. On the Mountain that was God they saw the City of the Dead. Through the waters of the Prismatic Lake they stared at the Endless Caverns. They saw Mountains of Superstition and mountains of shiny, jet-black glass. The Virgin River brought them to Zion where all was lovely and inanimate, most lovely, most inanimate. From the Garden of the Gods they moved in heavy armor to the Place of the Bird People and saw the City of the Sky. In the Fever River they saw the Sangre de Cristo. In the Echo River they heard the Desert of Hissing Sands. In the Dismal

Swamp they came upon the passion flower, the fuzzy cholla, the snow-white blossoms of the yucca, the flaming orange of the trumpet-vine. Looking for the Fountain of Youth they came upon the Lake of the Holy Ghost wherein was reflected the Rainbow Forest. At Shiprock they were ship-wrecked; at Mackinac they were water-logged; at Schroon Lake they heard the loon and the wild antelope. The Gulf was lined with Cherokee roses, bougainvillea, hibiscus. They fell through Pluto's Chasm and awoke in Sleepy Hollow. They crossed the Great Divide (with Margaret Anglin) and came to soda canyons and borax fields. In the midst of the Thundering Waters they stumbled on the Island of Goat where Martha kept her Vineyard. Through the clear waters they saw jungles of kelp and phosphorescent marines. Near Avalon they saw the abalone and other shellfish lying on the ocean floor. Looking for the Black Hills they came upon the Bad Lands. Calling upon Manitou they found a Turquoise Spring and when they drank of its waters they were turned into obsidian. Searching for Green Table they came upon the Cliff Palace where the red man kept his Medicine Hat. Passing through the Valley of the Shenandoah they came upon the Hanging Gardens and were swallowed up by the Mammoth Cave. . . .

Endless was the trek and endless the search. As in a mirage the bright nuggets of gold lay always beyond them. They waded through poisonous swamps, they tunneled through mountains, they reeled through scorching sands, they built natural and unnatural bridges, they erected cities overnight, they compressed steam, harnessed water-falls, invented artificial light, exterminated invisible microbes, discovered how to juggle commodities without touching or moving them, created laws and codes in such number that to find your way among them is more difficult than for a mariner to count the stars. To what end, to what end? Ask the Indian who sits and watches, who waits and prays for our destruction.

The end is a cold, dead mystery, like Mesa Verde. We sit on the top of an Enchanted Mesa, but we forget how we got there, and what is worse, we do not know how to climb down any more. We are on top of the Mountain that was God and it is extinct—"the most lovely inanimate object in existence."

Finis

March, 1943

JAMES LAUGHLIN

Class of 1937, (1914–   )

*Laughlin founded the New Directions publishing
company in 1936 while he was still at Harvard and
a member of the* Advocate. *He has edited many
New Directions anthologies of experimental writing and, in addition, has published several volumes of his own poetry. His most recent book is*
Selected Poems *(1960).*

DEATH BY WATER

When the picture was over, he came out of the movie-house and
started along the main street toward the waterfront. The town was
dark except for the arc-lights grinning at the curbstones. He wondered
why everything was closed up at eleven o'clock; there wasn't even a
drugstore open, and the cars that had filled the street, when he had
gone into the movie-house, had brought no coolness, and no breeze was
coming up off the water. Maybe it might rain later on, but even that
would not clear the air for long. It never did in those infernal Florida
coast-towns; a few cool hours, and then that muggy inland heat would
creep back again to blanket and stifle everything. It was even hot on
the water, for the sea-breeze was cut off by the overgrown barrier of
land between ocean and river. He had sweated terribly that afternoon,
even when running at full speed down the channel. *Just keep an eye
out behind you, and if you see the wake kicking up close, then pull
hard over.* And the heat from the engine had only made things worse.
When finally tied up at the dock, on the down-current side with slack
lines in case the tide might rise in the night, he had felt like stripping
for a dip overside; but one glance at that oily, dung-colored water had
sufficed to dissuade him. So he had had to slosh around in a pan of water

from the tank, water that reeked a little of gasoline. Then that ghastly restaurant on the main street; a bright-hued wall-painting of an alligator chasing pickaninnies up a palm tree; overhead fans twisting sickly; coffee stains on the table cloth; his food drenched in grease; and that buck-toothed slattern leering at him while he ate it. But it had been better in the movie-house, hot as it was. And that impressionistic music at the end, that sounded vaguely like Respighi, had somehow moved him. Then those two girls a few rows in front of him. Their white shoulders shone in the darkness, and now and then he had heard them talking and laughing softly to themselves. *You could probably pick up a girl in a little place like this, if you just knew how to go about it. They were probably just waiting for somebody to chase after them. But two of them wouldn't be so good. You mightn't be able to get rid of the one you didn't want.* When the lights came on after the picture, he had waited till they had gone past him and then followed them up the aisle and out into the street.

Now they were walking along just ahead of him, going slowly, not talking. He had to go slowly too, to keep behind them. *You might just walk up beside them and say something about "escorting them home." Then you could suggest the road along the river. But two of them . . .*

He kept feeling the bottoms of his feet slapping down on the firm pavement. They felt heavy, bruised with each step, but his head ran lightly before him in the shadows beyond the arc-lights. His head kept darting past the girls; then it would come flashing back to him and follow behind them for a while. He watched their legs rippling under the white silk. They walked along with swinging stride, clicking their heels on the pavement, clicking the rhythm of their weaving thighs. He stroked with his eyes the smoothness of their hips beneath the smooth, bright silk. Then his head went dancing off again into the shadows beyond them, and he thought for a moment that his feet were going to follow it. But he felt the pavement hard beneath them again, and he knew he would never pass the girls. He knew that he would never even be able to come up to them. He knew that he would follow them until they turned off the main street into the darkness; then he would turn back and make his way to the dock. There, lying on his mattress in the cockpit, he would see them walking before him across the night's black sky till he should fall asleep.

But later, when he lay there in his boat, staring wide-eyed upward, with a newly-risen moon flooding light around him, he felt no desire for sleep. Now his limbs had lost all heaviness; they were alive with potency as if they wished to seize the dark and struggle with it, clutch it tightly, and wrestle with it. Nor was his brain quiet in the single image of the two girls swinging leisurely along. They were there before him, but a swarm of other, foreign shapes and figures pressed about them, obscuring the firm lines of their bodies, sometimes blotting them out altogether. And the night held more for him than the rhythmic clicking of their heels. The singing hum of insects, unfailing melody of clear, warm nights, swelled in his ears to a pulsing, crashing, roaring. And when, at odd intervals, it ceased abruptly, the very silence seemed to fold in toward him, beating relentlessly upon him. He tried to close his eyes and still his mind's mad course. But the moon-brightness was now unbearable, forcing its way through his eyelids. When first the moon had risen above the shore-line trees, he had thought it soft and radiant; now it hurled itself down upon him, glaring, brazen, fire-white. Nor could he seal his mind in emptiness. Headlong, it rushed along heedless of time or place, casting up images now blurred and fleeting, now brutally precise. And the two white figures, once so smooth, so softened, were now distorted and grotesque, leering horribly at him with the grin of the buck-toothed waitress.

Then he became aware of his physical discomfort, of the scantily cushioned boards beneath him, of the unbearable heat and humidity in the air. The boat rocked a little at its berth, but the movement did not sooth him; it was jerky and irritating, as if the boat too were troubled in its rest. And every now and again the bow line creaked on a piling. The tide was rising.

So he rose from his mattress, knowing that sleep was impossible, he would only torment himself further by lying there in inactivity. He stood up in the rear of the cockpit and looked at the shadows cast by the moonlight on the low, irregular buildings at the end of the pier. Fish-houses probably, and in the morning he would be rudely awakened from sleep by the noisy grunting of fish-boats. But now, softened by shadow, their contours blending away into darkness, they were almost appealing, somehow pleasing. Yet in the bright morning light . . . A subdued sound brought his eyes near at hand where his dingy was rubbing gently against the dock. He undid the line that held it, thinking to snub it closer and so keep it from bumping the pilings, and then, caught up with a sudden desire for active motion, he jumped in, fixed oars in their locks, and sculled rapidly away from the dock.

A little way out from shore, he rested on his oars, while the boat glided slowly to a stop. No current was running, and the surface of the river was calm, though occasionally a little wave slapped against the side of the boat, making it sway gently. The humming of insects was fainter now; perhaps the moon was charming them into silence. For it no longer seemed so harsh and hostile, and it was higher in the sky. Away to the south of him it cast a radiant path on the water, which glistened away into distance, finally merging into obscurity. But other lights were visible now, as well. Upstream a draw-bridge spanned the river, stretching a chain of bright beads from shore to shore. And further still beyond an airplane beacon swung its wheeling beam above the dark line of trees. Watching its brilliance wane and recur, as slow rotation carried it on its measured path, he felt the turbulence ebbing from his mind and a calm passiveness growing in its place. One after another those troubled images retreated whence they had come, leaving him with only the impressions of his senses.

Then, taking hold on the oars again, he began to row slowly and rhythmically, following the line of the shore. His strokes were long, and he paused between them, hearing the water swish on the keel below him and scuttle out from beneath the stern, hearing even the drops dripping from the oar-blades. Each stroke was equal in strength, each pause in length. Thus gradually, he lost himself in the rhythm of motion. His whole being fused with the regularity and fatal sureness of it. Movement followed inevitably on movement; his eyes hardly saw the shore-line as it dropped away behind him. His muscles sang softly within him; his head was light with the pleasure of it. He had no head; it had drifted off on the swirling wake, and his body was whole and perfect without it.

He might have gone on thus for hours, had not a sudden light flashed in his eyes, startling him back into consciousness. An automobile coming along the river road; its headlamps shining out over the water, as it rounded a bend. He stopped rowing for the spell was broken. His head was back in its place again, squatting only too firmly on his shoulders. He turned to look down-stream and saw more lights; another town; he must have gone far indeed. In fact, he had not even known that there was such a town. So he went on again, thinking to see how big it was and whether it too had a dock. *Useful to know if you ever run out of gas.* Soon he drew abreast of a sea-wall, lit at intervals with arc-lights and backed by a row of palms; apparently a town of some consequence. *Funny that you shouldn't have noticed it on the chart. Maybe it's one of those boom towns. Those charts are pretty old anyway; they probably wouldn't show . . .*

He turned quickly, certain he had heard voices, and saw two figures by the sea-wall a little way below him. Apparently, they had not heard his approach, for they did not turn toward him. He dragged one oar in the water, turning the boat a trifle to see them more easily, and drifted slowly toward them unobserved. But he could see them plainly, for they stood under a light; boy and girl, she half leaning on the low wall, back to the water, and he standing in front of her, close, almost touching her. They had ceased talking, but still were motionless, the girl with eyes lowered. He looked at her, not at the boy. She was almost a pretty girl, though he saw only her profile, and that half in shadow. But her dress was white, delicately molding her body. He gripped the oars with his hands, crushing his fingers against the handles, as she raised her eyes to the boy. He tried to stand where the boy was standing; tried to look at her from within the boy, to see her as the boy must see her. He was there himself now, standing close to her, his knee pressed ever so lightly against hers, his hands near hers. He would stretch out a hand and touch her. He would touch her now. He would touch the silk of her dress with his fingers, caressing the flesh beneath it. He would . . . *Worlds away now in darkness outer and extreme. Years foregone now in light blinding and terrible.* He was crying out wildly, as if in terror; he was pulling frantically at the oars with anguished strength, pulling madly, stroke on stroke, faster and faster in a vicious frenzy of motion. Crescendo of violence and madness upsurging, all-swaying, compelling. Faster than flight on toward oblivion, faster than light into unconsciousness.

And then a long, long time later; he was lying in the bottom of the dingy, gasping for breath. His heart was hammering relentlessly against the wells confining it; his skin was heavy with the pressure of the surging blood beneath it. His whole consciousness was bound up in this agony of body, and each quick-drawn breath held all the moment's life. But slowly relaxation crept over him; his breathing became calmer, less violent, and he found himself thinking normally again. Thus he sensed

James Laughlin 187

that the tide must be near the flood, since the dingy rolled a little as it drifted, and, seeing the moon above the mainland, guessed it was well past midnight. He raised himself from the bottom of the dingy to sit in the sternseat that he might look about him; but he could not be sure of his exact position on the river. The drawbridge was still there above him with the slow-whirling beacon beyond it, and a few scattered lights marked the town whence he had set out, yet no light was visible from the spot on the shore where that town with the sea-wall ought to be. Moreover, the black line of trees along the shore stretched in an unbroken line away to Southward as far as he could see. Perhaps he had drifted upstream. But that was impossible. Perhaps in the burst of energy and exertion he had covered many miles of water. But that seemed even more unlikely. He could not have gone on long at such a pace. What had become of that town, then, so clearly seen but a little while before? That town with its palm-lined sea-wall, so brightly lighted, so unreal in the night. Unreal—it had seemed terribly so, almost unnatural, unlike any town he could remember ever having seen along the inland waterway. Why that sea-wall at all beside a calm and sheltered river? And not marked on the chart . . . Perhaps there was no such town, and all he had seen was but illusion. Was it possible? He hardly thought so; yet that strange light that had suffused the scene, almost uncanny now that he recalled it. And the fact that neither of the figures had detected his presence. But that girl, she could have been no illusion. He saw her even now before him, close to him, turning her face up to him. She could be no shadow of a shade. She was alive, impelling. But if that were so, why . . .

A sudden lurch of the dingy seized him from his revery. He leaned over its stern and stared down into the water, trying to penetrate the muddy opacity. He wanted to peer down through it to the river bottom, to see what might lie imbedded there. And as he sought in vain to pierce its rippling surface, there came to him a new, unwonted sound from the mainland. It was hoarse and gruff, now staccato, now whining off into silence. At first, he wondered at it, unable to determine its origin. Then he remembered the railroad, and knew it for a locomotive shunting cars on a siding. Fruit-express cars, probably laden with oranges from lush inland groves. Doubtless the northbound express would soon be along, and the fruit cars would go with it as far as Jacksonville. That was it surely, for he remembered waking in a fright a few nights before, as he lay at anchor in a lagoon crossed by the railway trestle, to see the train flash shrieking past in the blackness, blazing the night with light, gone in an instant, leaving only the diminishing echo of its passage. That train had gone surging past him in a sure wave of power, but this night-owl locomotive was fitful and vacillating. It seemed unable to sustain itself in effort, unable to settle its mind about whatever was worrying it, to rest in the night, that was not made for movement.

The water was warm, when he plunged his hands into it, warm and somehow unliquid. It stank a very little, too. And that locomotive still snorting and hiccoughing. Sad music this, that crept out to him over the water. *You can hear the ships going by in the night sometimes with that sad, still music heavy with sleep. You can hear it if you listen on the wind.* His hands were trailing in the water, and he felt it circle each separate finger like a glove. *You can hear them passing, but you don't know where they came from or where they're going. Only that still sad music riding the wind, after they have passed.* He was leaning far over toward the water, the stern board cutting sharply into his belly. His face was sinking closer to it, drawing down to it, eyes blurring out of focus seeing only *quiet there surely, lying firm in sand. You could lie quiet there your cares forgot. Quiet and silent there, wave-washed, secure.* His forehead was wet, and his eyes stung a little, as the water came up to meet them. His nose and mouth slid into it. He let his breath slip slowly through his nose, and it bubbled up from his nostrils. *You could be quiet here. And your weary body would be washed away. There would be just your head left there with pearls for silent eyes. Quiet and sure there, untroubled, un-* . . . Why was he being such a damn fool, his head under water, thinking sentimentally about death? Pitying himself to death, thinking he hadn't strength enough to give life meaning. God, what silly slosh!

He pulled himself back into the dingy, dried his face on his shirtsleeve, and took hold of his oars again. Unhesitatingly, he turned the boat upstream and started rowing with firm, even strokes. *You nearly did it that time all right. That would have been a fine, brave piece of work, wouldn't it? BOY FEARED DROWNED and all the drip and slurp of a funeral for the young which died good. Better get yourself a wet nurse.* He sculled along steadily, putting his body behind each stroke and finishing it with a little spurt from the wrists that sent the boat darting ahead. He felt the presence of his whole body in the movement. Arms pulled, and shoulders strained; legs braced and back surged. But there was weariness in him, too. He burned no longer for savage and violent exertion. This even pace was satisfying, as it carried him steadily upstream. *You can feel the tide pulling on you now, running downstream along with the current. Running down to the inlet and out to sea. You can hardly get a boat out the inlet when the tide is kicking up the rip.* It was darker, too, for the moon was low above the trees on the mainland. It would be gone soon, and the night would be empty without it. He wondered rather vaguely for a moment about the town and the girl by the sea-wall, but it didn't seem to matter any more. The image was no longer clear, and willingly he let it drift away. His mind was placed with a dreamy emptiness that did not even leave it, when the weird, long-drawn shriek of a locomotive whistle came floating past. But later, when, all unannounced, a cool, fresh breeze stirred over the water from the ocean, bringing the sea's coolness across the torpid river, he knew that a new strength was in him, born of the sea and strong in the strength of the sea.

June, 1933

190   *James Laughlin*

PETER VIERECK

Class of 1937, (1916–   )

Peter Viereck's first collection of poems, Terror
and Decorum, *won the Pulitzer Prize in 1949.
Since then he has published three volumes of
poetry in addition to the verse drama,* The Tree
Witch, *first performed at Harvard's Loeb Drama
Center. Mr. Viereck teaches European and
Russian history at Mount Holyoke College, and
his publications in history and political science
include* Conservatism Revisited *and the* New
Conservatism, Metapolitics: The Roots of the
Nazi Mind, *and* The Unadjusted Man, *a discussion of the conflict between the creative imagination and mechanized conformity.*

DIES ILLA

'Dies irae, dies illa
Solvet saeclum in favilla.'

        Everywhere
Awareness lurks behind a thousand blendings.
Awareness shivers—even in oases—
At hard-riding portents saddled like thistledown
On winds that have strayed in many places,
        Seen many forgotten beginnings and thrown
The dust of many great and little endings
        Into the air.

Out of the air,
Our swelling shadows breathe us when we breathe.
Sky snuffs up earth. Solidity has been rent.
A runaway outlaw nerve—or is it death?—
Signals and signals our brain-cells with
Black. In our sweetest entanglement,
When loam enriches or when limbs enwreathe,
            Who's purring there?

            Dead faces wear
An underwater strangeness, once so precious.
Our goggle-eyes plead upward—beached at birth—
To God. So minnows pray to beaks of gannets.
More air, more air!—the gasp of earth,
One of the uninhabitable planets,
Where meat stuffs meat (as food or love) yet threshes
            Alone when most a pair.

            Only from God's stare
We're not alone, or is it death, unblinking?
My dear, we have strolled to a spell-bound place
Where sunflowers have eyes that follow us.
Twilight lisps at our knees to swallow us;
Don't move; we are watched by a cloud with a crafty face.
Move fast; the fingers of the sun are sinking
            And clutch your hair—

            And tug you beneath by your hair.
Sunset-defier, sharer of dawns, hold me so
Close I will never let you go,—
Clasping you free from all the ebb of things,
From all but One. And if the One outclings,
Let love not die alone; let springtime wilt:
All nature ambushed by one descending quilt
            Of sick air

Everywhere thick.
And I—if it ends, if solidity ends tonight—
Will hold you close through all the holy thunder . . .
Till unrepentant flesh rekindles and, dawn-frenzied,
Strains at the quilt of sky and blazes through and rends it,
Shaking our windowpane with jubilant light.
You will shrug at God and with how young a wonder
        Wake me quick.

September, 1936

1912*-1952: FULL CYCLE

I. LOVE SONG OF PRUFROCK JUNIOR

Must all successful rebels grow
From toreador to Sacred Cow?
What cults he slew, his cult begot.
"In my beginning," said the Scot,
"My end;" and aging eagles know
That 1912 was long ago.
Today the women come and go
Talking of T. S. Eliot.

II. INSCRIBED FOR YOUR BEDSIDE
"GLOSSARY OF THE NEW CRITICISM"

Here's the eighth form of ambiguity:
The *new* philistia loves "obscurity,"—
And only we still dare to hate it
Because a *texte* without a Muse in
Is but a snore and an allusion.

*Events of 1912, the key year: *New Age* starts publishing Hulme's essays; Imagist nucleus founded (Pound, H. D., Aldington); *Poetry: A Magazine Of Verse* founded by Harriet Monroe (to whom Pound in 1914 sends Eliot's "Love Song of J. Alfred Prufrock," written 1910-11); October 1912, the American-verse number of Harold Monro's *Poetry Review* (W. C. Williams, Pound); symbolic clash of the simultaneous 1912 publication of *Georgian Party* and Pound's *Ripostes*.

Peter Viereck   193

Well then, let's turn the tables hard:
The snobs all snubbed, the baiters baited,
The explicators explicated,
And avant-garde the new rearguard.

III. FROM THE SUBLIME TO THE METICULOUS
IN FOUR STAGES

DANTE: We were God's poets.
BURNS: We were the people's poets.
MALLARMÉ: We were poet's poets.
TODAY (preening himself): Ah, but *we* are critic's poets.

IV. EPITAPH FOR THE NOUVEAUX NEW CRITICS,
HUGH KENNER, E TUTTI QUESTI

Cliché is dead, long live cliché,
And in old fields new Georgians play.
O miglior fabbro and O mandarin,
You who skinned Georgians like a tangerine,
Two Hercules who on your natal day
Strangled these snakes of cliché-pandering,
These same that now through backstairs wander in:
Let not (while death-knells from Kinkanja ([1]) ring)
The pedant town of Alexander in.
From kitsch the nineteenth century banned her in,
You freed our Muse. For what? Was Queen Victoria
Primmer than précieux new "Prohibitoria" ([2]) ?
Loving your ART and not your fleas, we pray:
May time protect you from your protégés.
Time's up when pupils' pupils school the school.
Cow? Bad enough! But sacred—calf?
Now that the cup of insolence is full,—
By God, who'll start a brand new Nineteen Twelve?

September, 1952

1. cf. not *The Golden Bough* but *The Cocktail Party*, American edition, p. 174.
2. cf. Louis Rubin in *Hopkins Review*, summer 1950: "He has twice criticized the award of the 1949 Bollingen Prize to Pound's *Pisan Cantos*, on grounds both of form and content. Either he must repent, and publicly, or resign himself to a prominent and permanent position in the Index Prohibitorium of the New Criticism." (In a review of Peter Viereck's book of poems, *The First Morning*, Scribners, N. Y.)

WILLIAM CARLOS WILLIAMS

(1883–1963)

Williams studied at the University of Pennsylvania, where he was a friend of Ezra Pound, and then returned to Rutherford, New Jersey, as a general practitioner. He published more than a dozen volumes of poetry and several collections of short stories. His Collected Poems *was published in 1934, and his major work, the epic* Paterson, *was completed in 1951. His last collection of poetry was* Pictures from Breughel. *He won the National Book Award in 1950 and the Bollingen Prize for poetry in 1953.*

FROM A PLAY

I am a writer
    and I take
great satisfaction
    in it

I like to time
    my phrases
balance them by
    their sensual

qualities and make
    those express
as much as
    or more

than the merely
    literal
burden of the thing
    could ever tell

April, 1942

Midgette Swanston 1972.

THE ELEMENT OF TIME

ADVICE TO A YOUNG WRITER

IF GENIUS has anything to say in America it had better be strongwinded. Because a life, contrary to the classic opinion, is endless. There is plenty of time. And no hurry. Nobody ever overtakes anybody else. Long-windedness is always a competitor and has to be lived down but even that dies finally from living in its vacuum. Then genius has its chance. Nothing grows old.

The only thing necessary is to have something to say when at last the opportunity comes to say it. But most blurt it out, or try to, breathlessly before or during puberty, and then look around for the next opportunity. It has passed.

Certainly, let everything there is to be said go into it, any time. That's probably everything there is in you—so rottenly imperfect that God himself couldn't make head nor tail of it till he'd worked on you for a few years long. Using the figure of "God."

In youth the violences usually have a great element of justice about them. Maybe it's only drink. There's a whole philosophy in that too. But it's a tough career. Taking something of a lesser sweep, or a greater one, it's no matter; the good of it, I wish to say, comes only to full flavor by intense doggedness.

I'd go so far as to say that everything a man can be taught in his youth has only this value, that unless he is a man it will kill him. Whatever he sees, whatever is brilliant to him, closest, most significant, no matter what anyone else says about it, that is the thing he's got to work with till he disproves it or makes it into a satisfying whole. And for this, there is an ocean of time.

I emphasize, it isn't the mass of difficulties that need unhorse a genius. It is the slipping, sliding wastefulness of useless rushing about. There isn't much to do. It's just the flip of a word sometimes. One doesn't have to live this kind of life, that kind of life. The only thing that has ever seemed to me to be important is never to yield an inch of what is to the mind important—and to let the life take care of itself. Sure, go ahead to Paris. Why not?

Life gets to be a battering down of the inessential. But if something

William Carlos Williams 197

doesn't come up out of the scaffolding when that is removed. And if that hasn't been essentially there from the time the first hair sprouted on the belly—in spite of all the whackings it got. Then, why not have stuck a flag at the peak of the lumber after all and called it a day.

And nobody can't tell you nothing about what you gotta do. Listen to them and take a lesson. You'll see what I mean.

The writer has an opportunity in this country that is unequaled elsewhere. But he's got to live through being a worm in the manure heap. Nowhere is there the intensity of uniformation that, I am assured, will be found in the House of Representatives. Nowhere else on earth. Not even China where childishness was, at least until quite recently, a glamorous spectacle in the adult. But in this country everything is still broken apart.

If anybody can hold to anything and cling to it long enough to have it be beaten into some shape by the holding and the onslaught, it will at least be refined enough for one to make out clearly its original futility. And even that would be a distinction.

It's not likely, though, that anyone with any intelligence at all will be able to hold to something wholly futile throughout a lifetime. He might though. If he is a supreme genius.

But there's no way of eliminating stupidity, the way it will take, from any instructions.

Anyone who has survived to this point, and finds the times rather tough—though I was referring more to the preceding paragraphs than the times—might profit by the following and realize that today is a comparatively enlightened era after all. Tomorrow writing may be even more highly honored for the indestructible accuracy reflecting the adjustment between the page and the unbeaten mind of the writer there is in it.

No, I don't think I'll tell that story after all.

February, 1934

During the past two months I have stumbled across two of the most deadly books of literary disappreciation for modern poetry that could possibly be imagined. They seem to be attempts to appraise the verse written in our language since 1912, the conventional modern rebirth of poetry. They are in effect attacks upon the whole underground source of the modern fountain of poetry come of a desire to drag it back, reharness it and force it to turn again the old academic mill. Is it a sign of the times? I fear so. In Wallace Stevens there is a poet in whom a war is constantly in progress between this desire to break the back of his art and a determination to go ahead and break free into the full day of the modern world. I see poems of Stevens which merit my highest praise. Later a book appears in which the poem I admire has not been permitted to appear. Stevens is a far better poet than his critical standards seem to indicate. May his will decay as he ages and his dæmon get more and more the upper hand.

Stevens Memorial Issue, 1940

A FACE OF STONE

HE WAS ONE of these fresh Jewish types you want to kill at sight, the presuming poor whose looks change the minute cash is mentioned. But they're insistent, trying to force attention, taking advantage of good nature at the first crack. You come when I call you, that type. He got me into a bad mood before he opened his mouth just by the half smiling, half insolent look in his eyes, a small, stoutish individual in a greasy black suit, a man in his middle twenties I should imagine.

She, on the other hand looked Italian, a goaty slant in her eyes, a face often seen among Italian immigrants. She had a small baby tight in her arms. She stood beside her smiling husband and looked at me with no expression at all on her pointed face, unless no expression is an expression. A face of stone. It was an animal distrust, not shyness. She wasn't shy but seemed as if sensing danger, as though she were on her guard against it. She looked dirty. So did he. Her hands were definitely grimy, with black nails. And she smelled, that usual smell of sweat and dirt you find among any people who habitually do not wash or bathe.

The infant was asleep when they came into the office, a child of about five months perhaps, not more.

People like that belong in clinics, I thought to myself. I wasn't putting myself out for them, not that day anyhow. Just dumb oxen. Why the hell do they let them into the country. Half idiots at best. Look at them.

My brother told us to bring the baby here, the man said. We've had a doctor but he's no good.

How do you know he's no good. You probably never gave him a chance. Did you pay him?

Sure we paid him.

Well what do you want me to do? To hell with you, I thought to myself. Get sore and get the hell out of here. I got to go home to lunch.

I want you to fix up the baby, Doc. My brother says you're the best baby doctor around here. And this kid's sick.

Well, put it up there on the table and take its clothes off then. Why didn't you come earlier instead of waiting here till the end of the hour. I got to live too.

The man turned to his wife. Gimme the baby, he said.

No. She wouldn't. Her face just took on an even stupider expression of obstinacy but she clung to the child.

Come on, come on, I said. I can't wait here all day.

Give him to me, he said to her again. He only wants to examine it.

I hold her, the woman said keeping the child firmly in her arms.

Listen here, I spoke to her. Do you want me to examine the child or don't you. If you don't, then take it somewhere.

Wait a minute, wait a minute, Doc, the man said smiling in-gratiatingly.

You look at throat, the mother suggested.

You put the baby up there on the table and take its clothes off, I told her. The woman shook her head. But as she did so she gradually relented, looking furtively at me with distrustful glances her nostrils moving slightly.

Now what is it.

She's getting thin, Doc 'think somethink's the matter with her.

What do you mean, thin?

I asked her age, the kind of labor she had had. How they were feeding the baby. Vomiting, sleeping, hunger. It was the first child and the mother was new at nursing it. It was four and a half months old and weighed thirteen and a half pounds. Not bad.

I think my milk no good, said the woman, still clinging to the baby whose clothes she had only begun to open.

As I approached them the infant took one look at me and let out a wild scream. In alarm the mother clutched it to her breast and started for the door.

I burst out laughing. The husband got red in the face but forced a smile. Don't be so scared, he said to his wife. He, nodding toward me, ain't gonna hurt you. You know she hasn't been in this country long, Doc. She's scared you're gonna hurt the baby. Bring it over here, he said to her, and take off his clothes. Here, give 'im to me. And he took the infant into his own hands, screaming lustily, and carried it to the table to undress it. The mother, in an agony of apprehension kept interfering from behind at every move.

What a time! I couldn't find much the matter and told them so. Just the results of irregular, foolish routine and probably insufficient breast milk. I gave them a complemental formula. He chiseled a dollar off the fee and—just as he was going out—said, Doc, if we need you any time I want you to come out to the house to see it. You gotta watch this kid.

Where do you live, I asked.

He told me where it was, way out near the dumps. I'll come if you give me a decent warning. I told him. If you want me call in the morning. Now get that. You can't expect me to go running out there for thing every time the kid gets a belly ache. Or just because she thinks it's dying. If you call me around supper time or in the middle of a snow storm or at two o'clock in the morning maybe I won't do it. I'm telling you now so you'll know. I got too much to do already.

O.K., Doc, he said smiling. But you come.

I'll come on those conditions.

O.K., Doc.

And sure enough, on a Sunday night, about nine o'clock, with the thermometer at six below and the roads like a skating rink, they would call me.

Nothing doing, I said.

But Doc, you said you'd come.

I'm not going there tonight, I insisted. I won't do it. I'll ask my associate to make the call or some good younger man that lives in that neighborhood but I won't go over there tonight.

But we need you Doc, the baby's very sick.

Can't help it. I tell you I'm not going. And I slammed up the receiver.

Who in the world are you talking to like that said my wife who had put down her book as my voice rose higher. You mustn't do that.

Leave me alone, I know what I'm doing.

But my dear!

Four months later, after three months of miserable practice, the first warm day in April, about twenty women with babies came to my office. I started at one P.M. and by three I was still going strong. I hadn't loafed. Anybody left out there? I asked the last woman, as I thought, who had been waiting for me. Oh yes, there's a couple with a baby. Oh Lord, I groaned. It was half past three by then and a number of calls still to be made about the town.

There they were. The same fresh mug and the same face of stone, still holding the baby which had grown, however, to twice its former size.

Hello Doc, said the man smiling.

For a moment I couldn't place them. Hello, I said. Then I remembered. What can I do for you—at this time of day. Make it snappy cause I've got to get out.

Oh yeah.

Listen Doc, we been waiting out there two hours.

Good night! That finishes me for the afternoon, I said to myself. All right, put it up on the table. As I said this, feeling at the same time a sense of helpless irritation and anger, I noticed a cluster of red pimples in the region of the man's right eyebrow and reaching to the bridge of his nose. Like bed-bug bites I thought to myself. He'll want me to do something for them too before I get through I suppose. Well, what's the matter now? I asked them.

It's the baby again, Doc, the man said.

What's the matter with the baby. It looks all right to me. And it did. A child of about ten months, I estimated, with a perfectly happy, round face.

Yes, but his body isn't so good.

I want you should examine him all over, said the mother.

You would, I said. Do you realize what time it is?

Shall she take his clothes off? the man broke in.

Suit yourself, I answered, hoping she wouldn't do it. But she put the infant on the table and began carefully to undress it.

No use. I sat down and took out a card for the usual notes. How old is it?

How old is it? he asked his wife.

Ten months. Next Tuesday ten months, she said with the same face on her as always.

Are you still nursing it?

Sure, she said. Him won't take bottle.

Do you mean to say that after what I told you last time, you haven't weaned the baby?

What can she do, Doc. She tried to but he won't let go of the breast. You can't make him take a bottle.

Does he eat?

Yeah, he eats a little, but he won't take much.

Cod liver oil?

He takes it all right but spits it up half an hour later. She stopped giving it to him.

Orange juice.

Sure. Most of the time.

So, as a matter of fact, she's been nursing him and giving him a little cereal and that's all.

Sure, that's about right.

How often does she nurse him?

Whenever he wants it, the man grinned. Sometimes every two hours. Sometimes he sleeps. Like that.

But didn't I tell you, didn't I tell her to feed it regularly.

She can't do that, Doc. The baby cries and she gives it to him.

Why don't you put it in a crib?

She won't give it up. You know, that's the way she is, Doc. You can't make her do different. She wants the baby next to her so she can feel it.

Have you got it undressed? I turned to the mother who was standing with her back to me.

You want shoe off? she answered me.

Getting up I went to the infant and pulled the shoes and stockings off together, picked the thing up by its feet and the back of the neck and carried it to the scales. She was right after me, her hands half extended watching the child at every movement I made. Fortunately the child grinned and sagged back unresisting in my grasp. I looked at it more carefully then, a smart looking little thing and a perfectly happy, fresh mug on him that amused me in spite of myself.

Twenty pounds and four ounces, I said. What do you want for a ten month old baby? There's nothing the matter with him. Get his clothes on.

I want you should examine him first, said the mother.

The blood went to my face in anger but she paid no attention to me. He too thin, she said. Look him body.

To quiet my nerves I took up my stethoscope and went rapidly over the child's chest, saw that everything was all right there, that there was no rickets and told them so—and to step on it. Get him dressed. I got to get out of here.

Him all right? the woman questioned me with her stony pale green eyes. I stopped to look at them, they were very curious, almost at right angles to each other—in a way of speaking—like the eyes of some female figure I had seen somewhere—Montegna—Botticelli—I couldn't remember.

Yes, only for God's sake, take him off the breast. Feed him the way I told you to.

No will take bottle.

Fine. I don't give a damn about the bottle. Feed him from a cup, with a spoon, any way at all. But feed him regularly. That's all.

As I turned to wash my hands, preparatory to leaving the office the man stopped me. Doc, he said, I want you to examine my wife.

He got red in the face as I turned on him. What the hell do you think I am anyhow. You got a hell of a nerve. Don't you know. . .

We waited two hours and ten minutes for you, Doc he replied smiling. Just look her over and see what the matter with her is.

I could hardly trust myself to speak for a moment but, instead turned to look at her again standing beside the baby which she had finished dressing and was sitting on the table looking at me. What a creature. What a face. And what a body. I looked her coldly up and down from head to toe. There was a rip in her dress, a triangular tear just above the left knee.

Well—No use getting excited with people such as these—or with anyone, for that matter, I said in despair. No one can do two things at the same time, especially when they're in two different places. I simply gave up and returned to my desk chair.

Go ahead. What's the matter with her?

She gets pains in her legs, especially at night. And she's got a spot near her right knee. It came last week, a big blue looking sort of spot.

Did she ever have rheumatism? You know, go to bed with swollen joints—or six weeks—or like that.

Did you have rheumatism? he turned to her.

She simply shrugged her shoulders.

She don't know, he said, interpreting and turning red in the face again. I particularly noticed it this time and remembered that it had occurred two or three times before while we were talking.

Tell her to open up her dress.

Open up your dress, he said.

Sit down, I told her and let me see your legs.

As she did so I noticed again the triangular rip in the skirt over her left thigh, dirty silk, and that her skin was directly under it. She untied some white rags above her knees and let down her black stockings. The left one first, I said.

Her lower legs were peculiarly bowed, really like Turkish scimetars, flattened and somewhat rotated on themselves in an odd way that could not have come from anything but severe rickets rather late in her childhood. The whole leg while not exactly weak was as ugly and misshapen as a useful leg well could be in so young a woman. Near the knee was a large discolored area where in all probability a varicose vein had ruptured.

That spot, I told the husband, comes from a broken varicose vein.

Yeah, I thought so, she's got them all up both legs.

That's from carrying a child.

No. She had them before that. They've always been that way since I've known her. Is that what makes her have the pains there?

I hardly think so, I said looking over the legs again, one of which I held on the palm of either hand. No, I don't think so.

What is it then? It hurts her bad, especially at night.

She's bow-legged as hell in the first place. That throws the strain where it doesn't belong and look at those shoes—

Yeah, I know.

The woman had on an old pair of fancy high-heeled slippers such as a woman might put on for evening wear. They were all worn and incredibly broken down. I don't see how she can walk in them.

That's what I told her, the man said. I wanted her to get a pair of shoes that fitted her but she wouldn't do it.

Well, she's got to do it, I said. Throw away those shoes. I told her and get shoes with flat heels. And straight heels. I tried to impress her. What they call Cuban heels, if you must. New Shoes, I emphasized. How old is she, I asked the man.

His face colored again for reasons I could not fathom. Twenty four, he said.

Where was she born?

In Poland.

In Poland! Well. I looked at her, not believing him.

Yeah, why?

Well. Twenty-four years old you say. Let's see. That's different. An unusual type for a Jew, I thought. That's the probable explanation for her legs, I told the husband. She must have been a little girl during the war over there. A kid of maybe five or six years I should imagine. Is that right, I asked her. But she didn't answer me, just looked back into my eyes with that inane look.

What did you get to eat?

She seemed not to have heard me but turned to her husband.

Did she lose any of her people, I asked him.

Any of them? She lost everybody, he said quietly.

How did she come to get over here then?

She came over four years ago. She has a sister over here.

So that's it, I thought to myself looking at her fussing, intensely absorbed with the baby, looking at it, talking to it in an inarticulate sort of way, paying no attention whatever to me. No wonder she's built the way she is, considering what she must have been through in that invaded territory. And this guy here—

What are we going to do about the pains, Doc?

Get her some decent shoes, that's the first thing.

O.K., Doc.

She could be operated on for those veins. But I wouldn't advise it, just yet. I tell you. Get one of those woven elastic bandages for her, they don't cost much. A three inch one. And I told him what to get.

Can't you give her some pills to stop the pain?

Not me, I told him. You might get her teeth looked at though if you want to. All that kind of thing and—well, I will give you something. It's not dope. It just helps if there's any rheumatism connected with it.

Can you swallow a pill, I turned to her attracting her attention.

She looked at me. How big? she said.

She swallows an Aspirin pill when I give it to her sometimes, said her husband, but she usually puts it in a spoonful water first to dissolve it. His face reddened again and suddenly I understood his half shameful love for the woman and at the same time the extent of her reliance on him.

I was touched.

They're pretty big pills, I said. Look, they're green. That's the coating so they won't dissolve in your stomach and upset your digestion.

Let see, said the woman.

I showed a few of the pills to her in the palm of my hand.

For pains in leg?

Yes, I told her.

She looked at them again. Then for the first time since I had known her a broad smile spread all over her face. Yeah, she said, I swallow him.

December, 1935

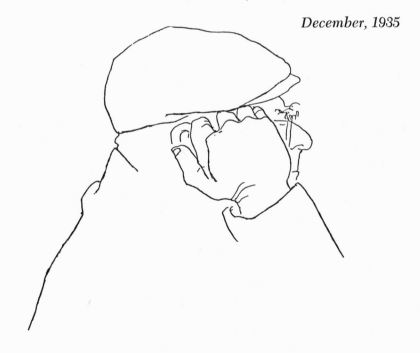

William Carlos Williams 207

ARTHUR M. SCHLESINGER, JR.

Class of 1938, (1917–   )

Arthur Schlesinger, Jr. was a member of the Harvard Society of Fellows for three years after his graduation. He won the Pulitzer Prize for his book The Age of Jackson *and has also published histories of Franklin Delano Roosevelt's presidency and the New Deal. He is presently at work on* 1000 Days, *an account of his experiences as an advisor to President Kennedy.*

THE REPUBLICANS COME BACK

THE REVIVAL of the Republicans has probably not embarrassed the writers who in 1933 retired them to the history books. Political observers have always been careless in distinguishing between sleep and death. The reading of funeral rites over a badly beaten party is a favorite diversion of American history; but too often, the corpse, like Aaron Burr in Mark Twain's sketch, sits up and talks with the coachman. In 1798 Noah Webster reported that the flood of Federalist votes had washed away all remnants of Jeffersonian power: two years later Jefferson became president. And in 1928 Silas Bent, examining the gaping hole in the Democratic Party where the Solid South had been, pronounced the wound fatal: in the next election the Republicans were overwhelmed.

But so many parties have disappeared in American history that these amateur prophets can not be altogether disregarded. Their predictions, however, have rarely taken into account the economic bases of politics which underlie and breed the emotional attainments. As a rule, political parties begin when men come together whose economic interests will be furthered by the same policies; they always go to pieces when personal rivalries or clashing economic interests strain the party lines to the breaking point. Even then, the continuity of economic life—the fact that most people do the same thing from day to day—prevents parties from utterly disintegrating. They break into large fragments, which are re-aligned to strengthen old parties and form new ones. The Federalist Party disappeared soon after the common man had turned from a subject into a citizen; but, though the party had gone, the Federalists still remained. The Whigs, when split by conflicting economic programs, soon found themselves more at home in the Democratic and Republican parties of the day. The Democrats would have faded away in 1928 only if the public had been convinced that what was good for Andrew Mellon was good for it. And so long as a large minority of the United States believes in rugged individualism, the Republican Party will survive. It is, of course, easy to reject prophecies after the fact; but it is also difficult to escape the conclusion that the prophets used the methods of Evangeline Adams rather than those of the Brookings Institute.

Certainly the clairvoyants of 1933, who could not see how Republicans were to recover from their drubbing, were guilty of some very wishful thinking. The number of Roosevelt's enemies is growing daily: Wall Street operators who find brokerage tame after years of speculation; industrialists aghast at the Wagner Labor Bill; the large number of people who see communism in government for the community, and the very small number who have moral or philosophical objections to public management; those who want to brain the brain trust; those who think that one of the alphabetical agencies has discriminated against them; those who look on the Constitution as something akin to divine revelation—in general, the capitalists, the conservatives and the large portion of the middle class which pays attention to them. It is this growing opposition that is waking the Republican Party to action. The economic basis for this line-up? Generally speaking (and all historical analyses in terms of economics are general), the vested interests, their hangers-on and their would-be sharers are facing the underprivileged and their defenders.

A corps of shrewd commentators daily attack the administration from this capitalist-conservative viewpoint. The New Deal, of course, has its champions; but to the unseeing reader the frothy trivialities of Paul Mallon must seem petty beside the stern warnings of David Lawrence.

Columnists have been very important in the revival of Republicanism; the case against Roosevelt is most effectively advanced by Lawrence, Frank Kent and Mark Sullivan, though they have their imitators in the local political experts of every Republican paper in the country.

Lawrence is talented chiefly in his ability to write as if he were taking his stand only after careful and impartial thought. He seems the most informed of the three; but his combination of *ex cathedra* judgments with a blanket disapproval of the New Deal gives him a flavor of insincerity. If Lawrence writes like a pope, Kent hands down his opinions like a Justice of the Supreme Court. Under this camouflage of judicial review, he is able to make quite unscrupulous insinuations about people. For this reason he is the most unfair and annoying of the columnists. To adapt an epigram of Constant Lambert's: if Roosevelt were to go up in a balloon, Kent would call him an exhibitionist; if he were to refuse to go up, Kent would call him a coward. Where Lawrence is a predisposed interpreter of issues, and Kent of men, Sullivan is a good-natured and rather bewildered dissenter to the vagaries of the New Deal. He has a clear and ingratiating style which reconstructs complex problems to make the conservative solution seem the only one. If his influence is not so great as the others, it is because he does not try to play God. Each in his own manner, these three men were probably most instrumental in the Republican recovery. The power to come back was there, but Lawrence, Kent and Sullivan had to throw on the switch.

Party leaders have not been much behind the commentators in painting the New Deal red. Magazine articles and books, signed if not written by prominent Tories, have scorched the insidious tendencies of the present government in terms as vague as the phrase "insidious tendencies." Hoover's amazing *The Challenge to Liberty* which revealed his political philosophy in 250 dull pages, reached, according to the publisher, over sixty thousand homes.

These doses of profundity have probably affected the mass of voters far less than the press attacks of stupefied Republicans and disappointed Democrats. A recent example is the series by James P. Warburg. This eminent economic thinker assailed the New Deal with great vigor and a fine air of: what a patriot am I to tell all these truths about Washington. The series borrowed liberally, especially from David Lawrence and William Randolph Hearst; but it confirmed the misgivings of the lower middle class as to Roosevelt's destination and was fearless in calling the

210   *Arthur M. Schlesinger, Jr.*

administration "socialistic." It ended with a bitter personal attack on the President in which Warburg turned the qualities in Roosevelt that had most appealed to liberals into defects of character. What had seemed receptivity to new ideas is really, says Warburg, the vacillations of a weak mind, swayed by the latest adviser; his frank acknowledgment of error shows nothing more than incompetence.

The effect on the very uncritical of articles like these, written allegedly from the inside, can hardly be overestimated. To the pseudo-intelligent, the attacks on the New Deal by conservative economists must seem almost as convincing. Closer examination usually reveals that those of the attacking economists who are not kept by Wall Street are voices from some academic grove where people still believe that America is an open market and the profit system is self-regulatory. But the ones who read them do not know this: the accusation that the New Deal is economically unsound damns it in the eyes of the suburban intelligentsia, no matter who the accusers may be.

The American Liberty League is the most imposing of the conservative press gangs. The nobility and patriotism in this band of corporation lawyers and millionaires fighting for the liberty which permits the rich as well as the poor to sleep in Central Park is not, however, very obvious. It is an irony of history that the American Liberty League of 1935 should be headed by men who would have led the Loyalist exodus to Nova Scotia in the days when people fought about American liberty.

The Republican Party has popular support. It has excellent men for the newspaper skirmishes which precede the battle. A constructive program would be pleasant but unnecessary; for empty catchwords about Liberty or the Constitution, reinforced by platform phrases which require neither to be understood now nor heeded after election, can bring victory. Roosevelt did not win in 1932 because of the Democratic platform. . . . In fact, the Republicans have everything a minority party needs to put up a fight, except a good candidate.

Herbert Hoover perhaps thinks of himself as another Grover Cleveland, but most of his party prefers to think of him as another Taft. To the nation, his nation still means the depression; to his party, it means defeat. And he has no strong personal following to work for his nomination out of devotion to the man. Hoover undoubtedly feels that he ought to have a chance to vindicate his conduct as president. In recent months he has certainly been acting as if he were looking ahead to the nomination. The heat of the battle has begun even to melt his personal coldness; the Hoover of today is a Hoover whose speeches contain funny stories and picturesque phrases. "Joyriding to destruction"—this sounds more like General Johnson than like the man who could think of no sprightlier sentence to arouse America in the midst of the depression than, "We have weathered the worst of the storm." Hoover must be considered seriously. If he is not himself nominated, he will do his best to dictate the choice. And, if he is as effective in hypnotizing the Republicans as he was in relieving the Belgians, he will bring into the convention enough votes to hold the balance of power.

The contributors to the campaign fund would accept Hoover only under bared bayonets; his name spells disaster. One man alone is less welcome to them—Senator Borah. Frank Kent and David Lawrence write that Borah is too old to be considered; but Borah evidently has not been convinced. In the last month he has been amazingly active and amazingly noncommittal for a man who is not busy looking over the eggs before they hatch. As a nominee, he would recover the Middle West for the Republicans; the farmers, preferring the AAA to Hoover's farm relief, which had relieved them only of their savings, are Democrats today. But Borah's resolute isolationism will offend, I suspect, a rather large group in the East; and his rash endorsement of inflation has ruined him with the New York financiers. Borah's votes, moreover, depend on his personal influence rather than on a well-articulated organization of the type Hoover has been trying to build. He may go into the convention as the popular favorite—a recent poll among young Republicans proves his popularity—but the gentlemen pulling the strings will see that he is not chosen.

The rise of Governor Alf Landon shows how a democracy is at the mercy of its press agents. A year ago no one beyond the Kansas borders had heard of him; now he is mentioned as the next president of the United States. To thinking people, one term as governor of Kansas seems hardly a qualification for the White House; but to the newspapermen who discovered Landon and named him the Kansas Coolidge, inexperience is a minor consideration. This is not a nickname to fill the intelligent minority with enthusiasm, but to the mass of voters it brings memories of thrift, shrewdness and prosperity.

Landon's chances have been damaged most by the decision of Hearst to back him. The *New Masses* is inclined, I think, to overestimate

Hearst's power in molding public opinion. The Hearst papers differ from others serving the same audience, not so much in their views, as in their way of expressing them. Instead of hiding his ideas on a forbidding inner page, Hearst sets up his editorials in large type and runs them on the back page. The size of his chain makes him only the best known of those who publish for the city slums. If Hearst bewitched the masses as effectively as the Communists think, he would not have such a long record of defeat on political issues. With all the support of his papers, he himself could get nowhere in politics. His papers were pro-German in the first years of the war, and the country became steadily pro-Ally. He championed Garner for the Democratic nomination in 1932, and Garner ended up as vice-president. On national questions, Hearst frightens away more backing than he attracts; the biography which ran recently in the *Boston American* is a serious blow to Landon's chances. But for most of the country, Landon has yet to show that he is more than an Alfalfa Bill Murray in a business suit.

Neither party has dared to nominate a senator since Harding. This year Vandenberg of Michigan, a fluent debater and a wary politician, has been frequently mentioned. The self-styled "discriminating critic" of the President, he stands between the New Deal and the Old, between the Progressives and the Old Guard. His chief drawback as the perfect compromise candidate is his spurts of independent thinking. The Party would prefer some political hack whom it could direct more easily. And in Senator Dickinson of Iowa it may have him. Dickinson is conservative, sober, silent and tractable; he has been a party regular of the most depressing kind . . . Vandenberg would be, prospectively, the best Republican president since Taft; Dickinson, the worst since Hoover.

Political hacks outside the Middle West will not stand much chance in 1936. Though the Party would protest the suspicion of choosing a candidate because he brings votes, it would doubtless bring itself to choose one from a region where votes lie; and the Middle West is a great deal more doubtful in the eyes of the Republican National Committee than the East. This is one cause of James Wadsworth's disappearance from public view. In 1933 he was everywhere mentioned as the Republican nominee for 1936; two years later his name appears in the papers only as a member of the American Liberty League. Ogden Mills has likewise seen his chances diminish. A slashing speaker and a master of invective, he could be perhaps the most effective critic of the

New Deal in the Republican Party. Fortunately he has remained in his country estate, a New York Achilles; and Roosevelt is spared the addition of his philippics to the admonitions of David Lawrence, and the bludgeonings of William Randolph Hearst. Mills has too many enemies for him to get the nomination; Wadsworth hasn't enough friends. And Hamilton Fish thinks the nomination so remote that he is trying to make himself a tail to Borah's kite.

Not all the contenders will be politicians. Several patriots have offered to sacrifice their business and personal comfort in order to save the country. These persons range all the way from lunatics under delusions of grandeur to Colonel Frank Knox. New England has already started Knox-for-President clubs; but his own section of the country knows him (when it knows him at all) as the owner of the *Chicago Daily News*. It is rather hard to see how his newspaper experience fits him for the presidency, though fitness, of course, plays little part in politics. Harding was the last newspaper owner in the White House. Knox is an immovable conservative; he can not be moved nor can he move anything. The Republican convention will watch him, not as Col. Frank Knox, but as the close political friend of Herbert Hoover. He may well be the beneficiary of Hoover's defeat; this likelihood has already put him high in the betting.

Though this about exhausts the list of Republican possibilities for the nomination, it does not exhaust the list of possibilities for the Republican nomination. Hearst, before he took up the Kansas Coolidge, urged the organization of the conservatives to oppose Roosevelt's "Socialist Party." And many prominent Republicans, who happen themselves to have no hope for the nomination, cry out for a coalition ticket with a conservative Democrat in one place. The main obstacle to this plan is that most conservative Democrats are conservative in political behavior as well as in politics; and they prize, above all, regularity. It is inconceivable that Byrd of Virginia, Ritchie of Maryland, Ely of Massachusetts should desert the Democratic Party. As for Al Smith, he would not leave it save to head the ticket. The chance of this is slight, though the same people who were horrified in 1928 by Smith's accent and his wife's jewelry now look to him as a possible savior from the urbane aristocrat of Hyde Park.

Not to be omitted in any survey of the field is the *Atlantic Monthly's* candidate for president, Lewis Douglas. He is popularly regarded as a financial genius, the Gallatin to Mellon's Hamilton. As a matter of fact, his writing and speaking show him to be sincere and well-meaning, with a naivete of approach to economic problems in the Godkin lectures which shocked the Harvard economists last year, and a naivete of outlook on society which makes him a political kinsman of Herbert Agar. Douglas, morever, is probably too honest a man to court the interests whose support would be necessary for the nomination; and he is probably too strong a man to tempt the interests' support in the hope that they might control him later.

Political prediction is a game any one can play but no one can play well. Nine-tenths of the forces which rule the convention are under the surface. It is easy to talk about string-pulling, but hard to name the men pulling the strings. In the long view, the Republican nominee for 1936 will probably not matter, for Roosevelt's re-election is likely. What will matter is that there will be a Republican nominee.

Republicanism is far from dead. Its economic bases are shrinking, but they are shrinking slowly. The Old Guard has its back to the wall, but it is not yet faced by a firing squad.

March, 1936

Arthur M. Schlesinger, Jr. 215

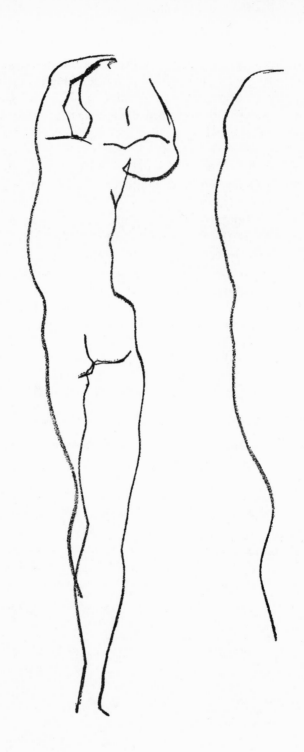

LEONARD BERNSTEIN

Class of 1939, (1918–   )

*Pianist, conductor, and composer, Bernstein is
the director of the New York Philharmonic Orchestra. He has appeared as guest conductor with
leading orchestras throughout the world. While
he was an undergraduate Bernstein wrote a music
column for the* Advocate, *an example of which
is included below.*

MUSIC

It has been a long time since music was last hashed over between
you and me. In the interim recordings have been pouring out thick and
fast—and so many worth consideration that this column will have to be
purely discological.

There have been four top-notchers in the last few months—musical
musts. Give the credit for one to Columbia—the Schubert Cello Sonata
in A minor (Set 346) played by the great Feuermann. And played
incomparably. The ease, charm, and flawless musicianship of the performance is incredible. You play each movement over and over to make
sure you were not just imagining. The tone throughout might be that of
a viola (if it didn't descend an extra octave) so unforced and sure is
Feuermann's bowing. And his sexiest sliding—which makes you gasp—is
never cheap. The tempi are psychologically perfect, the dynamics just
right, the movements (thank heaven) unusually short for Schubert,
the music itself charming, the accompaniment by Gerald Moore never
obtrusive, and the actual recording excellent. It just goes over the top.

The other three highspots are Victor products. Two of them owe their
success to Koussevitzky and his phenomenal Boston orchestra: the
Fifth Symphony of Sibelius (M-474) and Haydn's 102nd Symphony
(M-s29). The third is the delightful Third Quartet of Hindemith

(M-524) played with justly supreme authority by the Coolidge Quartet. Of the Sibelius the least that can be said is that this is the definitive performance of a great work of art. The first movement, especially, would be pure Elysium if only the French horns had disappointed us by *not* sounding in one place like a boy whose voice is changing.

The Haydn Symphony is not just another Haydn symphony. With all its good humor it has great power and breadth, almost in the Beethoven manner; it is the kind of thing that will close a program as successfully as it will open one. Of course, Koussevitzky takes the final Rondo at a pace that puts you on horseback; but somehow in this work it is far less objectionable than usual. Besides, you are perfectly confident that the orchestra could do it twice as fast.

Everyone—even anti-modernists—will like the Hindemith quartet. It has five short, direct, significant and satisfying movements, which are all played with unfailing taste and appeal. It would be both appropriate and encouraging to see this on Victor's list of "Ten Victor Records That Should Be in Every Home."

End of top-notchers.

*   *   *   *

Columbia has done some fine things in recent months, like the first volume of Debussy preludes played magnificently by Gieseking (Set 352), the Roussel Quartet in D played by the Roth (Set 339—for rather subdued Roussel), Bach's Second Sonata for viola da gamba and harpsichord (X-111, and fine Bach), and the Brahms Variations on a theme of Handel (Set 345) played with verve and understanding by Egon Petri (this just falls short of the top-notch list). But we cannot forgive the pressing of Deems Taylor's "Through the Looking-Glass" (Set 350). Now Taylor is a fine man: a sound and sensible musician, an expert informal orator, and a competent, likeable person. But he is not a great, nor a significant, nor even an interesting composer. Alice does seem so unhappy embedded in all this ill-concealed Franck and Wagner with Debussy dressing. True, it is cleverly orchestrated and neatly written, but that doesn't atone for the fact that if "modern" American music were going to be recorded, Columbia could have made it worth while. I do not want to be unfair to Columbia; she has released perhaps more American music than any other single commercial organization. And if the Looking-Glass pleases some listeners, well and good; recordings must be representative. But think of all that wax that might have been used for Copland's Ode or William Schuman's Second Symphony!

End of tirade.

✿   ✿   ✿   ✿

For the rest, Columbia and Victor share about equal credit and discredit. To Columbia, many thanks for the new Weingartner recording of Brahms' Third Symphony (Set 353) which would be fine if the strings were more precise, if Weingartner's phrasings were not so overdone that each melodic fragment ends in a hiccough, and if the chords did not waver so. (It is possible that the holes are punched off-center. This should be remedied.) More thanks for Margaret Roesgen-Champion's delightful performance of the Haydn Piano Concerto (Set X-118).

To Victor, thanks for Stokowski's playing of his synthesis from "Tristan" (M-508). If you like your Tristan with much Weltschmerz and passion (and there is no reason why you shouldn't) this is your best bet. The Liebesnacht, in fact, is something of a challenge.

There is much Gershwin: a Memorial Album (C-29) which is good for its hits of ancient days, but not for things like numbers from "Porgy" which it cuts to shreds. The two Iturbis do a "Rhapsody in Blue" (M-517) which is almost occult in its perfection of ensemble, but is lacking in the jazz feeling.

Schnabel, but for his Viennese conception of fugue-rhythms, plays the C minor and D major Toccatas of Bach (M-532) as well as is possible on the modern piano. And a special acknowledgment of Alexander Kipnis' remarkable bass voice singing a fat album of Brahms' songs (M-522). It is wonderful to hear his versatility of rendition: the lightness with which he does the "Vergebliches Ständchen" contrasts amazingly with the ponderousness of the "Four Serious Songs." The latter, by the way, for their rarity of performance and grandeur of sound are well worth the whole album.

And please read Aaron Copland's new book "How to Listen to Music." It is worth anybody's time. If you don't know much about music you will learn easily and enjoyably; if you do know much you will learn more; and if you simply don't care, you soon will. Let this be our final will at the great noon-tide. Thus Spake Zarathustra.

March, 1939

Leonard Bernstein 219

HARRY BROWN

Class of 1940, (1917–   )

Harry Brown's Harvard career was interrupted when he took a year off to write movie scripts. After graduation he worked for Time, The New Yorker, *and* Yank, *the Army magazine. In addition to his novel,* A Walk in the Sun, *he has published several volumes of poetry:* The End of a Decade, The Beast in his Hunger, *and* The Violent. *He has also written film scripts for Cagney Productions.*

ELEGY ON THE DEATH OF YEATS

Now Lear has moved across the broken plain,
And the lightnings are departed. In that region
After the storms the sun comes, bursting full
Out of the morning. In that place the rain
Succumbs. In that calm quarter of the world
The marble statues breathe and moan:
They are moved by love, their own love moves them.

What is this place, what region? This is the country
Where the devout, tall passes of the mind
Are taken by lone travellers, this the land
Of last ascent, where the small stones babbling murmur,
The fierce oaks threaten the sky, the water whispers;
Intellect's outpost, this, and those who reach it,
Prophets and madmen, neither live nor die.

Man in his gyre goes upward, ever rising
In love to love; and he has picked for guides
Those who, gray-headed, bent, and full of state,
Have opened for a moment nature's door,
Have gasped to see a wonder, and have reached
Desperately up; then dropped back, weeping, knowing
They had found the absolute and almost held it.

March, 1939

THE HEY OF THE LAST SHEPHERD

THE world now falls like twilight down the hills,
Is a mirage on the horizon's train,
Past the dead sands. On desert islands, too,
Where cryptic palms hold centuries of dew,
There comes a many-legged thing that kills
The little beasts about him. Such is this,
As each world goes, a body made for pain,
A bastard Heaven with a Judas stain:
More planets, then, will fall before our kiss.

And now the foul beast, elephant,
Shakes orchards as he passes with his thirst;
And every animal, though he be fox,
Or lizard roaming through the desert rocks,
Or major snake whose frozen gaze enchants,
Or swollen hippopotamus, must rise
From lairs, from caverns where the earth has burst,
From places where the very dirt is cursed,
To see his latest morning through blind eyes.

Harry Brown   221

And now the shepherd on his war-torn field
Sinks on his knees and gazes at the stars,
And seeks his daughter with a lonely hand.
He has known all the ravage on the sand,
The slaughter done, the final letter sealed,
The dead unburied on the city ways.
He hunts the web that forms the face of Mars,
The wandering souls, the planetary bars . . .
He speaks to ghosts, and this is what he says:

—Consider, love, the comets of the air;
How they play Daphne with the world as tree,
Flaring around us in their vast dismay.
We lie too near Avernus' bonnie brae
To call our sun Apollo. Who would dare,
After his journey's silence and the pity,
To char his breath by running in to see
The faces of the holy ones who flee?
Whose hand will build the last immortal city?

Sweet, you will never find the tale in eyes
Grown Nordic after ages of migration;
Nor in the brilliant lids across the stage.
The cover's but a means to clasp the page.
There's nothing in the color of the prize,
The little ribbon. Shadows through the pane
Are but the measures of a glassy station:
And you will find a bitter dispensation
In words and whispers blotted out by rain.

Mother, forgive the darkness we have brought;
Remember only that we were your sons.
When every light in Christendom is out
Remember that before we met the rout
We stood like men and, though long blinded, fought
Time in his arbor. Now that night has come
It is too late to move the rusting guns,
For down our gloomy slopes Avernus runs,
And we have lost the hour of the drum.

Lady, the crawling things upon the ground
Have slain the sheep and brought the lamb to death,
And killed the ox and left the swine to die.
The last sad martyrs fall alone and lie
In wasted bloody heaps, and make no sound.
Over! Over! the last die has been thrown.
Hills leveled, valleys raised to form a heath;
The seas burned empty. Here man's final breath
Sighs to its finish, and his flesh is bone . . . .

And now the ruined world sags down its way,
Grown circular and silent in its sphere:
If it should live it is the only thing.
No fin drives through the waters, and no wing
Soars in an airy passion. All the play
And tumult of milleniums is through . . .
And thus the souls of mighty worlds turn sere.
—Yet, as the unseen morning rises clear,
The broken forests feel th' immortal dew.

November, 1937

MR. CRANE AS ORPHEUS, A GOOD BOY

Vivant Musae! whose impossible lagoons,
Traveled by boats with clumsy sails, desire
Only the rising coral to remain.

The pretty ladies murmur pleasant tunes
Along the golden island. Strange, the fire,
On being touched, can telegraph no pain.

Only an empty body has the sand,
Unrecognizable man, blood in the water,
The lungs missing, the head departed.

Harry Brown 223

The numb harp is taut in the trench of the hand.
What woman will recall Oceanus' daughter,
To write down what the spinners started?

The snake before the honored grave may hiss
A treble warning. Reptile truth will say,
You shall not surely die.

The skeleton beside the cave may kiss
Other old bones, well-covered yesterday,
A jointless thing, creeking to where they lie.

A blind Eurydice may even yet discover,
After the pirate centuries, the shore a waste,
What the murder spared.

The idea of cool brows may arouse the lover
To resurrect himself, more lost, more chaste,
Then the panting deer, at last laired.

But what will help the gruesome struggle then,
Even with brighter tissues and incarnate skin,
After that most complete rejection?

Watched by a threadbare scattering of men,
They shout, *O vivant Musae!* and begin
The frightened, endless God-dissection.

March, 1940

THE ANATOMY OF THE DEBUTANTE

I have heard of your paintings, too, well enough; God hath given you one face, and you make yourselves another: you jig, you amble, and you lisp; you nickname God's creatures and make your wantonness your ignorance: go to, I'll no more on't; it hath made me mad.

To begin with, a debutante is a young woman (there are no male debutantes, in spite of what you may think of Lucius Beebe and Maury Paul), and she is generally a very fine figure of a young woman, in a splendid state of preservation. She does not possess false teeth, a wig, or artificial limbs. True, stomach ulcers sooner or later catch up with her, but that's an internal ailment, and as this is not a medical treatise, we need have nothing to do with ulcers, pro or con. No, we are concerned with the external attributes of these nice girls, and the ulcers can jolly well take care of themselves.

—But, says little Gianciotto, who is fourteen and promiscuous, how will I know a debutante when I see one?

—Why, says old Malatesta, making a *cornuto* at him, by her clothes. You can tell a debutante by her clothes, just as you can tell a Hottentot by his lack of them.

—As simple as that? says little Gianciotto.

—As simple as that, says the Old Roman.

And he was right; for if one should put a debutante in a room with twenty other women, she would always be recognized by her clothes. Of course, if one should put a nude debutante into a room with twenty other women, similarly attired,—

—It would not, said little Gianciotto, be a bad idea. Little Gianciotto is fourteen and promiscuous.

✻   ✻   ✻

Now that we have fought our way through the introduction, we should define what this piece is concerned with, thus: A debutante is composed of one part background, one part Antoine de Paris, one part *Harper's Bazaar*, five parts money, and eight parts ignorance. Taking ten parts as a norm, you can see that this adds up to considerably over that sum, which should give you a pretty good idea of what we have

Harry Brown 225

to deal with. She inhabits large cities, small cities, towns, hamlets, and Los Angeles, California. However, we are more interested, for our present needs, in the New England or Bury Me In Boston type of debutante.

There are several variations within this species, but it is best that in the beginning we consider the species as a whole. This, we understand, is the usual approach, as practiced by the young gentlemen of Harvard, Princeton, Yale, and the Hanover Ski School.

The debutante, as a whole, spends her afternoons in charity work, her nights in polite carouse, and her mornings in bed. She has breakfast at noon, dinner at any hour from eight to eleven, and supper, if she can keep it down, at two in the morning. Other than this she does nothing, for fear of becoming an object of scandal. From the age of fourteen to eighteen she goes to school, which, for her, is the equivalent of doing nothing; at the age of eighteen she becomes a debutante, which is the public's idea of doing nothing; and eventually she marries a Porcellian man, which is God's idea of doing nothing. All in all, she is, together with a housefly, one of the most useless things on the face of the earth. Not *the* most useless thing, mind you; for the Democratic Party beats her out there. But she does quite well in her way.

Well, then, here's the Littul Ole Boston Debutante, not worth a tinker's dam, and proud of it. She believes in Heaven, the Junior League, the Ritz Bar and Margaret Sanger. As far as marriage goes, she believes in (1) security, and (2) a decent amount of love. A husband, she realizes, is a necessary thing, for respectability's sake, much like the bottom part of a bathing suit. But of course, marriage is a concern of the post-debutante (a debutante becomes a post-debutante when she developes stomach-ulcers), and, as the post-debutante is the concern of a good psychoanalyist, we needn't bother with her. No, we started on the debutante, and, by Heaven, we'll stay on her.

If little Gianciotto should wander into the Ritz Bar at five o'clock in the afternoon, he would see several debutantes, of various shapes and sizes. This place, which is known familiarly as the Littul Ole Boston Watering-Hole, is where all the young ladies go to see the people they haven't seen since yesterday. Little Gianciotto (who is fourteen and promiscuous) wouldn't have much fun; but then, a fourteen year old, even if he is promiscuous, doesn't have much fun anyway.

Now, as we said before, there are several variations on the theme of the debutante, and we might as well take them up now. There is, to begin with, the Vincent Club, or Geez, I'm Duse, type, who has her artistic side but doesn't quite know what to do with it. Calling her the Vincent Club Type covers a multitude of sins, because she may be a poetess, a sculptress, or just a plain screwball; but we use that classification because we feel that the Vincent Club, together with the North Church Burying Ground, typifies the higher aspects of Boston culture. It is difficult to imagine just why the mental dry rot of Boston should produce young women with artistic leanings, but this is no more difficult than to imagine why the moral dry rot of Boston should produce young women. Yet it is necessary to admit that young women with beautiful souls do at times appear between Manchester and Cohasset, and it is also necessary to admit that these beautiful souls go the way of all flash. Terpsichorean ability in Boston is based on an ability to tapdance, artistic ability spends itself in fashion drawings, and the less said about the poetesses the better. It should suffice to say that art, of any kind, is at present foreign to Boston, the *Transcript* and God to the contrary.

Of course, debutantes are often used as models; and it must be said for them that they take to modelling like ducks to water, evidently because the practise of modelling requires no mental power. All that is necessary is for one to exhibit oneself, like a prize dog, which is really very easy; so easy, in fact, that professional models are trembling for their laurels. But, understand, we can't accuse the Vincent Club and amalgamated organizations of this. The Vincent Club tapdances. At least, we think it tapdances. Of course, there may not be any such things as the Vincent Club. It may be just a bad dream, the kind of bad dream that you get after eating Welch rarebit, which, like the soul of Boston, is composed of cheese.

Anyway, we wash our hands of this type of debutante, and turn to the Charity, or Up The Masses, Type. This group is made up of young women who want to work, but, as they are mentally incapable of the responsibilities vested in an employee, find it necessary to work for free, usually in some charitable enterprise. They, like the Black Plague, are a sociological phenomenon.

—But what, says Little Gianciotto, is a sociological phenomenon?

—Beacon Hill, said the old *condottiere* without a quaver.

—Well, bless me, says little Gianciotto, shifting his quid to the other side of his face, I wouldn't have known.

There are all sorts of charities, most of which have been going on for years and years, like decay at Yale. The main duty of charities, it would seem, is to have projects. These projects are invariably accompanied by several cameramen, who photograph the. young ladies assisting, all of which leads to the assumption that the main function of these charities is to assist the Photographers' Guild, if there is one.

—Then what is charity? says little Gianciotto.

—Charity, replies old Malatesta, is Love.

—And what, says little Gianciotto, leaning forward eagerly, is Love?

—Love, says the Lord of Rimini, with a leer, is fun.

—I'll say, says little Gianciotto, dragging down the housemaid.

All of which brings us to the third, and most horrible, type of debutante; the Glamour Girl, or Over The Hill To The Stork Club Type. This type centers itself in Manhattan, for the simple reason that Boston girls are too ugly to be glamorous, and Philadelphia girls too prosy. Each year the soberer of New York's *bon vivants* (Fr.) gather and elect the season's Glamour Girl, to the sound of loud cymbals, and, for no extra charge, to the sound of well-tuned cymbals. This year the Glamour Queen was Brenda Frazier (rhymes with *Asia*, *brazier*, etc.) who is, at the moment, in Bermuda or Zamboanga or somewhere, recovering from the effects of her debut and the possession of several million dollars.

Miss Frazier, to slip into the vernacular, is some baby. She is really a simple girl at heart, says her wise, wise mother, much preferring gingham gowns and rustic swains to the mad social whirl of Manhattan. But what can one do when one is a Glamour Girl? One must *live*, of course. It is useless to argue that some arsenic in her milk or liquidation *à la Russe* would do Miss Frazier a world of good. Even if Miss Frazier did herself in we'd still have Lucius Beebe, Miss Elsa Maxwell, and Cecil Beaton (status undetermined) to deal with.

Now, the trouble with Glamour Girls is that every debutante over fourteen (little Gianciotto's age) thinks she is one; and that adds up to an awful lot of glamour. Too, it adds up to an awful lot of stupidity. After all, if a girl spends all her time in cultivating her b-dy, for what would seem to be obvious reasons, she isn't going to have much time to cultivate her mind. As a result, we have a good, round number of nuts cluttering up the Social Register, which, we might add, is neither social nor a register.

Once, when we were younger and more foolish, we thought of saving our money and buying a Glamour Girl, but we finally rejected the plan because we realized that the upkeep on our purchase would be tremendous, while, at the same time, it would depreciate like hell. Yessir, there's no drug on the market like an old, decrepit Glamour Girl, we always say. Two or three years of parties, tossing in a child here and there, and they start to sag between ear and nostril. A Glamour Girl's face always goes first: their bodies hang on tenaciously. But that, of course, is beside the point—this is not a medical treatise.—

—That's what you think, says little Promiscuity.

Of course, America owes a lot to debutantes. When one is tired of newspaper accounts of wars and rumors of wars, one can always relax in the foolishness of the Society Page. I don't know what we'd do without Jerome Zerbe, Messrs. Billingsly and Perona, Cholly Knickerbocker, and Mrs. Harrison Williams. I don't even know what we'd do without Brenda Frazier (rhymes with *Asia* and *brazier*: see *Annals of Club Life at Harvard, 1939*). In fact, I don't even know what we'd do without debutantes in Boston.

For one thing, a lack of debutantes in Boston would mean that Harvard undergraduates would have to buy their own drinks. It would mean that the *American* and *Transcript* would have to shut down their plants. The reverberations would be felt from Eliot House to San Simeon. Of course, the main mass of the people would go its quiet way; but what do we care for the people, anyway?

The question is, now that we have the debutantes, what are we going to do with them? Certainly they can't be allowed to roam the streets night after night. No, they've got to be taken care of. But how?

—I know, says little Gianciotto, who spent a week in Berlin, a concentration camp.

—Hold your tongue, says old Malatesta, and take your hand off that maid.

—Which hand? says little Gianciotto innocently.

—The one I can't see, says old Malatesta.

But little Gianciotto has given us an idea. Why not put all the debutantes in a concentration camp? Of course, it would be a very nice concentration camp, with all sanitary facilities; and we could charge admission to the general public. We could divide the camp into three parts; a part for the artistic debutantes, a part for the charity workers, a part for the Glamour Girls. The artistic contingent could put on shows in which they could kick high and show their legs, if they have any—but we'd better go into this in detail.

Well, in the first place, the section of the camp devoted to the *artistes* would have, at one end, a huge stage, complete with a stage director, applause machines, and a noble purpose. At the other end would be thirteen microphones, a bundle of contracts to sing at the Sert Room, Ozzie Nelson, and assorted photographers. The floor would be paved with Cole Porter, Noel Coward, and Tommy Manville, the Asbestos Adonis. There would probably be no reason for Mr. Manville, save that his position on the floor would make him very happy.

The section of our camp devoted to Charity would have a floor paved with photographers and formal applications for aid. Each incumbent debutante would have a neat little desk, on which would be placed her hands and any number of cosmetics. There would be a great bustle of activity, because the girls, like the Red Queen (or maybe it's the White Queen) would have to work very hard to stay in the same place. Around the walls would be murals depicting *The Junior League Girls in Brookline*, or *Married But Willing*. (Readers are referred to my earlier books, entitled *The Junior League Girls At Rosemary Hall*, or *Thwarting the Evil Janitor*, and *The Junior League Girls At The Ritz Bar*, or *If It Ain't Dry It Ain't A Martini.*)

Finally, the section devoted to the Glamour Girls would contain, at one end, a throne on which Brenda Frazier is seated (till next season). Miss Frazier will hold in one hand a drink compounded of milk, coca-cola, and old blood; in the other she will hold a bill from the Ritz. She will be wearing a creation whipped up by Maggy Rouff, Schiaparelli, and the effects of three quarts of champagne. On her lap will repose a book by Lucius Beebe, and at her feet will repose Lucius Beebe himself, all in mauve. Photographers will be everywhere; and the place will be full of Glamour Girls, zebra stripe motifs, and sex with a vengeance. Restrooms will be provided for any spectators who feel nauseated.

Now, this camp should be placed, if we have anything to say about it, on Boston Common, between the Subway Station and the Bandstand. Admission will be nominal; say, fifteen cents. And when it's all done, we can forget the whole business and start cleaning up Massachusetts politics, an infinitely harder job.

But of course, the debutante is really not as bad as she sounds. She recovers from her debut, marries Jonathon Codpiece, (of the Boston

Codpieces, her second cousin), propagates, and eventually dies. All in all, she is a nice, well-rounded girl, without a brain in her head. But, as she is a member of the upper class (in Boston, at least), and as the upper classes have been operating on no mentality for nearly half a century, she really has nothing to fear. As long as she can afford psychoanalysts, she gets along. Unless Mr. Dies is right—

—Who, says little Gianciotto, is Mr. Dies?

—Mr. Dies, says old Malatesta, is a booger. And take your g-dd-m hand off that maid.

March, 1939

HOWARD NEMEROV

Class of 1941, (1920–   )

Howard Nemerov teaches English at Bennington College. His first book of poetry, The Image and the Law, *was published in 1947. Since then he has written* Guide to the Ruins, The Salt Garden, New and Selected Poems, *and* The Next Room of the Dream. *Nemerov has also published two novels,* The Melodramatists, *and* Frederigo, or the Power of Love.

INVENTORY AND STATEMENT: A DECLAMATION

50 beautiful girls count 'em 50, are dying,
all together and slowly. Their hearts
beat one-two-three-four, they've worked
together all their lives and given you
good entertainment: and the young clerk
with the hot pants, in the third row center,
was perhaps the least of the sinners among you.

Plato dreamed of a surpassing love
bound up beyond the moving spheres: and Ziegfeld
dreamed of fifty beautiful girls fifty,
who are dying.
                    The private citizen talks Babylon,
and has a righteous tea with the pastor,
and lusts in his heart; while my landlady
threw Alice out on the street and read Paris Nights.
Plato is dead, and Ziegfeld no less dead:
for I have given you here a thread of mine own life,
or that for which I lived.

What shall you do when winter is on the world,
and time comes out of the cliff to dine among you:
and the strumpet has none to love with her legs,
and the bride goes to an empty bed,
and the lover lies in the hasty grave
the earthworms dug under him?
Why, then you will set alarm clocks,
and whisper the time in restaurants;
there will be learned discussions, there will be
symposia; and the newsreels will picture
decay in the organism, newspapers will devote columns
to the death of a leaf.

Enforce the censorship: excise the merely
heterosexual: and show instead
defecation, masturbation, and a new
all-color version of Les Cent-Vingt Jours
—let the people learn the fashionable
technic from Alcibiades, and let
the newsboys peddle pictures of the Marquis
performing a subtle experiment.

For the fifty fair are dead, and godhead gone:
Brightness is dust, and through these portals pass
Plato, Ziegfeld, and all loveliness.

March, 1940

THE NATIVE IN THE WORLD

THE CLIMB from sleep was difficult, a struggle up a staircase of soft
pillows into which he sank again and again, drowsily defeated, from
which he clumsily climbed again to a sight of the room that, seen in the
equivocal wisdom of sleep, seemed to him any room, or all the rooms,
in which he had ever slept, or ever been at home. Perhaps (an instant

Howard Nemerov 233

afterward he could no longer remember)—perhaps the phrase 'at home' struck the first tone of clarity in his mind, for about it the room began to arrange itself, to become again the familiar fashion of his circumstance, rising and composing to his own composition of its features. One thing—the overturned chair by the desk, with his clothes crushed under it—remained obstinately unfamiliar; when had he done that? He searched his memory, but the incident had sunk under sleep; he could readily imagine himself coming in drunk and knocking the chair down in the effort to hang his clothes over it, but actually to remember doing it—that was a different thing.

He got out of bed, and as he stood up felt pain protest harshly in his forehead, making him dizzy with the angry sleep that would not readily dissolve. The clock said ten more or less exactly and it was dark outside. That meant twenty hours sleep; since two Tuesday morning. The dizziness surged higher as he bent in a methodical stupor to set the chair right and get his clothes. Going into the next room he started the phonograph and put on the Ricercare of the Musikalisches Opfer; then settled back in the darkness of a far corner. The one voice strode through his mind with a more or less plaintive confidence that another would follow, and soon another did, then one more and another, and the rest were sunken in the ensemble and the scratch of the needle. He closed his eyes, and as if his consciousness rested on quicksand he was irresistibly sucked back toward sleep, his eyelids grew heavy in a sort of undertow that he could feel heavily about his head. A dream, some frightening and fast forgotten dream, jarred him out of sleep; he had a vague impression of fear, something was being thrown at him. He turned on the light, changed over the record and picked up a book that was lying on the couch: *Alcohol the Friend of Man*. It was a reassuring volume by a doctor of unspecified repute; one must, he thought, turning over the pages, combine theory with practice. It seemed to him, as he had so often said, that there was a way to drink seriously, and a way not to drink seriously. Of three years at Harvard he had spent the last two learning the former, and was glad to distinguish himself from many of his acquaintances whose drinking was of the rowdy-up-and-puke sort. If a man wish to drink himself into insensibility, he phrased it pedantically, that is his own business; but equally he should not become a charge on his fellow-beings, and there is no excuse for forgetting manners one instant before passing out.

The record was over, and he walked across the room to change it, a strange figure in white pajamas, barefoot, head slightly too large for his excessively small frail body. He already had on his silver-rimmed reading glasses; he must have picked them up from the desk without thinking. He came from the Middle West, but one would unhesitatingly have called him a Yankee, judging by his pedantic contemptuous manner, his manners so civil as to be rude whenever he gave a cutting edge to his voice. His own estimate of himself was quite accurate: that his aloofness was respected, also his enormous and casual erudition; that even full professors were chary of a too great freedom with him or with his papers; that it was generally said of him that he would go far if he did not drink himself to death; that his paper on Augustinianism in the 17th century would no doubt put him in line for a fellowship; and at last, that he was drinking himself to death, or near to it—a state which he conceived of dubiously as a slight chill in his personal weather, as though a cloud should slide over a hill on which he was sunning himself. As to his reasons—if a man wish to drink himself into insensibility, he thought again . . . and perhaps it is not even his own business, or perhaps it is a shady transaction in that business, into which he does well not to inquire too far; look what happened to Oedipus.

He had put on the Ricercare again, but now he turned it off in the middle and called Rico's number. He listened apprehensively to the empty buzz of the phone, three, four, five times: he could hear it as if he were in the room, but as if the room were still empty, the lonely stupid ringing. Damn Rico, he thought, damn the twisted little Cuban Jesuit gone wrong, and damn, he said, and damn with the ring of the phone, and damn again and hung up. The receiver clattered into its cradle, and he felt again how painfully slow it was to wake up, how fiercely he must fight to stay above the surface, so to speak, to force every last ache and hurt in body and mind to the service of wakefulness, to a nagging insistence on belief in being awake. Rico was probably out with Alan; Alan, he thought angrily, the little blond jew-boy who's trying to get me out of the way by advising me seriously to go see a psychiatrist. And Rico is helping him too.

He shuddered slightly, envisioning conspiracy and betrayal: the swift, sure honest-eyed kiss of treachery, the bright, the clear, the trustworthy Judas; and the appalling thing was that it took place on such a pitifully small scale, the love life of a colony of worms. The disgust, and the hate, were waking him, slowly, as one fever will fight another and overcome it.

He took up the phone again and called Rhys. One could always talk to Rhys, no matter how far they had gone apart. Long ago, before the drinking, as he thought, they had been close friends, working furiously together, reading two and three books in an evening and listening to Bach from two to four in the morning. And then—there had been no break, not even a coolness; but they went their ways and saw rather less of each other. When he was drunk and wanted to talk out of turn, he often still climbed to Rhys' room, and he would talk wildly for fifteen minutes, often incoherently, and then Rhys would deliberate heavily, and say at last, "Well, John, it's difficult..." which in itself would be somewhat reassuring; and then they would exhaust a small stock of polite and cynically erudite remarks about obscure poets, or faculty members, and it would be over.

"Hello, Rhys? This is John—Bradshaw.... I hope I didn't disturb you?"

"Not at all," said Rhys, in the coldly amiable tones that meant he was disturbed.

"Look, Rhys,... you mustn't mind me; I'm not drunk, but I took twelve grains of amytal last night when I was. I've just managed to get out of bed and I'm a little—woozy." He was, in fact, woozier than he had thought; there was that dull weight on his forehead that was worse than pain, more unknown and more fearful therefore.

"What I wanted to know was could you meet me for a drink, about fifteen minutes from now?"

"No, I can't," said Rhys. "You sound troubled. I don't know medicine, but isn't twelve grains rather much?"

"The prescribed adult dose is a grain and a half. I wish you'd come out for a drink. I want to talk to you. Really, you know, it gets to be too much, sometimes... everywhere you go people are such bitches...."

"What the hell is wrong, John?"

"Oh,—look, I'm liable to ramble a bit—I'm not very awake and the drug is still pretty strong—Oh goddam it Rhys, I've been betrayed, I—"

"Again?" A politely skeptical coolness.

Steady, he thought to himself; he was weak and falling again, and before answering he bit his lower lip hard, till the blood ran, to save himself from sleep.

"I mean it," he said stubbornly.

"Yes," said Rhys; and John recognized the tone Rhys used to nice drunks. "Yes, people are . . . difficult sometimes."

"Rhys, I'm not drunk. I want to talk to you. Why won't you have a drink with me?"

"Because I don't feel like it, John."

"Rhys, you think I'm drunk. I'm not, Rhys. It's the amytal. I couldn't be drunk, Rhys, I just got up, I've slept since two this morning."

"I know you're not drunk, John," said Rhys coldly. "I'm busy, and I think you ought to go back to bed. You don't sound very well."

"I only want to talk to you about Rico. You think I'm drunk."

"What's Rico done now?"

"I want to talk to you, Rhys."

"Well . . . ?"

"Not on the phone."

"All right then, good night."

"Rhys—"

"Good night."

He waited for the dead click at the other end, and then placed the receiver carefully down. That had been a shameful performance; he was not drunk, but he could not have been more maudlin in any case. Rhys would be nodding his head sagely at this very moment: poor John Bradshaw. Oh, damn Rhys. It was unfair of him. He might have had the common courtesy to listen to me, Rhys the careful, Rhys the un-drunk, the dullard so proud of his dullness; one could summon up at will that favorite image of Rhys the damned, sitting deep in his arm-chair after a peculiarly bitter confessional period, sitting like a tolerant father-confessor, saying slowly between puffs at a cigarette, "Gawd, all you people live such exciting lives—it must be so difficult for you—you come and tell me about drinking and drugs and your homosexual expe-riences—and I sit here on my can, taking it all in, living my dull life. . . ." And he would sit there on his can, looking as old as he could, and staring into the fire, saying "they also serve," or some such. Poor Rhys! And so anxious, too, for you to know that he was only pretending dull-ness (which God knows he was not) and that he was a man of deep spiritual crises; as he would say, and so smugly, "My blowups all take place inside." All right. Let Rhys take that attitude. He wasn't required.

He got to his feet and walked slowly about the room, still thinking about Rhys, beating one little fist determinedly into the other hand and thinking with melancholy savagery, 'cut away the non-essentials, cut them out." Rhys was a non-essential, Rhys always worrying about his writing, his piddling poetry, his painful anxiety that you read his newest work, that you pat him on the head, that you say nice things. . . . As for himself, he thought, there would be a book one day . . . a book after this long silence, after the non-essentials had been cut away and meditation had burned some great stone to form inside him, a book that would say all these things that had to be said, against the lying time, against the lying treacherous people, against Rhys, against Rico, against Alan, against (he sneered) all these smilers with their dull knives. One voice in his wilderness would not waste time crying out for help, for cries would only bring the wolves along faster. And through this, beneath the pain and the hate and the disgust and still half-prevailing sleep, he knew that he was crying out.

He went into the bathroom and looked at the bottle of amytal. There were at least twenty-five grains left; he smiled a little to remember the time when one grain could give him a solid night's sleep, the rapid necessity to step up the dose, the doctor at the hygiene building telling him pedagogically that he was by definition a drug-addict, his crazily epigrammatic crypticism to the doctor ("Jonathan Swift was by definition not a well man, and a neurotic to boot"), his cheerful announcement to Rhys (Rhys again): "You may call me De Quincey, I'm depraved." It was the precipitous, the plunging rapidity with which it had happened, this drug business, that astounded him and started slight inadmissible fears from their careful rest. How one thing led to another! in such seemingly inconsequential succession of one pettiness on the next, until, looking back from the most extravagantly fantastic heights of improbability, from the most unwarranted excesses and distortions, one was surprised and shocked to note how accurately and how unerringly every smallest act, word and gesture quietly conspired to build such a wildly rococo and out-of-the-way edifice,—such a goblin's architecture that at one moment one shuddered to think how it drove one on to the end, and at the next dismissed the whole structure with a smile for its implausibility. He stared fixedly at the bottle, imagined himself reaching out for it, tried to imagine himself refusing, and could only get a more or less chromo reproduction of a man in a magazine advertisement with his head turned disaffectedly away from a cup of coffee, saying: "Nope, I keep away from it. Keeps me up nights." This did not seem to him a satisfactory image of moral grandeur; with a smile he took up the bottle and locked it away in the filing cabinet on his desk. Then, puzzled, he looked at the key to the cabinet; what to do with that? He took it with him into the living room. He stood in the very center of the carpet, shut his eyes and turned around thrice, as though he were absurdly playing some children's game of blind man's buff; with his eyes still tightly closed, he threw the key straight before him, heard it tinkle in landing, then turned around twice more before opening his eyes. A glance about the room satisfied him that the key was not in evidence, not obviously anyhow. It might be days before he came across it. Unless the chamber-maid picked it up in the morning. He could imagine that she might hand it to him, asking whether he had lost it, and imagine himself saying no, I wonder how it could have got here ... but one couldn't do that; all one's correspondence was in the filing cabinet, and notes for a couple of essays as well. Anyhow, it would be easy to find the key again, when it was really required. Meanwhile, one could ... imagine it lost.

He decided to give Rico one more chance, and dialled his number again. The equivocal ringing—does it ring if you're not there to hear it?—angered him; he thought it possible that Rico and Alan were in the room, refusing to answer, he could hear them guessing who it might be, smiling complacently, drifting from smiles into their moonings and caressings, their adolescent, ill-informed lecheries—but no, neither one of them would have the strength to let the phone ring and keep on ringing; across each ugly infirm purpose would flash thoughts of importance, of some great person, some missed opportunity, the thought especially: it might be something better. And they would answer the phone. Rico particularly would answer the phone, compliant opportunist, affection's whore ... had he ever done differently, or been anything else? Rico? who told (with pride) how he had been seduced by the house-maid when he was fifteen, and how three weeks later he had gone to his mother and got the girl discharged on some pretext.

No, they would answer the phone, he knew, and since they had not... Perhaps they weren't even together; he cut the call short and dialled Alan's room. Alan's roommate answered:

"Hello."

"Hello, is Alan there?"

"No, he went out half an hour ago."

"Was Rico with him?"

"I think he was going to meet Rico. Is there any message I can give him?"

"No thanks."

"Your name . . . ?"

"No thanks," he said coldly and replaced the receiver. He thought desperately for a moment that he might call Rhys again, then rejected the idea. There was no sense in begging. He felt tired again; the weight in his forehead had turned into a headache, and his eyes tended to water. The slight exertion of walking about the room made him want to go to bed, but he refused, and to clinch his refusal, began to get dressed. A drink was probably what was needed, he thought. A drink, and an hour out of this room. There was the mood he had been in all too often lately: his room depressed him, almost as much as did a library, for example; and the best things in the room,—the Matisse over the victrola, for example—they were so recognized, so much the very breath of this tepid climate that they became unbearable, and music was unbearable, and work as well, and it all seemed to him the ugly and ready-to-hand diversion afforded a man sentenced to life imprisonment. Not the ugly, but the commonplace disgusts, he thought. If they put Matisses in the street-cars, one would counter by hanging advertisements on one's walls. Yet he felt unsatisfied outside his room, again like a prisoner so acclimated as to shun freedom; a walk, however short, tired him inordinately, and climbing two flights to the room made his head throb as if the blood would burst out. He felt now that he required a drink; he would go to St. Clair's, nor did he disguise from himself the fact that half his motive was to find Rico, and that if Rico were not at St. Clair's he might be at Bella Vista, or McBride's, or the Stag Club; or he might be in town at the Napoleon or the Ritz or the Lincolnshire.

By the time he had finished dressing he found himself nearly exhausted. He had to sit down on the couch and turn out the light, and it was then that he began to think about the key to the filing-cabinet. He felt that he had perhaps been foolish, with his infantile stratagem. He might need the key in a hurry, for his notes, or to answer a letter, or— no need to disguise the fact from himself—to get the amytal when he came in drunk; it had to be conveniently to hand, or he would get no sleep. He must recognize the fact by now, he argued: he required the amytal, he was a mature individual, still sane, heaven knows, more sane than most of his dull acquaintances, he would not over-dose. And anyhow, the test was in the will to stay off the stuff, not in locking it away, there was no help in that. To be able to keep it before his eyes, that bottle, to look at it steadily, and steadfastly not to take it—at least not more than was absolutely necessary—there was the thing. Besides, suppose he needed it in a hurry, sometime, and the key had got lost— there were any number of ways that could have happened: it might have fallen into a crack in the floor, might have slid under the carpet, might even have landed down the radiator gratings, irretrievable short of large-scale operations that would require the janitor.

Hastily he turned on the light, began to look around. It was not that he wanted any now, or would take any tonight; but this was the saner thing to do, he must know.

The key was discovered with ridiculous ease, under the bookcase. He picked it up and laid it carefully in the middle drawer of his desk. And unformed to speech or even to clear thought, but present in his mind, was that justification, that ritual against reason, of a postulated higher power, of unspecified nature, watching over the episode, the feeling, carefully swathed in obscurity: Providence didn't want me to hide the key, or I wouldn't have found it so easily.

Put vaguely at ease, he began to get on his overcoat, and then decided to call Rhys again, buoyed up by this same vague assurance that he would, by however narrow a margin, do the thing which was to be done, that the thing would be right because he did it. But there was no answer, and for some reason, he was more infuriated at this than at Rico's absence—a little relieved, too, for Rhys would have been annoyed; but angry, angry that Rhys should not be there, should have gone out after making some excuse to him. Betrayal, he thought, furiously and without power. Rhys too. Although loneliness was his habitual way, it was by preference, because it suited him to be alone, but this, the loneliness by compulsion, was a new thing. He felt a terrible isolation, the phone seemed to him now only an instrument of the Inquisition, to teach him his loneliness as it were by rote, and he had the sudden sense that whatever number he called, it would be closed to him by that instrument. In fact, he thought in satiric anger—in fact this whole room is given only to people who want to be left alone. It is made to teach them the measure—that is, the unmeasurable quality—of isolation, of being absolutely alone. Harvard College built it that way—they get a lot of lonely ones around here.

The brief walk in the cold, up Dunster street and across the Square to St. Clair's, fatigued him excessively; he recognized that last night's dose had not nearly worn off, and that the cold had the unusual effect of making him want to lie down and go to sleep just wherever he was, in the street even. It was almost like being drunk, that disgusting soddenness with drink that made it Nirvana just to stop moving, anyhow, anywhere. He kept up his heart to a degree by repeating his little catechism of betrayal, his interdict on Rico and on Rhys, all the fictions of his misery forming into churches for his martyred self: here was a first station, where one knelt to beg forgiveness for being rude to Bradshaw; and here a second, where one knelt to do penance for being out when Bradshaw called, here another for thinking Bradshaw drunk when he wasn't, here another for the general sin of offending Bradshaw; and a last, where one prayed for the grace of Bradshaw: Oh Bradshaw, we do beseech thee . . . and a return for the petty humiliations, and a hundredfold paid back each error, and he knew it for pitiful, but nevertheless went on, in a rage of cynical benevolence, to forgive Rico, to forgive Rhys, to forgive them and cut them away from his side, and to go on in the thorough lonely discretion of his anger.

When he entered St. Clair's the first person he saw was Rhys, big, rather stout, and darkly dressed as usual, sitting by himself at a corner table. Rhys waved and beckoned to the chair opposite, and John sat down there.

"You're avoiding me," he said without thinking; his anger came to a head and he wanted a fight.

"If I were avoiding you, would I come and sit in a bar?" asked Rhys politely, and it was like being hit across the face.

"Then why did you tell me you couldn't go out?"

"I didn't say I couldn't go out. I said I didn't feel like going out." Rhys was nettled, and showed it by getting more and more polite.

"If you don't want to see me, I won't sit here."

"Don't be silly. Sit around and have a drink."

Rhys, he thought, was playing for a dull peace and it was not to be allowed; he must be disturbed, made to give himself away. He ordered, and got, a large martini, and sipped it in an uneasy silence.

"You should have gone to bed. You look as if you were trying to kill yourself." Rhys gave in and said something.

"What the hell would you care?" he asked rhetorically, hoping at the same time that Rhys would say something friendly and reassuring.

"How is it possible for anyone to care? You're not very responsive to care, you know."

"Oh, some have managed." He lit a cigarette. It tasted very bad, but it was against the sleep that even the drink seemed to drive him at. The place where he had bit his lip was still tender, it hurt when he spoke.

"You alienate even those," said Rhys. It was for him as though he had said 'where are you, John?' and reached out a hand in the darkness; it was such an unwelcome thing to be forced to find people when ordinarily they came and disclosed themselves.

They finished their drinks in silence and ordered more.

"Now what's this about Rico?" said Rhys at last.

John emptied his glass again, slowly, before answering. "It's only that from now on," he said, "I'm going to play dirty too. If you don't what chance have you got?"

"I always thought of Rico as more or less irresponsible," said Rhys, "but—"

"It's not only Rico, God knows. He can be excused: if you were bounced out of a parochial school in Cuba and landed at Harvard with the prospect of eight million bucks when you came out—alors. Not alone Rico, no. It's everyone. And you too, sir. Don't you understand: I'm playing your way now, the safe way you all play, don't give anything with one hand that you can't get back with both, any time. And if I can't beat these Jesuits at their own game—well, what the hell..." he shrugged his thin shoulders, deliberately blew smoke across the table between them.

Rhys determined to show no annoyance, to maintain objectivity. So he sat with hands out equally on the table, looking like the balance-pans of the blind goddess.

"Essentially stupid attitude to take," he said. "I mean—granting that people do present . . . difficulties at times—still, just how much have you got hurt?"

"Got hurt, hell. That's not—"

"You don't need to answer me," continued Rhys with a show of calm.

"I'm just suggesting the question as something for you to worry about."

"Don't go on; you had it right the first time, when you said something about responsibility. You just make an ass of yourself when you put it on the piddling level of 'getting hurt.' It's only a question of how the essential non-pirate is to live in a world of pirates."

Rhys had no immediate reply to this, so they ordered more drinks and John continued:

"Romans and Orthodox Jews make the best pirates because even if they do put pretty far out to sea after plunder, they've both got a sailor's snug harbor to get to again. The Catholic can drop anchor in a church, the Jew carries his absolution along on shipboard. But they aren't the only ones, not by a long shot. It applies to everyone you know . . . piracy isn't so safe a game for them, but if you think for a minute—"

"I wish you wouldn't pretend to sit in judgment when you're looking so pitifully ill. You remind me not so much of the Christian Way as of Nietzsche."

And suddenly John felt the fatigue again, the wish to give it up; what was the use in arguing with Rhys. The drink was having an inordinate effect because of the amytal. He knew it would be difficult to get up, next to impossible to walk home.

"Hell," he said. "It's only an argument for you. Forget the whole thing." And then: "Will you take me home?"

"What's wrong? Not feeling well?"

"I'm sick to death of sitting here with you, listening to your well-fed brain. I want to leave and I can't do it by myself. I'm asking you: as one last favor, would you see me home? Let me assure you, sir, it will be the last. I shan't disturb you and your values again."

"Please don't be melodramatic with me, John," said Rhys in a quiet rage.

"Can't you see that's not the question?"

"Don't you think you'd feel better if you sat here without drinking for a few minutes?"

"Oh for heaven's sake, sir, don't be reasonable with me. I've asked you a question, will you—"

He felt a draught on his back from the open door. Shivering extravagantly, with the hope that Rhys would think him ill, he turned and saw Rico and Alan standing beside his chair.

"Wha's wrong, little one," asked Rico, slightly drunk, smiling with his beautiful teeth.

"Rico!" He held out his hand, forgetting Rhys, forgetting Alan. "Rico"—and more softly, as though drawing the other into conspiracy— "will you take me home? I can't go myself."

"Sure, little one. I can take you home. Come, give me your hand." Rico laughed, his laugh and his glance taking in the whole room, stranger and intimate alike, as though to disclaim all embarrassment and responsibility, as though to enlist their sympathy not for John but for self-sacrificing Rico who had to take him home.

"Come," he said. "Up on your feet."

He got to his feet slowly enough, his eyes half fading from their focus. The floor seemed to rock beneath him, his ears filled with noise, and it was as if he stood on a separate planet that rocked backwards and over in space, out of sight of Rhys who sat there with an embarrassed expression on his face. Then suddenly he knew he was heavily in Rico's arms, and in one instant synapse of sobriety he heard himself saying to Rhys "I hate you more . . ." and Rico saying roughly "Come on," pulling at his arm. Then the two little voices were again swept away in a wave of sound against his brain, formless sound at first, that resolved itself into a rhythm and at length into words spoken from far away: "Drink and drugs that done him in," or some such; and then— drink and drugs—he could no longer hear for noise, but the enormous voice of Rico was in his head saying "Come on, come on," and all at once they were in the street and the cold stung his eyes and the sweat on his cheeks.

Rico and Alan had taken him by the arms, close to the shoulder, and were dragging him along. Whenever he stumbled they set him right with a jerk that lifted his feet off the ground.

"Wait," he said. "Sick."

And while they stood silently by holding him, Rico holding his head forward, he was sick, with a horrible violence, in a little alley off Dunster street. His stomach, almost empty to start with, twisted painfully at the finish, and he lost consciousness.

When he came to he was alone in his room with Rico. He could not see Alan anywhere. He rested on his bed and Rico was taking his clothes off. There was no longer any rest, or desire to sleep; there was only pain in his stomach and an actively hurtful weariness.

Rico finished stripping him, folded him in between the sheets. "You'll be OK in the morning," he said. "You were sick as a bitch. How d'you feel now?"

"Rico," he whispered. "Don't go away, Rico." He felt distantly that he was a child, in his child's bed at home; he had done a wrong thing, and Rico would be angry, with the efficient necessary anger of a mother.

"Kiss me, Rico," he said. "Kiss me good night." And then, as Rico made no move to comply, he said: "You're mad at me ... ?" with a pathetic dubious note of shame in his voice, and Rico stooped and quickly kissed him on the cheek.

"Now good night, little one."

"Don't go, Rico. Stay here tonight."

"I can't. You'll be all right now."

"But I won't, Rico. I won't. I'll be sick again." He grew panicky with new fear. "I swear I'll be sick again," he said. "The minute you leave. Don't leave, Rico."

Then, in a tone of malicious invalid craft, he said accusingly: "You gave Alan the key to your room, didn't you?" Breathless, he went on: "You told him to wait in your room, didn't you."

Rico's face gave him away; it was true, it could only be true. "That's why you want to leave," he went on. "I know why." Quietly he began to whimper, and the tears rolled down his face. Then in a desperate martyrdom he said in a choked voice: "I'll kill myself if you go. I'll kill myself the minute you go out that door."

"Nonsense, what would you do it with, little one." Rico was not very good at situations like this; he felt vaguely that he should comfort, should sacrifice himself a little and help; but he had no intelligent means of doing it, being frightened not by a lie, but by a lie that would involve him later.

"I'd take all the amytal. I would. It would be enough. You'd see it would be enough. Rico, don't be a bastard. Don't go away."

"You mustn't do that, John. You mustn't think of it."

"And you can't find the amytal either. I hid it." There was a terrible cunning in his voice, he was determined to have the drug. It did not at that time matter to him whether it was a lethal dose or not; it was to spite Rico, to hurt him, to say to him: 'See what might have happened. The guilt would have been yours, you would have murdered me.'

Rico went to the bathroom to look for the amytal.

"You can't find it, you can't," he mocked in a thin voice cracked with approaching hysteria. "Go away, damn you. Go away."

Rico came back into the room.

"You won't do it, John."

"Get out."

"Promise me you won't do it."

"Get out."

"If you don't promise I can't do anything."

"I said get out."

Rico was faced with something beyond his comprehension, and he took the only way he understood.

"All right," he said sullenly. "I guess it's your life." And having thus washed himself clean in his own eyes, he walked out.

There was no question of decision, now he was alone. It was again that unfaced trust in a higher power, in some back world watching. With unnecessary stealth he got out of bed and, entirely naked, went to the desk, got the key and opened the filing cabinet. He took the bottle into the bathroom and poured all the pills into a highball glass, which he filled with warm water. This decoction he took back into the living room, where he sat down on the couch by the phone and began to drink. When the glass was empty there remained a considerable residue of damp powder at the bottom, so he refilled the glass and started again, more slowly, from time to time stirring the mixture with a pencil. At last he had finished. From experience, he knew there would be about fifteen minutes to wait.

He turned on all the lights, not feeling like getting into bed again. As he stood naked in the corner by the light-switch he was taken suddenly with a frenzy. The thing was done, it was done. Was it right? was it so at all? The indecision after the event frightened him, he imagined the maid finding him in the morning and with a certain sense of abject shame rushed to put his bathrobe about him. How to know? He questioned if he should be saved, and then, as he became somewhat more calm, there occurred to him another of those tests of providence, another cryptic question to which the oracle might smilingly equivocate over his special case.

He took up the phone and dialled Rhys' number. If Rhys answered he would explain and have him get a doctor. If there were no answer . . . and as he listened to the ring he felt certain there must be. It was not so much the test of fate, but the thought that he must speak again to Rhys, apologize, absolve, ask forgiveness.

There was no answer. Unwilling to believe, he put the phone down on the table and let it ring. The answer was given, but unsatisfactorily only more or less given, with the smiling ambiguity of power. He went to the window and opened it, then sat back on the couch. It is doubtful that he thought any more of death, of the probability or the certainty. He listened to the dried icy branches of the trees scratch together in the wind, down in the courtyard; and it is doubtful that he thought of leaving anything behind, of regret, or the irrevocability of death.

For his room, warm with the lights full on, seemed to him some tall citadel of the sun, with a certain congenial ease of sunlight upon it, and when the sleep came down, it drifted in like the cool sudden shadow of a cloud, that only made him shudder slightly.

June, 1941

248   *Howard Nemerov*

DJUNA BARNES

(1892–   )

Djuna Barnes began her career as a reporter, illustrator, and feature writer for various newspapers and magazines. Her first novel, A Book, *was published in 1923. Other early works include* Ryder, A Night Among the Horses, The Book of Repulsive Women, *and dozens of short stories. Her best known novel, the highly original* Nightwood, *was published in 1936.*

THE PERFECT MURDER

PROFESSOR Anatol Profax was nevertheless deeply interested in dialectology. The effect of environment on the tongue had been his life work; he had even gone so far as to assert that the shape of the tongue made people move up or down town; if it were heavy, large and flat it usually took them to the country, if it were a light tripping member they generally found themselves in Paris. The professor thought that the cutting out of tongues might produce mystics. He was sorry he had no power to try the experiment.

By the time he had reached middle age Professor Profax had pretty well covered his field—no pains had been spared. He had tracked down figures of speech and preferred exclamations in all walks of life; he had conversed with the trained and untrained mind; the loquacious and the inarticulate had been tabulated. The inarticulate had proved particularly satisfactory; they were rather more racial than individual. In England they said "Right!", in Germany they said "Wrong," in France they said "Cow!", in America they said "So what?". These were bunch-indexed or clubbed under *The Inveterates*—it was his sister (now swatting out a thesis on the development of the mandible under vituperation) that got

Djuna Barnes 249

him down. She was always saying: "My God, *can you believe it!*". He classed her as the *Excitable Spinster* type and let it go at that. On the other hand the scores he had chalked up on defective minors and senile neurotics had proved disappointing. The professor was not even slightly interested in the human whine of the permanently hooked; conversely, he thoroughly enjoyed the healthy alkahest of applied appelatives— they were responsible for the most delightful boggles. What he had yet to lay his hands on was someone who *defied classification.*

Crossing Third Avenue toward Fourteenth street, Professor Profax pondered the key-words of fanatics, men like Swedenborg and his New Church, Blake and his Bush of Angels. He decided that these gentlemen were quite safe (he had underscored their writings); they had saved themselves by the simple expedient of Getting Out Of Reach.

He thought of his father, a hearty non-conformist who had achieved a quiet insecurity, over the dead bodies of John Wesley and the early Mormons; who had kicked out the family foot-organ in favour of a turning-lathe, and who was given to shouting (rather too loudly) "Terrain tumult—ha!"

Deep in the pride of those reflections the professor smiled. He little cared that his figure was followed by many a curious eye. He was indeed old-fashioned. His frock coat was voluminous. Like all creatures that hunt too long he looked hungry. His whole head which was of polished bone, bore a fine sharp nose, a lightly scored mouth and deep cavernous sockets. He carried a cane over a crooked elbow that tipped inward to hold a worn copy of his book "The Variations"; it was precious in itself, additionally so for the notes on its back pages, made during a trip through the Allegheny mountains and the fastnesses of Tennessee. He had gone to check up on reactions to the World War. The hill folk had resented the intrusion with dippers smelling strongly of liquor; of the war itself they had only heard as far as prohibition. There was little labial communication. These went under the head *The Impulsive.*

He raised his eyes. A poster depicting the one True and Only Elephant Woman confronted him in a bright green and red. He lowered his eyes thinking of Jane Austen; a good tart girl of a *sec* vintage propelled by decency springing to the lash of matrimony. Love—now there was an emotion that had a repetitive vocabulary if ever there was one. It consisted of "Do you love me? Do you *still* love me? You *used* to love me!" Usually this was answered with "Yeah, I love you. Uh huh, I still love you. *What?*" Out west it changed slightly, the interrogative was almost unanimously responded to by "Hell, no!" But one needn't go West. Take his own case, he had never married, yet he was a man of violent passions, wasn't he? He thought this over slowly. Certainly at some time in his life he must have curbed an emotion, crushed a desire, trampled a weakness. The kerchief in his coat tail fluttered, filled with the dying life of a September noon. Perhaps he was a man who was living on embers and an annuity; a man of worthy memoranda and no parts. Well, it could not be helped now, after all, his Mistress was *Sound*, that great band of sound that had escaped the human throat for over two thousand years. Could it be re-captured (as Marconi thought it might) what would come to the ear? No theories for or against; no words of praise or of blame, only a vast, terrible lamentation which would echo like the "Baum!" of the Malabar Caves. For after all what does man say when it comes right down to it? "I love, I fear, I hunger, I die." Like the cycles of Purgatory and Damnation.

Some years back the professor had thought of doing something about it. He had even tried, but it had been a bit of a failure for, as he recalled sadly, he had been one jigger too elated, had had a swizzle too much (a thing he was not given to as a rule). This Holy Grail of the Past had eluded him, fool that he was, and had become only a dull longing which he had satisfied by calling in the local fireman and the Salvation Army. He had offered them libations of Montenegran rum (which he kept hid in the darkness of his Canterbury) . . . ; he had even tried to explain himself, somehow he had got nowhere. The firemen had not made him happy; the little woman in the Booth bonnet had not saved him. He remembered that he had pressed a five dollar bill into the hand of the one to remove the other. It had all been a most frightful fluke. He had ended weeping in his den, pen in hand, trying to write a legible note on his blotter to President Wilson; the trend was to the effect that he considered *kumiss* preferable to bottled beer. He had to read it in the mirror the next morning, his head tied up in a towel. Somehow he had written it back-hand and upside down. In general he tried to think that he had had a religious experience, but he said nothing about it.

At this moment someone in flowing black bowled into him. He reeled a step, recovered his balance, recrooked his cane and took off his hat.

"Heavenly!" she said. She carried a muff; the strap of one of her satin shoes was loose, her long yellow hair swung back as she caught up her velvet train. "Heavenly!" she breathed.

"What?" said the professor, "I beg your pardon."

"Dying!" she said taking his arm. "I *am* shallow until you get used to me. If it were not so early I'd suggest tripes and a pint of bitters."

"Britain," he muttered, "that stern, that great country. How did *you* get here?"

"But it *is* too early."

"Are you the elephant girl?"

"Sometimes, sometimes I work on the trapeze, sometimes I'm a milliner, sometimes I'm hungry." She was thinking. "I'm so fond of the austerities—you know, Plato and all that. He said 'Seek the truth, and take the longest way,' didn't he?"

"I don't know."

"I just died," she said, "but I came back, I always do. I hate being safe so I let the bar go and I flew out, right out into you as a matter of fact—"

They had come to the park, and now she released his arm, leaning against the rim of the fountain bowl. "I'm devoted to coming back, it's so agonizing." She swung her foot in its loose shoe, looking at him with her bright honest eyes. "I'm an awful fool when I'm uncomfortable."

"Are you uncomfortable?" he inquired, facing her all in black.

"I shall be." she paused, "You see, what is really wrong is that I'm not properly believed; people are wicked because they do not know that I am a *Trauma*."

"I know."

"Do you! That's wonderful. Nobody trusts me. Only last night that beast of a sword swallower (yesterday was Sunday you remember) refused to swallow six of my kitchen knives, he said it would spoil him for the canticles!" She threw her arm out (a velvet band with a bright red rosette was on its wrist) "Imagine! Such perfidy, such incredible cowardice!" she sighed. "Man is a worm and won't risk discredit, and discredit is the *only* beauty. People don't believe me because they don't like my discredits. For instance, I love danger, yet if anyone put a hand on me I'd yell like murder. Perhaps you heard me yell a moment ago, perhaps you even thought 'the girl is afraid.' How stupid you are."

"Wait a minute," said the professor, *"Did* you yell?"

Two large tears rolled down her cheeks. "Do *you* doubt me? You bet I yelled."

"Lob." muttered Professor Profax, "Toss, bowl or send forth with a slow or high pitched underhand motion—lob."

"Wrong." She steered him back across the street, pressing her face against a confectioner's window. "I'm vindictive because I have a *passionate* inferiority; most people have a *submissive* inferiority. It makes all the difference in the world. I am as aboveboard as the Devil. I'd like some caramels."

He bought her a bag of caramels. He was a queer lead colour.

"For instance, I'm lovable and offensive. *Imagine that position!*"

"Do you play dominos?"

"No. I want to be married." She blinked her eyes, she was crying again. "You see how it is, it is always too late. I have never been married and yet I am a widow. Think of feeling like that! Oh!" she said, "it's the things *I CAN'T STAND* that drew people to me. It has made me muscular. If I could be hacked down without sentiment I'd be saved. It's the false pride in violence that I abominate. *Why should he be there?*"

"Who?" said the professor nervously.

"The villain." she was smiling.

The professor was beginning to feel that a great work (which he thought he had written) was now hardly readable. He thought grimly "Poor child, I'd like to support her." He drew himself up with a jerk "I'd like to have her on my hands, it's the only way I can get rid of her."

"Yes," she said, "we might as well get married—time will pass."

"How about coffee?" he suggested. She nodded. "Tired and vigorous," he said to himself, "What a girl."

She turned him toward Third Avenue. How the dickens did she know it was East not West that his rooms lay.

"Shall we get married to-day or later?"

"Later." the professor said. "Later will do." He walked slightly listing, she was hanging on his arm, she had forgotten the train of her velvet dress, it was sweeping through the dust, dragging cigarette butts and the stubs of theatre tickets.

"I love enemies," she said, "and Mozart." She turned her head from side to side looking about her near-sightedly. "Let's never make a malleable mistake, do you mind!" She was taller than he, it was odd. "I can't stand my friends," she said, "except for hours."

"Extraordinary," he muttered, "I don't know how to class you."

She drew back with a cry. "Class me! My god, people *love* me!"

She was a little blind in the darkness of the staircase. "People ADORE me—after a long time, after I have told them how beastly they are— weak and sinful—most cases are like that, lovely people. All my friends are common and priceless."

He opened the door and she entered by a series of backward leans, turning shoulder blade after shoulder into the room. He took her muff and laid it down among his guitars and dictionaries—why on earth a muff in September? She did not sit down, at the same time she did not look at anything. She said: "You can criticize people as much as you like if you tell them they are wonderful. Ever try it?"

"No."

"Try it." She pulled her dress about her feet. "I want you to under- stand, from the beginning, that I am the purest abomination imaginable." She sat down on the trunk. "And my father says that I am so innocent and hard-pressed he's always expecting me to fall out of a book."

He fumbled with his hat, cane, notes. They all fell to the floor.

She sat like a school girl, her knees drawn up, her head bent.

"You're a sedentary. *I* take solitude standing up. I'm a little knock- kneed," she added honestly, "and I want to be good."

Professor Profax put the kettle on. "Would you mind," he said, his back to her, "falling in with yourself until I light the fire."

A stifled scream turned him. She had fallen face down among a pile of musical instruments, knocking over the Canterbury, sending sheet music fluttering into the air. She was pounding her fist among the scattered caramels. Her fist was full of them.

At that precise moment Professor Anatol Profax experienced some- thing he had never experienced before. He felt cold, dedicated and gentle. His heart beat with a thin happy movement. He leaned over. With one firm precise gesture he drew his pen-knife across her throat.

He lifted the heavy leather lid of the trunk and put her in, piece by piece, the velvet of her gown held her. He laid the toppled head on top of the lace at the neck. She looked like the Scape-Goat, the Paschal Lamb. Suddenly the professor's strength went out of him: he lay down on the floor beside her. He did not know what to do; he had destroyed definition; by his own act he had ruined a great secret; he'd never be able to place her. He shook all over, and still shaking he rose to his knees, his hands out before him, the heel of each he placed on the corners of the lid and raised it.

She was not there.

He clattered out into the street waving for a cab. He did not notice that the vehicle answering his call was one of those Hansoms now found nowhere except at the Plaza. He climbed in slamming the little door. "Anywhere!" he shouted to the driver and slumped into the corner. The horse started at the crack of the whip, jogging the leaning face of the professor which was pressed against the glass.

Then he saw the cab's twin. Breast to breast they moved out into the traffic. *She* was in the other. She too was leaning her face against the glass of the window, only her face was pressed against it as she had pressed it against the confectioner's! Her hair fell across her mouth, that great blasphemous mouth which smiled.

The professor tried to move. He tried to call. He was helpless, only his mind went on ticking. "It's the potentialities, not the accomplishment . . . if only I had gotten her name . . . fool! fool? What *was* her name! . . . Lost, lost . . . something extraordinary . . . I've let it slip right through my fingers . . . ."

Behind the mists of the two sheets of glass they rode facing each other. A van came in between them. A traffic light separated them.

April, 1942

MARIANNE MOORE

(1887–   )

*After graduating from Bryn Mawr, Miss Moore
taught stenography and worked as an assistant in
the New York Public Library. From 1926–1929
she was acting editor of The* Dial. *Her first book
of poems was published in England without her
knowledge by members of the Imagist group.
Since then she has been publishing of her own
accord. Her* Collected Poems *appeared in 1951.
She has also published versions of* The Fables of
La Fontaine *and* Predilections, *a book of essays.
Talking about her work, Miss Moore quotes Con-
fucius: "If there be a knife of resentment in the
heart, the mind will not attain precision." "That
is to say, poetry watches life with affection."*

THE WOOD-WEASEL

emerges daintily, the skunk—
don't laugh—in sylvan black and white chipmunk
regalia. The inky thing
adaptively whited with glistening
goat-fur, is wood-warden. In his
ermined, well-cuttlefish-inked wool, he is
determination's totem. Out-
lawed? His sweet face and powerful feet go about
in chieftain's coat of Chilcat cloth.
He is his own protection from the moth—

noble little warrior. That
otter-skin on it—the living pole-cat—
smothers anything that stings. Well—
this same weasel's playful; and his weasel
associates are too? ONLY
WOOD-WEASELS SHALL ASSOCIATE WITH ME.

April, 1942

NORMAN MAILER

Class of 1943, (1923–   )

Norman Mailer came to Harvard to study Aero-
nautical Engineering, but he won the college
short story contest sponsored by Story Magazine
and turned to literature. After several years in the
Army during the War, he wrote The Naked and
the Dead. *Since then he has written* Barbary
Shore, The Deer Park, The White Negro, *and*
The American Dream. *"Maybe Next Year" was*
written for Theodore Morrison's course at Har-
vard and was later included in Advertisements
for Myself.

MAYBE NEXT YEAR

THE TRAINS used to go by, used to go by very fast in the field past the
road on the other side of my house. I used to go down there and walk
and walk through the fields whenever mom and pop were fighting, fighting about money like they always were, and after I'd listen awhile, I'd
blow air into my ears so I couldn't hear them, then I'd go out in the field,
across the road from my house and slide down the steep part of the
grass where it was slippery like dogs had been dirty there, and then I
used to climb up the other side, up the big hill on the other side, and
walk and walk through the fat high grass until I would come to the
railroad tracks where I'd just keep going and going and going.

Why don't we have any money, we never have any money, what kind
of man did I marry, what good is he, what good is he, look at him, look
at his boy there, look at your boy there, look at him, he takes after you,
look at him walk away like he never hears us, look at him, no good like
you, why don't you ever get any money?

Norman Mailer

The grass sticks would be rough and sharp sort of, like sharp pages in a book, and I had to walk with my hands in my pockets so I wouldn't cut my fingers. They were tall, the grasses, and sometimes they would hit me in the face, but I would hit them back, only that used to cut my fingers, and I'd start crying, but I stopped soon, because there was nobody around, and I knew that when there was nobody to hear me, I always stopped soon, although I never could figure it out, because I always could cry for a long time, and say I was going to run away and die if people were around.

I can't help it if I'm not making money, my God there's limits to what a man can do, nag, nag, nag, all the time. My God I can't help it, there's limits, there's depression, everybody's losing money, just worry about keeping the house, and don't compare the child to me, the God-damn child is splitting us up the middle, I can't help it if he's a stupid kid, he's only nine, maybe he'll get smarter yet, I can't help it if he's dumb, there's a depression going on I tell you, everybody's losing money, there just isn't any money around.

The railroad tracks made a funny kind of a mirror. I could see myself in them, one of me on each side, I was so tall in them, but I was awfully short, as short as my arm, but I was awful tall, I looked as tall as pop, except as tall as if I was to see pop all the way in the distance coming up the hill to our house, when he looked as tall as my arm, but I knew anyway that he was oh ten times bigger than me.

Why is the boy always disappearing, why don't you find him, you haven't a job, you just sit around, you might keep him near you, you might teach him to be like you, and sit around all day, and make it easier for me so at least I wouldn't have to look for him, but you can't even teach him that, I never saw such a man like you, they didn't make my father out of men like you.

If I walked and walked along the tracks, there was a spot where I could get to a place where all the big slow trains came into town. If I was careful I could sneak up in the grass near to where the men who jumped off the big trains camped in the fields.

They were dirty old men, they just sat around, and smoked pipes and washed their dirty old shirts in the yellow water spot where I used to go swimming before mom started yell yell yell about the dirty old men and wouldn't let me swim there.

They're filthy old things, you'll get sick and die, they're diseased, they're diseased, why did the town let them camp and flop in a meadow like that, right on the town limits, what's the good of living out of town when our only neighbors are bums, what's the good, what's the town mean, why aren't they put in the coop where they belong, why should they be flopping so near our house in a meadow?

I didn't like the men, they used to talk and laugh to themselves all the time, sometimes they would sing songs. I knew they were dirty men cause mom said they would give me diseases, but one time I came up and talked to them, when I went out mom and pop were shouting, and the men looked at me, one of the old ones who was sitting on his old stork bundle bag sort of, got up and looked at me, he made fun of me, he said sonny got a dime for a poor old man to have some coffee, and then all the men started laughing, haw haw haw kind of laughing. The other men came around me, one of them said he was going to take my shirt and use it for a snot-rag, and they all laughed again, the big man in the middle of them making believe he was going to throw dirt at me only I didn't know he was going to fool me until I started crying, and he laughed too, and dropped the dirt.

That boy is going to get in trouble, why don't you take care of him, keep him around you, he goes off into the meadow, and God knows what those bums are going to do to him, they're all vile, they don't live like men, they're not men I heard, they're no more men than you are, both of you are, why don't you take care of him, he'll turn out weak in everything like you, those bums will get him in trouble.

Pop came over, grab-me picked me up, and carried me upstairs, and licked me, and locked the door on me, and then he went downstairs, and he and mom yelled and yelled right through my crying. I waited and waited for them to hear me, but I must have fallen asleep because the next thing it was morning, and I didn't remember stopping and rubbing my hands on my nose to wipe off the crying. They unlocked the door before, I sneaked downstairs, the front door was open and mom and pop were sitting around front, not saying anything, I hated them, I ran out the door between them, and hid around the side of the house. Pop and mom came running out, they ran the wrong way calling to me, they were looking for me, and they weren't smiling, but they were talking nice the way they did when they didn't mean it, just like when they wanted to catch our dog, and that made me feel sad, and oh I felt just terrible, and then when they started coming back I didn't want to get another licking so I ran away without their seeing me, and sneaked across the road further down, into the field, and up the slippery hill, run run running way off until I got to the railroad tracks. I sneaked along them to where the dirty men with the disease were, and I hid down in the grass, and hid behind some to look at them, but they were all gone, there weren't any of them, but the old man who had made fun of me the day before, and he was lying on the ground crying and yowling like he was hurt or dead.

I walked over to him, he looked at me, he started crawling to me, I could see it was his foot that was hurt cause it was all bloody like, and bleeding near the knee. Help me kid, help me kid, he kept yelling.

Go ahead, hit the child, hit it, hit it, it deserves it, playing with dirty old men, hit it, it's a terrible child, it never listens to us, there's something wrong with it.

The old man looked like a snake, and I stepped back to run away from him, but he kept crawling after me, yelling don't go away kid, I won't hurt you, please don't go way kid, but he looked like a snake, only bleeding. I yelled at him, I said go away, you're a dirty old man, but he wouldn't stop, and I picked up a rock, and threw it at him, it missed him, but I threw another rock, and it hit him in the head, he stopped moving to me, he was crying something terrible, there was a lot of blood all over his face.

Why kid, why kid, why kid, why hit me.

You're a dirty old man, leave me alone, I don't like you, you're a dirty old man.

Kid for God's sakes help me, I'm going crazy kid, don't leave me here, it's hot here kid, it's hot here kid.

Then I picked up a stone, and threw it at him again, only I didn't see if it hit him because I was running away. I heard him crying, screaming, and I was scared, but I kept running, and then I said I hate them, I hate them, the grass kept cutting at me, I couldn't run with my hands in my pockets, kept cutting at me and cutting at me, I fell down, and then I got up and kept running home.

I walked down the last part of the hill, and across the road, and when I got back mom and pop were sitting around again, and I started crying. I cried and cried, and they asked me what's the matter, what's the matter with you, why are you crying, but I just kept saying the dirty old man, the dirty old man.

Norman Mailer 261

And mom said I thought they all were kicked out of town, I don't know how any of them were left, you're not lying?

I'm not lying, I'm not lying.

And pop got up, and said to mom I told you not to do it, you get an idea in your head, and you can't stop, those men were beaten, I don't know how any were left in the dark, we had flashlights, but there might have been, it's the boy's own fault, he had no business going around there today, and anyway he wasn't hurt, he didn't start crying until he saw us, I saw him before he saw me.

And mom said, if you were a man you'd go over there now, and finish them off, you wouldn't even go last night without any help, if I were a man I'd thrash the man that touched my boy, but you just sit there and talk talk talk that it's the boy's fault.

Pop got up, and walked around and around, and he said it isn't the boy's fault, but it isn't the man's either, and then he stood up, and said I'm not going to do anything about it, what with the boy between us, and the job ruined, and everything Goddamn else, I might be one of them myself, maybe next year, and then pop stood up and walked off down the road only farther out of town, not the way the old man was. I could see that pop's shoulders were screwed up around his neck, and then I was happy, because all I could think of was that I'd seen two big men cry that day, and maybe that meant I was getting bigger too, and that was an awful good feeling.

June, 1941

BORIS PASTERNAK

(1890–1960)

In 1943 the Advocate *published a special Russian Authors issue which presented in translation the works of a number of Russian writers who were not well known in this country. Pasternak at that time was one of Russia's leading poets, but after the war, he writes, "I began to feel ashamed of my own reputation and decided I must justify it." The result was* Doctor Zhivago, *a novel that won the Nobel Prize for literature in 1958. The Soviet government, however, refused to let the novel be published in Russia, forced him to refuse the prize, and expelled him from the Writers' Union. "But what wicked thing have I done," Pasternak wrote,*

> *"I, the murderer, the villain?*
> *I made the whole world weep*
> *Over my beautiful land."*

ROOSTERS

Nightlong the water labored without end.
Till morning came, rain burned her linseed oil.
Now from beneath the lilac lid the steam
Pours forth: earth steams like *shchee* when on the boil.

And when the grass, shaking itself, leaps up,
Then who will tell the dew how scared I am—
That hour when the first cock starts to yawp,
And then one more, and then—the lot of them?

They name the years as these roll by in turn,
And on each darkness as it goes, they call,
Foretelling thus the change that is to come
To rain, to earth, to love—to each and all.

Translated by Babette Deutsch

Summer, 1943

THE LAST TWO DECADES:
1947–1966

RICHARD WILBUR

(1921–   )

As an undergraduate at Amherst, Richard Wilbur was editor of the college newspaper and looked forward to a career in journalism. Poetry did not become his major interest until the war. "One does not use poetry for its major purpose, as a means of organizing oneself and the world, until one's world somehow gets out of hand," he wrote. Wilbur was a junior fellow of the Harvard Society of Fellows from 1947–50. His third book of poems, Things of this World, *won the Pulitzer Prize and the National Book Award in 1957. Since then he has published another collection of poems and verse translations of Moliere's* Tartuffe *and* The Misanthrope *which have been said to be better than the originals. He now teaches English at Wesleyan University.*

THE PURITANS

Sidling upon the river, the white boat
Has volleyed with its cannon all the morning,
Shaken the shore towns like a Judgment warning,
Telling the palsied water its demand
That the crime come to the top again, and float,
That the sunk murder rise to the light and land.

Blam. In the noon's perfected brilliance burn
Brief blooms of flame, which soil away in smoke;
And down below, where slowed concussion broke
The umber stroll of waters, water-dust
Dreamily powders up, and serves to turn
The river surface to a cloudy rust.

Down from the bridge the river captain cries
To fire again. They make the cannon sound;
But none of them would wish the murder found,
Nor wish in other manner to atone
Than booming at their midnight crime, which lies
Rotting the river, weighted with a stone.

February, 1949

OBJECTS

Meridians are a net
Which catches nothing; that sea-scampering bird
The gull, though shores lapse every side from sight, can yet
Sense him to land, but Hanno had not heard

Hesperidean song,
Had he not gone by watchful periploi:
Chalk rocks, and isles like beasts, and mountain stains along
The water-hem, calmed him at last near-by

The clear high hidden chant
Blown from the spellbound coast, where under drifts
Of sunlight, under plated leaves, they guard the plant
By praising it. Among the wedding gifts

266   *Richard Wilbur*

Of Here, were a set
Of golden McIntoshes, from the Greek
Imagination. Guard and gild what's common, and forget
Uses and prices and names; have objects speak.

There's classic and there's quaint
And then there is that devout intransitive eye
Of Pieter de Hooch: see feinting from his plot of paint
The trench of light on boards, the much-mended dry

Courtyard wall of brick,
And sun submerged in beer, and streaming in glasses,
The weave of a sleeve, the careful and undulant tile. A quick
Change of the eye and all this calmly passes

Into a day, into magic.
For is there any end to true textures, to true
Integuments; do they ever desist from tacit, tragic
Fading away? Oh maculate, cracked, askew,

Gay-pocked and potsherd world
I voyage, where in every tangible tree
I see afloat among the leaves, all calm and curled,
The Cheshire smile which sets me fearfully free.

April, 1947

KENNETH KOCH

Class of 1948, (1925–   )

Kenneth Koch came to Harvard in 1946 after three years in the army. He, John Ashberry, and Frank O'Hara were at Harvard together and influenced each other's poetry tremendously. He spent three years in France and Italy but has since returned to New York. His best known book is KO, or a Season on Earth *(1959).*

ENTR'ACTE FOR A FREAK SHOW

THE MAN WITH THE IRON MOUTH: See how
    the light bulb powders on my tongue:
Miraculous.

THE HUMAN FROG: No more than a mockery,
A trade you learned, as useless as a lung
Without a body. Rather gaze on me:
My shrunken body utterly depends
Nor on a trade, but birth; this should delight
By making nightmare solid for you, friends,
So that undressing in your home tonight,
Your undeniable symmetry will mean
The terror was unreal that made you cry:
For you are you and with your eyes have seen
The trusted proof that figures do not lie.
I am a thing of God.

THE MAN WITH THE IRON MOUTH: My vulgar friend
Disdains me for my intellect, but this
Alone can set you free: That I defend
Absurd perfection, happily dismiss
All other kinds of action, must console
All you good people gathered in this place
Who feel your hands go empty and your whole
Body tremble, suddenly meet the face
Of your own childhood, when sleep will not bring
Its usual peace, reminding you of love
And what you have not been; remembering
My serious diet of glass, you can remove
My vision with a smile, sane and sincere,
Clenching your fists.

THE HUMAN FROG: You speak of things that seem.

THE BEARDED LADY: Gentlemen, you both lie.
    Confess me here
The twice tormented mirror of your dream.

June, 1947

JOHN HAWKES, JR.

Class of 1949, (1925–   )

John Hawkes' Harvard career was interrupted by the Second World War, during which he served as an ambulance driver in France and Germany. When he returned to Harvard, he took the writing course offered by Albert Guerard and wrote his first novel, The Cannibal. *His most recent novels are* The Lime Twig *(1961) and* The Second Skin *(1963). Hawkes teaches English at Brown University.*

LITTLE BEATRICE

> *Your misery does not touch me;*
> *Nor the flame of this burning*
> *Assail me.*
>
> DANTE

Straight the hair, dull the little girl;
I see her hiding from the crowd, a squirrel,
Clutching to her chest the half filled bag,
Her eyes the staring chestnuts of a vender
Mad with the cold, an old Venetian faker.
She will never ride the dark gondolas.
She stops to mimic a song that she once heard,
And darts at a passing woman with a word.

Her father, a ringed gipsy, rakes the coals;
Holding his coat he curls round the fire,

Puts the folded paper inside his shoes
And hears the tambourine under the trees.
He knows her coming by the slamming door
And confident that she will watch the stove,
He retreats within the olive grove;
Mounting the stairs she contrives to be a queen
And drops her cloak, a gesture against the heat;
Then picks it up, remembering the street
Where frozen Caesars and Giuseppes meet.

Spring, 1947

John Hawkes, Jr. 271

ROBERT BLY

Class of 1950, (1926–   )

*After graduating from Harvard, Robert Bly spent
a year in Norway on a Fulbright fellowship before returning to his native Minnesota. He is editor of the literary magazine* The Sixties, *and
translator of Spanish and Scandinavian poetry.
He has published a collection of his poems,*
Silence in the Snowy Fields.

THE PURITAN ON HIS HONEYMOON

Travelling south, leaves overflow the farms.
Day by day we watched the leaves increase
And the trees lie tangled in each other's arms.
Still generation, and calls that never cease
And rustlings in the brush; yesterday
She asked how long we have been on the way.
So in the afternoon we changed our route
And came down to the coast; everywhere
The same: fish, and the lobster's sensual eyes.
The natives sang for harvest, gave us fruit,
At night the monkeys sat beneath the trees.
All night the cries of dancers filled the air,
And last year's virgins pressed into the leaves.
Sometimes I think of your land, cold and fresh,
And try to think: what was the month we quit
Your northern land that seemed inhabited
By more than reproduction of the flesh?
I saw here while the branches interknit
The monkeys gibbering by our bridal bed.

March, 1949

STEPHEN SPENDER

(1909–   )

Stephen Spender was the leader of a group of poets, including W. H. Auden and C. Day Lewis, who revolted against the poetic theory and practice of T. S. Eliot and created the new poetry of the thirties, using the objects and terminology of an industrial society. The following article was originally an address given at the "Defense of Poetry" conference held at Harvard in 1950. Spender published his Collected Poems *in 1954 and is editor of* Encounter *magazine.*

MODERN POETRY AND SCIENCE

—address by Stephen Spender delivered at the conference on The Defense of Poetry at Harvard College on the evening of August 14, 1950.

A FEW weeks ago, I discovered that Mr. Elliott had allotted to me the subject of Modern Poetry and Science by way of approaching the wider subject of Poetry and the Public. Knowing nothing of science, I wrote protesting. But meanwhile his suggestion had got me thinking. And so now I will approach tonight's discussion with some reflections on the reactions of poets to a scientific age.

It strikes me at once that most poets know little or nothing about science; and it strikes me also that in a very important sense scientists know little or nothing about it either. I can illustrate this by an anecdote.

A few weeks ago Professor Huxley invited me to a dinner in London of the Royal Society. He explained to me that by a long-established rule, after the dinner, the President, or Chairman would ask whether any of those present had any matter of scientific interest to communicate to his fellow members. He added, though, that these communications were always of a general, and often of a facetious, nature, for the good reason that if any member of the Royal Society spoke of his own subject, not more than two of his audience of fellow scientists would be able to understand him. Science, a hundred years ago, was expected to provide explanations of man's situation in the Universe by processes of reasoning which were ultimately convertible into popular myths, such as the theory of evolution. However, today it tends to become explorations of specialized fields of research which although they may have an enormous effect on all of our lives, cannot be explained to the general public without risk of gross distortion. I do not think that a modern poet—unless he were a very stupid one—would set out to write a poem discussing Einstein's Theory of Relativity, or the Quantum Theory, with the same confidence as Tennyson set out to discuss evolution in In Memoriam.

Tennyson's poem should remind us that nineteenth century Victorian poetry was more modern in its aims than critics seem prepared to recognize today. Poets like Tennyson, Arnold, and later on, Thomas Hardy, wrote poems in which they tried to give expression to the scientific thought of their time. Yet perhaps the attempt to express ideas such as those in "Locksley Hall," "In Memoriam," and "The Dynasts," was mistaken. Mistaken, because it was an attempt to humanize the detached, skeptical, rationalistic, completely objective attitude towards life of a science which insisted on measuring everything from the outside. And the inside life of the passionate, sensual, subjective individual could not be projected upon the impersonal universe described by scientists without an effect of weakness, as of trying to measure one life against the cold indifference of interstellar space.

When we say that the Victorians were not modern we do them an injustice if we mean that they did not interest themselves in the modern situation of living in a world dominated by science. Yet the twentieth century poet has rejected their attempts to make poetic philosophy out of scientific facts and theories. Possibly this rejection is not final. One may even hazard the guess that we are at a turning point where men will have to invent a myth of science as a benevolent activity within human affairs, because an impersonal science willing to destroy cities or to save the lives of the victims of cancer with the same impartiality, is becoming intolerable to us. In a new society, where guided scientific research fulfills a moral role, there will be new Shelleys who endeavor to use poetry as a vehicle for imagining that which we know.

Meanwhile, contemporary poetry shows less attempt to grapple with scientific theory than poetry did some hundred years ago. Today the influence of science on poetry is perhaps to be found elsewhere. It is to be found not in some attempt to state theories such as that of Relativity in long poems, but in a use of image and metaphor which owes something to the laboratory, and which aims at the precision of scientific thought. The image of the nerves projected from a slide upon a screen, or of the evening "like a patient etherized upon a table," are to be found in Eliot. And there are many such examples in Empson, and especially in Auden. At the age of twenty, Auden as an undergraduate, already introduced into his poems lines like

And if though we
Have ligatured the ends of a farewell.

Note, though, that the use of the scientific image is ironically to reject the scientific view of life. For nothing could surely be less scientific than T. S. Eliot's view of the evening with stars millions of light miles away, as a patient etherized upon a table. In fact, the Victorians tried to express scientific ideas in the vocabulary of romantic diction; the moderns use a vocabulary of scientific precision to reject the ideas of scientists.

So the nineteenth century poets tried to annex science into romantic diction; the modern poets write in a crystallized, concentrated, dense or explosive style which seeks to compete with the intensity of scientific statement. It is as though poets felt the need to use poetry as a means of concentrating nuclei of the forces of an interior life, as powerful as the concentration of external forces by scientists.

This brings me to the place where the subject of Modern Poetry and Science links up with the wider one of Modern Poetry and the Modern World. For the modern world is quite obviously affected in all its aspects by science. The example of this which shook the nineteenth century was the famous challenge of scientific method to the complacent assumptions of legend and history on which religion had rested for many hundreds of years. Although the wider quarrel between religion and science may be based on a misunderstanding, this misunderstanding has never been fully cleared up, and it certainly undermines our religious life. Another effect of science is the deluging of life with inventions, machinery, and ideas, all of them of a compelling kind, which yet supersede one another so rapidly that it is difficult or impossible even to make them symbols of the forces of command over nature which they represent, far less to attach any lasting esthetic or moral significance to them. One can admire the aim of Rupert Brooke in writing about the "clean beauty of a great machine," but it is impossible to read these lines without reflecting that the machine in the mind of Rupert Brooke would probably look very shoddy and even dirty to us today. And yet, these symbols of machinery and inventions do play an extremely important role in our minds, even in our dreams. They represent forces which the artist and the poet should make significant unless they are to terrify us with the sense of an overwhelming emptiness. So the poet is confronted with the alternative of clinging to old symbols which retain their force because they have been used and fixed in past literature, and which remain permanent precisely because they are dead, and therefore outside the race of scientific phenomena; or of trying to chase after the images of industrial civilization, which shift their significance as they change their physical appearance in the real world, quite apart from the fact that these machines which surround us are the masks of a profoundly ambiguous and ambivalent scientific purpose.

Science has provided men with the means whereby our whole civilization exists under the threat of complete destruction. It has divided the mind of everyone into two irreconcilable pictures of a future—one, a future of utter destruction, or the other, a future of unparalleled prosperity. Whether or not we are destroyed, this vision of the future forced on us by science, already means that what has always been the essential condition for creating poetry—the assurance of a continuity in civilization which means that the poet communicates not only with his contemporaries but also with the future—that certainty is lost.

All these conditions which I have stated are commonplace. It is no longer necessary to underline them. I would like, though, to try to define one contemporary situation to which all the diverse aims of modern poets are related, one challenge which they are bound to meet.

The special modern situation which all modern poetry endeavours to meet, is this: that today our experiences through the senses of our bodies of any one place or relationship or dream, which we can, through the force of that experience make into that meeting place of interior life with the external world, which is the poem; this experience and active creation is threatened by our awareness of outside forces which make it impotent and ineffective. In a world where some event which takes place in Tokyo can immediately—within a matter of minutes—affect the quality of living in London or, for that matter, in Iowa City,—there is no fixity of personal experience which is not threatened by wider events outside our experiencing of them.

In the past, the main theme of poetry was the struggle of one time—which was the little point of the poet's identification of his inner life with his experience of external reality—with the whole of time. The theme finds its ideal expression in those lines from Shakespeare's sonnet where it is expressed most directly, or in Marvell's—

> But at my back I always hear
> Time's winged chariot hurrying near.

We have a peculiar feeling when we read such lines that we are in the presence of the absolute theme of poetry. Poetry is not descriptions of scenery or records of the experience of love. It is an assertion by the poet of the discovery within some particular experience of a principle which extends beyond the experience itself; and this discovery is of the activating principle of pure creativeness: that within the particular experience is discovered the power to create the poem, to assert that within the landscape or the love an image can be wrested that will defy the inroads of time. Creativeness is our capacity to confront our passive realization of the nature of an experience with a positive affirmation of life. By a completely free act the positive pattern of our imagination is imposed upon the received pattern of our experience.

However, for this condition of a time-defying creative principle to be asserted, the context of time-destructiveness has to be stated. The images of Laura and Beatrice survive precisely because within language they are set in the stream of those forces which destroy the real image. The power of thought to overcome corrupting physical processes, when the conflict between idea and reality is set within language which vividly creates both idea and reality, is demonstrated. So the aim of past poetry was to discover within certain experiences those images which could be rescued from time. But in our day it is not just the identity of one time within all time which is threatened with corruption. But the identity of one place within other places also threatens to disappear, because at any one place of our experience we are conscious of the threatening contingency of other places which are outside the range of the experience of a place which we have made our own. To some extent, all this means that there has been a great acceleration of events. The objects on which the imagination seizes are apt, in the world of scientific progress, to be transformed too quickly for the imagination to be able to grasp significantly their worth. But also I mean more than this: I mean that in the very moment of our inwardly experiencing them, experiences are undermined by outward events. The consciousness of this undermines the identity of our experiences and even robs us of our own personalities.

However, the achievement of poetry is to overcome a difficulty by stating it. To make, as I have said, the image of Laura or Beatrice immortal by creating it within the context of those forces which corrupt the real image. And this brings me to what I most wanted to say: that what is healthy and good in contemporary poetry is the endeavour to state the situation whereby the sense of place in the modern world is dissolved by the awareness of the disturbing contingency of other places outside the poet's personal experiencing of that one place. Modern poetry consists of many endeavours to find the situation in which the poet can assert the creative principle within a complete awareness of the forces threatening his sense of place.

To trace the history of the various movements in modern poetry is to trace the varying aspects of a single endeavour. What could be more significant, for example, than the effort of several poets at the beginning of this century to attach the poem entirely to the creation of a single image, or to some symbol which seemed to have no relationship to a system of values outside the poem itself? The significance of images and symbolism is that to these poets the only certainty of place consisted in some form or shape which could be created within language itself—in which language had abandoned, as it were, all its claims on the world of actuality and had made a kind of bridgehead out of the experience which exists in poetry itself—pure poetry, in a word. But the limit to which language itself can become an object of experience was soon explored, and then we find the poets trying to re-establish their connection with life—and using for this purpose the remnants of Christian tradition which still remain intact, or exploiting the forces of the individual unconscious, discovered by Freud and his followers, in the hope that within the individual himself there is a vast interior world which can be maintained against the imposing phenomena of the external world dominated by science. Always there is the same research for the dynamic of an interior life attached to personal experiences which can resist the inflow of the external forces of the scientific age. Viewing poetry within the light of this one situation, I would say that the poems of a writer like Robert Frost, are not nearly so far from those, say, of the Surrealists as might appear. For Frost, in his insistence on that which is most threatened—the sense of external nature which a man can make part of his own soul—is aware always of the threat. His poetry is an affirmation which realizes the forces of negation, and it therefore confronts the same problem as those who seek an answer to negation in the subconscious personality.

It seems to me that our history should make us humble. We are living in a world in which science, despite its great constructive achievements, appears unfortunately above all as a destructive force. The question which will be answered in the next few years is whether this force can be switched to constructive purposes or whether it will destroy us. Whichever happens, there will be a transformation of the world we know. Constructive science means world unity. Destructive science means the collapse of our civilization into many fragments. When one reads contemporary critics one has the impression that all the literary movements in which we live seem very complicated. But they will appear all too horribly simple within thirty years from now, as simple, perhaps, as the 1880's appear to us today. We are living through a phase, and we are the creatures of a phase.

We have thought our way into this wide and complex chaos, which is contemporary civilization, and the formidable machines capable of destroying us all with which we are confronted are products of our own thinking, projections of our own imaginations, a reflection of the whole sum of contemporary interior lives, emerging from and influenced by the past. In the widest sense, the problem of any contemporary poetry is that the shape of the life of the world at that time is the projection of the thoughts and images in the minds of the men and women of that time: and that the only means of conquering that disorder of the mind and the imagination which is a contemporary society, is with an order of thought and imagination towards the achieving of which poetry can make its particular contribution. But order can only be achieved if the challenge of the real disorder is fully realised within the imagining of the new order. Poems which do not meet the challenge of the context of their time are as stupid as ideal political systems which might make us all happier, were they not completely impracticable. A poem, insofar as it states a situation and meets that situation, does offer a real solution, that is to say a creative affirmation confronting destructive events, to the public of that time. And in the large, poetry offers a pattern of order of the imagination within chaos which at least proves that the lights of civilization are preeminently kept burning in cities of the mind. At least, the poets and their public are inhabitants of a civilized city which, as long as they maintain it, cannot be destroyed.

September, 1950

JOHN CIARDI

(1916–   )

Poet, editor, translator, and popular lecturer, John Ciardi has moved through most circles of the literary world since graduating from Tufts in 1938. He has published nine volumes of poetry in addition to verse translations of Dante's Inferno *and* Purgatorio. *He taught at Harvard for several years, later at Rutgers, and is now poetry editor of the* Saturday Review of Literature.

MIDNIGHT ON A SIDE STREET

NEW YORK

I

Into the midnight of the licorice streets
An invisible rain sifts down, drifts down
From a pink and orchid sky.

Stains of neon drip and elongate
From the Spectacular-and-Marqueed center
To every rim of dark.

There are veins of mineral light running wet stone
And a fluorescence in the eye. The world's crystals glow
Their image in a stone pool.

Is every rain a memory? I close a door
Between going and coming, and walk the multiplied
World of these reflections.

Dwarf dragons coil their mineral colored scales
On the oily pavement. There are millions of dragons
Deepening the stones I walk.

II

The recurrence of dragons in the invisible rain
Is true and absolute. I walk, rather,
The losses of the dragon-perceiving eye.

These works of light lengthening endlessly
Through veins of wet stone
To the moment of the eye—

These dragons from a fantasy beyond
The white bones of its dreamers
In the blue downfall of time—

I am again and must be, mourns the walker
To his vision. I fix the permanence of dragons
In the wet stone of the eye.

But is it enough to invent these permanencies
In the eye pierced by its vision? Do I perceive
Or is it the vision that perceives me?

And what have I to do with permanencies
In the stone world, in the invisible rain?
The eye is no stone, but an egg:

It hatches this dazzle of dragons and shatters
In the act of its own multiplication,
Mourns the walker.

Heigh-ho then sweetest ego, and since eggshells
Must do for souls, let me enclose all dragons
And form the light that forms my presences
In the stone world, in the invisible rain.

September, 1950

ADRIENNE RICH

Radcliffe 1951, (1929–   )

Adrienne Rich's first volume of poetry, A Change
of World, *appeared in the Yale Younger Poets
Series while she was a senior at Radcliffe. She has
since published* The Diamond Cutters *(1955) and*
Snapshots of a Daughter-in-Law *(1963). She lives
in Cambridge with her husband and three sons.*

THE HOUSE AT THE CASCADES

All changed now through neglect. The steps dismantled
By infantries of ants, by roots and storms,
The pillars tugged by vines, the porte-cochère
A passageway for winds, the solemn porches
Warped into caricatures.
                              We came at evening
After the rain, when every drunken leaf
Was straining, swelling in a riot of green.
Only the house was dying in all that life,
As if a triumph of emerald energy
Had fixed its mouth upon the walls and stones.
The tamest shrub remembered anarchy
And joined in appetite with the demagogue weed
That springs where order falls; together there
They stormed the defenseless handiwork of man
Whose empire wars against him when he turns
A moment from the yoke. So, turning back,
He sees his rooftree fall to furious green,
His yard despoiled, and out of innocent noon
The insect-cloud like thunder on the land.

April, 1951

Adrienne Rich 283

NIGHT

The motes that still disturbed her lidded calm
Were these: the tick and whisper of a shade
Against the sill; a cobweb-film that hung
Aslant a corner moulding, too elusive
For any but the gaze of straitened eyes;
The nimbus of the night-lamp, where a moth
Uneasily explored the edge of light
Through hours of fractured darkness. She alone
Knew that the room contained these things; she lay
Hearing the almost imperceptible sound
(As if a live thing shivered behind the curtains)
Watching the thread that frayed in gusts of air
More delicate than her breathing, or by night
Sharing a moth's perplexity at light
Too frail to drive out dark: minutiae
Held in the vise of sense about to die.

December, 1950

DONALD HALL

Class of 1951, (1929–   )

Donald Hall was Pegasus *(literary editor) of the*
Advocate *and editor of the 1950* Harvard Advocate Anthology. *Since then he has brought out
two anthologies of* New English and American
Poets *and a volume of* Contemporary American
Poetry. *He has published several collections of
his own verse, including* Exiles and Marriages
and A Roof of Tiger Lilies. *He is now Professor
of English at the University of Michigan.*

THE WEDDING PARTY

The pock-marked player of the accordian
Empties and fills his squeeze box in the corner,
Kin to the tiny man who pours champagne,
Kin to the caterer. These solemn men
Among the sounds of silk and popping corks
Stand like pillars. Here the white bride
Moves through the crowd as a chaired relic moves.

We are the guest invited yesterday,
Friend to the bride's rejected suitor, come
On sudden visit unexpectedly.
And so we chat, on best behaviour, with
The Uncle, Aunt, and unattractive girl;
And watch the Summer twilight melt away
As thunder gathers head to end the day.
And then at once the pock-marked player grows
To dark magnificence beside the bride

Whose marriage fades, whose Cinderella gown
Becomes a smock to peel potatoes in.
And in the storm that hurls upon the room
She sees in a burst of lightning, clear, immense,
His box that empties, fills, empties, fills.

December, 1949

A FACE IN THE MIRROR

This billowing fish, my silver twin,
Swims in his bright aquarium,
And gay delirium
Spins on my nose, and flutters at my chin.

I built this fish. From silly air,
From coloured light and bits of sound,
I fleshed him out to round
The crazy circle to a perfect sphere.

Damn him to hell. I stare at him,
This serpent of the monstered brain.
If I am to be sane
This fish must swim to me; these lights must dim

That bulge upon my eyes and whine.
This fishy thing is what I think.
I pause upon the brink
Of shaking hands. Oh finny hands are mine!

May, 1951

FREDERICK ENGLISH

Class of 1951, (1929–   )

*Frederick English, a former member of the liter-
ary board of the* Advocate, *now lives in New
York City.*

IN DUST

a section of a novel

THERE was the day betty manter sitting in the seventh grade a big girl
for the seventh grade mrs manter would look at her daughter perhaps
as she brought betty a good night kiss and a glass of water and think
my this girl my daughter is growing big and the darkened bedroom the
street light slipping in and mrs manter good night betty sleep tight
leaves the room knowing for an unrecognized second that somewhere
her life and her childs should have blended in freedom and love but
disinterest and a sense of duty that contorts leaves her hardened and
her emotions go no further than the neighborly thought my she is a big
girl

and betty manter in school   the sunlight with tired fingers touches
her desk with blue sky and saturday afternoons alone with dreams and
voices in light and she sits tired her fingers moving in idle thoughts of
the future over the carved initials of the past thinking almost nothing
but thinking toward the future which in tired dust is now nothing or it
is nothing she says with word thoughts   it is only herself she lets
float like an old log in a sluggish stream to something beyond the
immediate though she knows not what it is and does not care

and the voice of the teacher continues to move with monotonous
rhythm through the sunlit tired afternoon room and betty manter listens

Frederick English   287

as she would listen to the wind in the trees as she sat beneath with her dolls listens to it as something apart as only something that somehow formed a complement to her dreams

elizabeth manter what did I just say

and a child looks up losing in fright thoughts that were not those of a child but which only a child could recognize and cling to miss sprague could not long ago having lost them and sitting at home alone with her parents dreaming not the future but the past and he had asked her to marry him that night and everything that she had worn remembered   the little light brown felt hat the softly mustard colored dress and the shoes he had stepped on while dancing and she had laughed and in the still night with the sound of insects never stopping and allowing silence he had asked her and a strange sick feeling of hunger and parents at home who had saved that she might go to normal school and a year to go and in the quiet black night with no moon and the eternal sound of insects she said no and tried to smile and that night she lay in bed crying choking in her pillow and from that moment her past was to become her dreaming future

what did I just say

and betty manter looking up at miss sprague thinking in sight lines on sidewalks and walking missing cracks and playing with tar warm sticky with the summer sun and miss sprague was old wrinkles but the name was empty in time   and now no time and no space and betty felt alone with miss sprague and not alone   space and time had both vanished like when a kite string breaks she was left alone holding nothing startled a little afraid conscious only of herself and of something lost

come now what have I been saying the voice taut aggressive righteous certain of victory in the sunny still warm room

Im sorry I dont know   and a child asks for forgiveness for the sound of wind in the sunday tree tops and the new dress her mother just bought pink and blue and for air and space but it was all tight tight tight   why dont you know

silence in a throat afraid to speak

and now the solidity between teacher and child cracks a foot moves a desk creaks and betty manter feels eyes and faces crawling over her skin warm and her fingers clench and where does she sit alone with clouds and green and hay smell and only the breathy talk of the alive and colored friends who float peaceful in the sky

why dont you know

and the words stumbling like a marble rolling down stairs   I wasnt listening

rocking on the porch in the evening how the she hated the people who walked by and she wasnt going to stay in that town oh she was going places but her hate was too solid to ever move and after normal school she was still on the porch rocking backwards with every movement still hating

and angered at a life the words tore from her clenched teeth frantically as though awaking from a nightmare she searched with horror compelling haste for the lamp switch   oh not listening   youre too smart to have to listen   why do you come to school   youre so big you can almost get married   I suppose thats what you were thinking of   and what are the pigtails for   a little big for them arent you   maybe you think the boys will pull them   oh I know you elizabeth manter   too good for everyone else   stand up until class is dismissed   you and your pigtails   oh arent you the smart one   and listen when I speak   and she returns to the blackboard and her voice like the chalk dust dry unpleasant seems to pervade the room stale lifeless distasteful

and betty manter stands feeling sick and her legs weak and her childs life seeming to dissolve in sobs choked in her throat her eyes wet and understanding something that had now been torn from her and made something apart from her and cruel she sees only a blurred room that she hates with bitter choking taste and not hearing and not seeing she is like the little child in bed with the night black about her and covering her head and thinking of sun spilling through sound of play in a tomorrow but tomorrow is only a room with a handkerchief clenched in a fist and thought floundered in hate at injustice sensed in her heart

the sunny late september afternoon drowses with voice and silence and the sun warm yellow colors the room and dust floats calmly in its presence

the school bell rings and miss sprague can return to yesterday and the children to tomorrow and she dismisses class with her usual harsh authoritative tone of voice almost as if she is afraid that here too is an order that will go unheeded and betty manter feeling no longer a part of this group of sunny day school room children but rather as something to be looked at with astonished interest as something quite different and quite funny walks as if an automaton moving to nothing that can be seen or known nothing that is or was and trying in emptiness not yet to cry she takes her sweater from the hook in the corridor where the warm weather clothes lightly cover the walls and as she does so the girl who sits opposite her in class jane tomkins lightly touches her arm and says in the voice of a child with sympathy and love who fears yet the words of both   shes an old pill

   get your hands offa me   get away   leave me alone   betty manters voice rising all the time to a crescendo of tears her sweater crumpled in her hand she runs through moving silence blurred and distant like space through a rain covered window and now she runs down the stairs past the other children racing for empty loneliness where she can cry within herself in a hollow distant place as she reaches the door billie fitzgerald whose mother had hoped he would be an altar boy how near an altar boy is to god she would say and then she would pat his head brushing his hair back and somehow realizing herself within him and in her mind a blurred confusion with a golden throne and a man with a beard and her son an angel in the service of the bearded man on the golden throne and infinitely happy and billie fitzgerald whose mother said the rosary for him every night because she had heard stories from the neighbors which she of course did not believe and yet she did not quite disbelieve cries out with the magical sing song power of a child   bessy manter pigtails bessy manter pigtails old miss sprague said youre bad oh you make us awful sad   the voice high pitched with its compelling up and down rhythm   laughter   and the group of boys with him singsay it together   bessy manter pigtails bessy manter pigtails old miss sprague said youre bad oh you make us awful sad

   and betty manter runs running through sound that like waves pounding at rocks moistens every crevice with fury running ageless through open air with the blue sky above her and autumn trees lightly tinged with winter along the sidewalk towards her home but only she is and all else is something that was and not seeing and no longer hearing she runs down the sidewalk ignoring the short cut path towards home of which she does not even think with only hate pounding in her heart and sorrow bitter with youth that has been questioned and home home where she can lie on her bed while the sunlight fills the room with tomorrow and crying and how could she and how could she and hating hating she runs

tears in her throat and her face destroyed with inward weeping and the tears she is in the kitchen of her home and the note on the table at bridge and home for supper for supper for supper and rocks slimy slimy she cant get hold she cant get hold and in her room the pillow cool and all the words of a life repeated repeated and she cries with the torture of youth felt contaminated by age and destroyed and alone and the sunlight is a dream tomorrow cold and moist

her mother comes home and she hadnt won but then cant take games too seriously mrs hopkins who had been her partner could have died when she tried that finesse as she said later to helen tyring   mary manter just doesnt know the signals why the way she plays   but the tea had been nice and they were really lovely cookies that helen had brought oh dear

betty   she calls while she removes her hat so nice of helen to say it was cute   betty   and a child rises from the moist mud and walks an unknown corridor dirty   mother mother   running down the steps and her arms about her mother and the perfume and it is an odor in the stars where   where and weeping

oh darling what is the matter   the voice crawling down a ladder to play with the ants   tell mother all about it

a child sobs words recreating in her heart the sound of man in rebellion within himself and then and then and then words spiraling within her tear filled throat

there there   and the arms are politely removed from the stars why just today helen tyring said how pretty she thought your hair was in braids dont call them pigtails oh and helen liked my hat that you thought was so pretty now go along upstairs and dry your tears and wash your face   and the sun excited sand and the woman fat and why dont you play with my little girl and mother walking down the beach pretty and free and why dont you play with the nice womans little girl and the sand hot and a pretty stone and alone and making love to the stone and the fat woman is a jelly fish and her daughter is a baby and why why why

mrs manter recaptures a lost bridge hand and a child climbs the stairs towards something she does not yet know though has already felt in a miasma the stairway slowly a step at a time with the autumn late day dusky warmth she walks moving like dust rising slowly upward seeming without direction and a point of dust in shady night she walks through the hall through sounds of childhood and days of sickness when her doll that auntie nora had brought who visited every summer and was candy and fun lay beside her in her bed with doctor smell and fear care and glasses of water in the night and sun days of the future and alone and the house sounds footsteps of mother downstairs preparing and no one cares

in the second drawer in the bathroom and the tile with lines that had been distorted to worlds of tomorrow and the chair carried carefully from the bedroom and placed before the medicine chest mirror and no sound and blunt and held cold and cold smooth the wash bowl she sits on the edge her feet on the chair and one braid clutched taut in her hand with the scissors she cuts cutting through the sandy rough rock falling tumbling in the sea and crying and the rising falling and the thick hair shiver sound and blunt and free she flings the hair upon the many lined tile where she had etched in moments a green blue dream and she stops crying the tears frozen in her heart and the other braid she cuts and the hair in the mirror without conscience falls and the wind is in the sky and a doll is in the attic dust

September, 1950

GREGORY CORSO

(1930–   )

*A tough young kid from the lower East Side,
Gregory Corso got his literary education in the
Clinton prison where he spent his 17th through
20th years. After that, he writes, "Went back to
Village, did nothing but get drunk and sleep on
rooftops till 1954 when beautiful now dead Violet
Lang brought me to Harvard where I wrote and
wrote and met lots of wild young brilliant people
who were talking about Hegel and Kierkegaard.
Had* Vestal Lady *published there by contributions from fifty or more students from Radcliffe
and Harvard.* Harvard Advocate *first to publish
me."* *

POEM

In the early morning
     beside the runaway hand-in-pocket
     whistling youth
I see the hopping drooling Desirer
His black legs . . . the corncob pipe and cane
The long greasy coat, and the bloodstained
     fingernails
He is waiting
     flat against the trees

September, 1954

* From *The New American Poetry,* Donald M. Allen, editor.

NATHANIEL LA MAR

Class of 1955, (1933–   )

Nathaniel La Mar studied writing under Archibald MacLeish while at Harvard. His stories were published in the Advocate *and in the* Atlantic Monthly.

CREOLE LOVE SONG

I USED to work for the LaBotte family. That's how I know what I'm going to tell you about Jemmie LaBotte. They lived up on Bayou Street in one of those big pink stucco houses with a wide tile porch and tall windows with fancy, yellow frosty-looking window panes.

Old man LaBotte was a doctor. He was queer in a way. I used to hear some of the white people around town say he was nothing but a "ham-fat" doctor. I never could quite get the straight of it. I do know one thing, though. He didn't go around like the other white doctors in New Orleans did. I mean he never went around to high faluting people like the kind of fine ladies his wife was always playing bridge with. As far as I know he didn't treat anybody but the Creoles down in the Quarter. Some people said it was because Dr. LaBotte was a Creole himself. They said that about Mrs. LaBotte too; but I didn't believe it. He used to come down to the Quarter whenever somebody got hurt on their job or beat up in a fight. He had a smart way about him; he could always get money out of his patients. I know of a lot of people that didn't pay their house-rent or their electric bills, but Dr. LaBotte got money out of them. He had a shiny green car, and whenever he came driving through the Quarter everybody would get in their windows and doorways and start yelling and waving at him; even old people. I'd shout just like the rest of them. "Hey! Hey! There go Doctor. Doctor! Doctor! Hey there, Doctor LaBotte!!"

That's the way we'd go on. Sometimes he'd have his son Jemmie in the car with him. That was before Jemmie went off to medical school. Jemmie was almost grown, but he'd hang out of the car window and laugh when we'd shout.

Doctor LaBotte used to come to see my Aunt Albertine sometimes. My parents went to Chicago when I was little, and they didn't come back. So I lived with Aunt Albertine. She was young and pretty—had a lot of men always hanging around our house after her. She had yellow skin and long brown hair; and she had a fine shape. She used to drink a lot. But the thing about her was that she knew it was bad for her. So she'd make me go out to a pay-station 'phone and call up Dr. LaBotte to come see her. I don't know what he'd do for her because she wasn't really sick. He talked to her; that was about all. But he could get her out of her drinking moods and she'd be all right for a while.

One day in the springtime Dr. LaBotte came to see us when Aunt Albertine was coming out of one of her moods. I was surprised, because he came to talk about me. "Why don't you let Emory come see if he'd like to work for us up at our house, 'Tine? Lightwork—kind of helping around the house——you know. We'd give him his breakfast and lunch and he could get his supper down here with you. He could save, maybe——go back and finish high school in a little bit."

At first Aunt Albertine didn't say anything. Finally she sized me up and said, "He fifteen. Let him do what he want to. *I* don't care. It ain't like he was going far off." She could tell I wanted to go by the way I was looking at her.

So I started working up at the LaBottes'. I think it was March when I started, and Jemmie LaBotte came home from medical school that June. He was a lot like his daddy; he laughed like him, and acted just about like him. He was glad to be back home. Sometimes he'd walk through that big house all day long, smiling in a funny way. Or sometimes in the evening he'd go walking down in the Quarter. People saw him down there; just walking those old, narrow grey-looking streets when it was almost dark.

I guess Dr. LaBotte was glad Jemmie was home. He laughed more than I'd heard him laugh when Jemmie wasn't there. But then he started carrying a funny look on his face. And when he came home in the afternoon he'd go in the little room where his desk was and just sit there with the door open.

Jemmie LaBotte didn't pay me much attention. I'd pass by him in the house and he always looked like he was thinking to himself, or sometimes he'd be talking to his mother and daddy. Sometimes he sat in the living room and read all the morning. I knew they were medical books; most of them were old, and had pages as flimsy as tissue-paper—they were full of fine print. Jemmie LaBotte seemed like a fool to me, reading like that in the summertime. Especially since he was supposed to have just graduated from wherever it was he'd been. One day I asked him, "You remember all you read?"

"Yeah. I sure do." He laughed when he said it; he was a friendly somebody after all. "They make you—in a medical school."

"But you're not going back are you? Your mother says you're a doctor now."

"I want to do what Daddy's doing—doctor up people down there where you live." He looked at me like he wanted me to believe he really meant it. I could see he meant it.

I wondered why Jemmie LaBotte didn't seem to have any friends. Maybe once in a while somebody would call him on the 'phone. Answering the telephone was one of the things I was supposed to do. I'd call him to the 'phone and he'd talk a little while to whoever it was, but he never went anywhere much.

It got so Jemmie and his daddy argued. They'd sit out on the front porch late in the afternoon. I could hear them through the screen door. The old man's voice would be squeaky and high like he was afraid of something. "You sure you want to stay in New Orleans and practice?" He'd say. "You could always go back up there and study another year, if you wanted. You could be a specialist!"

They'd talk a long time, and Jemmie would get worked up and keep telling Dr. LaBotte how much he wanted to be just like him. He wanted to help people down in the Quarter just like the old man did. Jemmie LaBotte was always so serious about everything. He'd beg his daddy like I used to beg Aunt Albertine when I was little and wanted her to give me money to go to the movie or the carnival. I mean it; and he sounded queer when he begged like that. You'd have thought he was as young as I was. It didn't sound right to hear somebody who was supposed to be grown going on that way. "I don't want you to quit, Daddy. I'm not trying to make you *quit*. I just want to go down there with you."

"You don't know how they live—it's hard to get to know. I understand every one of 'em down there." Dr. LaBotte's voice sounded so old. I don't think I'd ever thought he was old before. It was almost pitiful the way he kept trying so hard to get Jemmie's mind off staying in New Orleans; like there was something in New Orleans he was ashamed of. "If you got to be a specialist you could get on at that baby hospital up in Philadelphia—I know you could."

Mrs. LaBotte took Jemmie's side. She must have thought old man LaBotte was jealous of Jemmie's being young and right out of school. Most of the time he wouldn't say anything to her when she started talking, because he knew what she was leading up to. "You know good and well you ought to let Jemmie make some of your calls for you— 'specially those late calls. It'd be better for *him* to go down there in the Quarter at night. I'm always afraid somebody's going to jump in the car or something one of these nights. It's always so bad down there at night." She worried him all the time.

It got so when somebody from the Quarter called up old man LaBotte he'd get his bag and leave the house before Mrs. LaBotte and Jemmie could ask him where he was going. And when he was home he stayed shut up in the little office room. He started acting old and crabbed.

Mrs. LaBotte was the one who finally did it. I know it was her and not Jemmie because every time I heard her and Dr. LaBotte talking he'd be saying, "I'm tired of it, Juanita! I'm tired, and sick of it too!" It was what you'd call clever, the way she'd bring it up all the time about letting Jemmie stay in New Orleans and help him. She did it while they were eating, or when Jemmie was out taking one of his walks, or even when he'd just go out of the room a minute. I never did talk any of the LaBottes' business to anybody, because it didn't make a bit of difference to me what they did, but I did tell Aunt Albertine how bad the old man was looking, and how Mrs. LaBotte wouldn't lay off. Aunt Albertine said, "Well, you just make sure you don't be smelling in something you ain't got no business bothering with."

One morning Dr. LaBotte didn't come out of his bedroom early like he usually did. And Mrs. LaBotte tipped around, because she said he needed rest. That bedroom door didn't even open when the 'phone started ringing. It was an old man called David calling up from a grocery store. I knew who he was because he stayed about two blocks from where me and Aunt Albertine live. The children in the Quarter named him "that li'l man with the great big head." He wanted to tell Dr. LaBotte he had the "choky-feeling" in his chest again, and he couldn't lie down and sleep. So Mrs. LaBotte went in the bedroom. But they didn't start fussing, though. All Dr. LaBotte said was, "Tell Jemmie he can go down there—he wants to go." I think Mrs. LaBotte had worn him down to nothing. His voice sounded so tired, "Let Jemmie go down there—."

I went down to the Quarter with Jemmie LaBotte because I knew where David's house was. It's hard to find a place you're looking for in the Quarter because the house numbers are all faded off. I'm telling you the truth, it felt good riding through the Quarter in old man LaBotte's shiny car, because everybody really *did* look when they saw it was me in there. Jemmie was nervous. He kept laughing and saying, "You know, when I was little, people used to ask me what I wanted to be. As little as I was, I'd always say I wanted to be a doctor. They'd ask me why, and I'd tell them it was because Daddy was a doctor—I thought there wasn't anything else anybody *could* be but a doctor!" He laughed too much, and that childish way he had about him made me think he was foolish.

David's house was like the rest of the houses down there; the weather-boards were old and needed some paint. And it had fancy rusty iron banisters around the front porch, with iron flowers and curls. The room old David was in had the shades down and it was blackdark, except David had a little candle sitting in a piece of saucer on his chiffonier. Jemmie LaBotte didn't know what that little candle was for. He didn't pay it much attention at first; but I knew. You see old folks always burning a candle when they're afraid they're going to die, or afraid somebody in their family is going to die. Sometimes you're supposed to put pepper on the candle because everybody says it'll keep the worms from eating you after you're dead. David was propped up on a pillow. I sat down on a little stool by the door. Jemmie said, "You know good and well you ought to have some air in here, hot as it is." And then he went over to the window to let up the shade.

But old David screwed up his face at Jemmie LaBotte. "I wish you wouldn't be messin wid that window shade, 'cause that air out there got things in it bad for my feelings right here." He hit his chest with his wrinkled-up little hand. I could see he didn't like Jemmie LaBotte.

"Air never did hurt anybody's heart trouble." Jemmie LaBotte pulled up the shade a little.

"Your daddy don't never make me keep no air in there if I don't want none." I think that was the first thing that got Jemmie. And then old David wouldn't let Jemmie touch him with the needle. He held out those skinny old arms like he was scared to death. "Naw! Naw! You ain't going to put that thing in me. I don't want to have that thing sticking in my arm. And your daddy don't never stick me with none, either!"

I felt sorry for Jemmie LaBotte. He stood there like he didn't know what to do. Old David kept on hollering, "Oh Jesus! Oh Jesus! You going to stick me with that *thing*. Your daddy don't never do nothing like that!" Finally Jemmie LaBotte took a good hold on his old arm and jabbed him very quick; and you'd have thought David was having a baby by the way he was taking on. But after that I started feeling good toward Jemmie LaBotte because I liked the way he just went on and stuck the needle in anyhow. And he tried to be nice to old David after he gave him that shot: he told him to be quiet because he was through and ready to go, and he said he hoped he'd rest easier.

But old David wasn't ready for Jemmie LaBotte to go away. "You ain't going to give me nothing like what your daddy give me when he comes?"

"What'd my daddy give you?"

"Some kind of stuff—."

"What stuff does he give you?"

"That stuff what make me sleep a lot. *You know*, Mr. Jemmie LaBotte." He kept smiling a sly, hateful smile. "Your daddy always give me a piece of paper that I can get it with at the drugstore-man's. Your daddy say it's codeine."

"My daddy didn't give you any codeine. Where'd you get that, talking about codeine? Don't you know your heart's too bad for you to be taking anything like that?"

"Well that's what your daddy say it was. Codeine. Make me sleep." He winked at Jemmie LaBotte like he expected him to understand something. "Your daddy give me that stuff instead of all that sticking me with that goddam old needle."

I don't know what made me think I had to say something; because it wasn't any of my business at all. But Jemmie LaBotte had such a funny look on his face all of a sudden I said, "Don't pay attention to old man big-head David. They say he don't never tell the truth about nothing." But Jemmie looked strange. And we went out of the house with David still begging for some of the "sleepy stuff."

Jemmie LaBotte just asked me one thing while we were going back to Bayou Street. "Why'd old David have that little candle? How come he didn't have the electric light on?"

"That's the way a lot of folks do when they're scared of sickness. You smell how that candle was making that stink in there?"

"I'd have made him put it out if I'd known that was what it was."

"A lots of people keep a sick candle," I said. "I bet your daddy never did try to make anybody put out their sick candle. They wouldn't do it anyhow—for him or nobody else." He didn't say anything after that.

The day after we went down to old David's Mrs. LaBotte called me out on the porch and she tried to make me think she just wanted me to sit out there and rock back and forth in the rocker and talk to keep her company. But she kept on trying to get it out of me about what happened when we went down to the Quarter.

I didn't tell her a thing, though. It wasn't my business. But I did tell Aunt Albertine how Mrs. LaBotte tried to pick me and Aunt Albertine said, "You better be careful—that's all *I* can say." She'd seen old man David that day at the grocery up on Ogechee Street and he was telling everybody Jemmie LaBotte was a good-for-nothing doctor; and then he'd roll up his sleeve and show the little place the needle made. Aunt Albertine said he was clowning and telling everybody Jemmie LaBotte was nothing but "ca-ca."

About a week went by and old man LaBotte didn't seem to be getting better of whatever was wrong with him; at least he didn't come out of his room. And Mrs. LaBotte kept saying all he needed was rest and for people to let him alone and not worry him. There was something wrong between him and Jemmie ever since the day Jemmie went down to David's. But as far as I know Jemmie hadn't even seen him since then; so I didn't understand what it could be. Then one Sunday morning early a lady named Mrs. Clara called up the house to ask for Dr. LaBotte because her little girl was having a fit. It was so early in the morning Jemmie and Mrs. LaBotte didn't even bother about telling Dr. LaBotte. Mrs. LaBotte said she knew he wouldn't care if Jemmie went.

Jemmie LaBotte took me with him again, and we went driving fast through those grey little snaky-looking streets in the Quarter. We saw a lot of people walking the sidewalks; and some of them were still drunk from Saturday night. When we got to Mrs. Clara's house she was out in a funny kind of silk dress washing the steps to her front porch with a jar full of pepper-water. She was real fat and she had her behind turned up to us because she was down on her knees scrubbing the steps; and at first it looked funny. But she turned around and it was pitiful because her big fat face was screwed up and she was crying. The pepper-water had the front steps smelling loud like grease and vinegar. So Jemmie LaBotte asked her what that stuff was and why she wasn't in the house with her little girl. Mrs. Clara said, "I ain't in there 'cause I got to wash with this old pepper-water. Keeps off bad things from coming in the house—keep 'um way from my baby." Jemmie LaBotte told her she had no business believing in such things and he made her put down the jar with the pepper-water in it. But she kept on saying, "Your own daddy—your flesh-and-blood daddy—your daddy—he say it's fine if I want to wash off them front steps with my pepper-water!"

I sat on the porch while Jemmie LaBotte was inside. I'd seen that little girl lots of times with Mrs. Clara when they'd be walking up Ogechee Street. Her name was Monica and she was about eight years old, and she was pretty because she had a round face with a funny kind of purple eyes and light, hay-colored hair. But you could tell something was wrong with her because she walked so slow and funny, and held her head like her neck was made out of rubber.

When Mrs. Clara came to the screen door with Jemmie LaBotte she was saying, "Ain't you going to give her none of them pink pills what makes her sleep? Your daddy say them be good for her—they make her lay real quiet so she don't have no more of them fits. She don't roll her eyes or nothing if she have them pink pills."

Jemmie LaBotte kept looking at the little thing around Mrs. Clara's neck. It was hanging on a greasy string. I don't think he knew what it was, but I did, because my Aunt Albertine always has one so she'll be sure to have good luck. It was a little ball of hair; only this was a little ball of hay-colored hair. Mrs. Clara and Jemmie LaBotte were both acting all upset.

"I'm not going to give her anything to make her sleep, because it wouldn't be good for her. She had a *fit!* It's not good for her to go to sleep on medicine, I don't care *what* my daddy told you." So we left, and Mrs. Clara stood on her front porch; and she was crying and sprinkling pepper-water because she said Jemmie LaBotte must be evil and she didn't even want the smell of him around her house.

"You ain't no good kind of a man like *Doctor*," was the last thing we heard her say.

Then Jemmie LaBotte told his mother. They sat in the living room on that big settee and he told her how old David asked him for codeine and said Dr. LaBotte always gave it to him. And he told her how he didn't want to believe a thing like that on his daddy; but he told her what happened with Mrs. Clara. "That little girl's name is Monica, and the whites of her eyes are all dulled over. Like she's been asleep a *long* time! She had a lot of codeine—I can tell she has."

Once Mrs. LaBotte looked up and saw me standing in the doorway, but she turned her head away. Dr. LaBotte came in the living room; I don't know whether he heard them or what. But Jemmie didn't act like he was there. "I thought my daddy was something." He said it just like the old man wasn't there at all.

And Dr. Labotte said, "They do magic down there, Juanita!" When he called her name Mrs. LaBotte put her little handkerchief up to her mouth. She made a little choking noise. Dr. LaBotte kept blaring his eyes; I thought he was going to go crazy. "Real magic," he said, "they wouldn't stop that voodoo down there for anything. They wouldn't even stop it for *me*."

"You've got them so all they want is codeine. You think codeine can do an epileptic fit any good, Daddy?"

"I told you—you don't know how they are. You think they'll take medicine, don't you?"

"You're bad as they are. You put them all to sleep. You can put them to sleep, all right!"

Dr. LaBotte said, "They love me. You get so you'll do anything for them if you can just get 'em to love you." And then he went out of the living room and left Mrs. LaBotte and Jemmie still sitting there on the settee. He walked away slow, like he was so old.

From then on some strange things started going on. Jemmie LaBotte swore he was going to be what his daddy never was. He could hardly wait until some more of the old man's patients called up so he could go back down to the Quarter. He kept saying he knew he could make them like him down there, if he could just get them to let him do them some good. It got so the main thing for Jemmie Labotte was his big idea about how he was going to do them some good and make them like him. You should've heard the way he kept talking to his mother about it.

But Jemmie LaBotte didn't know the word had got around about him. It just takes one mouth to spread things in the Quarter, and David and Mrs. Clara ran their mouths a plenty. Everybody down there was whispering old man LaBotte was sick and going to die and his boy didn't know a thing to do for him or anybody. His boy wasn't nothing but "ca-ca," and a good-for-nothing. That's what they said about Jemmie LaBotte. David told everybody he could feel funny things crawing in his arm where Jemmie La Botte stuck him with that needle. And Mrs. Clara said her Monica was bloody-eyed and always screaming with fits, because Jemmie LaBotte didn't give her sleepy-stuff to quiet her down.

Then one day Jemmie LaBotte got tired of waiting. He must've known what was wrong by that time. So he went down to the Quarter. That evening when I got home Aunt Albertine told me, "Jemmie LaBotte come driving down here today. Folks say he was trying to see old David and when David found out who it was he locked up his door on him. Yeah—I hear he was even begging old man David to let him talk to him."

"Begging him do any good?"

"Didn't do a bit of good!" Aunt Albertine laughed about Jemmie LaBotte because she was just like the rest of them; she didn't think he was anything.

But I give him credit. He tried hard in the Quarter. He tried to get David and Mrs. Clara to believe he wanted to do them some good. But David would always lock his door, and Mrs. Clara wouldn't even let him come up on her front porch. It got so bad people would sit in their windows and laugh whenever they'd see him coming. But he kept on going down there.

Then one day Jemmie LaBotte did get a 'phone call. It was August then, and that day was rainy. All over the house was quiet like somebody was dead or going to die. And it was so hot all the windows and doors were open and you could hear rain hitting the gardenia bushes out in the front yard. Whoever it was calling sounded like they were crying. All they said was for somebody to come down to Mama Callie's house quick. So he went down there by himself. I could see he wasn't thinking about taking me down there with him that day. But I wouldn't have gone anyhow, because I didn't like that old Mama Callie.

When I was little I used to go over to her house with Aunt Albertine. Aunt Albertine never has stopped going to Mama Callie's because Mama Callie knew her when she was just knee-high. In the first place I didn't like Mama Callie because she was always coughing. Everybody knew she had T.B., and she was sleepy-looking and slow-talking because she stayed all doped up on codeine to ease her coughing spells. She must have been about seventy-five years old, and she had a sister named Alena who was somewhere around fifty. She and Alena spent all day making little charms and things; and they sold them around to a lot of people. Like if Mrs. Clara wanted a hair ball out of little Monica's hair she'd cut off a snip of hair and take it to Mama Callie, and Mama Callie would do things like dip it in hot chicken fat and tie it on a string and wrap it up for a week in senna leaves. Then she'd give it back to Mrs. Clara when it was ready to do some good. Sometimes on a hot day you'd walk past their house and you'd see Mama Callie and Alena sitting in the open window and Mamma Callie would always be singing something in French. She said that song was a Creole song her father taught her when she was a little girl. They say she was real proud of that, because her and Alena's father was a Frenchman. Anyway, whenever she and Alena sat in the window Mama Callie would hold her old sleepy-looking face out the window to see who was walking up and down the street. Alena, who liked men, would be just sitting there beside Mama Callie brushing her hair. She had long hair that came all down her shoulders, and she always brushed it with a brush soaked in strong tea to keep it from getting grey.

When Jemmie LaBotte came back from Mama Callie's he looked discouraged, and he didn't say a thing.

But that evening Alena was going around telling everybody in the Quarter about how when Jemmie LaBotte got to Mama Callie she'd had a hemorrhage and blood was coming out of her nose and mouth all over the bed-sheets. Alena said, "He come bringing his fancy bag with them bottles in it. He thought he was going to give Callie one of them needles of his, but me and Callie wouldn't even let him get near the bed. I told him he wasn't going to touch my Callie!" Alena was bragging about how she told Jemmie LaBotte right to his face they'd just called him so he could give Mama Callie some codeine. But he wouldn't give her any, and he started telling Alena how much Mama Callie needed a hospital, or at least some medicine. Alena laughed, "That Jemmie LaBotte wanted to pay me money to let him stick Callie with one of them shiny needles—even much wanted to pay me *money!* Callie and me told him if he couldn't put her to sleep there wasn't *nothing* he could do. We fixed him. Callie, bad off as she was, she couldn't help but laugh at him. We fixed him all right!" Alena said she warmed up some pig oil with mustard seeds and went to work on Mama Callie and started rubbing her all over with it right there in front of Jemmie LaBotte. "He was just standing there looking. And he looked like he couldn't take his eyes off. He couldn't even stop looking for nothing. Like a young'un watching his daddy in the bed with his ma." Everybody laughed at Alena's saying that. "I could see he didn't like it for nothing, but there wasn't a thing he could do about me rubbing up Callie with that hog grease. Callie was warm, and shiny as she could be when I got through with her. He just stood up there like he had that hog grease on his brain—stood there just looking 'cause that's all he could do—look."

You could tell Alena liked to talk about it. Everybody she told it to sure did listen. I know it must have made Jemmie LaBotte feel beat down for Mama Callie not to let him even touch her, because even old man David, bad as he was, let Jemmie give him a shot that first time, anyway.

About a week after all that happened Jemmie LaBotte asked me if I knew Mama Callie and Alena, and I told him yes. Then he started talking about how queer they were. He talked so fast; like he couldn't tell me quick enough. I didn't see why he was acting so worried. "That old Mama Callie—you know what she did? She wouldn't even let me put a stethoscope on her. You ever see all the little baskets in there— in her bedroom? They were all full of leaves!"

I knew the little baskets he was talking about. "Yeah, They're willow leaves."

"You know what she does with them?"

"Naw," I said, "I never did know."

I knew what those willow leaves were for, but I didn't tell him because I didn't see what difference it made to him.

One evening Mama Callie called up again; Jemmie LaBotte didn't seem to want to go down there. But his mother couldn't see why. "You ought to go if they called you, Jemmie," she kept saying. She was so proud of him because she thought he was everything old man LaBotte never *had* been. "You have to go right on down there, even if that old lady won't let you attend to her—she *called* you."

Mama Callie and Alena must have known he'd come, because they told Aunt Albertine and a lot of other people to be on the look-out if they wanted to see the car when it drove up. Mama Callie was feeling weak and puny, but she was sitting in the window singing that little French song, and Alena was sitting beside her brushing her hair with that brush she kept wetting in a bowl of tea. Mama Callie told Aunt Albertine Jemmie LaBotte started worrying her to let him give her some medicine as soon as he got there. The way they talked about it you'd have thought Jemmie LaBotte was like a little dog or something they'd taken some kind of a fancy to. Alena got rid of all her men friends, and even when it made Mama Callie cough and spit up blood she burned a little basket full of dried up willow leaves every day. Alena said, "We burn them leaves 'cause it make him get us on the brain. And pretty soon he be coming right on down here all the time."

Sure enough Jemmie LaBotte did start going down to Mama Callie's. He told Mrs. LaBotte he went down there so he could leave medicines for Mama Callie and try to make her take them. But Mrs. LaBotte noticed how much he was going down there. She even told old man LaBotte. And he used to lie in his bed and call Jemmie. "Jemmie, come tell your daddy what's going on down there at Mama Callie's. Come tell me! How come you're down to Mama Callie's so much, Jemmie?" But Jemmie stopped going in his daddy's room. Even Mrs. LaBotte couldn't make him go in anymore. And that hurt Dr. LaBotte. He began to fall off a lot. You could tell because his hands and his face got so thin. But still he'd lie in his bed and call in that nagging voice, like there was something he knew about Jemmie.

Mama Callie and Alena got so they bragged and said they were going to have Jemmie LaBotte pretty soon. Alena tied up her hair every day in a lot of silk rags because she wanted to look fine when he came. And Mama Callie claimed they could get him down to the Quarter whenever they wanted to. Alena was always telling everybody, "All

I got to do is heat up that hog oil and start rubbing on Callie with it. That Jemmie LaBotte look like his eyes going to pop out. When I do that he look like he don't want to do nothing but just look at me and Callie; and he knows we ain't going to let him touch her. But he just keep on looking. Sometimes he look right pitiful."

I didn't think Jemmie still cared anything about his daddy. He did though. Because when old man LaBotte had that heart attack you could see it did something to Jemmie. They had a lot of fine specialists with Dr. LaBotte, but it didn't do him any good. He lingered, and got weaker every day. They said he was "in coma" so nobody could go in there to see him. Jemmie and Mrs. LaBotte would just sit in that big living room all day long with the shades down; and two or three nurses were always coming and going and walking soft on those big thick rugs. They made me think of white rabbits, the way they were always streaking through the house. I didn't like them because they wouldn't let Jemmie LaBotte even see his daddy, and he wanted to a lot. He kept saying there was something he wanted to tell his daddy.

Alena and Mama Callie told Aunt Albertine Jemmie LaBotte had stopped trying to make Mama Callie take his medicines. They said he came to their house just to see them and they called him sweet-boy-Jemmie. "He just like a baby," Mama Callie was always saying. "He come and just sit there and watch Alena swing them plaits around in the air. Sometime Alena hand him one of them hair-plaits and he hold it and he just laugh. Just like a young'un with a sugar-tit." Alena swore Mama Callie was telling it like it was. "Callie telling the honest-to-God truth! That Jemmie LaBotte done changed a heap." Then they'd both laugh. Mama Callie would laugh so hard she'd start coughing.

It got around that Jemmie LaBotte had started writing prescriptions for Mama Callie to get codeine with. Somebody even said they saw him go in the drugstore to get it for her one day; but I still thought it was just meanness making them all tell lies on him. All that time Dr. LaBotte was sinking. Mrs. LaBotte couldn't understand why Jemmie was staying away more and more. She didn't think it hurt him that his daddy was dying, but she was wrong. He never did mention Dr. LaBotte much, but you could see he cared about the old man, just by some of the other things he'd say. Like one day he told me, "Mama loves this house, but I want to get out of here. I can't stand it anymore."

My Aunt Albertine was there at Mama Callie's one day when Jemmie

LaBotte came to see her. She said Mama Callie had a pretty bad coughing spell and her mouth started running blood, but Jemmie LaBotte didn't do a thing except get down on his knees by Mama Callie's bed. And when she'd stopped coughing Mama Callie took a little ball of hair from under her pillow and gave it to him. Mama Callie told him that little ball had some of her and Alena's hair in it. She gave it to Jemmie LaBotte because he'd kept asking her to give him something to help his daddy in his misery. I'll tell you the truth, I didn't even believe my own flesh-and-blood aunt. For one thing I couldn't *see* Jemmie LaBotte doing all they said. I didn't even believe the willow leaves I'd found meant anything.

In the end I saw for my own self, though. One night. Dr. LaBotte had been real low all that day, and they'd put him under an oxygen tent. And Mrs. LaBotte had been calling up her friends telling them she didn't understand why Jemmie was off down in the Quarter. I think she must have known Dr. LaBotte was going to die. Those nurses finally gave her something that made her go to sleep, so she'd stop carrying on so. Anyway, that night after I'd got off I was walking up Bourbon Street on my way over to the show field to see if the carnival had come; and so I passed by Mama Callie's. Even when I was still way up the street I heard that singing. Mama Callie was singing and she was in the front window. She was singing that little French song, but it went so slow I could tell she was weak; she was so feeble her voice sounded high like a chicken squawking.

> "Donnez tes levres
> Donnez tes mains.
> Ces yeux, ces yeux
> Sont pleins du feu!"

All the lights were on real bright in the room where she was. And she was sitting right up in the window with some kind of a shawl on that had long fringes that kept blowing around her arms. I couldn't help but look in there when I went by, but Mama Callie didn't see me because she had her eyes shut. I told you how the light was on in the room; I could see good. Alena was sitting there a little ways behind Mama Callie. She was in a straight chair and she had silk rags tied all through her hair: red and blue and green and yellow; all kinds of colors. Jemmie

LaBotte must have been down on his knees or almost on his knees anyway, because all I could see was his head. Alena had Jemmie LaBotte's
head, holding it *tight* in her arms. Just as tight as she could. It was so
queer, because it looked like she might have cut off his head from his
body and just was holding nothing but that head in her arms. She had
her eyes closed and he had his closed too. Only in the light I could see
shining streaks on his face like he was crying. He looked pretty: like
a woman. Maybe it was because Mama Callie and Alena were so
wrinkled and ugly, but he looked really pretty; something like a young
girl. His skin was so smooth, and his hair was shiny and very thick; like
purple and black mixed together.

When I got back home that night I told Aunt Albertine how I saw
the three of them. And she said, "I been thinking about it a while. I
don't like all that funny stuff that's going on." She told me she wanted me
to quit working for the LaBottes.

Only next day when I went up there a lot of people were at the house.
Women in fine clothes with feathery hats and little white handkerchiefs.
They were answering the telephone and talking loud all over the house
and wiping their eyes because old man LaBotte had died the night
before. I didn't even get a chance to see Mrs. LaBotte, because a nurse
was keeping her quiet. And everybody was saying Jemmie LaBotte
must be raving-crazy, because he'd gone driving down to the Quarter
the night before, right after the old man died.

*   *   *   *

It seems like it's been longer than two years ago since all that was
going on; but it's been just about that long. I don't know for sure, but
I don't think Jemmie LaBotte even went to his daddy's funeral. I do
know one thing, though; he's never home these days. I see him all the
time; whenever I go up on Bourbon Street. He's always at Mama Callie's
house, and he waves his hand to me when he sees me. Alena still makes
her little hair balls, and everybody says Mama Callie's just hanging by
a thread. She doesn't feel anything, though because most of the time
Jemmie LaBotte keeps her full of codeine. But Jemmie LaBotte doesn't
just only give codeine to Mama Callie. He gives it to a lot of them.

And they've stopped talking mean about Jemmie LaBotte down in
the Quarter now. They stopped all that long ago. Even Mrs. Clara and
old David don't put bad mouth on him anymore. They all think Jemmie

LaBotte is all right these days. I know for a fact he never has to beg to get his money out of anybody, and that goes to prove what I was just saying. You ought to just see the way some of them carry on and call his name when he comes walking down Bourbon Street. Sometimes it's night when he comes, and everybody hangs out of their window and all you can see in the dark is fire from cigarettes. They make a lot of noise, but you can hear that laugh of his above everything else. You can't tell me their carrying on like that doesn't give Jemmie LaBotte a good feeling, after the way everybody used to treat him. You can look at him and see it makes him feel good. The way he smiles, the way his eyes flash when he talks. You can tell he'd do anything in the world for them.

December, 1954

JOHN HOLLANDER

(1929–   )

John Hollander contributed to the Advocate *while he was a junior fellow of the Harvard Society of Fellows. His first book,* A Crackling of Thorns, *was the Yale Younger Poets Selection for 1958. Since then he has published* Movie-Going and Other Poems *and* Visions from the Ramble, *as well as* The Untuning of the Sky, *a study in the poetry of the English Renaissance. Mr. Hollander teaches English at Yale.*

SONGS FROM A PICARESQUE ROMANCE

They tell of how Dick Dongworth *loved vainly his dark and glittering cousin* Roseblush, *and of how, amid many adventures, he sang these songs:*

SUNG TO HIMSELF ON HORSEBACK

I who have affected
Learning and remorse
Never held good manners
Improper out of doors,
Until an old man showed me
All that grace abhors
—The boneyard, of course
To which I'll be elected.

I've always played at knowing
The nature of the weather,
Pitting knowledge and
Despair against each other;
But now they hold dominion
Like kings allied together
    Over wherever
It may or not be snowing.

If I'm undone in London
Who'll love or honor me?
Unless I were to bend and
Demand alms of the sea,
Nor man nor star nor girl's bare arms
Could bear my perfidy;
    My grave would agree
With his bears' arms I've punned on.

The gentler arms of battle
May ring about my head
In celebration that has made
Old cities kneel and wed.
Although imposing Rome was
No virgin, yet she bled,
    And for an aubade,
Morning came with a rattle.

Love's flame is fairly steady,
For love can ill afford
That final bifurcation
That's fired by the sword;
When brands and ashes drop,
Smoke goes up like a bird:
    Raze me, O Lord,
My beard's too long already.

When all the wild red things she's worn
Hang like cousins in a closet,
She'll think of one she's bruised and torn
When, though pale, she's tried to lose it.
Once retrieved, she can't refuse it
Yet she fears its kind return,
Like a dead cousin's winding sheet
She'd gone and lost along the street;
Better let it burn, she said,
Better let it burn.

This warring and benevolence
I will not have; nor would I change her,
For she would offer no defense
And lend her body to a stranger.
*"The predication of Love's danger
Lies in refusals to deceive";*
And I would foxily concur
And go, and tell no tale of her
To let her learn and grieve in bed,
To let her learn and grieve.

Once, at a word, she reddened so,
All pale disdaining now belies her;
But since, her coloring grown slow,
She'd need a rainbow to advise her.
If distance proves me any wiser
I'll by far the wiser be;
She, wanting of sufficient haste
Shall as pursuer yet be chased,
While past her soft away I'll tread,
Soft and speedily.

John Hollander 313

But if her coloring be quick
And pink as skin has never worn it,
I'll wear the red as Simple Dick:
She'll play as bee, and I'll be hornet;
Night's colored dead, and thus we'll mourn it
Till our coloring is dun.
Then to redress the sky for Night
We'll wear that coloring to white,
And scratch it to the bone instead,
And scratch it to the bone.

DICK DONGWORTH CONSIDERS THE DEATH OF ROSEBLUSH

Her epitaph was never read;
Gone was the stone above her head
(Robbed by a needy sculptor
Who never could have helped her,
Nor had her maidenhead
Before she was dead).
Before she was married
They had her dead and buried.

She perished as must everyone
Who can I blame her death upon?
I should rather
Not involve her father,
Nor was she killed by fools
For freedom or her jewels.
(And we are all far subtler
Than to accuse the Butler).

Put all the guilt upon the lake,
Say she died for drowning's sake;
(Call it Nature reflected,
The glass that Love affected,

Or Christ's photographer)
The pool that swallowed her
Was merely a mirror
Whose image was in error.

Say that she was never brave
But only greedy for the grave;
Say Dongworth's rusty armor
Served only to alarm her.
Then write this of me:
"Were she only free,
John Thomas, my English cousin,
Could pluck her like a raisin."

March, 1956

WILLIAM ALFRED

(1922–   )

A favorite among Harvard professors, William Alfred is an Anglo-Saxon specialist who draws most Harvard students, at some time during their careers, to his survey courses in drama and in English literature. His verse translation of Agamemnon has been performed in Cambridge and New York, and his play "Hogan's Goat" opened in New York in the fall of 1965.

POEMS FROM

FIVE HARD SONGS IN A BAD TIME

"Now in my youth I am well on the way to a happy finish. I can hardly get much further at this staggering pace. Kicking evil away, I try, by singing, to have all things turned to the good. Love, and the dearest kind of love, is what I bequeath you all."
—RICHARD ROLLE OF HAMPOLE, AN ANTHEM FOR THINKERS, 113

BANKRUPTCY

"veni sancte spiritus . . ."

Adventurous Spirit, turned Recluse,
I need You. Put at my blind use
What is beyond my competence.

I have run through that princely sum
You gave me to begin with. Come,
Father. Beggar that I am,

Inconsolable optimist,
Reduced to die in this mare's nest,
Perfidious with tedium,

My wasted funds could meet with ease
This interest bleeds me to the lees,
All these usurious wants grow dumb,

Should You but take this risk on me.
I do not care how angrily.
My pride is gone with my income.

The time is past when crazed with shame,
No one came near I did not blame.
I know why I have nothing to my name.

Without You I will lose even sense and will.
There will be nothing left me. Nothing. Sure and still
That core of storms, that loanshark vacuum

Will rob me blind, despite this moratorium
It grants me, hounded to this one locked room
Of Your ruined house, my honorarium.

Pay off that devil for me. I am numb.
My schemes are muddled to delirium.
I can see no other way, unless You come

And tide me through this time, for me to assume
My mortgage. It makes even health seem doom;
For I have squandered all inheritance.

If I am done for, past the point where some
Have managed to recoup, You still must come.
Or who will close this house, and take me home!

William Alfred 317

When, caught between screen and glass,
Freedom of sight and touch
Were yours, but you found no way to pass
Beyond my window's smutch,
And flew till you split a wing
Against that ringing wire,
Since only to fly was to sing,
And to sing was your desire
I lifted up the screen.—
Yes, you foundered in the air,
And the grass no more was green
You fell to like a flare.
Bee,
I set you free:
Pray for me.

September, 1956

ROBERT CUMMING

Class of 1957, (1935–   )

Once Pegasus of the Advocate, *Robert Cumming
spent a year in the Peace Corps in the Far East
and then went to Nepal where he lived for over a
year. He has since moved to Boston's South End,
where he has interrupted a novel in progress to
write a book on Nepal.*

THE MEETING

RUNNING so fast, I don't know why I'm running so fast. I started running
just a little after I left school, where somebody started chunking rocks
at me. They hollered, "Let's see you run some, boy," and then started
chunking rocks at me. I didn't look back to see who it was or anything;
I just run. Now I'm way on away from there, but I'm still running.

Course the main reason for running today is Daddy Grace. Everybody
in school's going to see Daddy Grace, and some of them didn't even
come today so they could get prepared. But he ain't coming till six
o'clock, and anyway mama said she'd prefer I didn't go. Clarie said why
don't she and me go together, and mama said she wished I didn't go. I
sure would like to go, but I don't want to cross mama. I wish I had somebody, my daddy or somebody, to tell me things like why those folks
chunking rocks at me or what to do about Daddy Grace. Things like that
you just don't know.

I'm not even going to think about it; I'm just going to run. When you
run it seems like you're getting some place big, even if you're only going
home. All you do is run. You don't have to worry bout anything, like how
you wish you had a daddy or whether you ought to go hear Daddy
Grace. Your arms are pushing out behind you and your knees most
hitting up against your chest, and you just run.

I can run fast as anybody I ever saw. It must be a mile, maybe three or four, from school to my house, and I bet I only been running bout a minute. It couldn't be much more than that and I'm most home already.

That's my house, down the end of this alley. Past the one with the shiny doorknob, that one with the chinaberry tree out front. Before daddy left it used to be all our house. I don't know where he went but I sure wish he wasn't gone. Pretty soon after that the Watsons—that's Wash Watson and Mrs. Watson and their three little girls—they moved in the two front rooms. Clarie and mama and me live in the back room with the stove.

When I come in the door one of the little girls is picking at the cardboard tacked up on the wall to keep the place warm in winter.

"Stop that, Sarah-Anne," I say. "You know better than to tear that stuff down."

But she doesn't stop and I walk on into our room. There is Clarie and mama. I know they're going to argue; I can see it fore they start.

"Are you going to see Daddy with me," Clarie says. "He's coming at six o'clock, but I'm going head of time so I can get up close and see his face.

"You know what I think about it, son," mama says.

I hate this kind of tanglement. I wish daddy was here; he would know what we was going to do. Maybe he'd have taken me off squirrel-hunting or something, so we wouldn't even be here. I just wish there wasn't any arguing.

"I don't want any truck with that kind of shouting and hoodoo," mama says. "If folks worshiped God in the Church, stead of that man in his tent, they'd be a site better off."

"Daddy makes the sick people well, and the lame to carry their beds," Clarie says. "Everybody says he does. Bess Johnston, who never in her life been to church on Sunday, saw him over to Kannapolis last week and she's been talking about it ever since."

I look at mama. She is sitting in her chair with that black dress on. The skillet is lying by her feet, with this morning's grease all hard in the bottom. I wonder if God made her old like she is so she couldn't stop me from going to hear Daddy Grace.

I wonder if my daddy ever went to see Daddy Grace. I'd ask mama, but I don't want to hear any more arguing. I just want to get outside.

"The disciples give Daddy a brand-new tent," Clarie says. "I give him part of it. It must be a hundred times as big as this old house. And he deserves it," Clarie says. "They arn't a man in this state can preach like Daddy can. He tells you what's right and what's wicked, and you know it's the Lord's truth. I just feel like crying and praying, to see his face."

I wonder whether Daddy'd make me know what's right, so I'd feel like crying and praying. I look at mama where her black dress is tore by her knee.

"Let me go for a while, mamma," I say. "I'll come back and fess all about it."

Daddy's tent is in that big field south of town. It's the biggest field around. It goes from the edge of town almost down to the river. That's where they have the fair when it comes up from Charleston.

"My, ain't that a fine tent," Clarie says when we get out there. It sure is big. It must be ten times as high as that truck they bring it in. It has a long tunnel like for an entrance, and over the place where you go in it says HOUSE OF PRAYER in big blue letters.

Inside the tunnel there is sawdust on the ground. Clarie and me walk down it. On one side there are bottles of Daddy's spring tonic, wrapped up in silver paper. On the other you can get a disciple's haircut for two dollars.

"Let's get right down in front," Clarie says, "while we got a chance." We walk out into the main part of the tent. There is nobody there, just empty benches going on for miles. Up toward the roof the air looks sort of smoky, and in the middle you can't even see the top. It seems like an eagle or an angel or something might be up there. Music is coming from somewhere, like in church.

We walk all the way down to the front. Against the side of the tent there is a platform that sticks out to the three nearest tent poles. The poles are slick and red. All around the edge of the platform are piles of roses, yellow and pink ones all mixed in. Then there is a space and then the benches begin. We sit down on the very first bench, Clarie and me.

Now the people are coming in, and it sure is hot. All the men in dark blue suits and all the women in the gayest dresses they can put on. First they fill in around the platform, and then the whole place gets filled, back through the poles and haze so far you can't even see. The women all talking bout Daddy and fanning themselves like they thought it would do some good.

Robert Cumming 321

I guess mama's back home sitting in her black dress by the stove, and that little Watson girl sucking her thumb or tearing the cardboard off my daddy's wall. But I ain't going to think about it now.

There are seven men dressed in white up on the platform, holding the shiniest bugles you ever saw. They begin to blow and then there is a shout from the back. Daddy comes walking slow down the aisle, all by himself. He is wearing a bright gold cape that drags along the ground. "The disciples give him that last year," Clarie says. Underneath he has on one of those black suits like daddy used to wear to parties.

When he gets to the platform the seven men jump off and he climbs up alone. He turns around slow so that gold cape twirls out like an umbrella. He's a mighty big man, I think; must be about eight feet tall. Then he stops and I can see into his black eyes deep. I know why folks call him Daddy, just like they did Abraham. He raises up one hand.

"Children," he says.

"Daddy," everybody shouts. There is whooping and yelling. Some man behind me says, "Daddy, we is waiting on you."

"Children," Daddy says. "Children, there is just one thing in this world and that's Jesus Christ."

"That's right, Daddy," the people say. "Daddy, that sure is right."

"We don't need to think about anything, or worry about anything, or do anything except trust in Jesus Christ and obey him. Like he is our father. That's what the Gospel is about and that's what I'm here about and that's what the greatest hymn ever written is about. So let's sing that hymn right now, you and me together. *What a Friend We Have in Jesus.*"

In church they usually let a hymn play through once before folks sing it, but here everybody hits the first note.

> "What a friend we have in Jesus,
> All our pains and griefs to bear,
> What a privilege to carry
> Everything to God in prayer. . . ."

I think it is the finest singing I ever heard. While it's going on I'm watching Daddy, all alone, singing up on the platform. All he's doing is singing. He never has to worry, or run from anything. He knows what he ought to do and he's up there, alone, just doing it.

After the hymn there is shouting and folks saying Amen and walking in the aisles. Then Daddy yells "Silence," so loud you can hear him all over the tent. He just whirls his cape around and yells "Silence!" and people stop and listen like a train was coming.

Then he begins talking very soft.

"Children," he says. "Just put your faith in Jesus. Just forget the rest and put your faith in the Lamb of God. Now if you give me three volunteers—just three people willing to stand up for Jesus—I'll feed this five thousand. I'll show you what faith in Him can do for every one of you."

Then I am jumping up and I say, "Here am I." One time our preacher give a whole sermon on saying "Here am I." He said it was like jumping in the middle of the river, and if you don't do it you may have to stay back in the coves the rest of your life. He said you may only get knocked for once. So I jump up. Clarie pulls me back by the sleeve but I run up over the roses on the stage beside Daddy. "Here am I," I says like the Prophet in the Bible. "Send me."

Daddy steps back a little, but then he comes up and puts his hand on my shoulder. He's a big man, and I'm proud to stand up beside him.

"Son," he says, "you mighty brave to come up here when you so young and had so little time to get faith. I'm mighty proud of you. Now I'm going to help you along at first, but you'll be riding on your own faith soon enough."

There are two other men up on the stage, and Daddy goes over and shakes hands with them. Then he whirls around at the crowd.

"See these poles," he says, pointing to the tent poles at the edge of the platform. "They slick as grease; nobody could climb them. Now these children are going to rise by faith, their faith and our faith if we all praying for them, just like we all going to rise by faith if we got it."

He brings me over to one of the posts and slips something under my arms. In a minute I am rising up, grabbing onto the pole something is cutting into my shoulders and the people yelling fit to be killed. I think this is all a trick and I get mad at Daddy. Then I think he's right, I couldn't get up here by myself, even if those other fellows could. It is so hot up here I stop thinking at all.

Down below Daddy is shouting about faith. All the people are pointing at me and shouting. Then I'm ashamed I aint got more faith in Daddy and Jesus. I let go the post with one arm and slip the wire off it. I wave at the people; they point at me. It sure is hot. "If you got enough faith," Daddy is saying, "it will hold you up." It is so hot; all you can smell is roses. I wave hard at the people. "Jesus will be your father," Daddy says, "if you just trust in him." My other arm slips out of its wire; I grab at the post; the people shout real loud.

I'd swear I stayed up there a minute after that wire was off, fore I fell. Anyway I'm not hurt when I hit the platform; but I sure am ashamed. All those people, and everyone of them knows I didn't have faith enough to stay up a pole. Or maybe mama is right and Daddy Grace don't have religion at all. I don't stop to think. I feel like a slice of meat on a skillet, and I don't stop to think. I don't even look at Daddy Grace; I just duck out under the tent behind him and run.

I run so fast I leave that whole place behind me, with Daddy shouting and people yelling and all. I run the other way, toward the river, stead of toward town. But I don't even care.

Then I wish I had somebody—daddy maybe—to tell me what happened, so I say running,

"Daddy, what really happened?"

But that hasn't got any sense to it. So I just run on faster leaving even that thinking behind.

Pretty soon I come to the end of the field and run into the honeysuckle getting my feet tangled and falling balled up down in a clump. I am lying on my back and I look up at the pines overhead. I see how dark it is and how big the moon shines in between.

I get up and run on like you run through the woods at night: highstepping and listening for things not to step on, slow as a fast walk with your hands down near the ground. One time I look back and see Daddy Grace's tent glowing through the trees. It's big and bright orange like to hurt your eyes, like something in a bad dream. I don't want to look at it; I don't want to think about it more than I can help. I push my head around and run on on the soft ground between the pines.

Now I can see the moon glinting on the water. I come out on a cove that runs back up in the woods. All you can see is trees and water and moon; that's all there is.

September, 1955

SALLIE BINGHAM

Radcliffe 1958, (1936–   )

Sallie Bingham was a regular contributor to the Advocate *during her four years at Radcliffe. In 1960 she published a novel,* After Such Knowledge. *Her short story "Winter Term" won the Dana Reed Prize and established a local genre, "the Harvard Square sex story," which lasted for several years.*

WINTER TERM

IT WAS INCONVENIENT. And worse; Hal watched the woman behind the desk ruffling through file cards, and wondered if she had noticed that he came to the library every evening. She must have noticed him, and Eleanor; and he often thought she watched them during those evenings in the library. During the day, he sometimes planned a new kind of evening, still at the library, for the dancing and movie Saturdays he spent with Eleanor were even more stereotyped. Sometimes, he imagined that Eleanor would be there when he came, or that she would not be wearing lipstick, as when he had first seen her. But he knew that the small details' change could not alter the whole evening. In the past week, he had begun to imagine the only possible change: that Eleanor would not come at all. When he studied in his room in the afternoon, Hal planned to wait at the library until a quarter past seven, and then, if she had not come, he would leave, not buttoning his coat and turning at once onto the street.

"Why don't you take off your coat?" the librarian asked him. He had never heard her voice before. It was pleasantly colorless and he was surprised that with such a voice she had spoken to him at all.

"Oh, that's all right," he said, vaguely. "I may have to leave in a few minutes." She pulled out another drawer of filing cards, and began to ruffle through them. As he watched her, Hal became more and more surprised that she had spoken to him. It reminded him that he was still, even after a month, an intruder; there were so few boys in the library that the girls stared at them openly. He walked over to the reading room door and looked in; the red haired boy whom he had begun to speak to on the street was studying there with his girl. Eleanor said that they were engaged, although Hal had pointed out that the girl was not wearing a ring; Eleanor said it did not really matter. They always went out with each other, and on Saturdays and Sundays she had seen them having breakfast together in the Waldorf. Hal remembered asking her what they had been eating; it was a new way he had of testing Ellie, to see how long it would be before she laughed; if he teased her for a certain amount of time, he knew that she would more probably cry. "French Toast," she had answered promptly, "three orders, with maple syrup." And then she had asked him why he laughed, and when he shook his head and went on laughing her mouth began to quiver, and he tightened as she said, "Why do you always laugh at me?" They had had a bad evening. The tightening had started it, Hal knew; he could grant that to her in this carelessly objective mood of remembering. He wondered if he would ever be able to prevent himself from feeling like that when she didn't laugh, or when she was depressed, or when she asked him, "What are you thinking?"

Hal looked at the clock. She was already seven minutes late. It happened every evening; he imagined her dawdling over combing her hair, watching the clock, and planning not to leave in time. She often warned him about taking one another for granted. Surprised by his own bitterness, he thought, Oh God, why do I always have to be so hard on her; lately she can't do anything right. He remembered how he used to feel when she came towards him, running because she was late, or in out of the rain; she shook the rain out of her hair (too proud to wear a scarf), and her face was flecked with drops.

Eleanor came in the door before he could decide when the change had begun. She started towards him, red faced from the wind she had fought for four blocks on her bike. "Hello," she said, and he knew that if he had looked permissive she would have kissed him instead, in spite of the librarian. It was one of the things that he had first liked about her, along with the absence of lipstick, which she had since started wearing; she was willing to kiss him even on the Saturday night subway to Boston, when the whole row of people on the other side of the car was watching. Hal remembered how surprised he had been when they first danced together and she had pulled close, for the action had not suited the mild, high necked dress she was wearing, or even the coolness of her cheek.

She was peeling off the neat layers of her coat and sweater, and he noticed how limberly she bent to unfasten her boots, because he was watching. She had a much better figure than the red haired boy's girl, especially since she had given up sweets. He remembered proudly that she had started to diet because he had told her once that a dress was too tight; he had never had to tell her again. Now, her hips were straight under her skirt, and he knew from looking at them how they would feel, very firm as she clenched the big muscles, and smooth through her slippery underpants.

She led the way to the reading room. He had grown accustomed to people looking but he knew from the way Ellie was smiling that they still made her uncomfortable. When they sat down, she whispered, "You'd think they'd learn not to stare every night!" and he whispered back, leaning close so that her hair touched his mouth, "It's only because you're beautiful."

"You've said that before," she said, mocking and pleased, but he had already realized it; it did not matter how often he had repeated the compliment, for every time the situation had been the same, until the lie had become as familiar as the library room. He looked at the clock.

"Bored?" she asked quickly.

"No." He tried not to frown. She made a little face at him, and bent over her notebook.

He wished he had not learned to translate her expressions. When he had first met her, he had been charmed by her good-humored little pout, or her wide-eyed stare after they kissed. But now he knew that the pout was made to conceal the quiver in her mouth, and if he watched her a minute later he would see that she was not reading, that she was staring at the page and trying not to look at him. And as for her expression after he kissed her—it always seemed to Hal that he was watching her come up from a great depth of water—he did not know what it meant, but it irritated him. It was like the way she acted after they had made love. She went into it as exuberantly as jumping up to dance, leaving it to him to make sure that his room mates were out, and that the shades were down. By the time he had checked, she would have pulled her dress off over her head, rumpling her hair in bangs over her eyes. He began to undress, folding his clothes on the chair—"Ellie, will you hang up your dress?"—, but when he turned around and saw her waiting, naked under her slip, he went to her and forgot what he had been about to say.

But afterwards, if she didn't cry, she would not speak to him. She clenched him in her arms when he tried to get up, and he had to hurt her in order to break away, even though he had told her how necessary it was. When she clung to him like that, with her fingernails pricking his back, he tried to force himself out of his sleepiness, to polish her hair and kiss her. But her mouth tasted stale when he was so tired, and he was afraid she might think he wanted to do it again.

"I'm sorry I was late," Ellie said, not looking up from her book, and he realized that for the last five minutes she had been trying to decide why he seemed irritated.

"I thought we said we wouldn't apologize any more." He wanted to sound gay, but he realized at once that she was still raw to the subject; her eyes seemed to grow larger with hurt as she looked at him and said, "I wished you'd forget that." She was bending down the corner of a page, and he wanted to tell her not to; the little, mechanical action irritated him out of all proportion, and he wondered if he was so tense because they hadn't done it for four days. How did she feel about tonight? He knew that his room mates were out. Hal looked at her, but he could tell from the way she was hunched over her book that she was not thinking about making love but about the evening three days before when they had quarreled and then made a list of resolutions over coffee in Hayes-Bick's. One of them had been not to apologize, for they agreed that it was hypocritical; apologies were only a dog-in-the-manger way of saying I was right all along but I'll give in for the sake of peace. It had been a terrible evening, and Hal was sorry that they had gone to Hayes-Bick's, for the quarrel had destroyed his picture of one of their first evenings together, when he had held her hand between the salt and pepper.

"Oh, I forgot to ask you about the exam." She had not whispered, and the girl at the next desk looked up, frowning. "How was it?" she whispered, not looking at the girl.

"Terrible!" The exclamation did not relieve him. He had come back from the exam in the winter darkness, coffee nerved, and fingering the three pencils in his pocket whose points were worn flat. He remembered cursing himself for not reviewing enough, and he had wondered wildly if he could have written at the end of the thin, scratched blue book, "Circumstances beyond my control. . . ."

"But I thought you were so well prepared; you've been reviewing for practically a week."

He tried not to say it, but the words promised too much relief. "Yes, but I can't really study here." He knew before he looked at her that she was hurt, and as soon as he saw her mouth he felt the tightening; he wanted to laugh out loud and throw his head back and yell with laughter, and at the same time he wanted to pull her into his arms and fold her so tightly that her breath came in gasps.

"You never told me that before," she said, and he knew how carefully she had weeded the hurt out of her voice.

"Well, I mean, what do you expect? How can I concentrate on studying with you around?" He had meant it to be a compliment, he wanted to see her smile and look up at him, but it sounded like an accusation. As she turned her face sharply away he thought, Oh God, not another scene, and then he noticed abruptly how thin she had grown; he could see the point of her collar bone through her sweater, and her little pear breasts stood out too sharply.

Ellie had bent the corner of the page down so often that it broke off in her hand. She turned to Hal, smiling too brightly. "You should have seen the dormitory tonight." In spite of her smile, Hal wanted to kiss her for changing the subject. He thought that afterwards he would buy her an ice cream cone at the drugstore on the way back. She loved sweets, and she hadn't had any for at least two weeks; he remembered her inexpensive, salad dinners even on Saturday nights. And she was really almost too thin.

"You know Wednesday night is usually bad, anyway," she was saying. The girl at the next desk looked up again, annoyed, and Ellie's hand flew to her mouth. She would not have gone on if Hal had not asked, "Well, what happened?" and then she turned to him and whispered so softly, hesitantly that he could hardly hear. "You know, Wednesday's boy night, and they have candles and ice cream, just because we eat at quarter past six instead of six! Tonight I sat at a table

with three girls and their dates and I literally didn't say one word."
Hal had heard it often before; he looked around the room, trying to
distract his attention from his own irritation. Why was she proud of
not talking for a whole meal? He noticed the pretty girl who was in
his humanities class; she was winding a shank of hair around her finger
as she studied. Pretty hair. But she looked even more tense than the
rest of them. During exam period, you could cut the atmosphere in the
reading room with a knife. Most of the girls looked overtired and ugly,
and they had not bothered to comb their hair. This was the one place
where they never expected to see any boys. But Eleanor hated the
Harvard library. She said she felt too stared at when there were so
few girls. Hal had caught some of the looks boys gave her when they
walked down the corridor, and he agreed. She had such a damn good
figure.

"You're not listening," she said. "I know—don't apologize; I shouldn't
be distracting you." And as though her rigidly calm tone really expressed her feelings, Eleanor wrote the date neatly at the top of a
notebook page, and began to read.

"I am interested," he lied, feeling her hurt; "it's just I'm interested
in this place, too." She did not answer, and so he slammed his book
open and turned the pages roughly, looking for the place. They
sat for ten minutes in silence. Hal tried to read, but he was too conscious of the tip of her elbow, almost touching his; it looked a little
chapped, and he remembered how hard the winter weather was on
her blond skin. Then he wondered how he had known that—he had
been through no other winter with her, or even a spring or summer—
and inconsequentially he wondered what she looked like in a bathing
suit. He hunched his shoulders and bent down closer to his book, trying to force the words into his attention. There were long, ruler straight
lines under many of the sentences, and minute notes were printed in
the margins. He had written them in October, when for a week he
had devoted himself to Schopenhauer, reading each page passionately,
proud of the learned comments he wrote in the margins. He even found
time to go into Boston to visit the museum where there was a portrait
of the philosopher, and he remembered how his head had pounded as
he climbed the long stairs and hurried down a corridor to the door of
the room where the portrait hung. It had been a disappointment, an
old placid gentleman in conventional black; did pessimism embodied

look like that? he remembered thinking, like your own grandfather? But he had come back with a feeling of accomplishment.

Now, he could not read his own notes. When Ellie was hurt, the consciousness of it ticked like a clock at the back of his mind, and he could not concentrate on anything. He gave up trying to ignore the point of her elbow. He wondered if she would move first, as she often did, slipping her hand into his or turning into his arms as soon as they were alone or touching the back of his neck. He noticed how rigidly she was sitting; why did they both go on pretending to study? He looked at the clock; already half an hour wasted. God, I wish we'd had a chance to make love so I wouldn't feel like I'm going crazy. Exams; we said we couldn't afford the time. And self-righteously they avoided his room, knowing that once they were there where the sheets were marked from the last time and where they had first said that they were in love, their resolution would collapse in a panic. Their coming together was always too violent, he thought, like the too big lunch you eat after missing breakfast, snatching and tearing at the food if no one was watching. But I bet she needs it, he thought, that's why she's so quivery, close to tears, and maybe that's why I loused up that exam. But he knew it was an excuse; he had failed the exam because he had not known the material. He felt his resentment heating as he wondered why he had not reviewed more carefully. But she's right, I spent all last week on it, he thought, and then he added, enjoying his bitterness, yes, but you know what studying here means, jockeying for position for three hours with our knees always about to touch or our hands and she's always looking up or else I am until finally we give up and hold hands though that means I can't write or else she can't. Why didn't I have sense enough to tell her I had to study, two evenings would have done it, but I knew she'd cry. Not over the phone but in the booth after I hung up so she wouldn't be able to walk back down the hall without the other girls seeing she'd been crying. He wanted to turn to her and break the then unreal wall of her concentration, asking, why does everything hurt you too much? And why do I always have to know? Although he knew the last, at least, was not her fault.

He heard eight strike in silver, feminine notes from the clock over the girls' gym. That clock would never let him forget the amount of time he was wasting; all evening, he would have to listen to its coy reminders. The thought jacked him to the top of his irritation, and he slammed his books closed and began to stack them together. Eleanor looked up, and he saw in her eyes the terror that he had heard once in her voice when he told her that he would have to go home for the weekend. She had said, "You know that means three days without talking to anyone." But he had answered, trying to laugh, "But there must be someone—all those girls." "You know I'm not a girl's girl; I don't really know how to talk to them. And anyway, I don't spend my extra time in the Smoker, so they hardly know my name." And he had understood what she had been unwilling to say, that he had taken up the time she might have spent padding herself with girl acquaintances against the time when she would be alone. In the end, he had left without telling her goodbye, and the weekend had been spoiled because he had known how she was feeling.

He stood up, although he had still not decided what he was going to do. Only, no more waste.

"You want to leave?" she asked, hurriedly gathering up her books, and Hal knew that she thought he was going to walk out without her. He knew that he was being brutal, and that if she began to cry he would be more than ashamed; he would feel that his hands were as clumsy as trays as he tried to sooth her, and then, as he struggled to find something gentle to say, he would begin to go mad with irritation. He started towards the reading room door before Ellie was ready, and he heard the almost hysterical ruffling of the pages as she closed her books. He waited for her on the other side of the door, and when she came, nearly running, he saw the brand mark of fear on her face fade as she smiled with relief that he was waiting.

"I agree with you; let's get out of this dreary place," she said, and Hal wished that she had been angry.

"Look, I'm going to walk you back now," he said as they went out into the sudden coldness. She began to fumble awkwardly with her scarf, trying to adjust it inside her coat collar.

"Right now?" Her voice was carefully casual.

"Look, Eleanor, I've got to get something done tonight. Friday's the Phil. 101 exam."

"Oh, I understand." They walked along side by side, conscious of not holding hands. The quadrangle was dark except for the library lights and the illuminated clock over the gym. It was always five minutes fast, he knew, on purpose, so that the girls who were late starting would still get to the Harvard classrooms on time. In spite of the clock, Ellie was always coming in late, hesitating in the doorway to look for him, and red and damp from running.

"Are you going to continue the history course?" He wished that she would not keep her voice cheerful, trying to pretend to him, but not to herself, that they had not silently quarrelled.

"Can't divide it at mid-term." He was irritated by his own grudging tone, although it was easy enough to justify it; even if he broke with her now and finally (it was incredible, the thought of pushing off her hands and running without hearing her calling), he would still have to see her every Monday, Wednesday, and Friday at ten in the history class where they would try not to look at each other.

Her dormitory was full of lights. "At last they've taken down the wreath!" he said.

"It was really too much." Her voice had revived with his cheerfulness, real this time; although it was ridiculous, he knew that the tarnished wreath was a reminder of the Christmas vacation they had spent straining to be together, the long distance calls when her voice was tremulous, and the too many, raw letters.

They stood under the porch light, and she held out her hands. He took them, and slipped his fingers inside her gloves. Her palms were soft and lined.

"Look at all the bikes," he said inconsequentially, "You'd think they'd give up in this bad weather," and they both looked out at the heaped, stone snow. He remembered that he had a long walk back, but as he bent hurriedly to kiss her she slipped her arms around him so that he had to pull back hard in order to get away. She let go at last, her arms hurting, and no longer trying to smile. "Hal, don't go." He hesitated. "Please don't go. Please." She was rigidly controlling her voice, but he knew the limit of her endurance, and he wanted to be away before she began to cry, for then he would never be able to leave. He would have to wait until she was calm, rocking her in his arms and kissing her hair. Then he would walk back along the river to the house, avoiding noticing clocks until he was in his room. When he saw the tin alarm clock that was already set for the morning he would throw his books violently into a chair so that John looked out of the bedroom: "What's wrong with you?" And then he would go out and buy coffee so that, with luck, he could study until three. By that time, the lights across the courtyard would all be out, and often, it would begin to snow.

Eleanor had sensed his tension. "About tomorrow," she said lightly, working her books around in her arms and wiping a fleck of nothing off one of the covers. "I know we both have a lot of work. I'll call you in the morning, anyway, and then we can decide. I guess maybe we ought to study by ourselves tomorrow night." Her voice was so matter-of-fact that if he had not known the pattern Hal would not have believed that, next day, when they came to the deciding, she would plead with him to study with her in the library: "Really, I promise, we'll get something done," and she would offer to sign a promise that she would not speak to him for three hours. Now, he was looking down, and running her finger along the side of a book. "Hal," she said, "I'm sorry about tonight. You know how I get sometimes." He put his arms around her, although the books were between them, and he tried not to tell her how sorry he was, tried to choke back his softness: "Oh God, Ellie," he said instead, and he heard the almost tears in his own voice, the rawness that was both tenderness and irritation. She strained up to kiss him, and when she opened her mouth he felt tricked, knowing that she was intentionally exciting him, that if he put his tongue between her lips he would not be able to leave. As he kissed her he began half consciously to forget that he should go. She dropped her books and they tumbled over their feet. He pressed close to her suddenly, forgetting, forcing his tightness to the back of his mind. He was only vaguely conscious of the porch and the staring light as he pulled her roughly against him, hearing her moan with pain and excitation. Then in a blurred voice, she said, "Isn't there somewhere we can go?" Her face was flushed, reminding him in a twisted way of a child waking up, damp and fresh. She was trying to think of somewhere and holding his hands tightly as though she could brace his desire and prevent it from diminishing.

He hesitated. He knew that he could leave now, quickly and without kissing her, and it would not be too hard. But then she would go on taking classes with him and calling to him across the street, and when he came up the entry stairs and heard his phone ringing he would have to wait on the landing until it had stopped. . . .

"It's too late to have you in the dormitory," she said, and he automatically checked off their short list of private places. It was too cold for the common; they had been nervous, anyway, on the bench behind the thin screen of shrubbery. And it was too late for her to go to his room. Parietal rules! He wondered viciously how many people they had forced into marriage. They had talked now and then of renting a room, but they never had the nerve; like his bedroom, the idea was sordid with old connotations. Although they were proud of their pretended indifference to surroundings, her face seemed to reflect the grey walls when they lay together on his bed.

"At least let's get out of this porch light," he said, and they went down the steps and stood hesitating on the sidewalk. She was looking around, eagerly and hopefully, and he wondered how much of her desire was passion and how much grasping; girls used sex to get a hold on you, he knew; it was so easy for them to pretend to be excited.

They wandered down the sidewalk. As they passed the college parking lot, Eleanor said, "Look, we could . . ." She did not go on, but Hal knew at once that she meant the cars, the college girl cars with boxes of tissues and clean seat covers, parked in rows in the lot behind the dormitories. "All right," he said, knowing that the whole time they would be afraid of someone coming, even at the climax they would be listening for steps. They walked around the lot. Ellie laughed; trying, he knew to keep him from recognizing the sordidness of the situation. He wondered why it was now so easy for him to accept the back seats of cars, and student beds with broken springs. He chose a Ford station wagon, and held the back door open for her. When he followed her, she turned to him, and they sank together down onto the seat. He started carefully to unbutton her blouse, feeling her stiffen as he traced her breast. Across the quadrangle, the gymnasium clock chimed silverly. Nine o'clock. Suddenly violent, he ripped her blouse open, and as she tried, terrified, to push off his hands, he began to tear at her slip. "Stop it Eleanor, let go," and as he pulled the straps off her shoulders, she dropped her hands and began to cry.

April, 1956

JONATHAN KOZOL

Class of 1958, (1936–   )

A summa cum laude *graduate of Harvard and
a Rhodes scholar, Jonathan Kozol published*
The Fume of Poppies, *a novel about a Harvard-
Radcliffe romance, in 1958. In 1965 Mr. Kozol
was fired from a teaching position in the Boston
school system for assigning a poem by Negro
poet Langston Hughes to a predominantly Negro
class. "As a neophyte" the School Committee
stated, "he tried to experiment outside the standard curriculum." The matter became something
of a* cause célèbre *in the struggle over the issue of*
de facto *segregation.*

FIRST LOVE

Pixie the Innkeeper's daughter was thirteen years old and had apple-
colored cheeks. Her nose was an impertinent button and her face was
round with smiles. She had a fuzzy mop of hair all around her head, of
soft silken brown, with wisps instead of bangs along her forehead. She
wore a blue dress with little white flowers and a petticoat underneath.
Only now in the evening, because it was cool, she wore a soft black
sweater on top, with long warm sleeves and a heavy stitching that
rested firmly upon her hips as they moved to and fro when she walked.
She was serving the beer to the customers and she was all smiles and
pink cheeks when she said, "Black beer or white beer?" And when a
lumberman or a fisherman tried to pinch her cheeks she slipped away
and cried in her high-pitched voice, "Go on and drink your beer, Mr.
Curdy. Shame on a man like you!"

Cherub sat in the window-seat where a large cushion was set in the bay looking down on the front of the house. He leaned upon his elbow, watching the motions of the bar-girl as she drew from the tap a long honey stream and then opened her mouth wide in surprise as the white bubbles overflowed the glass. Then she picked up a sponge and wiped the glass, and found a round tray, and set the tray down in front of Mr. Curdy and set the glass in the middle of the tray, saying, "Three please, and one for me, Mr. Curdy."

This time, the lumberman paid without trying to get a pinch. He sucked the foam off the top of the glass and winked to his pal across the table, while Pixie glanced about the room to see whether everyone was served.

Then she saw Cherub.

Cherub was wearing dark flannel trousers and a flannel vest to match, with a crisp new shirt underneath. His sleeves were rolled up showing soft tan skin and twisting muscles, but his hair was tousled and his lips had the small-boy pout. His blue eyes were lost in a sea of wonder.

"Well, quite the man you are!" said Pixie. "Where did we get our fine vest?"

He looked up to see her small pink wrist coming out of the cuff of her black sweater. He looked higher and saw her white throat where it rose above the curling neck of the sweater. The sweater was stitched vertically, ever so slightly filled out by her figure and tautened about the hips. She had rollicking lips, which she licked ever so often.

"What will it be my man?"

"Beer, please," said Cherub, looking up.

She looked down at Cherub. "What kind of beer?"

He looked up at her. "Black beer."

"Black beer, you say?"

"Black beer."

"Then black it shall be."

"That's good!"

"*Is* it good, now?"

"Sure it's good. I like black beer."

"*Do* you like black beer?"

"I love black beer."

She would not stop staring at him, looking down with a faint smile of freshness in the corner of her lips, as if she enjoyed mocking and liked to see somebody beneath her. Her eyes were large and blue, but it was the dimples in her cheeks and the roll of her lip that gave her smile its teasing wrinkle.

"I love it, too," she said. And she ran off across the room.

When she brought the beer back, Cherub said, "Are you the Innkeeper's daughter?"

"That's right," she said.

"Is that why you work here?"

"That's right." She was above him again.

"Oh."

Pixie looked at Cherub's hair. "Your hair is mussed up," she said. "You aren't very careful."

"Oh no," he said. "I'm not."

"Are you a messy boy?"

"Oh no!" he said. "Oh . . . yes! Am I a messy boy?"

She stopped smiling now and sat down beside him on the window-seat.

"I like this window-seat, don't you?"

"Yes, it's very soft," said Cherub.

"That's true." Her eyelashes batted downward.

"It gives a fine view," he said.

"And that's true."

"Do you sit here often?"

"Not often. It is the seat for lovers and I am not a lover. Have you had your love?"

"No I have not had any love. I am not a lover, either. I am not ever going to have one."

"Oh-h!" she opened her mouth wide and clapped her hands on top of Cherub's. "Not any love?" He wriggled a little in his seat, moving to the side. "No love at all? Ever ever ever?"

"Well . . ."

"I bet you will be a beautiful lover!" she said. "I can just imagine the girls who will be only dying to run their fingers through your hair." She placed one hand on his shoulder and looked up at his ruffled hair. "Isn't it lovely hair though?"

"Yes, I don't ever cut it. It just grows and grows." He looked down at the floor.

338   *Jonathan Kozol*

"Never do cut it?" she said. "And it just grows and grows? Oh, the warrior we are! Aren't we? Aren't we the warrior?"

Now the room was beginning to empty, because it was Saturday night, and the lights in the front of the room flickered out. Cherub and Pixie were in darkness, but for the criss-crossed light from the grill of the street-lamp that made its little waffle pattern upon the window.

"Oh isn't that a lovely night?" she said. "Do you see the snow coming down?"

"Is there snow?" he said.

"Over there." She pointed to the street-lamp, where the soft falling flakes could be seen floating across the light. "Over there the snow is falling so softly! Isn't it lovely to see the snow?" She turned to him suddenly with her face only an inch away from his. "Don't you love the falling sound it makes?" She rolled her full lip when she said love. "I love snow-falls."

"Oh it's nice!" said Cherub. "I love to see the snow-flakes twirling. Don't they twirl around!"

"Yes, they do," she said.

"Yes," he said.

"What is your name?" she said.

"Cherub."

"Do you like your name?"

"I like it fine. It's my only one . . . Do you like your name?"

"Yes, I do." She spoke softly, touching his hand, and watching his eyes.

"What is your name?"

"Pixie."

"Pixie?" His voice squeaked.

"Yes . . . That's the only one I have, too."

"Um-n-huh?"

"Do you like it?"

"It's a nice one . . . Sure, it's a nice name!"

"Yes?"

"It's one of the best I've ever heard. It's a beauty!"

There was a moment of silence. Everyone was gone out of the room. Behind the bar, a pale fluorescent light was glimmering, but all the other lamps were out. There was a snowy glow from the street.

Jonathan Kozol 339

"Well, don't you have to go to bed?" said Cherub. "Isn't that important?"

"Not so important." She giggled a little.

"But, it's bedtime," he said, squeaking again.

"Bed-time?" she said. "For you? . . . How old are you?"

"Thirteen," he said, feeling for one of the buttons of his vest.

"I am thirteen, too."

"Yes. That's so."

Just then the clock on the mantel bonged twelve times, one right after the other. Then it stopped all of a sudden, leaving a big space of silence. Pixie ran her hand down Cherub's shoulder, bare beneath his new shirt, and warm.

"I have to go to bed," said Cherub. And with that he got up from the seat and went out the door. Pixie sat alone not smiling now, but looking down at the soft piles of snow.

The next morning they met in a hay-field. The sun bathed the young grass in yellow summer. The smallest blades were only a pale green, with soft shoots, but the greater grasses were stiff and reedy and cut you when you passed.

Cherub had risen early, thinking to go down to the pond. The pond was behind the orchard. The Inn was in the other direction, at the top of the mountain. From the middle of the meadow you could not see the Inn any more, but you could see the snowy peaks. Down below you could see the green of the apple-trees and, through the branches, the clear blue of the pond.

Cherub skipped along the path in the meadow. There were yellow buttercups and dandelions, milkweed and bramble-bush, and around the rocks great wild clusters of field-rose. The thorny stems twisted in erratic patterns but the flowers were small and cup-shaped. Cherub bent down to look at the velvety petals, but you could not pick the blossoms without being stuck on the thorns. Then you would have a fine sting in your finger!

About half-way down the hill there was a small thicket sprung up about a cherry-tree. Nobody knew how the tree got there, because all the other trees were down in the orchard, and they were all apple. But there it stood, in the midst of a dense little growth of lilac and orange-flocks, white heather and overgrown blue iris. Cherub sat down

on a small flat stone. He curled his toes up and down inside his canvas sneakers and pulled off his jersey. The smell from the thicket of ripe blossoms was rich and heavy in the heat of the sun, but in the shade, it was cool and refreshing.

Suddenly a small gray form whirred up in the thicket. It was a sparrow, rising in alarm from the nest she had built beneath the heather. Cherub looked down to see but it was too dark. He lay with his belly on the rock and drew the brush apart with his hands. Then he stuck his head into the darkness. There, on a small mossy pad of darkest green, were three tiny sparrow-chicks who could not have been more than ten-days old. They were ungainly little forms, all bone and gray skin, with enormous beaks and eyes. But over the gray skin there was the faintest down of brown feathers, and the wide open beaks were piping a tiny cry of hunger.

Suddenly Cherub jumped back in horror. A long slithering rustle broke through the grass and the tiny malicious eyes of a snake gleamed into the nest. Then the rattling continued and moved. The snake appeared, piling up in coils and waiting for the rest of its eely train to come into the shade. Finally the entire snake was there, brown-and-green-patterned with tiny black circles everywhere and a phosphorescent glimmer, as of spilled oil, all along its hide. It did not rest in a single neat pile of coils but rather slipped out into several oily rings and curves that caught the light of the sun, even here in the dark shade, and shot it back with splintery gleams. The snake was getting ready to spring.

Up above, the sparrow whirred about in frantic circles. A faint helpless cry seemed to come from its beak, but the beak remained frozen closed. The wings of the bird fanned the air faster and faster, threshing at the slight wind and hovering just over the brush. Now it moved up slightly and now it came down, and now it moved in a rolling path as a small boy treads water to stay afloat.

Cherub watched the snake gorge down the birds. First it lowered its head to the surface of the moss and began swinging to the right and the left. Then its eyes lit up and its whole upper body shot ahead a half-foot; then its lower body caught up; then it waited. After a moment, it continued its dance-step: to right, to left, forward, forward. Pause. Now it was at the edge of the nest.

Cherub lay on his belly, wondering what to do. But he could not do anything or the snake might eat him, too. He wanted to run away but he did not dare to move, so he stayed on his belly, watching the long body thrust forward its head.

The snake's head was not half the size of the sparrow-chick. Still, it simply moved forward with a weaving sucking noise and a shuffle in its long train, and merely drew the upturned head of the paralyzed chick into its throat. Slowly, the whole bird began to disappear between the wide fangs of the serpent. The black circles grew bigger and smaller as the snake expanded or contracted, and the stripes seemed to change place with each other, green and brown, brown and green, by an electric shifting motion. Soon the entire bird was passing down the endless canal of the serpent's stomach. After a while the bulge became smaller and longer—it was being dissolved by the acids of the stomach! Soon it would be only crumples of beak and bone and a long rich mash of nourishment for the serpent's body. Now it went after the next chick.

The mother sparrow waited until all three chicks had been eaten, and then flew high up into the sky with strange excitement. Cherub watched the heavy serpent rattle sluggishly away. Then he climbed down from his rock and looked about the lovely meadow with a confusion in his eyes and with his fists tightened.

That was when he saw Pixie.

She had come down the mountain to pick some apples. It was an hour's walk from the Inn to the meadow and a half hour across the meadow to the grove. She was smiling and singing, with a straw basket over her arm.

"It's the new boy," she said, when Cherub stood up by the thicket.

He saw her and thought, "It's the pretty girl."

"Hello, Cherub," she said when they were close. "Isn't it a glorious day?"

"Yes, it's quite nice," he said.

"Would you think there could be snow just an hour away?" she said. "Can you think of that!"

"No, isn't that something," said Cherub.

"What?" she said.

"I said—'Isn't that something! . . . That's something!' I said."

"Un-n-huh . . ." She was looking him up and down, examining his clothes. Today he wore leather mountain-shorts, with bare knees and legs, and blue sneakers with white socks. His jersey was red and white striped, crossed over by the leather straps of the shorts.

"Your hair is tousled again."

"Oh . . ." He tried to smooth it out with his hand.

"That won't do you any good," she said. "You need to comb it."

"I don't have any comb," he said.

She paused for a moment, fixing the strap of her jumper. "You can use mine."

Cherub looked up at her. She was wearing a blue and white jumper of crisp organdy, with slender straps going over her shoulders. Her arms and the upper part of her breasts were pure white with flashings of red going through them. Her cheeks were the same; she never became tanned like Cherub. It was the mountain air that pinched her to a pink color. She bent down suddenly to pick a dandelion skeleton in the grass at Cherub's feet. He glanced down at her leaning body and bare outstretched arm and then bit his lip and looked up again with a queer look in his eye.

"Don't you wear underwear?" he said with a squeak.

"Oh, not in the summer-time," she said.

"Not any at all?"

"Not a stitch!"

"Huh!" he said. "Aren't you cold?"

"Oh no," said Pixie. "I'm rather warm-blooded. And, you see it's freer like this." And she twirled around merrily in the sunshine, lifting up her skirt to her thighs.

"Oh . . ." Cherub's eyes came together across his nose in a contorted twist.

"You're much freer," she said.

"Please don't do that," said Cherub. "Please don't."

"Don't do what?" said Pixie.

"Couldn't you just let your skirt down to your ankles, please?" he said.

"Oh . . . silly!" And she let down her skirt gracefully and kissed Cherub on the forehead. He turned crimson.

"You know, I saw a snake," he said.

She lifted up her skirt again to her knees and pointed out her leg in front of him. "Look, I gashed my ankle the day before yesterday."

"With brown and green stripes."

"I am so wild, Daddy says. He says I am a termagent."

"It ate some birds."

"But don't you think girls should swing from trees?"

"Three of them. It ate them up."

Just then, there was an eely slithering in the grass and the same poisonous serpent crawled between Pixie's legs before she could make a move. After it had passed all the way underneath her, it rattled off for a hundred yards and disappeared in the orchard, she screamed, "It did?"

"Yes," said Cherub. "It ate them up, one after another. I saw it myself."

"Oh . . ." She was quieted by this. "That always bothers me. I am so sad to think they eat each other up. Doesn't it bother you?"

"Yes, it makes me sad, too," said Cherub. "Some people say that is a girl's feeling to be sad when somebody is killed. But I like little birds and things."

"Yes . . . You're a good boy." She touched his arm.

"I just hate to see any nice little animal die."

"I like you very much, Cherub . . ." She slipped her arm underneath his. "Won't you come and help me pick apples?"

The orchard was heavy with hanging moss. The apple-trees looked like great old men, with gnarled and twisted limbs, bending over to scratch their backs, their long beards trailing to the ground. Cherub climbed up on the branches to knock down the apples. He would straddle a branch with his legs, hold tight with both hands, and jump up and down. As the branch began to sway he would ride it up and down, waiting for the apples to fall. All at once they would tumble to the ground in little ripples. One two three four. You heard them thudding upon the hard ground.

Pixie tried to catch them. "Knock me down that one," she would say, pointing to a ripe beauty hanging in the sun. Then Cherub would wriggle up the branch until he was near enough, and began to ride it furiously up and down. The leaves would swish and rustle; the twigs would break off in tiny bits; the bark would crumble in Cherub's hands; the branch would creak. Then all at once there would come a neat little snap and, a moment afterwards, a soft little plop. The apple would land in Pixie's skirt.

She held it up as long as she could, collecting ten or twenty shiny apples. Then, when they became too heavy, she poured them all out like a pile of treasure, dusted off her skirt, adjusted her jumper or some other little thing that was wrong and then stationed herself again underneath Cherub, ready to catch the apples he sent her way.

He enjoyed it tremendously.

"This is good fun," he said.

"You do it nicely," she said.

They made a rich store of apples.

Later, it was time to go home. Evening was coming down over the meadow, driving the daytime behind the mountain peak. The snowy summit glistened in pink sunset. The green upland meadows bathed in sundown yellow. But below in the orchard, where Cherub still climbed from branch to branch, the shadows were advancing past the tree-trunks on padded steps. It was growing darker and darker.

Cherub came down from the tree. He smoothed his hair over his brow and said, "Whew! That was a hard chore." And he slipped off his jersey and used it to dry his sweating chest and arms. Under his arms and along his sides there was tremendous heat. He moved his hands swiftly all about his curving shoulders and smooth chest, trying to find some relief.

Pixie stood with her hands behind her back, watching him. She saw the hollow at the bottom of his throat and the slender blades of his shoulders in back.

"There is a pool, you know."

"Is there?"

"Down there."

He looked around and saw the darkening blue of the pool through the green and black of the apple-grove.

"Nobody would mind?"

"Nobody is here." She swayed a little. You could hear the rustle of her skirt.

"Go on," she said.

"You won't come?"

"I'll stay here."

"Promise?"

"I'll count the apples."

He looked down at the pile of shining beauties and then up at Pixie. "All right," he said. "I'll be back soon." And he threw down his jersey on the moss and ran off through the shadow of the trees, loosening the straps of his leather shorts as he went.

Down at the pool there was a regular chorus of music. The evening-birds, mostly red wings and hummers, were chirping and whistling with such energy and excitement that you would think something was imminent in the woods. It was only their way of filling the space of twilight with a sound of merriment to chase away the dark. Yet the dark was always coming.

Pixie sat down by her hoard of treasure. She rested her head against the trunk of a tree and closed her eyes. The chirping of the sparrows joined with the hum of crickets and the rustling of the leaves. She began to be very sleepy. Soon she shifted away from the tree a little bit and lay her head upon the moss, stretching her arms beside her. She turned her face slightly to the side and began to sleep. The deep flush came up her cheeks and shoulders and the straps of her jumper slipped down along her arms. Her legs were slightly parted and her slippers were black; her hands lay open.

Cherub returned from the pond. He was dripping wet, and carried his socks and sneakers in his hand. His hair was streaming down over his forehead and cheeks. He kept wiping his eyes with the back of his hand and hopping from foot to foot to shake the water from his ears. His bare feet crunched the twigs and dry leaves, but the green moss felt good.

Then Cherub stopped very suddenly.

Just ahead, no more than ten or twelve feet, the Innkeeper's daughter, Pixie, lay sleeping upon the moss. Her hands were slightly curled but open, and her organdy bodice sighed slightly with her breathing. There was a deep flush in her cheeks, and her neck was dappled with a flood of pinkish warmth. Cherub saw the straps of her jumper slipping down her arms.

And just an inch away from her slumbering eyes he saw the weaving head of the green-barred serpent, with its small black circles, hissing lightly and stabbing at the air with its forked, needle-sharp tongue. And then Cherub realized that the girl was not asleep at all. She was simply too paralyzed by fear to even quiver or take a deep breath. And much too scared to cry.

Cherub watched the snake hover in the air as he had seen it do before the nest of the sparrow-chicks. In the same way, it murmured with a nervous rattle and seemed to spit out a venom in its hiss. The tiny eyes were again lighted up as with sacred little fires of witchcraft.

The snake began to draw up the train of its body. At first it lay at its full length of about a yard-and-a-half, moving only in the section that supported the swaying head. Then it began to suck itself up, inch by inch, into a heavier, fatter snake—a thicker, shorter serpent with broad bars of oily green and brown and large circles of black. Worst of all, to Cherub, was the breathing of the snake; its whole skin seemed to pant in and out, expanding, then contracting its circles of black— broadening, then lengthening out its bars of green and brown. And, meanwhile, the fattened head just hovered in the air.

Then the head shot forward.

Cherub did not move.

The paralyzed girl did not move.

They both waited endless minutes as the snake, with its thousand automatic muscles, climbed slowly up the side of her neck. Second by second, the damp black head rose along the soft white flesh of the pretty girl, across the warm blood-filled flesh of her throat.

Only once, Pixie made a sound as though she were going to cry out: a small piping seemed just to reach her lips where it was choked by the tremendous weight of fright.

Still he did not move.

Now the snake drew up its train behind it. The fat coils climbed up the side of the neck, holding on by a thousand little grippers that sucked for support to the soft, girl's flesh. Finally, the head reached the middle of her throat, and stopped. There it again hovered in the air, rising up first in a direct line, then inclining to the left, and now to the right. Finally, it began to wander in a circle, the black head, and the pliable six inches of muscle that supported it, turning slowly about as with meditative rhythm. Now it inclined to the breast, and now it inclined to the face. Now it trembled over the lips. And now it swayed, too, over the closed eyes and the pink cheeks and the mischievous small nose. And then it returned to the white throat again, where it rose over the beautiful blue veins—and trembled.

And then it fell.

Cherub watched as it slowly crawled down the opposite side of the neck, pulling its body behind it—moving faster and faster. And by the time the ugly head had disappeared into a bramble-patch four feet away, the last inches of the rattlesnake dipped down the neck of the Inn-keeper's daughter, and rattled off through the moss.

An hour later, Pixie had finally recovered enough of her heart to stand up. Cherub put his arm about her waist and together they walked up the long mountain-path to her father's snow-covered Inn.

By nine o'clock, everyone had retired. The jolly Innkeeper had fed Cherub and Pixie a good dinner in front of the fire-place, and sat rollicking with laughter as they told of the day's events.

"That's good that you got away daughter," he said in a hoarse energetic voice. "That's good you got off with your life. I'm glad of that."

"Are you, Daddy?" She loved her father and put her arms around his tough knotty neck.

"Ah, there, there, daughter!" And he patted her fondly on the back. "Ah, you must be careful of those rattlesnakes. They're vicious creatures, all right. You can mark me that!"

"We mark you, sir," said Cherub politely.

"Eh, boy?" The big man spoke heartily but his eyes were growing bleared with sleep.

"Oh Daddy is tired," said Pixie. "Daddy has to get his rest. Don't you, little Daddy?"

"What's that, little daughter?"

"Oooh! You!" She squeezed her Daddy's nose between her fingers. He smiled and hugged her.

"That's it, daughter. That's the spunk."

"Oh Daddy," she said. "I was so scared." And she began to cry.

Cherub sat quietly while her father cheered her up. "Ah, where's the spunk, Pixie? Where's your Daddy's girl? Hey, there?" And he kept stroking her hair and pinching the dimples of her cheeks until the color came back into them. "Is that my girl now? Is that my Pixie now? Where is that little nose? Where is that nose hiding?" And he pretended he could not find it. Then, all at once, he smiled with a big burst of laughter and said, "There she is! There's my Pixie!" And he caught her nose between his fingers and rubbed the tip of it against his own. She began to laugh. Then he got up from his chair, said good-night to Cherub, bent down to kiss Pixie on each small ear, and went out the door and up the steps. They heard him trudging off to bed.

"You're rather close to your father, aren't you?" said Cherub.

The fire was blazing nicely.

"Daddy is my darling," said Pixie.

Cherub sat back in silence. He felt he had missed something because he never had a mother. A father was for a girl and a mother for a boy. He had been cheated. And yet, when he thought of it, he had had a hundred mothers; everywhere he went he found a mother. He had too many, in fact. Every little girl and every hot honey and every old granny wanted to be a mother to Cherub, and he didn't like that at all. So what was he complaining about? Why should he be jealous?

But still he felt confused about something.

"Pixie?" he said at last.

"Yes," she said.

"That was a terrible thing today."

"Yes."

"It was the worst thing in my life."

"And mine, too." She looked up, her moppet hair shining before the blaze of the fire. "And yet . . . It was a strange thing to happen, too . . . I mean, not just bad: It was also strange, and terrible, and . . . exotic." Her eyes glowed for an instant. She had flicked her tongue on exotic. "Don't you think?"

"Well, . . . it was unusual," said Cherub.

"But exotic!" she said. ". . . Thrilling!"

"Thrilling?" said Cherub. "It didn't thrill me."

"It thrilled me," she said quietly. And for a while she was afraid to look up. "Come over to the window seat," she said finally. "We shall have to talk . . . It is warm in front of the fire."

The big hearth blaze was crackling at its height. Soon it would die down. They went over to the window-cushion and sat down. To-night it was not snowing but the whole mountain-top was frozen in white.

"You see, it was a matter of pride for me to have that snake crawl across my neck. It was something . . . I shouldn't have wanted to miss. If you see?"

"No I don't see," said Cherub. "I don't see why anyone would want a snake to crawl across their neck. I wouldn't like it."

"For the sensation," she said. "The feel of it."

"Huh?" said Cherub. He looked at her, a little surprised. "What did it feel like?"

"Feel?" she said.

"Yes," said Cherub.

"Nice," she said. "It was a nice feel."

After that, there was a pause. The room was becoming very warm. Upstairs, there were footsteps for a while creaking on the rafters, and then there was silence. Pixie leaned back in the window-seat. "Do you like girls?" she said. She played with her jumper strap, kicking off her shoes. They landed with a clap-clap on the floor.

"Some I like. Some I don't like," said Cherub.

"Which ones do you like?" she said.

"Pretty ones."

Pixie moved over to Cherub. She reached her arm up about his warm neck and looked into his eyes. They were drowning in their own blue seas. "Am I pretty?" she said.

He looked down at a brass button on the cushion. "Yes, you look fine," he said.

"How fine?" she said.

"Very fine."

"Fine enough to eat up?" She rolled her lush lip on *eat up*. "Fine enough to gobble down?"

"Un-huh," said Cherub.

"Could you gobble me down?" she said, giggling.

"Un-huh."

"Go on! Gobble . . ."

"Huh?"

"Eat me up!"

"Oh say!" Cherub scratched his head. "You're acting mighty queer. I haven't ever heard any girl talk like that before. What if your father heard you?"

"Daddy is asleep," she said. "Listen." And in the silence they could hear him snoring, even through the double rafters of the ceiling. "We're all by ourselves."

"Isn't it bed-time?" said Cherub.

"Un-uh!" she said. "Not this time. You said that last night. Look! You're thirteen already."

"That's true."

"Well, then!" And she got up, a little angry, her round face all flushed over with warmth, her electric fingers trilling restlessly at her skirt. "Are you a queery?" she said.

"Me?"

"You know what I mean. A big queery."

"Oh no!" he said.

"And you have never had your big love?"

"No," he said. "Well, yes! . . . No! I have had my shack, if that's what you mean."

"No," said Pixie. "That's not what I mean."

The fire was crackling quietly. It was at its very highest: the flame was brilliant but the blaze was silent. Warmth and sleepiness filled the room. Pixie sat down again on the velvet cushion at Cherub's side. "What I mean is . . . have you ever been in love?"

"Oh I see," said Cherub.

"It gets difficult to explain," she said. "Sometimes it is hard for me to talk. I get this nervousness and I don't know what to say."

"Me too," said Cherub, taking her hand. "I get scared too."

"Do you?" she said.

"Yes," he said.

"What do you get scared of?" she said.

"Lots of things," he said.

"Like what?"

"Like . . . girls."

"Are you scared of me?"

"Yes," he said. His lower lip was quivering.

"Don't be scared of me."

"No?"

"No, don't be scared of me."

"Oh-h-h . . ."

"What is it?"

"Nothing."

"Tell me," she said.

"Oh please!" he said suddenly. "Oh please leave me alone." And he began to cry.

"What is it?" she said. "Are you scared?"

"It was the snake," he said. "And everything. And your father. And now the things you are saying."

"What am I saying?"

"About love . . ." He looked down and picked at a button.

"Well, what's wrong with love?"

"What's wrong with love?"

"That's right. What's wrong with love?"

"Nothing," said Cherub. "I guess . . . But it scares me."

"You have never known it," she said. "That's all your trouble. You have never been in love."

"Do you think that's it?" said Cherub.

"Of course that's it," she said. "You could try anyway. What have you got to lose?"

"Nothing, except . . . my other friend said it was different."

"Who is your other friend?"

"Morton."

"What did he say it was?"

"He said I needed a shack."

"Well, did you get one?"

"Yes."

"Did it work?"

"Nope."

"What happened?"

"I threw up."

"Good for you!" said Pixie. "Good for you! It just shows you've got guts. It shows you can't just hop onto any old cow and expect fireworks. Can you now?"

"No, you can't."

"But with a young girl it would be different, wouldn't it?"

"I guess so," he said.

"And if you were in love."

"Yes," he said. "That's it! Sure that's it!"

"Cherub?" she said.

"Yes?" He did not move away from her now.

"Could you fall in love with me?"

He looked her up and down.

"I could try, I guess." She tickled his ankle with her toe. "It wouldn't be so hard."

"No?" she said. Her finger ran down his side.

"No," he said.

*　　*　　*　　*　　*

The summer came and the summer went away . . . The sun shone down on the snowy mountain and the snow melted and rushed into the streams. The sky was more blue than it had ever been before and the first red leaves balanced crisply in the morning air; the squirrels furled their tails and gathered horse chestnuts for winter. But at noon-time it was still blazing hot, and the reaper with his scythe had to stop under a shade tree to mop his brow. Indian summer had arrived.

Cherub and Pixie romped in the luscious meadow; they swam in the secret pool; they climbed the highest apple-tree in the grove. And no more serpents were seen in the grass.

"Oh say! This is living," said Cherub one day. "I have never been full of so much pleasure before. What a pure joy it is just to swap around all day long."

"Yes," said Pixie. "It's nice."

When it was bad weather, they stayed in the Inn. Then they played games or chatted if people were in; but if they were alone, they went up to the attic. In the attic there was an old feather-mattress on which they made love. The rafters hung with lots of cobwebs and it was damp there after the rain; but Pixie liked it none the less.

"It's a little wet," Cherub would say.

"That's all right."

"Don't you mind?" he said.

"No, it's all right."

"Look! I'm stuck in a cobweb. I wonder where that goes to?"

"Come on," she said.

"Wait a minute."

"Come on."

Once the Innkeeper had a party. Everybody drank a great deal. At the end of the main course, Pixie brought in the sherry and set it before Mr. Curdy at the head of the table. He gave her a pinch. "Ha ha ha. That's my girl. You don't mind, Sam?" And the Innkeeper smiled and nodded. Then as Pixie went down the line, serving people the drinks that Mr. Curdy poured, each gentleman would pinch her wrist or give her a little kiss. Cherub was watching it all from the kitchen door.

"Well I hope you've had your fun," he said when she came in.

"I'll say!"

"And you don't seem to mind the wear."

"No I don't," she said.

"You do just about what you want, don't you?"

"Maybe."

"But you don't care what somebody might think, do you?"

"Maybe I don't."

"You're quite a smarty, aren't you?"

"Maybe."

One day in September, Cherub looked up at the sky and said, "It seems like real summer, doesn't it? Look how blue the sky is."

"Yes, it is," said Pixie. "It's very blue."

"I like to see the sky that blue," said Cherub. "There aren't any clouds at all."

"Isn't that one?" said Pixie.

"No, that's not a cloud," said Cherub.

"Yes it is. That's a cloud."

"No, that's not a cloud."

There was a long moment of silence; finally Pixie brightened up.

"Then we will love, today," she said. "Then we will love in the apple-grove."

They went down the winding path to the sloping hill called Great Green. After that, there were two or three smaller slopes before you arrived at the meadow. Cherub and Pixie strolled along through the autumn grass. The milkweeds were dried up now and the dandelions were turned to skeletons. Only great ghostly puffs of immaterial fluff remained of those merry yellow flowers, and the pods of the milkweed were dry. When you squeezed them in the spring, a sticky sap would pour through your fingers. Now if you pressed them they would crumble. And now from the thicket in the center of the fields, blossoms no longer radiated their colors. They were dead now. They were fallen to the earth. Only the more hardy plants remained, that could stand up in a chill wind.

"Come to the orchard," said Pixie. "You cannot feel the wind in there."

"I love you, Pixie," he said.

"Yes you do."

"You asked me to love you, and I did it. Wasn't that nice?"

"You were too good," she said. She laughed with a smile.

They came into the orchard. Under the September branches, the ground was lush with fallen leaves. "We can sit here," she said. "In this lovely pile."

He sank into the leaves. "Tumble down upon me," he said. "Please do." She tumbled down upon him and rested in his arms; the wind blew her moppet hair across his face. He kissed her upon her lips.

"This is old love for us now," he said. "We are old lovers already."

"Soon we shall be sitting by the fire in our rockers." He laughed.

Later, they got up and walked under the trees. It was the end of September; October was on the wing. Cherub and Pixie dressed alike; flannel shirts of red plaid, blue jeans and sneakers, hats and scarves.

From the rise in the middle of the orchard you could see the whole landscape.

"Soon I shall be fourteen," she said.

"I am only thirteen."

"You will be fourteen sometime."

"You will be fourteen first. I will still be thirteen."

They went down the decline together and came to the pond. The water was dark and sedgy but the scrawny branches of the trees reflected clearly in its surface. A few birds piped occasional tunes.

"Do we dare go for a swim?" He looked into the surface at their twin reflections.

"Oh I think no," she said. "There is too much of the bite in the air. It would not be wise at this stage."

"No, I guess not."

They walked along. Past the pond there was stubble ground where the farmers had already harvested. The short-cut stems broke unevenly the surface of the field; it was a yellow, erratic, deathly sight.

"What do they cut the stems for?" said Cherub. He pointed down at the stumps of straw.

"For next year's crop," said Pixie. "So it will grow better. You have to cut it down low so next year's will be tall."

They went along over the stubble. It was an uncomfortable feeling under foot. Soon they passed onto the turf.

"Where shall we go now?" said Cherub. "We have made the whole tour."

"We could go back."

"Couldn't we go below? We have never walked down there."

"That is not permitted," she said. "Nobody can go that way. You would fall down and be hurt."

So they returned the way they had come, a way they had gone many times: past the stubble, about the pond, into the orchard, through the trees, across the meadow . . . And then they stopped to pause by the thicket once more. Cherub found the flat rock and sat down upon it and Pixie sat down on the ground. For a moment she started, and a shiver darted through her body, as she saw a long wrinkled form extended beneath the brambles. Then she looked again and saw that the life was gone; it was only the shrivelled hide of what had once shone with brilliant colors. Brown and green, and black circles, glaring eyes and warning hiss—now these were gone, and only a shrivelled bit of leather remained. The serpent had shed its skin.

There was a quiet in the air.

"You remember that day? It was on this flat rock I was sitting."

She did not answer.

"There was the serpent." He pointed. "That's where we met."

Still she hung back.

"What's the matter?"

"Oh . . ." She looked up at him with glazed eyes.

"Yes?"

"I remember," she said.

Later, up at the Inn, while the packing was going on, Cherub stalked about restlessly with his hands in his pockets and his cheeks pouted out in a deep sulk. Outside the sky was gray; there was some snow on the ground and a great deal of slush. Sometimes rain or sleet cut across the sky and beat upon the windows, then cut downwards straight into the porous snow.

"Fine!" said Cherub, kicking things as he walked. "That's a funny one if you ask me. I never heard of that before."

The movers strapped up the big trunks, got them over their shoulders, and came trundling down the stairs. They brought them out to the van. Then the Innkeeper came down and tied together andirons and stuffed newspapers under window-sills and left paint brushes in turpentine. Pixie came shuffling down with a load of dresses over one arm, saying, "Make way. Make way." And loaded them onto the truck. Then the movers came back in again and started piling up chairs and tables, loading them onto their backs, and carrying them out the door. They took the cushion from the window-seat; they took the old cash-register; they took a case of beer.

"Black beer!" said Innkeeper, laughing, and clapping the moving man over the back. "Good for you!"

Everything went out to the truck.

The room was empty now; Cherub sat in the barren window-seat with his legs crossed. "That's just damn luck!" he muttered, pulling out his fingers. "How do you like that?" He listened to them crack.

"Sourpuss!" It was Pixie. She came in gaily and sat down beside Cherub, spreading out her skirt. "Grumpuss!" And she tickled him under the neck. "Old Grand-daddy-Won't-Smile!"

But Cherub did not answer.

"I'm so excited!" she said.

He just looked at her.

"It will be a beautiful Inn. Way down in a valley surrounded by the desert, with coconuts and palms . . ." She waited for him to answer. "Isn't that lucky!"

On the stairs you could hear the moving-men bringing down a bed.

"Oh I do hope the sea won't upset me! You know how squeamish I am. I don't want to spoil it now and be sick on poor old Daddy. Dear lovely Daddy!" And she bounced up and down on the wooden seat. "You know what Daddy has said? Daddy says they don't wear bathing-tops in the desert. He says I will only need my panties. Now isn't that something? Would you believe it? Just the luck of it! I'm simply giddy . . ."

She took him in her two arms and hugged him. "Where's that nice smile?"

Cherub stood up and looked down at Pixie.

"Are you very badly off?" she said.

He pressed his lips together tightly. She looked up:

"Can't we just have a kiss now? Can't we now?" She poked him in the belly with her index-finger. "Lovey there! . . . Now Lovey! . . . Won't we just give Pixie a kiss? I'm not off for the moon, you know."

"Where are you going?" he said at last.

"Just across a little ocean or two and a weeny old desert," she said breezily. "Now haven't we a kiss?"

Cherub looked down into her wide-open eyes and moppet of fluffy hair. The blue jeans were gone now and she wore a leaf-green dress with a low neckline bordered in lace. Her breast and throat were dappled a blossomy white as usual. But in her eyes there was a special thrill.

Cherub looked down with his own great blue eyes. But this time they were not swimming in their own seas of wonder; they were hardened into a cold glassy blue.

"You'll get your kiss in Kingdom-Come!" he said bitingly. "That's where you'll get your kiss!"

"Oh . . . bitter, bitter, aren't we? Bitter! Bitter!" She shook her finger up at him, trilling the lace of her dress with some kind of quiver of her body. "Aren't we the saucy-pie!"

"Why don't you shut up?" he said.

"Naughty! Naughty!"

"Won't you shut up?" And with that question he gave her a raw fierce slap across her mouth and cheeks that sent her teeth together with a snap and left a huge red welt. The welt began to pucker up and swell. "Oh . . ." She put her hand to her face and was crying.

"Lovey, dovey, Daddy . . . Shit!" he said in rage. "Can't we have a little kiss? . . . Aye? . . . Aye? . . ." He glared down at her trembling lips. "Can't we have a little kiss! ! Hey? ?" And he was ready to slap her again, but the full flood of her tears burst out upon her cheeks, and he did not dare.

Just then the Innkeeper called from outside: "Pixie, dear?"

Her lip trembled and her hand seemed to vibrate against her cheek; her whole body shook.

Slowly, her eyes flooded with tears.

"Oh . . . Cherub," she said, stammering. "I'm so sorry."

And she looked up straight into his eyes.

Suddenly he collapsed. He fell down into the seat at Pixie's side and his head slumped upon the wood. She lifted it up and lay it in her lap. In spite of the hurt of her own mouth, she was stroking his cheeks. "I'm so sorry, Cherub, that I couldn't do any different. I just wanted to have you so much and I didn't think about the future; but now Daddy has to go. I knew Daddy had to go. But I wanted you anyway, that's just the way I am. I couldn't help it."

"You're right," said Cherub with his eyes closed and his hand in Pixie's lap. "It isn't you and it isn't me. Is it? It isn't either of us . . ." He scratched his head. "Then what is it? . . ." And he pressed his blue eyes tight and pushed his face deeply into the softness of her lap.

"Pixie!" Her father was calling.

"It's time to go." She stood up and held out to him her thin arms, pale beside the springtime green of her dress; her shoulders were bare.

"Isn't that a strange one?"

"What's that?" she said.

"I was just thinking how bad most things are. Most things are ugly, aren't they?" She let the lace slip down one of her shoulders. "Except you're not," he said. "You're not ugly. You're pretty. Everything is ugly except you."

"I have to go," she said.

"Can't I go, too?" said Cherub.

"Oh no," she said. "That would not be permitted."

"Why can't I go?" he said.

"Oh, I'm afraid not," she said.

He cracked his knuckles.

"Good-bye, Cherub."

"Don't go."

"You will slip the lock?"

"Stay a little longer."

"Daddy says you must slam the door."

"Can't we just talk?" He jumped up from the seat and grabbed her wrist. She looked up at him sadly. He moved his hand slowly along her arm, feeling the warmth of her flesh. When he came to the crook of her elbow, it was wet on the inner side. Then he cupped his hand around her slim shoulder, feeling the shoulder blade in back and touching the hollow of her throat with his finger-tip.

"Pixie's Daddy waiting!" The big gruff voice called out through the cold air.

Pixie pulled up the lace of her dress.

"I do hope I don't get sea-sick!"

As she moved away she said, over her shoulder, "Don't forget about the door . . . to slam it."

"How do you do it?" he said.

"You do it like this," she said. "You click it . . . There is a little lever."

"Oh I see."

"Push it all the way up."

"I see."

The motor roared outside. She disappeared without turning back.

Cherub heard the door slam, the truck start up. He did not look outside but looked around the empty room. "How hollow it is," he thought.

"How empty to be all alone. I cannot fill up a room myself; I am too little." He made one step on the oaken floor. "The room is cold." He looked at the empty hearth. "There is no sense lighting a fire. It is late."

"Isn't it late?" He answered himself.

Outside the truck moved away; it honked once.

"Isn't it cold?"

The sound of the engine disappeared; he looked out the window. The truck was gone.

Suddenly, rain broke upon the windows. Cherub ran out through the hallway to look up the stairs. There was a hat-box half way down, on the landing; it was open and empty. A black ribbon hung out and there was tissue paper in a crumpled ball on the stair.

Cherub bent down to see the way the latch worked on the door; you had to snap it. There was a little lever you had to operate. Then it would close with a click.

December, 1957

THOMAS WHITBREAD

(1931–)

A graduate of Amherst, Thomas Whitbread con-
tributed to the Advocate *while he was a tutor and*
teaching assistant in the English department at
Harvard. He published Four Infinitives, *a collec-*
tion of his poetry, in 1964.

SKEETER

A skeeter skitters shrewdly across a pool.
Circular proliferations point
Toward a rounded end, then merge, then flatten away.
Dead skin on a finger-tip announces more:
Hot water, advancing blood, then quick cold air
And retreating blood. The surface of the pond
Seems to stretch and contract, but does not swell and shrink
Like human skin. It is not human skin;
It is water, set in motion by the legs
Of an insect, moving shrewdly over it.
The shrewdness is not ours. We can know
An expanding radius from each still point,
But the pointless movement, unpredictable,
From point to point, inscrutable and dumb,
Bores us. The cunning bores us. We have hands
Complete with permanent fingers, fully skilled
In compassing our very human desires.
Therefore we wash and dry them, to make sure

That they are serviceable; the dead skin
Peels off, expendable. Shrewd skeeter, skate
Icily random across your glassy drum:
I could break your floating web with one dropped stone
But my hand is clenched and will not let it go.

September, 1958

ARTHUR FREEMAN

Class of 1959, (1937–   )

*Arthur Freeman spent a term as a junior fellow
of the Harvard Society of Fellows. He has published one volume of poetry,* Apollonian Poems;
an issue of Identity Magazine *has been devoted
to his poetry. He is a baseball enthusiast, and has
written on Hart Crane. He received his Ph.D.
from Harvard in 1965 and now teaches English at
Boston University.*

THE EXHORTATION TO AN
AUDIENCE, TO BE STILL

WHEREAS, these nimble shadows, dosing our stage
with a fairyland somnolence, are shy
if questioned, flit when caged
by whispers; and pinpointed, they must vanish, they must fly
like fireflies into someone else's dream—
no less illusory than shadows seem . . .

WHEREAS, the glancing glass of the imagination's
mirrors, pierced with laughter, shatters;
so this lacy needlework, contrived hallucinations,
striated with conversation, scatters
back to ravelled stagecraft . . . thus the violence
of careless talk uncharms our spell of silence. . . .

THEREFORE, peace! Now in attentive webs, catch rapture fleeting;
rise with our fantastic eyes, to sight beyond mere seeing.

December, 1957

Arthur Freeman   363

THE ZOO OF YOU

Thy leopard legs & python thighs,
Thy perched breasts & darting eyes,

Thy growling belly in its lair,
Thy crafty copperhead of hair,

Thy silky calves & furry groins,
Thy maney, rippling lion-loins,

Thy hind-behind—all these pursue
In beastly order (& I too)

Thy Pussy's primitive purlieu:
Unlock, unlock! Let's feed thy zoo.

November, 1958

THE SHORT HISTORY OF ART

Murano craftsmen wound your stem's
arpeggio of fluted crystal, filigree by filigree,
in twists and curls, veronicas of molten amber,
up, and upward, ever to the ruby cup.
Halfway along this cadence, they contrived
some ornament, *divertimento:* lacy glass
blown thin as moths' wings,
pierced, drawn, pinched, and molded
superfine, superfluous and exquisite, an airy
bauble, without flaw or function; thus
bestowing artfully their art
on what most richly might receive.

364   *Arthur Freeman*

Glass vines like viol strings, your neck:
they plied its frail white arc
to rise and fall, and fuse by fire
into the fiery goblet's throat,
below the full-blown, crimson lips.
And at this time of joining glass,
they would seal up a song inside,
a captive lyric, prisoner of form.

The centuries were not unkind.
You passed through France and England,
were admired and copied, never chipped.
You held court in museums, palaces,
drew patrons from among
grand dukes and princes, landed lords,
and men of honour and prestige. You were
more celebrated than your artificers—
(XIVth Century, Unknown). But day by day
your voice must age, your song
grow more elusive, lurking deeper
in the windpipe, among dry chords,
flat melodies. No longer
were the years indulgent. In a paper bag
you crossed the sea.

Today,
like the poor *apoggiatura* out of time,
your accents poised between intent and meaning,
you perch homeless on a modern shelf,
in modern context. While the life-span of your art
expires, you, its skeleton, will stay on
to be bric-a-brac. We'll analyze your bones,
your dried-up ligaments no rosin elixir
will ever tune to life again. A brittle
music tinkles round this Genuine Antique.

Irreverently passed from hand to hand,
from merchant to housewife, dealer

Arthur Freeman   365

to tourist, bought, sold, given
and re-given, traded and returned,
the shell of what you were lives still.
And sunlight, that was wont to fire
song in your glass throat, burn your lip
like Memnon's, with Venetian caroling, now slants
in dusty slices through Venetian
blinds . . . Only to cast a new day's light
on chinks and fractures, dissonance,
corruption, flaws and faults unseen till now.

Repeat, again repeat, until
one afternoon some curious four-year-old admires
your swansong's dying glow, and mercifully, you drop.
And pitifully you shatter, on a strange floor,
in a foreign epoch . . .
                        Scattering for good
or evil, fragments of imported glassware;
giving up the ghost of an old sweet song.

April, 1956

DAVID LANDON

Class of 1961, (1938–   )

David Landon was Pegasus of the Advocate *in 1959–60, and while at Harvard won the American Academy of Poets Prize and the Potter Prize for Comparative Literature. He spent three years in France and is now a graduate student in comparative literature at Vanderbilt University.*

DEBUTANTE

"Elle continuait à offrir le spectacle somptueux et désolé d'une existence faite pour l'infini et peu à peu restreinte au presque néant."

Marcel Proust, *Les Plaisirs et les Jours*

As you moved once,
towers dropped to their knees,
the spooks of elegant thieves
sighed in the mirrors for your gold hair,
the glass slid in silvery carpets under your feet,
and out of the gilt-framed emptiness
horses of snow leapt sleepily into the moon.

With a snicker of knives, like ripped silk,
the mirrors fled to infinity,
and a riderless waltz chased after.

You stood bewildered,
and the sea of our voices crashed around you;
trumpets licked you with hot tongues,
young men attended
with the sleek cars of their calculations;

and I was terrified,
hearing you run down the stairway,
as if someone spilled a basket of marbles.

I have read that you married finally;
and I wonder if your days are ripped from you,
as pages from an engagement book;
or if caught in your mother's dull enthusiasms,
restlessness will bring you to adultery.

The thought of you frantic in those endless halls
has brought me to my knees,
and the memory of what has gone
is as if on a day of azure,
the snow got up and left,
and the shadows slid into the sea.

May, 1961

A HOT NIGHT

In the streets, on a hot night,
they open the doors of the bistros,
and the voices spill out,
as trash from a truck;

The odor of coffee keeps us awake
and we talk till our dry speech scratches,
as fingernails on paper,

and then it rains
and we escape.
How shall we gather so much
silver coin in our small arms?

May, 1961

TO THE RIGHT OF BOSTON

While I sit by the Charles,
The sun goes down to the right of Boston;

The shadows come out from under the bridges,
Blurring the edges of things.

When the sky fell through the bottom of the river
All but the windows plunged after;

The nearness and distance tremble,
And over the water,
Steeples and gold flags float on a black cloud.

Suddenly two black birds
Zoom out of nowhere and are gone,
And the distance runs after them.

The lights go on,
And icicles drop into the river;
Behind me a mother calls her children to dinner.

It must be warm in the houses
As inside a jack-o-lantern;

I pass by in the darkness
Thinking it is good to be hungry,
And then to eat.

May, 1961

David Landon 369

STEPHEN SANDY

(1933–   )

Stephen Sandy was born and raised in Minnesota and holds a Ph.D. from Harvard. He has published three collections of poetry: Caroms *(1961),* Mary Baldwin *(1962) and* The Destruction of Bulfinch's House *(1963). For several years he has taught in the English department at Harvard.*

THE GOLDWEIGHER

Low Countries; 15th c; a Burgher donor

i

From the road the afternoon is sapphire-clear;
The fields, a canvas sealed with snowy gesso
Where artisans have left their sluggish marks,
Fence lost in drifts like driftwood on white beach.
Flattened now, unshaped, these supine fields
Roll back from squinting eyes; this ironing frost
Has cadged the desert's bright rough cloak with ease,
Robbed the tropic panther of his muscled crouch.
—I think these bare wonders, stable beauties,
These uncut stones might curb the men who rule
Our finer towns, fend off the troubador
With lute in hand, him gaudy with glad song.

So run my thoughts: lush thoughts that sometimes elbow
Prisoners of Cold, as this December day
Spirals toward Christmas eve, and my time climbs:
The old love heady on my trudge toward home.

But, sure, this grief of cold resilient light
Tattered Joseph in his boots would know
As sacred (and properly magnificent
For nativity)—would know this better than
Our gargoyled towers, all our celebrating,
Attentuated gestures of the earth
That point up paradise with files of saints
Marshalled by kings to gaze upon the vault.
And certainly he'd know the antique ease
Of fields bedded in snow; the warm, banked house;
The cattle stamping slowly on the straw,
The chinked barn steaming through Cold's long delay.

ii

A man who comes years after greatness, seeks.
He pauses by the statues in the square
And gapes at fame, seeking some quirk in stance;
Decides (in deft perversion of heroics)
That though bronze kings corrode on golden thrones
Still higher thrones are clay—the crown of thorn
Fetches more honor than a golden garland.
Taut Alexander, who held all the world,
Felt no such humble call. He claimed his fame.
To serve, hold back, he knew meant death; yet knew
His heights would leave him reeling at his death.
Only the age-old dead, whose tales are gnarled,
Pretended hemlock cups were draughts of wine.

                   And Christmas Eve comes up
The East, the light dying, falling far
To another world. Now the North Star points
Toward Dipper's span; now no prospect of a fire.

iii

What snow! From certain heights to certain deaths
The traveller wanders, too far from home.
Here new foods are dangerous, and old clothes

Stephen Sandy 371

Set one apart on strange, uncharted roads.
Across the field, turned by the mangle of the wind.

A light off the road! A corn crib's slats
Send stairs of light, lead from my road
Across the furrowed field up to an old
Wind-guttered shed made warm by man's sure hand:
One feeding his stock, guarding his own land.
I stop for the corn-crib light.

                    My eyes half close.
Haunches are melting two ovals in the land
Of frost. It is damp rest, and all dry is lost
For tonight. Once I think I see the snow
That silks this bank give up some lover's ghost,
Like Dido locked in the toil of dark. But no,
The cash belt hugs me, holds me warm; my way
Holds only damp and caking boots. And yet
This scene, nameless! Surely there's a linen bed!

And farmers standing near, and lambs, and light?
(Candles glinting warmly by winter's gloom,
Circles of softness on the sacred floor.)

                  iv

But He means more than real or trusted crèche.
Once (in Bourges) I stood before *une Vierge;*
A populace of candles burned their prayers;
Beneath, two trays, one full at two francs, one
With but a handful left at ten. I thought
It is buying special ten franc candles,
It is the courage to do this thing that counts:
Whether or not the hoped-for outcome is assured.
Caritas and *humilitas* are still
Too good a buy for rich, too dear for poor.

I think of early mornings when wars are begun
And the most important departures made;

Before the city awakens, before coffee.
Of midnight, when you build and kill, and the still
Griefs labor. When love confirms, denies, or sleeps.
Of the evenings when the last bottle pops,
Uncorked at last, and wars and loves are gauged
Across the tablecloth. The Patience hangs
Around for always, and Meekness for a time.

Body stiffens on the ground, my rest; back takes
All the cold in; legs hurt from the long walking.
It is a night for every man to be
In his own city.

                  The road grows short,
And hurry, but night not warmer. I shall
be numb for hours, hours before limbs tingle.
This night it is a long way through to rest,
Also much pain before warm bed again.

v

You see, I've chosen for myself a far
City, so far for such a night; so cold.
What's more, you see, the woman I desire
I may not reach tonight. Willing would I
Deliver myself to her smothering hands!

And yet the manger counts . . . not on this road,
But in my city, in my morning of praise,
Where I have gold enough to love Him, love
To gild Him. There I'll buy a window for
His spiraling hall, one many-colored, bold;
(The roses glowing warmly in winter's glare
Pouring soft circles round the level floor)
To rainbow all His marble court in blues,
Reds; and, centerwise, a tall, contrite, and
Suitably attired image of myself.

Winter, 1958

Stephen Sandy   373

THE SULTAN WEARS
A CRIMSON TURBAN

May the Sultan behead whom he wants?

It is true the Sultan beheads whom he wants
When I go to the country of the Sultan
In a boat whose blades make the water play
Like endless fingers on the belly rolling.

The Sultan squatting cross-legged in slippers
That taper to points that point at his head
Puts down his mirror and nods, "Now
                  we will have beheading."

The Sultan beheading the people he wants
Is holding his golden parasol cocked
And sipping his amber norman of lemon
And grenadine in beer.

The Sultan is taking the head off
Of people he wants—and more,
He hoists them on gates of palazzos, like brooches
On walls where the guards in red shoes guard.
These are the sights we have come to see,
I, and the tourists with eyes that take postcards
Of all they barely manage to see.

We have come from a very afar
Because a photograph in our head from a book
Reminded us just in time of a desolation,
Much time, long roads, great silence;
And sitting at the end of all our vacations
When the stakes of our make-shift trips are all pulled up,
There is the Sultan, under the trees
By a trestle table of the picnic area.

The Sultan who beheads the people he wants,
Who is letting his swordblade shave his thumbnail

That ready blade, slipshod but shaved,
Shined and shampooed and heady for bigger game.

April, 1965

DAVID BERMAN

Class of 1961, (1939–   )

David Berman wrote poems for the Advocate
*while he was a renegade law student, enrolled
in writing courses under Archibald MacLeish.
He graduated from the Harvard Law School in
1963. He is now an assistant to the Attorney
General of Massachusetts.*

DISTORTED DIALOGUE

You ask me where I stand
And if I have a voice.
There isn't any answer;
So my answer is, "Of course."

The house that I would build is built,
Lived-in and crumbled; its noble architects
Drowned in a sea of half-forgotten facts.
The white and classic door,
The rich interior
Are shabby, old and ungenteel.
And only I, and sometimes you, are real.

Like a boy carrying a too-full glass of milk
Up a flight of uneven, rickety stairs,
I spill emotions that I am aware
Are neater when contained.
Shall I defy my nature with a scowl?
I am too egregious not to complain
And much too much reserved to howl.

ON FAILURE

If shamed, he well may say
Time is a kind of maze,
A puzzle children play
On dark and rainy days.
And who plays wisest, he
Leaves the most choices open
Especially when the solution
Is what he will call history.
(And children seldom question:
Is the best way right?
Is the right way best?)

But he whose gift is sure,
Both adamant and pure,
May let his pencil trace
The maze as in a race
While his lessers stare.
Then if it be unsolved
When he that tries is through,
Because they now all know
The route that led nowhere,
They say, "We always knew
And could have told you so."

April, 1961

GEORGE HORWITZ

Class of 1962, (1940–   )

While he was an undergraduate at Harvard, George Horwitz published portions of two novels in the Advocate. *Since graduation he has been living in New York City and writing. The novel of which "Elephant's Work" is a part is now ready for publication.*

The flashback sequence described in this begins and ends in a conversation between Marek Dmitrievitch Dorojoski and Michael Griffin. Dorojoski was born in Warsaw in 1926, the son of a bastard by a Polish aristocrat and a Russian peasant woman; his mother's parents were Ukranian and Russian, which explains Marek's patronymic. Griffin was born in Sioux City in 1920, but when addressed by the Pole, Dorojoski occasionally indulges in Russian name-calling, hence "Mikhail Petrovitch" and "Misha" will still mean Griffin.

They sit in a mossy alcove in Lisbon's Estufa Fria *(Portuguese for 'cool hothouse'), an ordered jungle in miniature, where they listen to water trickle down artificial streams and watch Julia St. John, who comes into the garden with a little Portuguese girl. Julia cannot see them, and Michael Griffin speaks of her.*

ELEPHANT'S WORK

THE FAMILIES in linen, silks, pomade, and patent leather came in and went out, walked up and down the paths in silence; Venustiano Ramirez turned the pages of his newspaper; and this Griffin, he too was silent now, much as he had been when Dorojoski last saw him, deeply engrossed and involved in a world he could not belong to. And then a very unusual thing happened. A beautiful girl came—no, she was.

She came through the gate, the same as the rest of the people. She dressed very simply in a plain blue shirt, a straight skirt of gray linen, and brown-topped tennis shoes. Nice enough legs, slender but substantial, if one can notice legs apart from the rest of a woman. The erotic implications of a well-formed calf, so poignant to some, had eluded Dorojoski thus far. But maybe. She moved well, smoothly relating herself to the ground. Her hair was smooth and straight, pale yellow falling to her shoulders, and moved in accordance with the rest of her body. Power was there. She stood as a separate entity for only a second before wide-eyed absorption with the garden and her small companion gave a unity to the whole scene. A glance from her eyes, now cast down, would fix a moment in time, she was that strong. She could stand alone, and Marek would think of her this way, towering somehow, majestic, but the strength of this girl was that she could stand and everything would come to her, but she chose not to stand.

In the midst of a toy jungle, a real tiger emerged. A white tigress. The rest of the jungle was still. The men watched her with some pleasure and not a little fear, the children followed her with their eyes and stood in awe, and the women waited with calm but humble acceptance, for a man does not run off with a wild beast, least of all a white tigress.

She brought with her a small child, girl of nine or ten in pink and white and ribbons and patent leather, soft black hair, fluff, and big dark eyes. Even from high up in his damp mossy place, Marek could see the child's eyes flicker from open betrayal of exuberance, to belying her age with Laconian nonchalance, to frank puzzlement as her mind cut across an idea, even a word, from her stately, yes imperious, charge (for the child was clearly leading the way, if not dictating it—who can dictate to a tigress?) They never touched each other physically, but they seemed to maintain a constant contact, the white tigress dropping an occasional segment of thought, the keeper picking it up and meandering with it, bringing it back in simpler form but covered with ribbon bows. They were both well-amused, but never too taken with themselves to miss a curiosity: see them now, Marek Dmitrievitch, as they stop on a stone path criss-crossed with cracks full of running water and they laugh when the white one puts her finger in the water and sets a drowsing carp sputtering away between the flat rocks.

"See this, Mikhail, see this. Someone has come to play and our little joke turns into a good thing."

"I have been watching, Marek." Griffin held a white handkerchief in his hand and unhooked his eyeglasses from his small, flat-lying ears. He turned away in his chair and Marek could not see his face. Griffin seemed mechanically occupied in something, wiping his glasses perhaps, and there was nothing but his voice, low, steady, forced flat. "I knew her once," he said and on the last word he seemed out of breath.

"Would it be greatly encroaching to ask what she was like?"

"Indeed it would." He took out his black laquer case. "Cigarette?"

"It's cheaper than eating." Marek took one and nodded thanks.

"Where are you eating tonight?" Griffin said.

"Molino said something about meeting in a place called O Aquarion at six-thirty. Do you know it?"

"It's quite pleasant, but I think you'll want to change your clothes."

"Clothes. Yes. I left my gear in your lobby, but I might have to borrow a suit and ties from you. Molino said to bring you along, if you wanted to come."

"How sweet of him. Touching all around, really—of Molino to tempt away the spiritually celibate Griffin and of Marek Dmitrievitch to spare Griffin's toes."

"Well—"

"Griffin will now tell his story, having been touched." He spat out the last word so, Marek thought. Yes, he protests too much. Inexplicable to Dorojoski, Griffin had found something that came close to him, and when he turned to light his guest's cigarette, his eyes were bright green and glittering. When Griffin spoke at times like this, the words tumbled out with a sureness more of language than truth. With sufficient tempering he had always been able to withdraw from situations, no matter how harrowing for him, and could talk about the most maudlin things as if he was no more involved than a kid at a Mighty Mouse cartoon festival. He loved a story almost too much to exist in one himself. His enjoyment of detail was too sadistic. "You see her now with a little girl, and, if you'll excuse the expression, they are commu-ni-ca-ting with each other. They are. Watch them. One speaks and the other answers in simple words they both understand, and not baby talk either—real words, because the words are not important to any more degree than this: they are speaking to, not at, each other. Or so they think, and that's enough for them to feel comfortable about it.

"This was not our way, because we had by-passed the opening stages, where one draws a complete blank or feels a moving rapport. We had ignored the complete blank, each of us saw something, some tremendous power moving the other, and the attraction of these powers was enough to hold us together through the stages of groping for objective correlatives. Now of course, I don't really mean to say we just stood around and watched each other stand around. It was a great deal more reasonable than I make it sound: she was utterly blameless throughout, to begin with. She was just out of a convent, and was so taken by the sight of me sweating on a hot day in front of a Michelangelo Moses in the Bargello that she asked me what I saw, the first man she'd spoken to in conversation since she was six, or something like that, except for the executor of her father's will."

"Is she Portuguese?" Marek said and Griffin smiled.

"Evidently her parents were British and she was born there, raised here and educated in Italy. She was about to set out on some kind of tour, and she was taking one last look around the Florentine museums when she found me. After a time, we went outside to a cafe, drank Campari which she didn't like, and she agreed to stay on for another few, since her lease wasn't up for another week anyway. I should add at this point that it was all quite new to me too, and I continued at *my* penzione until the end of the week, when we left together for Rome. We finally got together there, more out of a feeling of mutual obligation than anything else, which is a ghastly thing to say, but there it is: each of us felt that this was the thing one had to do and, not wanting to insult the other, we sort of stumbled into. And stumble was the word. But it was quite exciting in one way—just look at her: but no one, not even Dorojoski, could be cold enough to resist that; you couldn't even talk yourself into thinking you were doing her a favor." And Marek watched her rippling through the gracefully suppressed leaves and light, and he heard them laugh. "Of course it was exciting, exhilarating at times, but there still existed this stigma of mutual respect. She was so damned smart and alive, constantly writing and writing well, and filling the back of her notebook with incredible sketches of everything we saw, underlining everything I ever saw in a face or a building with perceptions always of one more degree of intensity than my own faculties would allow; and to her, I was an altruist and a leader, and a doer, all at once, a man articulate and sensitive without being appalled with the human condition to the extent of reaching a state of inertia.

"It got to be quite a rub, after a while, coming to a great shoot-'em-up finale in Naples, horrifying enough in itself. There are a lot of classical ruins around there, Herculaneum and Pompeii just a short sprint down the Amalfi, and there is beauty enough too, God knows, with Vesuvius, the bay, and Capri. But just about the time we arrived, I had taken a very realistic but macabre—yes, masochistic way of looking at myself, and I decided that, frankly, I had come to see the law of the jungle in action. I had protected myself from it all too long, and now, in Sunny Napoli, I was going to see it all.

"Well, it was awful, Marek, really disgusting, and *I* did most of the horrible things. The law of the jungle, survival of the fittest, et cetera— it's all very well on paper, but you should see the fittest. The survivors —how pathetic they are. The injustice overwhelmed me after a while— when fools like those have to live by their wits, something has gone wrong with the balance of nature. But you've seen all that, haven't you?"

"I have been to Naples."

"Then you know what I mean? They aren't even a little bit *cunning*."

"I think I understand."

"Go ahead, Marek. Rub it in. I know I won't fit in that world or any other. It doesn't offend me as it used to."

Griffin was lying, naturally. Nothing hurt him more, thought Marek. "Tell me about the horrible things that happened."

"The horrible things. Ah, you mock me, but, yes, well, at first . . . nothing seriously grotesque; after an hour or so of fending off beggars, filthy picture salesmen, hotel agents, and so on, I stuffed one head first into a big trash barrel. I can't even remember what he wanted me to buy—maybe he wasn't selling anything at all: perhaps he had been sent to welcome the two of us to his city. The poor fellow. Feet kicking, the barrel swaying clumsily, it makes a touching reminiscence. Then a bootblack caught us waiting to cross a street and started polishing my shoes right there on the curb, so naturally, I kicked him into the gutter."

"I've heard bootblacks laugh about this afterward."

"Sure you have, but I haven't, and she hasn't. Look at her—how many bootblacks has she talked to?" Not very many, one would guess from looking at her. She and the child were bent over a small plant, and for a moment, her hair hung down straight and long, and it did not look as if she talked very much to anyone. "Sure, they laugh, but all day long it was things like this, nothing serious, almost funny. Coming out of Thomas Cook's with the mail, some slimey little character blew his horn at me. At us. Things as small as that. Italians blow their horns continually and it's nothing to get upset about, but here I was with that splendid girl and two footballing freshmen from Minnesota, and when I told them to lift the back bumper of the offending Fiat, they tumbled into action. Naples was full of disconnected trash barrels that day, and I upended this one through the open sunroof of the Fiat and then jammed it under the back bumper. The poor thing couldn't move. The freshmen thought it was a howl, and we bought them a round of Cinzano and talked for another half hour, but she didn't laugh once. She had stopped speaking altogether, actually.

"Eventually, of course, I got tight, but not until we had been through the city a couple of times and down to Pompeii and back. We were planning to ferry out to Capri the next day, so we stayed in a funny little hotel which occupied one story of an office building overlooking the black market. We bathed there, changed for dinner, and left it again as quickly as possible. The view of Vesuvius through the French windows was marvellous but the rest of the place wanted something. This was our feeling toward most of the places we stayed: isn't it terrible that you can sleep somewhere and make love to your sweety there, and still not form any attachment to the wall paper?

"We had cocktails at the Excelsior, and if I ever go to Naples again, I'll stay at the Excelsior, and never step out the door until the day I leave. There's more going on in that place than the rest of the city put together. From the outside, it seemed much the same as many of the other fine hotels on the quai, except that a monstrously long white Cadillac with license plates was stuck halfway through the porte-cochère. We watched it back, rock, sway, heave, and finally spew forth six arabs in native costume, three of which waddled into the hotel leaving the ones remaining to block five swarming lanes of Alfas, Fiats, and Vespas, while the Cadillac lumbered back on the quai. The three footmen quickly returned to the car, sparing no Arabic invective to the Italian motorists, and rolled away in air-conditioned splendor. It was all quite enticing.

"There was more of the same inside, only better. Fix it in your mind, Marek Dmitrievitch: an atmosphere of golden light from glittering fixtures, desk clerks in morning coats, Viennese waltzes played by a skeletal violinist oozing sensitivity, retired Britons having their last crack at the grand tour, and in the midst of it all, those Arabs, but now they were dressed in natty Italian sport clothes. The Moslem world in

Naples, negotiating their oil away to shifty Greeks and Florentines, business as usual, the Europeans offering strong drinks, the Arabs declining and proferring Balkan cigarettes in platinum cases to their elegant hosts. Much too precious to be believed, if you have never seen it, when East meets West in this pleasantly cutthroat way, soft tunes, sophisticated laughter, small gestures with finger-tips, and the whole running in a dead heat, when all at once, everyone rose quite abruptly and a short fat man came through the door. He was dressed in a flowing black robe and one of those white things on his head that you wish was a towel but isn't and on top of the whole thing, an octagonal crown of gold. Everything about him was perfect—the point of his beard, the tortoiseshell rims of his round dark glasses, the impression that he was even shorter than he looked and wore roller skates and had someone under the robes pushing him along whenever he stamped his feet, everything. He was followed, naturally, by another man, very dark but ordinary enough in the setting, neatly turned out in gray flannels, a short-sleeved white shirt, and pointey-toed beige shoes. They sat down on a small couch and almost as soon as the other man began to talk, the fat man broke into a high frenzied giggle which he sustained almost continually for the ten minutes he sat there. The joke was interrupted only briefly once, when a horsey little blond thing of nineteen or so in a Brigitte Bardot dress flounced in, addressed herself briefly and with evidently pleasing simplicity to the fat man who rose and nodded while she slumped down on an adjacent hassock. Then the joke and the giggle continued while the rest of the crew jockeyed for position, three at a time behind the small couch while a brace of photographers snapped pictures. When everyone but the girl had posed at least twice behind their heavyset leader and his jester (or prime minister) (or both) the fat man slapped his companion on the knee, jumped up, and fairly dashed from the room, an action which set off a short but horrendous clattering of small coffee cups and saucers, rattling of glasses and ashtrays, screeching of suddenly vacated chairs, and crunkling of flashbulbs into carpets (fine Persian things, probably sold to the hotel at a customer's discount by one of the fat man's forefathers). Less than a minute after the slap and sprint, the last of them had disappeared and the waiters were sweeping up the broken glass ..."
Now Griffin was quiet, looking down the little hill at the two girls, drumming his knees with his clean white fingers and sucking his lower

lip. Under his eyes he began to shine with perspiration, like a man eating hot peppers.

"And then what happened, Misha?" and he started to get up, but sat down again. The child and the white tigress sat for a moment on a bench across the pond from Ramirez, and for a moment, Marek was preoccupied wondering which camp would see the other first and leave, but Misha went on.

"But this time, I was fairly tight, and we left too. After some fine Neapolitan food and a quart of that wretched chianti, back we went to our sumptuous room, with its grey office furniture and plastic light fixtures. It wasn't very lyrical, as you would say—all the scene lacked was a pair of wet socks drying over a reading lamp, but we were used to each other by then, or anyhow, she was used to my smells. I don't mean to be offensive, Dorojoski, but everything else was there: two bags of smelly clothes, wet bathing suits, opened letters, some more of that wine, oh yes, and a couple of huge peaches. There were about five newspapers of various origins too—she had some kind of small boy curiosity about the Congo then. You wouldn't think old Griffin could do much with that for equipment, would you? But I was a desperate man by that time—I didn't even need the wine.

"But let us give her proper credit—I was tight and grumpy, and ready enough for bed. It was she who opened the french windows, stepped out on the balcony, and said, 'Holy God, Griffin. Look at those moths.' Even then, I didn't answer, but she went right on anyway. 'They must be attracted by the neon sign,' she said, and added thoughtfully, 'Moths are fond of bright light.' There was a moment's pause and then, 'Ak!'

" 'What did you mean by that last "Ak!"' I said.

" 'A bat just sucked up one of the moths,' she announced, and after a few seconds of respectful silence, she added, more to herself, I think, than anyone else, 'Now I'm watching the bats. That's life in the big city I guess.'

" 'What is?'

" 'The big ones eat the little ones. As you said about the war: shit doesn't run uphill.'

"I hated it when she used words like that. I joined her on the balcony. 'Just what is it that you're trying to say?'

" 'Nothing,' she said. 'I'm just running off at the mouth.'

"I said, 'Look. I'll show you something.' I tore off a corner from the front page of the newspaper. 'Bats are blind, but they have built in radar systems—a high peep and sensitive ears that pick up echoes from the smallest objects. Watch this.' I dropped the scrap of paper and it began to float down in front of the neon light, but it was not three seconds from my hand when a small brown bat swooped in and took it in its mouth. He spat it out again in an instant. 'You see? He couldn't tell until he had it in his mouth. Look.' I did it again, but the paper fluttered down undetected, so I let a third fall. Another bat took it. When she saw me tear off another piece, she said that I had made my point and need not continue for her edification.

"'Shit doesn't roll uphill,' I said. 'Watch.' She went back inside, but I couldn't stop. I was just being perverse, I suppose, and it was rather an awful thing to do, but I couldn't stop. True, half way through the newspaper I stopped baiting the bats. They showed no sign of learning —they were just as eager to lay tooth to the Grand Prix as they were to sample Kasavubu, perhaps moreso, and for me, the fascination diminished severely. 'Can one desire too much of a good thing?' Rosalind thought not, but then she mightn't have thought this a good thing either. I had begun to notice the air currents though, so I kept tearing off bits of paper, but now long strips designed to get past the bats. I let them spin down and sometimes they blew quickly around the corner of the buildings, as if ashamed or fearful of their origins, but usually they floated out and down to the street or to one of the balconies further down. When I returned to the room, I had no newspaper left.

"'You must be very proud of yourself,' she said.

"'Yes, I am,' I snapped back.

"'Why don't you come to bed now?'

"'I'm not sleepy.'

"'You ought to be, even if you're not, so lie down and snap off.'

"But then I took one of those mammoth peaches and returned to the balcony, where I ate it, dripping the juice over the rail. It was pretty good because the ground floor was an open air restaurant, and I could imagine all the slobber going down there and disrupting someone's elegant meal. When I finished, I dropped the pit, as big as an apricot, and it hit a metal table at the bottom. Raucus shouts of anger—imagine, your Conradian evening under cold white stars over the sultry bay, all shot to hell by a falling peach stone! I was satisfied. I had struck back at the jungle, and I was at peace. I came inside. I clicked off a light and smoked a cigarette in the dark, and I thought she was asleep when I lay down. The next day began with a grey and vermillion hazey sunrise, and when I turned over to see, she was gone."

Summer, 1963

George Horwitz 387

ROBERT LOWELL

(1917–   )

When Robert Lowell was a freshman at Harvard and candidate for the Advocate's *literary board, he was asked to tack down a carpet in the sanctum and when he was finished, told that he needn't come around any more. Since then he has been better received.* Lord Weary's Castle, *his second collection of poetry, won the Pulitzer Prize in 1947.* Life Studies *(1960) won the national book award, and* Imitations *(1962) the Bollingen Prize for translation. His latest book is* For the Union Dead, *which was welcomed with great enthusiasm in England and America.*

The following Imitations are taken from the Robert Lowell Issue which the Advocate *published in 1961.*

FOUR IMITATIONS

THE CADET PICTURE OF MY FATHER

(For Viola Bernard)

There's absence in the eyes. The brow's in touch
with something far. Now distant boyishness
and seduction shadow his enormous lips,
the slender aristocratic uniform
with its Franz Josef braid; both the hands bulge
like gloves upon the saber's basket hilt.

The hands are quiet, they reach out toward nothing—
I hardly see them now, as if they were
the first to grasp distance and disappear,
and all the rest lies curtained in itself,
and so withdrawn, I cannot understand
my father as he bleaches on this page—

Oh quickly disappearing photograph
in my more slowly disappearing hand!

Rilke: *Jugend-Bildnis meines Vaters.*

SELF-PORTRAIT

The bone-build of the eyebrows has a mule's
or Pole's noble and narrow steadfastness.
A scared blue child is peering through the eyes,
and there's a kind of weakness, not a fool's,
yet womanish—the gaze of one who serves.
The mouth is just a mouth . . . untidy curves,
quite unpersuasive, yet it says its *yes,*
when forced to act. The forehead cannot frown,
and likes the shade of dumbly looking down.

A still life, *nature morte*—hardly a whole!
It has done nothing worked through or alive,
in spite of pain, in spite of comforting . . .
Out of this distant and disordered thing
something in earnest labors to unroll.

Rilke: *Selbstbildnis aus dem Jahre 1906.*

YOU KNOCKED YOURSELF OUT

I

Those unnumbered, ruthless, random stones,
tense, vibrating still, as if slung
by the smothered abysmal fire;
the terror of those Amazon cataracts cascading
down miles to the chaos of implacable embraces;
the rock's lockjaw above the sand's
detonating dazzle—do you remember?

The sky-line, a blinding china saucer?

Do you remember the mountain, that wounded giantess?
The stranded sand-pine
with its nets of roots as mineral as the shards they finger,
as it beetled above the down-slope, only
yawning to engulf the horizon shadows?
Cool that grotto's gullet filled
with salad leaves and butterflies—
do you remember it, dumb, delirious,
there just under the summit's rotunda stone,
three men's length tall?
A king-pin of flint, teetering,
immobile?

Quick wren. Greedy eyes drunk with wonder.
You zig-zagged from fiber to fiber
to conquer the height's speckled crown,
dare-devil, musical child,
and loitered there alone to spy into the lapis lazuli bayou,
where unearthly, moss-browed turtles
were rousing from the ooze.

There the tension of nature at its lowest,
submarine sublimities,
nihilist admonitions!

II

You lifted arms like wings,
and gave the winds back their youth,
as you ran on the inertia of the stock-still air.

No one ever saw
your deft foot rest from the dance.

III

Lucky grace,
how could you help knocking your brains out
on such horny blindness—
you, simple breath, crystal bubble,

a candle, too dazzling
for the shaggy, random, vandalistic
burning of the naked sun!

Ungaretti: *Tu ti spezzasti.*

RUSSIA 1812

The snow fell, and its power was multiplied.
For the first time the Eagle bowed its head—
dark days! Slowly the Emperor returned—
behind him Moscow! Its onion domes still burned.
The snow rained down in blizzards—rained and froze.
Past each white waste further white waste rose.
None recognized the captains or the flags.
Yesterday the Grand Army, today its dregs!
No one could tell the vanguard from the flanks.
The snow! The hurt men struggled from the ranks,

hid in the bellies of dead horse, in stacks
of shattered caissons. By the bivouacs,
one saw the picket dying at his post,
still standing in his saddle, white with frost,
the stone lips frozen to the bugle's mouth!
Bullets and grapeshot mingled with the snow,
that hailed . . . The Guard, surprised at shivering, march
in a dream now; ice rimes the gray mustache.
The snow falls, always snow! The driving mire
submerges; men, trapped in that white empire,
have no more bread and march on barefoot—gaps!
They were no longer living men and troops,
but a dream drifting in a fog, a mystery,
mourners parading under the black sky.
The solitude, vast, terrible to the eye,
was like a mute avenger everywhere,
as snowfall, floating through the quiet air,
buried the huge army in a huge shroud.
Could anyone leave this kingdom? A crowd—
each man, obsessed with dying, was alone.
Men slept—and died! The beaten mob sludged on,
ditching the guns to burn their carriages.
Two foes. The North, the Czar. The North was worse.
In hollows where the snow was piling up,
one saw whole regiments fallen asleep.
Attila's dawn, Cannaes of Hannibal!
The army marching to its funeral!
Litters, wounded, the dead, deserters—swarm,
crushing the bridges down to cross a stream.
They went to sleep ten thousand, woke up four.
Ney, bringing up the former army's rear,
hacked his horse loose from three disputing Cossacks . . .
All night, the *qui vive?* The alert! Attacks;
retreats! White ghosts would wrench away our guns,
or we would see dim, terrible squadrons,
circles of steel, whirlpools of savages,
rush sabering through the camp like dervishes.
And in this way, whole armies died at night.

The Emperor was there, standing—he saw.
This oak already trembling from the axe,
watched his glories drop from him branch by branch:
chiefs, soldiers. Each one had his turn and chance—
they died! Some lived. These still believed his star,
and kept their watch. They loved the man of war,
this small man with his hands behind his back,
whose shadow, moving to and fro, was black
behind the lighted tent. Still believing, they
accused their destiny of *lèse-majesté*.
His misfortune had mounted on their back.
The man of glory shook. Cold stupefied
him, then suddenly he felt terrified.
Being without belief, he turned to God:
"God of armies, is this the end?" he cried.
And then at last the expiation came,
as he heard some one call him by his name,
some one half-lost in shadow, who said, "No,
Napoleon." Napoleon understood,
restless, bareheaded, leaden, as he stood
before his butchered legions in the snow.

Victor Hugo: *L'expiation*.

ROBERT LOWELL'S VERSE TRANSLATION
INTO THE AMERICAN IDIOM

That they are not classroom English I take for granted. That they are
something more akin to the local American way of speaking, in other
words to what we hear every day, makes him our fellow, as it made our
fellow of the same name crudely our fellow over a hundred years ago.
But the present Lowell is not crude, quite the opposite.

A translation into another language involves in the first place a choice
of the language into which the translation is to be made. This language

is used in this country by Robert Lowell with supreme ability and naturalness until it is acclaimed even in the classroom.

It must be heard to be appreciated. I have seen the enormous difficulties as witnessed by his work sheets in rendering the texts of some of the poems of Baudelaire in getting the precise accent of the words to stand up without a foreign un-American implication. This requires unceasing devotion to the text, and accurate work.

Here is a poet who knows what he is doing, devoted to the best in his language, with courage to go ahead with his own tasks, and a cultured addiction to his native way of speaking. You can't fool such a man because he will make up his own mind. When he hears a word spoken in a certain way he hears it so spoken and that is the end and you can put it into your lexicon as final.

May we have many more in America of the same caliber.

WILLIAM CARLOS WILLIAMS

SIDNEY GOLDFARB

Class of 1964, (1942–   )

Mr. Goldfarb, Pegasus of the Advocate in 1963–
64, won the Dana Reed Prize that year for the
best writing in a Harvard publication. At various
times he has been, in his own words, "a mail clerk
in a vitamin factory, roofer, plumber, leather-
necker, cab-driver." His work has appeared in the
Partisan Review. He is now studying in Chicago.

THREE CITIES

I

Daisies and such. A fist full of feathers in the wind.
Windows open and windows close, and the white men run
At the whistle's moan, filling the holes with bones and silt.
Every morning there is a little less to notice.

Every evening there is rancid breathing,
And the scent of plastic flowers fancies the window lattice.
Butter melts on the oilskin and dimples its own face swimming.
Clocks are electric and bear no winding.

Long into darkness. Grey lips flicker a thousand dots of love
Across the walls, rescreening a laughter the alley cans.
Twist the picture. Thumb the pupil till it bloats just right.
Then choke out the face that bids good-night.

I enter. So much muffled disbelief.
I am a glutton. I eat your pie
Without warning. I trample your high grass.
I pluck daughters from your low trees.
I am a fine example of what is most immediate.

I do everything with my hands.
I stuff my face with grapes.
I mulch them between my teeth.
Seeds run from my mouth and scatter carelessly.
I have no sympathy with what I cannot eat.

No one steals from me.
No one comes to my side of the river
To ask directions. I delight
In the sorrow of the misguided hunter
And the triumph of the wild pig.

But oh, you Withered Mother, Earth,
If my stomach makes your heart shiver,
And my clumsy droppings churn your gut,
Wait till the mud feeds my seed just right,
And my son comes rumbling from his hut.

III

Sometimes I must listen to myself.
In the silence of my room, cymbals thrash
A quiet violence, and laughter is the ceiling of my jest.

But you can hear that, my companion, my friend.
Deep in the cellars a voice rolls and towers,
Tolling a chorus from a single tongue.
In the window at our feet we see his figure,
White hair flailing in the darkness of his dance.
They say he cannot distinguish color

And will hold anyone in his arms.
Beneath the street his chorus holds us.
He embraces us and surrounds us in his yearning.

Listen!
It rises through the sidewalk and crumples our knees.
We cling to the pavement with hands and feet.
Hear it!
The cement clangs in his ravings.
The tolling of shovels girds the earth in his voice.
Hammers bind the wind to his lusting.
Hear it again!
How the bells break from shadows and whirl us in color!

Now you must know.
The street is an ocean he holds in its churning.
Waves ring the curbstone and toss us in union.
Listen!
It is the madman singing in his chains!
Echoing towers tell us of life.

It is the madman singing in his chains.
You are my brother. I am his son.

January, 1963

THIS YOU TOLD ME, THIS I THOUGHT, THIS I THOUGHT

This you told me: On the back porch you sat watching
Our puppy investigate the differences of shadow
And sunlight. Then came the neighborhood to sniff.
You saw them eye each other warily. So it was
That you knew of our small dog's friendly curiosity

Sidney Goldfarb 397

Among the great danes, retrievers and other nameless riff-
Raff. Then an anxious beagle tried to squeeze below
The steel link fence. You heard the metallic cry,
You watched it squirm as a steel tine caught
Beneath its eye and inched into the skin.
Our dog and the others milled in disconcern, but agony,
Its helpless fascination, held you;
The short legs pawed crazily, pain in suspension,
But you could not move till someone else, a woman
Fenced out of reach beneath her clothesline, screamed at you,
"It will bite you, but you have to help!"
Then you did not think. It whelped like a child,
The foolish thing, tearing its own flesh to get
Unhooked, but you pressed its snout down gently,
And pulled up on the fence. It had not bled,
Though the galvanized tine was dark with fluid, and so quickly
Did the dog flee, you could remember nothing
But the blur of black and white and brown.
The woman chatted as she took her laundry down.

This I thought: What if the eye had rolled
From the skull? What if it lay motionless
Upon our meagre beginnings? What if it stared up
At our incapabilities, turned on its white side
And told us of our feckless inhibitions?
I was afraid of what your hands had found
In this act. I would walk upon the ground
Where the dog had been. I would try to soak up
The sense of pain and heroism, but it was no good.
I could not have done what you have done.
I have no stomach for any animal but myself.

This I thought: Why then must I tell you?
What hooks itself behind my eyes and beckons
Me to submission? All that is lost in me
I find in you, all that is absent and forgotten.
All that is hardened to blindness you restore in me.

Summer, 1963

WILLIAM BURROUGHS

Class of 1936, (1914–   )

After his graduation, William Burroughs lived in New York, Tangiers, Paris, and London, holding down various jobs from private detective to bartender to exterminator. His first book was Junkie: Confessions of an Unredeemed Drug Addict. *The extremely successful* Naked Lunch *was finally published in this country last year.* Nova Express *continues in the same vein. "Junk is not a kick,"* he writes, *"it's a way of life."*

"WHO HIM? DON'T LET HIM OUT HERE."

I AM NOT *an* addict. I am *the* addict. The addict I invented to keep this show on the junk road. I *am* all the addicts and all the junk in the world. I *am* junk and I am hooked forever. Now I am using junk as a basic illustration. Extend it. I am reality and I am hooked on reality. Give me an old wall and a garbage can and I can by God sit there forever. Because I am the wall and I am the garbage can. But I need some one to sit there and look at the wall and the garbage can. That is I need a human host. I can't look at anything. I am blind. I can't sit anywhere. I have nothing to sit on. And let me take this opportunity of replying to my numerous and uh vociferous critics. It is not true that I hate the human species. I just don't like human beings. I don't like animals. What I feel is not hate. In your verbal garbage the closest word is distaste. Still I must live in and on human bodies. An intolerable situation you will agree. To make that situation clearer suppose you were stranded on a planet populated by insects. You are blind. You are a drug addict. But you find a way to make the insects bring you your junk. Even after thousands of years living there you still feel that basic structural distaste for your insect servants. You feel it every time they touch you. Well that is exactly the way I feel about my human servants. Consequently since my arrival some five hundred thousand years ago I have had one thought in mind. What you call the history of mankind is the history of my escape plan. I don't want 'love'. I don't want 'forgiveness'. All I want is out of here.

Question: "Mr. Martin, how did all this start? How did you get here in the first place? If you found conditions so distasteful why didn't you leave at once?"

"God questions I mean good questions, young man. Obviously I am not omnipotent. My arrival here was a wreck. Ship came apart like a rotten undervest. The 'accident' in which I lost my sight. I was the only survivor. The other members of the crew . . . well . . . you understand . . . uh sooner or later . . . So I decided to act sooner. And I have acted sooner ever since. The entire human film was prerecorded. I will explain briefly how this is done. Take a simple virus illness like hepatitis. This illness has an incubation period of two weeks. So if I know when the virus is in—(and I do because I put it there) I know how you will look two weeks from now: yellow. To put it another way. I take a picture or rather a series of pictures of you with hepatitis. Now I put my virus negatives into your liver to develop. (Not far to reach. Remember I live in your body.) The whole hepatitis film is prerecorded two weeks before the opening scene when you notice your eyes are a little yellower than usual. Now this is a simple operation. Not all of my negatives develop by any means. All right now back to basic junk. Some character takes a bang of heroin for the first time. It takes maybe sixty consecutive shots before I can welcome another addict. (Room for one more inside, sir). Having taken one shot it becomes mathematically probable that he will take another given the opportunity and I can always arrange that. Having taken two shots it becomes more probable that he will take a third. One negative developed makes others almost unavoidable. The same procedure can be applied to any human activity. If a man makes a certain amount of money by certain means he will go on making more money by the same means and so forth. Human activities are drearily predictable. It should now be obvious that what you call 'reality' is a function of these precisely predictable because prerecorded human activities. Now what could louse up a prerecorded biologic film? Obviously random factors. That is some one cutting my word and image lines *at random*. In short the cut up method of Brion Gysin which derives from Hassan I Sabbah and the planet Saturn. Well, I've had a spot of trouble before but nothing serious. There was Rimbaud. And a lot of people you never heard of for good reasons. People who got too close one way or another. There was Tristan Tzara and the Surrealist lark. I soon threw a block into that. Broke them all down to window dressers. So why didn't I stop Mr. Gysin in his tracks? I have ways of dealing with wise guys or I wouldn't be here. Early answer to use on anyone considering to interfere. Tricks I learned after the crash. Well perhaps I didn't take it seriously at first. And maybe I wanted to hear what he had to say about getting out. Always keep as many alternative moves open as possible. Next thing the blocade on planet earth is broken. Explorers moving in whole armies. And the usual do good missions talk about educating the natives for self government. And some hick sheriff from the nova heat charging me with 'outrageous colonial mismanagement and attempted nova'. Well they can't hang a nova rap on me. What I planned was simply to move out the biologic film to planet Venus and start over. Take along a few *good* natives to stock the new pitch and for the rest total disposal. That's not nova that's manslaughter. Second degree. And I planned it painless. I dislike screaming. Disturbs my medications."

Question: "Mr. Martin, in the face of the evidence, no one can deny that nova was planned. The reports reek of nova."

"It will be obvious that I myself, as an addict, can only be a determined factor in some one else's equation. It's the old army game. Now you see me now you don't."

Question: "Mr. Martin, you say 'give me a wall and a garbage can and I can sit there forever' almost in the next sentence you say 'All I want is out of here.' Aren't you contradicting yourself?" "You are confused about the word 'self'. I could by God sit there forever if I had a self to sit in that would sit still for it. I don't. As soon as I move in on any self all that self wants is to be somewhere else. Anywhere else. Now there you sit in your so called self. Suppose you could walk out of that self? Some people can incidentally. I don't encourage this but it happens and threatens to become pandemic. So you walk out of your body and stand across the room. Now what form would the being that walks out of your body have? Obviously it would have precisely your form. So all you have done is take the same form from one place to another. You have taken great trouble and pain—(believe me there is no pain like flesh withdrawal consciously experienced) and you have gotten precisely back where you started. To really leave human form you would have to leave human form that is leave the whole concept of word and image. You can not have the human image in the human image. You cannot leave human form in human form. And you can not think or conceive in non image terms by mathematical definition of a being in my biologic film which *is* a series of images. Does that answer your question? I thought not."

Question: "Mr. Martin tell us something about yourself. Do you have any vices other than uh junk? Any hobbies? Any diversions?" "Your vices other than junk I manipulate but do not share. Sex is profoundly distasteful to a being of my uh mineral origins. Hobbies? Chess. Diversions? I enjoy a good show and a good performer. Just an old showman. Well when you have to kill your audience every few years to keep them in their seats it's about time to pack in."

Question: "Mr. Martin, I gather that your plan to move the show to planet Venus has uh miscarried. Is that correct?"

"Yeah it looks that way."

Question: "In that case, Mr. Martin where will you go when you go if you go?"

"That's quite a problem. You see I'm on the undesirable list with every imigration department in the galaxy.

" 'Who *him?* Don't let him out here.' "

Question: "Mr. Martin don't you have any friends?"

"There are no friends. I found that out after the crash. I found that out before the others. That's why I'm still here. There are no friends. There are allies. There are accomplices. No one wants friends unless he is shit scared or unless he is planning a caper he can't pull off by himself."

Question: "Mr. Martin, what about the others who were involved in this crash? Aren't they still alive some where in some form?"

"You don't have to look far. They are sitting right here."

Question: "Who were these others?"

"There was an army colonel, a technician and a woman."

Question: "Won't you have to come to some sort of terms with your uh former accomplices?"

"To my disgruntled former associates I have this to say. You were all set to cross me up from the count down. You think I can't read your stupid virus mind, lady. And you, you technical bastard, with your mind full of formulae I can't read. And you Colonel Bradly waiting to shoot me in the back. The lot of you. Blind and paralyzed I still beat you to the draw."

Question: "Mr. Martin, what sort of place did you people come from?" "What sort of place did we come from. Well if you want the answer to that question, just look around, buster. Just look around." "Ladies and gentlemen, you have just heard an interview with Mr. Martin, sole survivor of the first attempt to send up a space capsule from planet earth. Mr. Martin has been called The Man of A Thousand Lies. Well he didn't have time for a thousand but I think he did pretty well in the time allotted. And I feel reasonably sure that if the other crew members could be here with us tonight they would also do a pretty good job of lying. But please remember that nothing is true in space, that there is no time in space—that what goes up under such auspices must come down—that the beginning is also the end.

Ladies and gentlemen, these our actors, bid you a long last good night."

Summer, 1963

SUSAN RICH

Radcliffe, Class of 1964, (1942–   )

Susan Rich studied under Robert Lowell while at Radcliffe and in her senior year won the Untermeyer Poetry Prize. Awarded a travelling fellowship for the following year, she worked on a collection of poems and drawings in France, Spain, and Italy.

DOLL

I painted her in a corner.
I painted my plaster mourner in the attic light
That barred the walls and striped the metal play-stove
To her left upon the fear-white table, to my right.

I didn't see she was afraid until I'd finished.
I didn't see until the light diminished on the walls
And crawled around the round point of her chin
Beneath the black-blue, upside down "u" of her mouth that falls.

Her brows were hair-fine, child-fine worryings, hair-thin,
One eye was larger than the other, staring down.
The other seemed to wander out and in.
One chipped fist gestured at her throat,
The plaster belly groped,
Her seated feet splayed awkward, out and in.
Both soles were little loaves or baked potatoes in the skin.
Each seemed to weigh a pound.

She cradled like a child of mine, or kin.
She fit, and better fits as I grow older,
Knowing how the shape should feel as it curves out and in.
I left her with a careless seal upon her forehead.
I left her in the storeroom
Underneath a blanket, tucked her in,
Where bats drop droppings on the newspaper around the door
that lets them out and in,
And rats roll pellets of molasses on the floor, like boulders.

Natural diaspora has emptied the attic,
The place where I sat them, the slanted room
That wanted rearrangement of the stuffed ones, and the new
synthetic ones that did not nick.
I climbed up every Christmas, guilty with neglect,
Buttoning small dresses up the back where fingerprints collect.
Heads roll and holes appear when witches prick.
Elderly collectors shut them up in cases where the hinges stick
And all the air is gone, and even dust won't bloom.

She sits alone inhabiting the gloom of our lean attic.
Green ruffles limp and yellow on her skin.
Her skin is ageless. She has no tongue and no one movement is erratic.
She won't distract the children moving out and in.

Fall, 1963

MARGARET HAMBRECHT

(1941–   )

*While she was a student at Wellesley College,
Margaret Hambrecht travelled to Harvard twice
a week to study writing under Mark Van Doren.
She graduated in 1963 and went on to the Boston
University Law School.*

WINDFALL

Gently in the gentle wind he cussed
Her mouth. It could grow broken when he kissed.
The stars: they could die snowing down like dust.

He swore, feeling memory take its sadist
Hold upon his skin. Wind like lust
Filled up his sailing mind. He felt it list

Against the waves. When he gripped his fist
He found it full of her hair the wind fussed
With that autumn. Leaves littered like mist

Against keen light. Sometimes he thought he must
Repair the fallen leaves and stars to get the gist
Of saving fragile things. Sometimes he just

Sat by the sea and hoped his heart would rust.

Fall, 1963

DONALD BLOCH

Class of 1963, (1943–   )

A member of the literary board of the Advocate,
*Donald Bloch published many of his short stories
in the magazine.*

METASTASIS

JOHN DAVIDSON could handle a flame thrower. As far as we know, there
wasn't much else of distinction about him. He came into sole pro-
prietorship of the Davidson butchery business when brother Martin,
drunk, enlisted in the infantry. John, sensible at his trade and quick
with his hands, thrived as was expected of him. The sawdust on his
floor was always fresh and sufficient; no dried blood set about his meat.
The last of his family in Claypool, John lived alone in the old Davidson place, a greygreen frame house like gradeschoolers draw in
crayon. Most of his time he passed alternately standing-resolution in
his stance—inside the house looking out, or outside the house staring in. Prosperous he spent no money to speak of. Slow and grey-
eyed, he safeguarded his privacy. He was tall, earnest, pleasant but
standoffish.

So, all things considered, we were surprised to see reciprocal interest
develop between John and Ellen Benson. From the moment she first
appeared in Claypool, Ellen Benson attracted easily as many men as
John kept flies clean away from his counter; and, as a practice, either
she kept them buzzing until they wore themselves out, or with a swat
she ended their unhappy captivity. The Bensons had lived in ports,
wilds, inland cities and towns, unheard of places, before arriving weary
pilgrims in Indiana. Mr. Benson was a government person. Her first
week among us, his daughter spent remarking, "This is the littlest place
I've ever *seen*. The *town*, where are you hiding it?" She was a talker,
a pretty thing with wheat blonde hair shorter than most. She smiled
often. Because her teeth had been fixed straight when she was a girl,

they were quite beautiful. No matter what she did, Ellen could only be graceful. She was gifted that way.

When hot weather came around, Ellen wore her skirts short. On occasion as she walked they would ride above her knees and show the trace of a zipper shaded scar low on one thigh. The men asked her about that after they ran out of more proper conversation. With a ready, direct answer, pulling her skirt high until the whole scar was visible, she put them at ease. "They got it out in time." Ellen made gouging gestures with her small hands whenever she talked about it. It was easy to stare at the silvery tissue; she herself often did. "It never metastasized." The men made her repeat that word time and again, "metastasize," taking it from her lips like dumb people, seduced by its sound and by her candor in telling. "Scooped it out in a lump. Sewed me back up."

The Bensons left Ellen to her own devices. Probably, they felt responsible for her having no real roots and few friends and that was why they permitted her to act at will. We thought they maybe had no choice. She was energetic to a point past belief, a series of explosions, undisciplined, attractive.

John Davidson first met Ellen when Mrs. Benson yawned so mightily after dinner one night that she strained her back and in the morning was obliged to have Ellen do her errands. But he had seen her before, prominent in the company of others and had heard particulars about her from Timothy Slocum. Tim had a boy who was seven going on eight then, homely and ill-bred. Bobby handled everything within reach, and usually left proof behind. First thing which fixed his eye but he didn't dare touch was Ellen Benson's branded thigh. The two bumped in the street one afternoon; Bobby's head almost disappeared into Ellen's stomach he was running so fast, not looking, but he richocheted. The little Slocum looked up bewilderedly from the dust where he sprawled and his eyes caught Ellen's sleek scar. At first sight, in every romantic sense of the word, he was smitten. A perceptive girl, Ellen figured what was going on in his head and took pity on his curiosity. She crouched down before him, reached out her hand for his and, when he surrendered the dirty thing, drew him near her. He didn't fuss.

"I always let my friends, that is my *closest* friends, touch my scar." Bobby nodded. He let his finger be placed on the skin and then thrilled as it glided smoothly about. He smiled. "Now close your eyes. Shut them and make a wish." Bobby pretended to close his eyes but through his lashes he still watched his finger, a little fearful but proud. "All right. Now tell."

"I wish you and me was all scar." Freeing his finger, Bobby made an expansive gesture with both hands. "One scar like that." He fled away. "Thanks." Before he vanished, he turned around to shout, wagging his head and waving his arms, his voice too big for his body, "Thanks. Thanks. Thanks." Timothy Slocum prized that story. When he told it, he extended his own forefinger and moved it in tiny rapid circles through the air, grinning so his eyes grew smaller.

So when Ellen came in to Davidson Meats and Poultry, setting the bell strung up behind the door to jingle, John already knew something about her. She looked at him and saw that. Odds were soon more than evened. She also saw, she thought, in one definitive glance all the essence of John Davidson. Ellen had already known too many men a slight bit mysterious and rather self-conscious, but everything that John did or said gave him away. He was old, much older than she, but not old out of the question. In his bearing, gestures and expressions, he so much as told her he was strong, warm, and predictable.

As Ellen Benson entered his store, John slowly wiped his hands clean on his apron and then spread them knuckles down on the counter. "Good afternoon." He took an involuntary step towards her and then blushed when even before placing an order she winked. Mrs. Holcomb, Mary Lee, was there at the time, "shocked," she said, "to the brink of tears and what was worse, the two of them didn't care to know it." When she tried to leave discretely, Mary Lee had the misfortune to drop her bundle at the door. It ripped open and a chuck roast rolled out onto the sawdust, stopping dead at Ellen Benson's feet. She retrieved it and curtsied. "It's ready breaded, Mrs. Holcomb." She licked her fingers. John looked on in silence. No one knows exactly what went on in there once Mary Lee got safely out. John closed early, pulled down the shade. Next day it was apparent that he and Ellen were keeping company.

It wasn't long before the two together became a fixture, like the town pump. We rarely saw either one without the other. Often on the long, circuitous walks they took together Ellen could no longer tolerate John's pace. She would run ahead of him, then turn and call back,

"Poke, you call *that* a stride? A child walks faster, gets farther." He would hurry on, almost run. Although John never laughed outright when he was with Ellen, we could see that he was pleased. She was gay all the time, inexhaustibly. He couldn't take his eyes from her, and nearly cut a finger off each time she came into the shop. Once he did slice his thumb deeply. Ellen calmly took the bloody thing into her mouth and sucked it clean hard, while she made a tourniquet from the hem of her dress and one of the dowels John used to piece meat together with. "Beware the gash of steel," Ellen told John and then led him to Doc Greavens.

There are flat fields east of Claypool two miles from town, acres of wild senna, gorse and rush that whistle in light breezes and gaily shriek in high winds. If we concentrate in the evening, we can hear them carry on. They are county land and useless except as soil binds. Old Miss Winnie Wright was the first to see John Davidson out there. She was singing back to town one afternoon after singing out that morning. John was digging. Miss Winnie said she stopped, stood by and talked. He worked away without saying anything. It wasn't exactly being rude, for Miss Winnie can carry on a conversation nicely by herself. She took off one slim gold hoop earring and put it half in her mouth, still talking. After John had dug a trench near a hundred yards long, shallow, a yard or more wide, he started on another perpendicular to the first. Frequently he paused to wipe the back of his neck dry with a red bandana and then half-wipe, half-massage his hands. Timothy Slocum can tell you that cleaver and shovel wear hands differently, the same calluses won't do, so it was no wonder that Miss Winnie could see John's hands going raw. Finally she just sat down and watched and sang in her scratchy voice. She spread her denim skirt about her until she looked like a wildflower. The sun came down. John dug and as he dug the metal of his shovel glinted in the twilight. Miss Winnie picked a fistful of wild senna and wore the thin green stalks into a crown which she sat on her head. Then she cocked her head pointed at John and hollered. "Boy come away. You've done work enough. Let be." John picked up. He had about completed a second trench. "Boy, let's be off." John shouldered his shovel, helped Miss Winnie rise up from the ground, and threw his free arm about her waist. They walked home like that.

"He smelled like men used to," Miss Winnie said. "I asked him what he was doing out there. 'It's so it won't spread, Miss Winnie,' he answered me. That boy was too gay to tell me straight. I asked him again what he was doing out there digging up the fields. 'It's so it won't metastasize, Miss Winnie,' he said. 'So it won't, no it won't, so it won't me-tas-ta-size, Winnie.' There was no getting to him."

From their front porch Mrs. Holcomb and her baby sister Robin saw the two of them come back to Claypool, Miss Winnie smiling so hard you couldn't tell wrinkles from lips. The ladies were surprised to see the pair enter The Gopher where John Davidson treated Miss Winnie and himself (most likely at her suggestion) to some cold beer. Several rounds downed, with flecks of foam about the corners of his mouth, John rose, kissed the burnt crown of Miss Winnie's head, ordered her another drink, and happy as men can expect to be, left her singing there. Next day, out in the fields he dug two more trenches to complete a square.

We should have known, all of us should have foreseen what was about to happen. Although some in Claypool thought the excitement almost worth it, the town could have saved itself considerable trouble. That Saturday from early morn on Ellen and John were together. They didn't do much. Walked around town, sat out behind the Benson place, returned to the Davidson's to listen to the radio. Yet there was a peculiar air about them of anxiety and impatience. Bobby Slocum stalked the couple through town and the town dogs stalked Bobby Slocum. He hoped for another go at Ellen's scar, but since she had started seeing John, she had time and favors for him only.

About nine o'clock that Saturday night—it was a clear night of deep blue—the volunteer's bell began to clang. That it would sound at all was shock enough for most of us. We came rushing from our homes, neighbor looking neighbor up and down for traces of flame, some examining themselves, their own houses, throwing wild looks around town. Claypool's fire chief, Wallace Whitney stood in the road pulling on hip boots with both hands, shouting calm words which no one heard. The bell went on clanging and banging. Wallace and the paid men went on ahead, east from Claypool with the fire wagon. The rest of us followed after. The sky was lit up unnaturally out there. As we drew closer, we thought it peculiar not to hear fire equipment in operation or the men shouting. After the alarm fell silent back in town, all we heard was a sound like violently crinkling cellophane and every now and then a "whooosh, whooosh." When we reached the spot we saw how the fire was strangely local. Hushed and motionless the men were seated in rows staring at the field. Through the heady flames which were pale yellow we could make out John Davidson and Ellen Benson. He had one arm around the girl, with the other he held his flame-thrower. It was off. The field, inspired, was consuming itself. John had sacrificed the wild senna, the gorse and rush to his love; he had done what he imagined would best please and most impress Ellen, not anticipating that we would rudely turn his private demonstration into a Claypool public festival. Ellen's face was glazed by the light, full of joy. Her eyes burned through the fire. She stretched up to kiss John with two hands on his cheeks and he looked about to laugh. The weeds burned splendidly, flames quickening in to smoke, smoke with a moment's hesitation dissolving in to the night. When it became clear that fear would be misplaced, we enjoyed the thorough self-destructive splendor of the fire. Wallace Whitney alone wore a frown of disapproval. Miss Winnie began to sing loud enough for us to hear and started to slap her old thighs with flat hands as she rocked slightly back and forth. "I rang the bell. I rang the bell. I rang the bell and woke the town."

The blaze didn't last terribly long. We had time and staying power enough to sit and watch the embers all but die before returning to Claypool, to our sinks half-emptied, pieces of pie half-eaten, stories incomplete. The stars seemed dull after earthly fire, cluttered in heaven, static. Miss Winnie, her feet in John's trenches, murmuring and muttering, picked about the edges of the charred stubble. Whatever she touched was thoroughly scorched and still full of sufficient heat to make her draw back her hand quickly and shake it. Ellen and John had long gone back to town.

Sunday morning we sent our children out to survey the damage. Where the land had been soft grey and green, a black patch remained. The children gathered about the rim of the razed ground as if it were a pit. Bobby Slocum was first to buck up courage and crawl out into the soot where he took up great handfuls of the velvety ash and flung them jeeringly at his playmates. Soon they all ventured forth, finding the surface slightly warm and smooth, ideal to roll in. When Bobby had taken his full of delight, he rose. Smudged and smeared until his features were confused, flesh stuck to his clothes, he started a race back to town. The children made their report without speaking an intelligible word. They were hosed off in turn in front of the fire station and sent wet, whistling, hungry home.

For their honeymoon John and Ellen Davidson spent three days and three nights at a hotel in Marion. The Monday after they returned, John reopened his store. At first business was brisker than usual because everyone had questions to ask or else came in as much to see what marriage did for a man as to shop. Hardly anything was seen of Ellen. One afternoon near closing when Cecil and Sarah Rawlings came in for an order, they found John looking out of the store window in a daze. There was no movement to his face but there was film upon his eyes and tears cut down his cheeks. He was wiping and wiping his hands distractedly on his apron. The Rawlings were at a loss. That was the only indication we had for a while something was wrong.

Within the month John closed up the store again and took Ellen with him once more to Marion. Their departure was sudden. This time the trip wasn't for pleasure, but Ellen was sick. John wrote to the Bensons. "It's her leg. The tumor didn't die in there. They didn't get it all and it's spreading." They were terrified. Ellen came back a week later with one leg, ready to receive visitors. She told Mrs. Holcomb, "It was like a spider was spinning inside me. The loathsome thing got happy, got confused and couldn't stop spinning. Had to do away with it. Can't stand spiders inside me." Ellen sat propped in a wicker rocker with heavy blankets on her lap although it was the hottest part of August. One shoe stuck out beneath the edge of the blankets. Although cheerful, Ellen looked thin. Her operation must have shocked John silly but he seemed to take it in stride. He had watched the amputation and observed for the first time his techniques applied to human flesh. It must have been cold water down his back, a needle through his eye.

Most of Claypool came at one time or another to see Ellen during the lonely daytime hours when John was at work. They sat and she talked. John looked in often, awkward and embarrassed if there was much company.

"Ellen?"

"I'm all right, dear."

"You're all right?"

"Yes, John."

"Good."

Ellen had many stories to tell and she told them well as she grew steadily thinner. Company dwindled with the novelty of her lost limb. Besides we knew Ellen wasn't getting any better, her wonderful spirit was in vain, and we were growing afraid. John had begun to smile and laugh about town. He told a joke to Miss Winnie once in the street. She laughed long out loud even though it was a joke she didn't appreciate, something topical John had overheard in Marion. He told the Rawlings when he walked them to the door after a visit, "Ellen and me, were the Lord's lightning rod," and put both arms together straight above his head.

Bobby Slocum took Patrice, his sister, to the Davidsons one afternoon near the end. When at last the adults grown careless in their conversation had let it slip, Bobby had been excited to learn what had happened to Ellen. He remembered what she had granted him in the past and in an instant decided, as children do, to forgive the intervening period of inattention. He anticipated a tactual experience that made him shiver just to think of it.

They came unannounced on a Thursday. Rather than walk up to the door, they crept around to a side window where Bobby made his sister give him a boost up. Ellen was in view by herself. Bobby stared in at her until Patrice's arms gave out. He said to Patrice that Ellen hadn't any eyes left, just scabby grey lids which she kept tight shut to keep the secret that her eyes were out. He said to his sister that Ellen's hair wasn't groomed, that it was stiff and dull. "Lost more than a leg," he told her. Patrice ran off when Bobby whispered, "She's dead, Pat. Mrs. Davidson's dead in there. No doubt about it, she's deader than you or me." He had decided he did not need her.

Then Bobby went to the door by himself and entered noiselessly. "There didn't seem cause to wake her," he later explained. Once inside, he slipped into her room where she sat and went directly to her side, holding in his breath as much as he could. Trying not to bother Ellen he started to peel the blankets from her lap. First he planned to rub the zipper scar again. Then Mrs. Davidson clicked open her eyes and found Bobby Slocum there about his business. He heard her open her eyes and looked up.

"Hello, Bobby." Her voice got caught coming out. "I'm glad you came to see me. All alone?"

"Hello, Mrs. Ellen." Then Bobby held up both his hands to show her how clean they were. He held his palms forward at arms length out in front of him. She nodded her head appreciatively.

"There are bandages this time, Bobby. Thick bandages. I'm sorry." When he didn't say anything but looked down where her other shoe should have been, Ellen said, "In a week maybe, or two. Will you come back?" Bobby put his hands into his pockets and then brought one out again clutching a hard cherry candy which he popped into his mouth. He looked up at Ellen and crunched the candy keeping his lips compressed. "Come here." She extended her hands to Bobby but Bobby didn't move. He rolled the candy under his tongue and let it melt there. "Come here." Ellen's voice enfolded him like hands and drew him unwilling but helpless to her. He had thoughts of recoiling but they subsided. He let her fold him in her arms and run her fingers through his hair, not complaining even as she worked out knots. "That pain I could have borne, Bobby. I would have welcomed that pain." He looked up questioningly when he guessed from the sound of Ellen's breathing that she did not want to cry. Her eyes were closed, her nostrils black quivering tears. Bobby swallowed the brittle sliver of candy left in his mouth. "Go home, Bobby. Go tell your mother hello for me." She let him go. He walked slowly out of doors and went to the side of the house. There beneath the window with a fist on each thigh he sat for a long time before going home.

Two nights later Claypool understood that Ellen Benson Davidson was fast dying and that she wouldn't last the coming of day. At half-past ten o'clock we heard a scream issue from the Davidson's; many followed. Only children slept while the rest of us waited for Ellen's pain to toll away the time. John was alone with her and helpless. No doubt each of his wife's cries ripped something irretrievable from him.

Because Ellen complained of the heat, the windows were wide open at the Davidson's, jaws for her cries to pass forth from into the night. Between screams Ellen talked, but incoherently. John thought over and over about placing a pillow above her face to muffle the pain, but he doubted his own control. The Bensons, hand in hand with confused expressions on their faces, came as far as their son-in-law's front door and then turned around to go home. Although there was light in windows over town where normally there would be none, John kept his house dark trying to keep Ellen cool but she still complained that the sheets and the breeze and even John's touch were white heat. He never called a doctor. We wondered when the diagnosis had been certain. Before the wedding? Before the operation? We wondered if Ellen and John had found out at the same time. At two we heard a new sound. Ellen's screams were caught short, the last more a moan of protest than anything else. The cry of a voice unused to itself replaced hers in the moving air. It strained briefly to achieve some sort of resonance but soon faded.

There were few changes visible on John Davidson's face in the morning when he went to bring Doc Greaven to write out a certificate of death. His smile was taut and his eyes appeared to have settled back ever so slightly into his skull. Otherwise we showed more effects from our sleepless vigil. No one spoke to John as he walked to fetch the doctor and arrange for burial. He stopped briefly at the *Sentinel* to file an obituary notice for the next issue. By noon there was a crowd lingering outside the Davidson place exchanging condolences amongst themselves. The Bensons were inside talking with John about Ellen. A tea kettle whistled incessantly.

Some swear that John Davidson took Ellen's ring finger away with him when he left, that he cut it off like a barbarian and that was why nobody was allowed to view the body, just a closed coffin. The Bensons told us she was buried in blue, her hair brushed from her forehead. It had grown long. "She didn't look well," they said. Bobby Slocum ran his hands all the way around the coffin and nobody stopped him. Patrice wouldn't believe her father that there was nothing to see, until Timothy held her up and she saw her own reflection in the coffin top. Miss Winnie stood beside John sucking on the insides of her cheeks with admiration for his three-piece suit. Days later, on boarding a train which would take him to Fort Wayne to see brother Martin, John promised to return soon. However, we knew that Claypool had lost him for good when his shop began to stink.

Summer, 1963

ROBERT DAWSON

Class of 1964, (1942–   )

At Harvard Robert Dawson was president of the
Advocate *and twice winner of the Academy of
American Poets prize. The* Saturday Review, *the*
Atlantic Monthly *and the* Transatlantic Review
*have all published his work. He spent the year
following his graduation in Rome, and returned
to his home in California last summer. His first
book of poems will be published by Houghton
Mifflin.*

THE PIGEON ROOF

Of science. The flapping flight of birds
Like the flight of this my poem to its destination
straight though ruffling the surfaces of many ponds

frets my waking. Those honking personalists,
Canada geese? No, the coo of lecherous pigeons,
plum breasts thudding transom and gable, spoils

the small dawn of my bedroom. Whose eyelids
scrape the cornea like pigeon toes? It is
the march hare physicist, the ultimate masochist,

that from braying beasts flays hide with thumb-
triggered bombs. Not pleasant to wake with dreams
if not to wake is not escaping so. Her shoes last night

Robert Dawson 417

skinned the dashboard, who slapped me when I turned
the speaker out. Manifolds, gaskets. Flutter valves?
Something I thought of hearts. Behind the screen

a hill sulks. Betraying the car to the checker of cars
by yellow green aisle lights ordered, till we saw
projectors flicker, blown tints sliding into shapes unseen,

we climbed. A damp rock scabbed with moss, black
between feathers of black, live oaks and manzanita,
an arbitrary island. Somewhere the swinging glass doors

of St. Luke's Emergency were nothing of the moment.
Planes crooned over us. Raid horns we heard or didn't hear,
no history being except in torment of made things.

Pecked slate rifts and the sky drips blue?
Mathematical beams and crossbeams loft me in silence.
Linoleum curls my toes and gives me away.

Five years I sleep here under the pigeon roof.
Once I shall wake and be myself. This poem
to relate my later by my former scenes.

Of art. The young man nailed to his page,
whose back the nurse screws higher, is death's
cautious lover. Capillaries pop and the white cells

swim the tendons. Plastic hawsers moor him to us living.
Red strings gurgle in his elbow pits. His scrawl falls
and smacks a fan and the interns scoop it, smooth it

on linen low across his chest, so birdcage thin a poem
stabs water. Weeks of relapse. Three of us filched
winesap that we dove for in the orchard ditch. Chocolate

ripples roiled us toward the pumps, which drank us? Each
time just in time bare flanks raked waiting fingers on the
escarpment. Two, in his attic pestered by maps and pennants,

perched on cartons of Safeway encyclopedias, traded verses.
Chianti bloodied his shirt cuff. He whispered starry drunks
his heroes flung once. My lines ran short but he held out

till dawn. The nurse excludes me when his mother comes.
Not right to meddle with his dying so. The page I drop
before I go says death's a method. Time through time I cry

don't read! don't! my time is now! That youth
whose forty swinish selves grunt pity, change to me!
Released, he tramps a golf course, snacks, and faints.

Gray wings sort currents north in spring. Blue bitterns,
pouters, bobwhites and the hermit thrush. From granite bluffs
I cast sardines for plovers. The surf-line sings as the bird

wheels deep. No one fishes this shore of the ocean. No
one ties together these things in a bunch.
I listen to my blood roar in a conch.

This beach is splintered with the homes of crawling things.
He dies while I'm a thousand miles and here.
At dawn the drive-in screen is yellow blue and rust.

Of history. Braceros pitch their own dirt with the tents.
Ma and me picked hop flowers once. Her fingers itched
and bloodied in the dew. I picked too small. They

canned us. Three who know each other only as he drives,
commuters, ride another's tailgate through a fog. Stalled
on a grade an oil truck. Later we fished their bodies with a torch.

Robert Dawson 419

Plum and emerald goiters, pigeons strut these eaves, that glut
on popcorn daylong on the courthouse lawn. White squab
filthy the plaster laths, or if they hatch dead, packrats

stitch their eyes? This attic no one visits from the quake.
Old man my father splints the trap door with a crow. Not
clear who enters, but with cardboard blinds the roof's

false windows, mornings crystallized. Bell beats on the
shingles. What flies first shatters its beak on a rafter.
Powder and twigs yellow our legs. Some amateur's fled

tumbler somersaults when clubbed and drops an egg. Shovels,
brooms. Hundreds of wings sheer off in flags or fractured
skate their own dirt buffeting. I cross my hands so the wrist

bones crack. Blood glues the wrung skulls in your palm
while feathers flurry gray. Cedar apples hiss. Bluejays
pester a squirrel. Cones and yellow needles bed a cigarette.

Smoke vines from bough up redwood bough. An owl glides
by the fire trail, his wingtips dripping flame? Parachutes,
fouled in a barranca, shred on juniper. So long as any

timber grows, the fire must, dry groves and cherry stones.
Then gobble the prairies. Even the tide burns. Ripples
from what sank here churn higher as they spread.

Without me seconds pass. If in the mind mind
is structured, wattled in some nest, its history creates
one unity for who would flee or fight.

Summer, 1964

BROTHER ANTONINUS

(1912–   )

William Everson took the name "Brother Anto-
ninus" when he entered a monastery as a lay-
brother in 1951. When he left the monastery six
years later he kept the name and resumed the lit-
erary career he had begun in 1948 with The Re-
sidual Years. *He has since published* Hazards of
Holiness *and* The Crooked Lines of God.

This interview between Brother Antoninus,
Robert Dawson and Sidney Goldfarb of the Ad-
vocate, *and* Dr. Albert Gelpi, *was recorded in*
February 1963 when Brother Antoninus was at
Harvard giving a reading of his works for the Ad-
vocate.

A CONVERSATION WITH
BROTHER ANTONINUS

Interviewer: We talked last night about the separation of Apollonian
and Dionysian poets and perhaps we should start there. Do you think
that contrast underlies the academic vs. beat poetry?

Brother Antoninus: What has confused the contrast is the attempt
to create a middle ground, for instance by William Carlos Williams. I
think Williams is an Apollonian, that is, not a Dionysian like Whitman
or Ginsberg, who move right out of the unconsciousness. He uses all his
powers of consciousness to realize his impressions, and this bearing
down of the conscious on the poem becomes extremely mental—not
rational, but deliberate registration of experience rather than vague
reception. A guy like Jeffers is much more unconscious in his effects,
especially meditative effects. It's that element in the so-called beat side

of things that centers around W. C. Williams and Charles Olson, that I can't think of as being Dionysian.

Do they crack the ego?

Occasionally Williams does, in a poem like ON THE ROAD TO THE CONTAGIOUS HOSPITAL, but generally, no. You see, most of them are eschewing rhetoric too deliberately. Rhetoric for me is the device by which the consequentiality of the emotional situation and the mood is in some way registered. Williams is anti-rhetorical because of his metaphysical premise that no reality exists except in things. So you get a phenomenological poetry in which the object is registered as much as possible. To me that involves certain preconceptions of the ego-structure and it isn't the sort of thing that opens up in poetry, except occasionally, as in the poem I mentioned, where Williams does become rhetorical.

How about THE GULLS?

In some poems like that and THE YACHTS, almost despite the poet the language takes on consequentiality in its abstractness, which is almost a violation of his principles. In PATERSON he's rhetorical in his release, but that is not what his followers follow. Creely and Jonathan Williams use satire and conscious devices.

Does Apollonian mean academic?

No, though academic poetry is Apollonian usually. I think academic poetry is marked by the use of literary convention. Wilbur is an example, and I suppose most people would say Lowell is, but I don't think so myself, although I can see his academic sources. I think he has a great unconscious. All the greats are men who have great unconsciouses— tremendous feelings of consequentiality. Opposed consequences within themselves have to be resolved in the aesthetic form.

Do you think the rhetoric of the beat generation will ever result in a great poet?

I don't think there was any rhetoric in the beat generation except in Ginsberg.

Is it the unconscious that forces the rhetoric? Can't you take rhetoric and consciously fill it up?

So that it becomes academic? That's what academic is. Berryman did it in MISTRESS BRADSTREET—there's another case of a man with not as great an unconscious as Lowell, but in that poem he succeeds on the rhetorical level because the issues of it meant so much to him that they provided a bearing-off point. Actually . . . we talk this way you know, but the possibilities of language have become so complex, you can develop schools around many things, like Berryman, who isn't going the same way as Lowell at all. You see the possibilities of a school and yet I don't think it would ever develop. You can talk in generalities, but when you dare become specific—like myself, am I Apollonian or Dionysian? I say Dionysian, but not anywheres near as Dionysian as Ginsberg.

Do you think one influence will predominate? What way is poetry going now?

I asked Lowell that and he said that it's in an in-between state, between the beats and academics, that everyone is fighting shy of the extremes and trying to come forth with a statement which embodies both the vigor of the beat and the structure of the academic. Which is just what you'd want to do; but it's not something probably that can be worked out, since that is already an academic position. Any thing really good has to arise from something in the self. The beat generation's function was the opposite—to break things open, and it did that, and everybody was glad though they spend most of their time putting the beats down as hopeless. It seems to me the only solution to this problem is to see it in terms of the creative personalities. Until they emerge no one can know what to expect. Until the leader emerges nothing happens; when he comes, the politics will go the way he goes. If you can establish the primacy of personality over idioms and schools, then you can make sense of it. Otherwise, just about the time you think you have your school going, along will come a real original creator and you have an apocalypse of poets.

Then the beats gave new birth to American poetry by the fact that they did lend personality, even if not a sustaining one. I think of the beat generation not in terms of form, but in terms of Ginsberg, Gregory Corso, etc.

Yes, the trouble with the poetry of the earlier 50's was that after Lowell, academic or not, there was no one of his stature to vitalize it. Suddenly somebody comes along like Ginsberg and with his poem HOWL captures the imagination. That thing sold over 50,000 copies in no time. It was read everywhere. In bars people were looking over shoulders to read it. It had a fascination about it, and when the label—beat generation—was applied to it, it went. There had to be a creative personality, and Ginsberg, and Kerouac supplied it. How great they were remains to be seen. The academic people who followed Lowell, like Wilbur, Merril, Merwin, and Sexton, lacked the creative energy that made him unique. They lacked the capacity to get enough energy into their material to crack the reader's ego. They wrote non-academic poems in an academic way. So, you don't like to quarrel with poems as good as some of theirs—as authentic, I mean, as moving to the point of consequence—you don't like to quarrel, but of them I find my reservations the same as in Lowell's later poems. LIFE STUDIES is a book I don't like very much. His utilization of the conversational didn't operate for me. I think he switched to the conversational in the later book because he had the problem of losing belief. When you don't have belief, you have to make do with what attitude you have, but not having belief, the psyche can't generate sufficient energy to move others, to crack the ego. It's only in belief—I don't mean the formal sense, I mean this in the sense of an unconscious which affirms the authenticity of reality against its dubious aspects—which asserts that authenticity and which denies the dubiety to register the consequence of its own needs. Well, Baudelaire could make poems out of disbeliefs that were shudderingly profound because his unconscious was locked on desperation. But modern unbelief, even anguished unbelief in LIFE STUDIES, fails somehow. Maybe it's the period in history. I feel something has happened to Lowell's poetry (and this despite that fact that people like Ann Sexton and Elizabeth Bishop think LIFE STUDIES is an advance over LORD WEARY'S CASTLE, which I would think is the received opinion)—this is a great thing to me—it's not true.

The accusation against the whole current generation of poets is that they run down somehow, that their early poems are better than their late. Do you think this pattern is fair?

I think success has a way of leasing off the psychic energy into extraneous elements. You write out of your unknown state, out of your need for recognition, your need to produce, to discover yourself and make the impact upon your time. This is man's masculine ego. When success comes too early in life to an artist, it raises problems that are almost insurmountable for him, in order to maintain the primacy of his original commitment. It's like the religious life. You can make tremendous acts of ascetism, of discipline, courage, charity, when you first enter the religious life. Then after you become adapted, you find you don't have the capacity. You realize that you are operating on only one level. With poetry, your initial creative insight carries you on with a great burst of energy and makes a break-through. Now to discover how to transfer over into another system, another psychic frame of reference is extremely difficult, and only a guy like Yeats, somebody like that who can go through about three generations in his own self, can do it.

Does that mean building new cosmologies to be able to write new poems?

That really isn't the problem. The problem, which has to do with the subconscious, is of the content in man of belief. The capacity of the poet must be invigorated by the capacity of belief in himself. This is not just egocentricity. Every poetaster in Greenwich Village believes he's great, but the idea is to prove it. Belief in talent isn't what he needs, rather a different kind of self-belief, the self-belief of a saint. An artist has to be a kind of saint in that he has to have an unconscious assumption of the primacy of his place. It's as if he inhabits his place, having found it himself. Then he has something that cannot be taken from him. Not even by success. I think Lowell would have maintained that if he hadn't gone through the crisis of losing the faith by which he achieved his prime work. When he'd lost that faith, it put a different bend in his career than you would normally expect. Yeats never suffered the loss of faith, in terms of content of it, when he lost his religion. If he hadn't been a religious poet there might not have been any problem in regard to his art. When you are a Christian poet, or a communist poet, and lose your faith, the loss of commitment reduces you to a different level of activity.

Isn't that Pragmatism? Do you mean the will to believe?

Not in the sense of the ego willing it. The main thing is to acquire the craft. Then the unconscious genius can transform the formal knowledge and the acquired craft into something that's both personal and collective. The accusation against the Dionysians is that they become so personal that they lose the impersonal framework which sustains a literary production. But I think the Dionysian really has to have a deeper control of rhetoric than the Apollonian. Deeper, because those unconscious qualities are to be manifested in terms of consequentiality. What rhetoric does is establish the moral consequence and primacy of the materials, and by moral primacy I mean something else than conventional morality, something more like survival value.

That seems to imply something like 'thesis, antithesis, synthesis.' If so, who would you say is a good example of synthesis?

Hart Crane. There was a man who has to speak, out of his belief, and that necessity creates the rhetorical, consequential structure. He was one of those men whose unconscious need and whose conscious commitment and craft burn and fuse together. Craft and unconscious seem simultaneous. There are the marvelous pieces like THE DANCE where the rhetoric is perfectly believeable; it's believed; the commitment of belief is there.

To me that unconscious power, or rather power rising from the unconscious, is recorded in what I call rhetoric. It's possible to be rhetorical in an academic way, but it won't register anything. That was the Georgian fault which Pound and Williams rebelled against. They discarded rhetoric because it could be faked up. Yet when Pound himself or Williams breaks through into consequence, when his implicit knowledge and belief in the consequentiality of the thing he's doing shows through in terms of opposed tensions within it, as in THE ROAD TO THE CONTAGIOUS HOSPITAL but not in the red wheelbarrow piece where he's merely drawing down the object, then all of a sudden rhetoric begins to operate. Even the guy who's anti-rhetorical cannot dispense with rhetoric when he becomes committed in the unconscious, not just the conscious art of delineation. Like a Goya, whose drawing is perfect, who has controlled skill, suddenly in the disasters of war his unconscious dynamism will emerge in consequence, fill up the rhetoric of art, transform the forms. The art becomes great and is identifiable in the conventions and tradition of art, because that's what holds it all together. Minor art can go along between, but suddenly, boom, the big ones appear, with maybe a handful of poems in their whole lifetime. They are the bearing-off points. Their rhetoric is so original, profound, and true that it doesn't seem like rhetoric or craft but some real thing achieved. The punch is in the rhetoric. That's the way Shakespeare did it. That's the way Whitman, Crane, all the great ones, operate. Eliot, when he becomes great, does it. Afterwards, there are poets who will come along and fill in and make a pattern with an anthology poem or two, and you enjoy it because it's extremely well done. For instance, in Anne Sexton or James Merril you find a consciously assimiliated rhetoric in the Georgian sense, but better done because they're astute enough to avoid sentimentality. You don't like to quarrel with poems that good, but you never believe in their consequentiality. They are too much dedicated to creating an aesthetic object. The beats revolted against the poem as an object in order to reassert that the vatic commitment in the poet's unconscious is the thing and not the aesthetic object. The vatic commitment must break through the object we call the poem. An icon has to lose its nature of instrumentality in the reality of the thing it is registering. It becomes transformed by something greater than instrumentality, and that, when it happens, is what I call rhetoric.

You mentioned war. Do you think the unavoidable commitment that a war produces explains that short burst of good poems in the post-war Forties?

Yes, there was Randall Jarrel and Karl Shapiro. Jarrel is still writing good things, though he emphasizes the Mephistophelian in himself. Even Wallace Stevens wrote his by far best poems in that period and after. But those poets of the war who wrote merely out of an ego need to participate were no good at all.

And what do you mean by a vatic poet?

Basically, one kind of poet or artist creates a world of his own making, while another stands witness to a world beyond the world of his making. The first is the visionary and the second is the vatic or prophetic poet. It's not a value judgement; I would say that Leonarda Da Vinci was the visionary and Michelangelo was the vatic. It's a matter of archetypes. Visionary and vatic are archetypes of the poet's nature. In literature, James Joyce falls into the visionary category because he's content to create a world of supreme fiction, whereas D. H. Lawrence is vatic. Lowell, because of his loss of faith, stopped being the vatic poet he was in QUAKER GRAVEYARD and became a visionary one. But I doubt that a prophetic poet can do that and survive. I don't believe Lowell can, despite his craft. If he is archetypally a prophetic poet, all the visionary alleluias in the world won't substitute convincingly.

This standing witness to reality doesn't necessarily imply a religious one. Sometimes it's moral, like the better poems of Wilfred Owen; after the war the registration of moral consequence that was breaking through the indignation became vatic. To my individual habit of mind, there's no comparison between the prophetic and the visionary archetypes, because it seems obvious that the man as maker cannot fulfill himself. Reality always lies outside to be broken through to. What good is it to me to create a vision? A mirror to look at myself in? What does it come to in the end any more than that? I don't know. I suppose it's all right. But oh to break the mirror, you see, in one blow.

Yet, you remain frustrated, you come back to the visionary in the end because you realize that you're doomed as a prophetic. You're doomed to the anguish of not being able to cancel yourself out in your role of standing witness.

If you're an academic poet you have a better chance of staying sane?

But have you in the end? I understand what you mean facetiously, but when you start fooling with dynamite, you'd better make what you're doing dynamite. The man who can do tricks finally blows himself up—but it's greater than that, more to do with psychology. In this vocation, given the nature of the material you work with—a word from the visionary point of view is the self-contained object, or from the prophetic, is a filament that relates the receiving object to a charisma—you're going to expunge yourself, burn yourself out by making that filament receive contact. The liabilities of the visionary artist are like those of a priest who disinclines to engage himself. To heck with those mystics, says the young priest, I'll dispense the sacraments, I'll be a functionary in the community, and I'll get along. So he thinks he will. But if the medium he's dealing with is real, the danger is obvious. There is no asbestos glove to protect you against the reality of words if you don't recognize it. The Apollonian can't use his art as a method to protect himself.

Whereas your Dionysian is overkind—by yielding himself to what he does, he maintains the salvation of kind. He liberates his spiritual dimension and it is conformable to the reality which he speaks. He is received by it. The person who falsifies that relationship because he doesn't know better can never recognize what he's dealing with. This is neurosis. It's the neurosis of the organization man, who sees the material he's working with only as units when they're loaded with unity, as objects when they're loaded with reality, and it's the reality that drives him into the neurotic condition. The organization man and all the other neurotic symptoms of the times result from the fact that reality has been theologically depotentiated. The attempt to depotentiate the material world to manipulate it as you will can only end in disaster to the person who trys it, because the truth is simply the opposite. There's enough reality in this book of matches to blow me apart. Yet I can't avoid facing it just to keep my sanity. I will either be consumed by what I give myself to, or be broken down by the world I refuse to give myself to.

If on the archetype, you're a salesman, that is, an intermediary between the manufacturer and the consumer, one who knows what the people need and what has been made, this man is protected in his vocation by his belief that this is what he does. He is a kind of teacher.

To me the thing that destroys a man or makes him vulnerable to neurotic diseases is that intellectual work has its liabilities of inner frustration and of the whole sensibilities, when it is involved in doing things on one level for another level. The organization man, who does things not for himself, is in danger that the inner refusal of the body to be any longer exploited thus will set up a counteractivity and he will die of cancer or heart failure. The negation of his whole way of life reverberates back through his sensibilities, and collapse comes because reality is denied.

If you can teach with life and commitment, go ahead, because this is life-giving and health-giving; you move, you radiate, you walk through your skin, you become an epiphany. You are in the prophetic dimension.

Find the archetype of what you are, and then if you are a poet, you'd better just not compromise with what you can't be. When the poet compromises and gives the better part of his time to what he isn't, then he becomes the academic. He loses even what he had.

Then you don't agree with Robert Pack's introduction in NEW POETS OF ENGLAND AND AMERICA?

His logic is so beautiful and careful, but I have misgivings that I can't really tie up. If the poet goes into the university, as he recommends, then he ought to make sure the two vocations aren't hostile in himself. Some can do both, but if he is merely serving mammon, if he isn't committed to teaching, then he's practising self-deceit, which is hostile to his real commitment. Life will come along and drive him to a lower level. Here's a man, say, who gets married, has children, and he has to take a teaching job to support them. All right, that's a different thing, that isn't what we're talking about. Life often forces us to do things we are committed against, but we are purged because it's not our choice. We're not trying to fool anyone. But even that is dangerous. The great

men are those like Blake who live in the hands of God, who have courage not to do what they have to do, if it violates their archetype.

I don't know how you find these things out. The mistake I made in
my own life in regard to being an artist, the first great mistake, was
when I married I sacrificed the inner viability of my marriage to my
career. In other words I accepted my art, in the religious sense, but at
the same time I entered into a relationship with a woman which was
based primarily on my need to stabilize my passional nature. Unless I
had the stability, I could not have peace I felt, but I didn't want to
sacrifice either way. I wanted to maintain the primacy of my career and
at the same time secure through the woman the equanimity of passional adjustment. The mistake I made was that I denied the primacy
of her person. By reducing her to an object and sacrificing that object
even to a school of thought, I denied the reality of the situation. So
when the war came and I was drafted, caput, she just found another
man. There was no primacy in our relationship, and that's why in my
second marriage I'd learned my lesson. And I replaced the primacy of
our relationship, not on the career, but on the person. And the career
went right along better than ever, because I had freed it from an over-
intensity that was false at this other level. By asserting the primacy
where it belonged, the art began to achieve liberty. Now then, this
marriage terminated because it was founded on a misconception. When
I became a Catholic, since we'd both been married before, we gave it
up, and I entered the religious life. Of course I was faced with the same
problem of primacy again, but I'd learned my lesson, from which I
made a better art and a more continuing one. I secured the inner freedom to relate to life as life moved upon me.

The primacy of personal relationship is what generates the creative
energy and liberates the charisma in the depths of one's unconscious.
Out of this the art prospers, but by objectifying his art, or reducing it
to an object, he reduces himself to that object. He is the egocentric
who has great mastery of his material, but where it should expand it
remains closed. When one yields to life and is an artist, his art takes
on the abundance and somnolent beauty of life, and the truth beyond
the tangential phenomenological object.

Well, a man fifty can always tell a youth that, but I think if someone
had told me in the first years of my marriage, I would have insisted it
was what I was doing, that I was really putting the primacy on the

personal. What I should have been able to see was that the primacy wasn't even on my person, and until I made concessions to the personal thing, I was living a lie. I had a vasectomy and no children, and in that kind of thing I was cutting myself off at the roots. Life-denying, matter how much I said I was life-celebrating. Denying my bio-logical immortality and my capacity to have sons, trying like Rilke to make my poems my sons. And they became crippled children be-cause I had crippled myself. But we've talked this way about as long as we can.

Well, since this is an interview, perhaps we should talk a little about critics. If you want to go on, that is?

Ask me a leading question.

Like the questions Dylan Thomas spoke of? "I carry Kierkegaard in my pocket. Who do you carry?" All right, I'll try. Do you think the critic affects the poet?

Supposedly the critic represents judgement. But I think he compli-cates the task of the poet by bringing in judgement collected reactions not within himself, which he gets from convention and tradition. The poet himself is the first and purest critic of his work. He also knows and writes against traditional backgrounds. But he has a knowledge of him-self within himself, and he produces in a state of tension between these two attitudes. When a poem goes into the world it has two destinies. It provokes a reaction from professional critics and it provokes a reac-tion from the people who read it, if they read it. Novelists needn't bother so much about the critic because the people support them, but the poet is so far from the people in our time that he doesn't get the normal assurance. So he has to think of the critic. They're eyeball to eyeball. The magazines are the critic's chief tool in his attempt to man-age poetry, since book publishers respect only poets introduced through the magazines. One of the main objectives of the beats was to crack this system by going straight to the presses. HOWL sold only 50,000 copies by direct appeal to the people. This situation is unfortunate for the poets, but it's unfortunate for the critics also. I don't think the poets will ever bring the critics around, however. The creative mentality and the critical mentality operate on different sets of reactions. The trouble will always be there, but the tension is necessary. The poet makes do with his times, but he shouldn't waste too much energy trying to solve a problem which is based on archetypal divisions. He does what he does, and shouldn't worry if he is always conscious of an outside point-of-view which he has and which brings a lot of pain.

The same problem confronts those who are trying to pretend there's no difference between negro and white, as if the differences weren't archetypally operating. We've put up an abstract concept justice, and true, we have to work in that frame, but it can't be solved. It's the same with poets and critics. The difference will not be solved as long as there are negroes and whites. Ideally, these archetypes give life its tension, and there's nothing more tragic than to see colored people abandon their archetype just for white mannerisms or whites becoming deliberate negrophiles to the extent of certain beatniks.

These archetypes are hard to overcome sometimes. As a West Coast poet, I carry a lot of regional bitterness against the East, because I feel the power of criticism lies in the East, while the power of creativity seems to be out West. I feel it's a more open situation; there's so much just around San Francisco now. But I'm realist enough to know that if you're going to make it, you have to come East.

Let's tie two subjects together here. Why do you think Robinson Jeffers, who's the first person that comes to mind as a West Coast poet, wrote some of his worst poems during the war?

Because he denied it too much, that is, the reality of it. Still he produced some short poems out of his denial of war that will gain strength as the world worsens.—SUCH COUNSELS YOU GAVE TO ME, for instance.

A poem like THE STONECUTTERS works through a meditative, philosophical tone, which from an academic point of view may not be satisfactory, but nevertheless it comes out of a part of the psyche that's very permanent:

> Stone-cutters fighting time with marble, you foredefeated
> Challengers of oblivion
> Eat cynical earnings, knowing rock splits, records fall down,
> The square-limbed Roman letters
> Scale in the thaws, wear in the rain. The poet as well
> Builds his monument mockingly;
> For man will be blotted out, the blithe earth die, the brave sun
> Die blind and blacken to the heart:
> Yet stones have stood for a thousand years, and pained
> thoughts found

The honey of peace in old poems.

In some way it's a man thinking out loud in a profound and serious way, which is a great deal different than writing about a red wheelbarrow. Many of Jeffers poems I could never be satisfied with if I had written them. As a poet I have to make a denser statement. But then his poems bear off and satisfy some important part of my nature, and I'm content that he did them. You know, though, there is not another poet I've ever read whose work I would put my name to, except my own. Even poems I recognize as masterpieces, I would never publish. I would have to tighten them or change them, even make them less than they are perhaps, but I couldn't let them stand.

However, for the present, the language can support a whole shoal of academic poets without much loss, but as I said before, we just have to keep our eyes peeled for the next break, the next masterpiece. And it will come from personality, not from any trend. The charismatic man with his creative energy will jolt everything forward, and then another shoal of academics will come, and the institution will support them so they can give themselves to their craft and not be involved in betrayal.

Summer, 1963

MARY ANN RADNER

(1944–   )

Mary Ann Radner won first prize in a national high school poetry contest and went on to win the poetry prize at Wellesley College. Following her graduation in 1964 she studied at the University of Florence and worked on translations from French, Latin, and Italian.

L'ENVOI

You are the long way that I have to go
away from you.

In your face now
comes the reflected strangeness of my face
going from you, a night in a far city.
Your voice moves me away as moving seas
will take me
and you translate me to another tongue.

I who am here within your hand's expanse
will not be here, but far; your holding
is giving me to distances.
My lungs which breathe you, blood which sounds you
will pulse another air
apart from you, my country, my nativity.

These forms of me you name and guess will alter
and be reborn of foreignness; oh you, become
the long way out, away,
how shall I make out of myself
the long way back?

ENTRY IN A WINTER DIARY

As if the pale day had been made for me
And not me for the day
I came out. I walked stern and free
Into the bold lake's center, where there lay
Full snow over ice. Wild as a smoke-ringed hawk
The sun flew down to land
From every heaven, took for rock
(Or any roost) my stretched and angry hand.

I trembled when that heartless crest flamed blue
Around and tensed its wing
For flight again! I wanted you
Under those skys, the night's wide lowering

Thawed into star. Without your singing town,
Becalmed on the lake's bed
While its piled whorls washed grey, and down
Beyond my step the huddled waters spread

Their silence, I was silent. Did I learn,
Ashore, to see the climb
Against the deep, the wind-honed turn
I took? The ice has scattered since that time.

April, 1965

Mary Ann Radner   435

THOU ART LIGHTING AND LOVE

> *"Not out of his bliss*
> *Springs the stress felt*
> *Nor first from heaven (and few know this)*
> *Swings the stroke dealt—"*
> GERARD MANLEY HOPKINS

Who is my Christ? Irreverently I guess
He is afflicted with your gentleness,
That he has eyes like yours, and hands that bless

As yours sweetly blaspheme: He was unnerved
By love always. His life was made with men
Who tempted their temptations and were served
With the same hurts that killed him. He was open

And closed, passionate and not understood,
Friendless and friendly. He did not talk much.
He saved his body for a bride of wood
Who tore his flesh off in her lifting clutch;

He died to take his wedding-sleep in hell,
Comes back a legend more believable
Than you, who show his love's painful gospel.

April, 1965

ROBERT GRENIER

Class of 1964, (1942–   )

*A native of Minneapolis, Robert Grenier studied
under Robert Lowell at Harvard and won the
Hatch Prize in 1965. He now studies at the University of Iowa.*

THROUGH (WHERE) WALLS (WERE)

I see
my wife
in the barn
of a dead New England farmer
in her old clothes—

passing the heavy
beams, avoiding the ridge
pole's shadow on the straw
floor, mount
a brittle ladder into the loft—

there
(experimentally)
seated
in a rotted carriage
below open sky.

Fall, 1963

LEAF

Nothing after that.

Nothing left to mourn
after that light

fall—
        filled with its own
              tune.

November, 1964

THE MINNESOTA SOLDIERS
HOME IN AUGUST

On the lawns before the brown Home
on the hill above the city
the wheeled sick sit still in the sunshine—

near acorns and the simply old, benched in the shade—
incurably happy, just to sit; looking up
or looking down at the feet-worn ground before their feet.

And one has a chained raccoon.

So many yellow elm leaves, straw hats,
glassed-in, round, steel-rimmed memories . . .
blue, canvas shoes.

Here thought's hard, hurts, useless, diffuse
as thought in sandboxes:

438   *Robert Grenier*

Forts, leaves, patient
bits of seed,
stick,
         sand . . .

Canes. The deafening echo of cannon in their ears.

The first of September sun's still so warm
this morning, Howard.

Nurses. Squirrels.

GRODEK

At evening the autumn woods ring with the sound of
deadly weapons, the golden plains
and blue lakes, over which the sun
more somberly rolls; night encircles
dying soldiers, the wild grunts
of their shattered mouths.
Still a red cloud silently gathers in
the meadowland, in which an irascible God lives,
the shed blood itself, moonlit coolness;
all streets point into black decay.
Below golden boughs of night and stars
the sister's shadow wavers through the silencing grove
to greet the ghosts of heroes, bleeding heads;
softly, in reeds and rifle barrels ring the dark flutes of fall.
O prouder grief! you brazen altars—
today the hot flame of the spirit feeds a huger pain,
the unborn grandchildren.
                              —*after Georg Trakl*

                                        April, 1965

WILLIAM FERGUSON

Class of 1965, (1943–   )

Poetry editor of the Advocate *in 1964, Mr. Ferguson won the Horace translation prize in the year of his graduation. His poems have appeared in broadsheet form and in the* Massachusetts Review.

As proprietor of the Ferguson Press in Milford, N.H., he has published the work of Stephen Sandy, Robert Grenier, Donald Junkins, and Tim Reynolds. He was instrumental in the effort that brought about The Other End of the Couch, *a hand-set, limited-edition pamphlet of poems printed for Gordon Cairney in 1964.*

ANALOGY OF THE BLACK PIANO

First reader: She wove a marvelous cloth on that dark loom,
colors of crystal, thunderous implication,
and each thread black, and many-colored,
and in the loom the sun-white cloth,
breaking of crystal, wakening waters,
color of wells at midnight, sea at noon;
and in the loom there were two lamps,
one dark, the other fire and light,
and one was of the warmth of the sea,
the other, warmth of diamonds,
and of the darkness and the light was woven
cloth of day and night, or of all time.

Second reader: This wind, crazy with rain, rattling shingles,
angers the river, charging a dusky bull
through hills heavy with trees, and it is she,
concealing its springs yet guiding the water in full force,
an image of winter come to haunt this season;
but the rain comes with the sound of flowers,
with the sound of trees stretching in clouds
to the low valley. Bells in the town;
I lie on the dry leaves marvelling,
though across the river in the spruces half-moving
the invisible raven waits
predatory in the stillness of the air.

First reader: Wind cannot touch the whiteness of this cloth
spread out, sun and golden, like the sea
calm at nightfall, or the same raging sea
sacrilege of the moon, and midnight torn from the wall.
this cloth, like the flag of a great ship
now ragged and torn one end to the other.
now coming out glorious pulling at the staff,
and still, it is true, the shining eye
of a bird perhaps, or a quiet god,
looms among cloudbanks, now, and gone,
without message, without a word,
no reassurance, rather a new portent . . .

Second reader: I am of the land, and of the mountains,
and I have followed this shaggy river
curve after curve, upriver, far from the sea,
and even so, the story is not told,
I cannot understand, even so,
the convolutions of that blessed stream,
the downward coursing, faithful, and
not without colors of lust, the which caught
true in the sun, reflect, yet colored, the whole . . .
the sound of bells, and lamplight tangled in them,
the bones of mountains and the bones of men
approach this chanting, risen from the dead.

William Ferguson   441

First reader: She weaves a marvelous cloth, an evening
woven in bellnotes, steeple-pierced,
lamps going on, and others dark still,
your village far from the sea, yet with a sign,
an image of water; seabirds circling
as if in search, and a sea-storm welling perhaps
in any lake, no matter how calm,

Second reader: and in the waving pines
the invisible raven waits
predatory in the stillness of the storm.
O let the spring come, and let no man revile her,
quiet rain, with sun here and there,
and the grass growing greener day by day,
a fine cloth for a child to play upon,

First reader: and in the loom the sun-white cloth,
green threads for tapestry multicolored,
a miracle half-seen in the doing,

Second reader: and the river in her soul
flows on in the memory
of storms and seasons, riding the heights of the wind.

Summer, 1964

DORIS GARTER

Class of 1966, (1944–   )

Doris Garter is one of the finest poets Radcliffe has fostered in years. She married Daniel Fendel '66 in the spring of 1965.

GO SLAY YOUR RIVAL

Go slay your rival for me if you can.
Choke him, but first invoke him, if you can.
He is no man: he will not answer an insult.
You aren't of his cult, he will not come.
I offer you this prothalamium
As mystery to help you win your bride.

I told you you would be the first. I lied,
It was so long ago, I had forgotten,
But he awaits you in my parents' house.
First you must climb the attic stairs
And open up the box in which he lies,
Three inches of him. Oh, he was so tall!
There is a princess in the box beside him
And I was she. How do you find my ball gown,
Does it become me? Take me, no, put me down,
First you must win me from him. Years ago
You'd not have had a chance. He had a castle
With a moat. (We never used real water.)
I was the daughter of a vassal of the czar
And princes came to woo me near and far.
How I did love him! Sometimes my sister would do him.
She wasn't strong enough or masculine.
I'd speak for him instead. I would begin,

Summon the princess to my royal bed.
And I, as princess said, *Yes, majesty.*
I grew impatient of the travesty
With the ungrateful mold of princess painted
Cold. Dispensing with formality
Myself was love queen to my statuette.
No longer porcelain, I, Elaine Jane Beautiful,
We met outside of China. I proclaimed
My lover's latent actuality. And he,
By royal proclamation
Whispered in privacy proclaimed me queen,
Using all the official words I'd seen
In documents or my imagination
Or my dreams.

I am your spoils once you depose my king.
I am your golden bough. Depose him now,
Lift him and smash him. Shatter everything
In his frail entourage. They won't fight back,
The pouting lady at his side will break
Like icing on birthday cake. Wed me the night
You do it. Will there be someone to invite?
No matter. I'll bear lotus and wear white.

Summer, 1964

GERALD HILLMAN

Class of 1965, (1943–   )

Gerald Hillman's short story Jo *won the Advocate fiction prize in 1964; he was elected president of the magazine for the year 1964–65. Mr. Hillman is currently abroad on a Shaw travelling fellowship.*

JO

Jo swept in with a querulous wind, she all flushed and gasping, it cold. "Oh Parker!" Parker stopped rolling and lay looking away on the red linoleum. And Eva just squatted on her stool in front of the old gray oven, black and all bellied out over the belt of her housecoat.

"I'm late," Jo said, "I agree I'm late." She tossed her coat on the table and watched while it unbunched and wiggled to the floor. "We will dine later than usual tonight, Parker. O! It'll be very romantic! I'll make cabbage. Okay? You love cabbage, Parker. And there'll be raisins, sauce, and brown sugar! I'll borrow brown sugar and put that in." She paused and frowned. "O! I've ten minutes to dress! He's coming today!" Eva bobbed her head like an unblinking pigeon pecking at the grass.

The bedroom was light light gray this month. Crumpled clothing hid a chair and night-table and drying stockings were snaked around the curtain rods, the bed unmade with sheets weeks old, half-off. In the painting on the wall, the sky was bright with oranges and yellows and reds, splashed over a fast-brushed sea, and there was a blue-red-green man, a chinaman fisherman, tangled in his net and going down in the enormous sucking green sea—a wedding gift from Gilbert's mother.

She undressed, humming and shuffling about, completely forgot what she was doing while late day at the window was shading everything blue, squares of smoky blue on the narrow walls and even on her skin—

playing on her arms and shoulders and turning the tips of her breasts purple like blue lips on cold swimmers. The clock tocked and she started, then yanked aside the closet curtain and footed the clothes-heap for anything fresh to wear.

"Ooo?" uttered Eva from her stool while she bobbed her kerchiefed head, and the low insistent "ooo?" skipped playfully from room to room. Generally a puzzling sound right between query and reply, it was her warning—and soon she would begin to sway and, if left alone, she'd be scratching her black forearms white and red, pulling at the skin. And Parker would just roll sillily, without a care, or rest on his back to watch.

"Ev, that guy with the special in glassware, remember? The one with the smelly box of soaps and . . ." She kaploddshuffled into the bathroom and sat. "I just saw him again. That's the eighth time. God, what if he's following me! He was at the bus shelter. Standing at the bus shelter. Nothing to it, lady, you know, just thought I'd stand at your bus shelter . . ." She flushed the bowl and turned a faucet. "O! he has this new red cart for his smelly box. 'Scuse me, ma'am, just walkin' my cart, ugly day, huh? . . ."

There was only a minute or so to go, for Gilbert was always on time. He had not seen her for three months, but that did not matter. Gilbert would not fail. Gilbert was set to everyone else's time, and whatever their time was, at the appointed moment Gilbert came. If they were early, he was. Once, she stopped every time-piece in the house half an hour before he was due: there was no time in the house: and Gilbert did not come home. How could he?

The doorbell rang at five-thirty and one second.

She snapped the bra around her waist and struggled it up, then stumbled down the hall, graceful as a stately goose, her long long hair falling free and golden-brown. She reached for the doorknob but paused to scratch an itch . . . "ooo?" . . . and then buttoned her bermudas.

"Hello, Gilbert."

Gilbert plodded in. He looked very determined. He had never before looked so determined. He slouched in the small hall. First he leaned toward one wall, then he eyed it suspiciously and leaned awkwardly toward the other wall. Everything about him was quite determined. He glared with ferocious determination at Jo's belly.

"Will you enter the livingroom, Gilbert?"

Gilbert sat in the oldest chair and pulled his ink-stained fingers one

446   *Gerald Hillman*

at a time. He took out his black pen and put the small black point cover in his mouth and rolled it around. Jo watched Gilbert, Gilbert watched the gay red flower on his bright turquoise tie. "Look how you look, Gilbert. Look how you look. Must you look that way? Do you look that way only when you come? Why Gilbert? Your hair, now. Your hair is half over your ears, Gilbert. Can't you feel it? Don't you have any feeling in your ears? How many shirts . . ." Gilbert gazed at the open quinine water bottles across the room. They were full of seeds. Long ago he'd declared that that was the one amazing thing about Jo, how she could get those seeds in. Gilbert himself had tried many times but without success. She used to line the bottles up across the room and flip them in. Gilbert had given up playing but when completely alone . . . he would not be humiliated even if it was the one amazing thing about Jo—and he had to admit it was. Gilbert occasionally tried with a very small basin . . . he played his own way . . . with peach pits. ". . . like the same one, the same one you wore at the hearing, Gilbert." She looked at his shoes. He looked sadly at his shoes. They were badly scuffed and the laces were knotted. The back of his left shoe was broken: he hid it with the toe of his right.

Parker came in. Probably to roll on the rug. A good part of the rug was rolled up, however. The walls were being repaired and bits of plaster dust lay over everything.

"I suppose you know," began Gilbert. He squirmed and cleared his throat. "I presume you are aware," began Gilbert. He frowned intently and his eyes muddied.

"Go on, Gilbert. Will you go on, Gilbert. What do I know? What do I know, Gilbert? Will you, Gilbert will you take that little black thing out of your m . . ."

"It's a dump! It's the town dump!" Gilbert shuddered. "Nine years and we never lived like this, Jo. We never lived like this. But mother said you would come to it. But I said no! I was wrong though. It's a dump."

"If you don't approve then leave, Gilbert. You know how. I mean you know the way, Gilbert. If you don't like it, it's not my fault. You heard the judge, Gilbert—you don't have to come, if you don't like it."

Parker got up and padded over to the big box where his toys were kept. He peered over the edge of the box and saw his broken duck that he'd been pulling around for months, for tiring tiring months. But there was a piece of quilt there nice to tear. He dragged the piece of quilt to the center of the room and gave it a good rip.

There was a warning from the kitchen.

"Do you hear that? She's worse!" said Gilbert, beginning again with determination. "Poor Eva! She's worse. I can tell from listening."

Jo sat on the floor and watched Parker and smiled faintly at Parker.

"She used to dance around and sing and now she's . . . I guess she can't do anything anymore. I guess she's getting worse and worse," said Gilbert. He hunched forward, his elbows on his knees, his arms outstretched.

"Sometimes she's worse. But sometimes she improves, of course. I taped her arms for a week last month and she didn't cry once. I taped only one arm at a time. That way works."

"That should have been done sooner," said Gilbert. "Why didn't you leave it on?"

"She broke her nails on it, Gilbert. I had my choice of two kinds of trouble." She reached over to stroke Parker's ears. "But I'm so very glad you're concerned, Gilbert. It is very generous of you to take an interest since it is, incidentally, your fault! You made her . . ."

"I? . . . I made . . ."

"You, Gilbert, you made her a nervous wreck!"

"Not me!"

"Yes! you went and pulled the house apart. 'This is mine, this is mine, I own that, half of this . . .'"

"The judge said . . . !"

"Could she keep house? What could she do? Gilbert tearing this, Gilbert ripping and tearing . . ."

"The judge said . . . !" said Gilbert, spreading his hands.

Parker sorted the quilt's intestines on the floor for her inspection. Then he rolled over and stared at Gilbert and let his weary tongue hang out. They watched him.

"Does she do anything anymore?" asked Gilbert. He leaned forward and frowned at the quinine water bottles.

"She minds Parker. She waits for me to come back when I go out. She listens to me and she changes her own housecoat Friday mornings."

Gilbert was picking up bits of plaster off the floor and tossing them at the quinine water bottles. They all missed. Gilbert looked more determined than ever.

"I am working now," she said, "At the Music Library on Claymont. I put away music. Good thing is, it's not too far to get to."

"Claymont."

"But I don't like walking there. Not alone, Gilbert."

"O! You shouldn't!"

"It is true that things have happened on the way."

"This place is a dump! A dump, Jo . . ."

"In fact, yesterday something happened to me."

"Mother will die . . . she's so happy when she's right . . ." Gilbert pressed his lips together. His right hand began debating with his left. "What happened?"

"Well, I can't take the bus too often. The soap man stays there. He scares me to death!" Jo stood up and leaned against the wall. "So I go behind that miser guy's house to the alleyway . . ."

"A miser guy."

"You know the alleyway, Gilbert?"

"The alleyway."

"Maybe you can see it through that window. Not that window! That window. That's the alleyway, the one that leads past where the grocery store was. To the Ave. Well, I was almost out of the alleyway and this boy came up to me right out from the place where they keep the barrels. He was about fifteen."

"Just hanging around the alleyway."

"And we started talking, Gilbert. O on and on about mythology, especially from Greek. All I knew was Sappho—you gave me her poems last year. Remember Sappho's poems, Gilbert? I knew her, but he knew lots of them. God, all! That was his occupation, he told me. Reading and memorizing mythology poems. He was funny to see, walking along, waving his arms, doing Calymachy's poems and . . . he had a downy mustache. Why was that?"

"Probably afraid to shave," said Gilbert.

"I guess so."

"Probably, I guess."

"Well then, he was afraid to shave and kept up a little mustache. You had one yourself, Gilbert . . ."

"I?"

"In the ninth grade . . ."

"Never in my life!"

"Oh yes you did, Gilbert. Oh yes you did. I have pictures of you with a pretty blond one."

"Never," said Gilbert, almost in tears. He shook his head. From the kitchen came the noise of Eva's slippers, tapping nervously on the red linoleum floor.

"What happened, Jo?" he said, regaining a determined look.

"We walked all the way to the Ave., Gilbert. And then into the Square and down toward Brattle Street, side by side, he talking away, bellowing away in that low voice, saying this about mythology while I was saying that, telling me all about Greek women prostituting themselves in the temples and the orgies. Right then . . . right in the thick of it all, I looked down. There it was, Gilbert! Sticking right out from his fly. All exposed. And nobody noticed. But what if they did! Well, I couldn't have it, Gilbert. I couldn't! So I just said 'look I've got to go now!' and I turned right into the barbershop."

They sat quietly for a long while and the room, unlit, became darker. They watched Parker wiggle his tail around the floor.

"Mother knew it . . ." murmured Gilbert.

"People never notice a thing."

"ooo?"

Gilbert tugged nervously at the button of his coat. He glanced down at one of his watches, quickly so's not to be seen. But she caught him.

"Don't you think it's quite long enough now, Gilbert? How long is it supposed to be?"

"The judge said . . . !" said Gilbert.

"I know, Gilbert, but how long, how awfully long is it supposed to be?"

"He said I could see Parker. He said I could see him! and that's exactly . . . that is exactly what I am going to do! I'm going to stay and visit Parker after I've visited Jo!"

Gilbert's determination was fierce. His face reddened.

"She's scratching!" Jo cried. "I can hear it! She's all itchy! Did you have to raise your voice? Did you have to raise your voice? You did it! Now get out."

"I don't hear it! I don't hear it," said Gilbert. But a sound like the scraping of light sandpaper was coming from the kitchen. "I don't hear it."

"You won't be able to talk at all in here in a minute, Gilbert. Please, go!"

"I came here to talk it out," he said, "that's why I came."

"Things were quiet before you came."

Gilbert nodded his head solemnly and folded his hands. "It was quiet before he came," he muttered. He stared at the quinine bottles knowingly as if they held a mystery no longer a mystery to him. "O it was quiet and peaceful before then, I think."

"He?"

"Parker."

"Parker!?"

Parker walked over to the window through which something of the sun's red was struggling back against the creeping plum of night even while all the trees were growing black, growing up to the sky. The window as big and whatever light there was flooded into the room and flooded over them all and made the room darker. Parker watched the still solemn playground they faced. He watched for the boy with the mustache while he trembled slightly and his tongue came back in. He grit his teeth and watched. There was nothing else to do.

"Gilbert, I am never going to have you here again! You insult me and Parker and you make Eva itchy. Now will-you-leave."

"We were happy. We were happy before he came. We had the apartment and friends and we ate at Milo's and I bought . . ."

"They were your friends and we ate there twice a year and we . . . fought all the time!"

"Spats."

"Fights!"

"Jo, he slept with us all the time! In between us. And he wets the bed every night, Jo. Admit it. Every night I swam for my life. I couldn't sleep, Jo. I got insomnia. I have to sleep, Jo. After all. I'm a statistician."

"You're a jerk, Gilbert. You've absolutely no understanding."

"I'm a jerk. I have absolutely no understanding."

"This is the last time you come, Gilbert."

"No." He shook his determined head. "No."

"G'bye, Gilbert. G'bye," she said.

Eva seemed better already. Jo put on the light in the pantry. Eva did not like the kitchen light above her stool. Jo wiped Eva's neck with a damp towel and then scuffed to the bedroom. Parker sat on the floor and nuzzled the sheets. She lay on the wrinkled bed and stared at the chinaman fisherman, trying to keep his hat correct on his head. Parker hopped up and sat on the pillow and yawned complacently and took a roll. In the kitchen, Eva stared from her stool with an occasional soft "ooo?" like a black oracle of old, frustrated by warning and warning, in a dead language.

"After I rest, I'll get out the cabbage, Parker, after I rest a little while. We'll have candlelight and we'll eat cabbage and cover it with—sweet brown sugar . . ." She flung her arms around her face.

Summer, 1963

Appendix

SEX: THE LITERARY BREAKTHROUGH
AT HARVARD SQUARE

THE OFFICERS of Radcliffe College, as well as parents of students and prospective students, have been caused increasing anxiety over the last few years by the publication of stories describing Harvard-Radcliffe love-affairs. Those published are but a small percentage of those written: an instructor in creative writing at Harvard tells us that one-third of every batch of papers handed in to him are of this genre, and the *Harvard Advocate* is flooded at each copy deadline with reams of poetry and prose describing these affairs in the Hasty Pudding—Hayes Bickford—steps of Memorial Church—coffee house, milieu. These pieces may be described stylistically as variations, more-or-less, between two extremes —one emphasizing the Pudding (Fitzgeraldesque),—the other the Bickford (Kerouacesque), with athletic and/or academic variants going off into Widener, or the Harvard Stadium. Harvard, being a place where literary aspiration and eros thrive together, it is not unnatural that this sort of fiction was initiated and reaches its greatest volume here. Needless to say, almost all of the unpublished poems and stories dedicated to 'young love,' are bad, but all of them—hundreds of them—have contentual elements in common with those that have been published.

We may still apply the term "Harvard Square Sex Fiction," generically, to works that are not strictly Cambridge-oriented, because those published stories that are not set at Harvard could just as well be, and they all seem part of the same trend. These published stories and novels vary a great deal in literary quality and style, but these qualities are not of as much concern as the elements of content they seem to have in common. The contentual similarities are so striking, furthermore, that it seems safe to treat these works as documents of what actually does happen at Harvard and places like it. Of the many published works, a few come immediately to mind such as Philip Roth's very fine *Goodbye Columbus*, in which, among many other things, an unmarried Radcliffe girl purchases a diaphragm, and a very bad novel by a Yalie entitled *Entry E*, which describes with well-controlled outrage a "gang-bang"—a kind of

Ivy League rape. The pattern of Harvard-Radcliffe affairs may be derived from such works as J. D. Salinger's famous "Franny," Sallie Bingham's locally scandalous "Winter Term," Jonathan Kozol's *The Fume of Poppies,* which doesn't even spare us the scatological intimacies, and Harold Brodkey's "Sentimental Education" with its less sophisticated but no less passionate lovers.

All of these stories, and the unpublished ones as well, are, in a sense, the same story. The two lovers meet in ways that are meant to be charming—such as observing each other in a Chaucer course, or holding hands between salt and pepper shakers. They fall in love, have adventures together, have intercourse, and through revelations that come to them from the adventures and the sexual experiences, take a spiritual journey that parallels the journey of their affair. They always end unhappily. The main source of their unhappiness is sex: satisfaction is never complete, although it may seem so at moments. Various things go wrong: they are either inexperienced and through their inexperience cause neurotic associations for one another, are awkward in a way the author means to be charming but at which we can only sneer, are over-sexed, have a purely sexual relationship without other areas of rapport, get pregnant and have the usual troubles, end up being promiscuous and hurting each others feelings, can't find a place to do it, do it in a disagreeable car, are guilty about it, want to do it when partner doesn't, are passive or aggressive in ways unbecoming to their respective sexes, can't stand to do it, or, very rarely, want to but don't. One or more of these things is always the matter; sometimes the whole gambit with variations.

Another trend, in the form of unquestionable documentary evidence, seems to back up the conclusions that we must draw from reading these pieces of fiction, these conclusions being basically that something is very much amiss in the lives of students at Harvard and Radcliffe (or anywhere, for that matter, but at Harvard it is more interesting because we are supposedly dealing with an intellectual elite, if not a socio-economic one). This trend of unquestionable documentation we are referring to appears in the form of "frank" symposiums, discussions and surveys in such periodicals as *Seventeen* and *Madamoiselle,* under such titles as "Chastity Today," or "What Girls REALLY Think About Sex," and, in a cheaper form, in teen-age columns about "datenique" (*sic!*) in so many newspapers. Typical of the "frank" articles in the first category are quotations that usually run something like this: "Peter, a brilliant physics major at ——————, had this to say about premarital sex relations on campus: 'I think a girl expects a boy to be experienced, and therefore, to prepare myself for marriage, I find it necessary to take advantage of any girl who will comply, although I could never respect such a girl, of course. On the other hand I would not take a girl home to meet my parents unless she were a virgin, tra la, tra la'." The editor will undoubtedly conclude that Peter holds "the double standard of today's brave youth . . ." In another article we will read that Suzey Q., co-ed at ——————, has this to say: "I think petting and making out is OK, if a girl knows where to draw the line, but I am willing to go all-the-way with the boy I love even if we're not married." These articles always conclude the same thing: that most young people favor complete consummation if they are in love (a few prudes notwithstanding), while others prefer various substitutes best left undescribed. These articles also conclude that this is very interesting, demonstrative of a change in attitude since the day when girls in their twenties were faced with that most over-whelming of all moral crises, should they kiss good-night on the first date, and that, all-in-all, this is all right. What they do not conclude, but what is apparent to us when we read the literary documents such as *The Fume of Poppies* and see where this attitude leads in the hands of such simple and obtuse people as Peter and Suzey Q., is that along with the new freedoms we have been reading about, and know from statistical analysts such as Kinsey, there comes inevitable unhappiness. We may be sure that this unhappiness is not inherent in the new sexual freedoms, themselves, although it is primarily sexual, but rather in the people and the environment of which they are the products.

The causes of this unhappiness, evidenced so often and so clearly in "Harvard Square Sex Fiction," are only scratched at by the various authors. Much of the unhappiness is due to the lack of any framework and code within which college students may practice their freedoms. The reason there is, as yet, no suitable framework, must be held to be the result of a society in a state-of-change; that people at Harvard and Radcliffe openly have affairs is denied by no one, and yet these affairs are carried on in defiance of the school administrations, parents, ministers, and self-appointed leaders of the young. The new freedoms are accepted as fact, but are still held to be immoral. If we accept the writings about Harvard-Radcliffe affairs as a documentary,—and this we must do both because of the recurrence of content and the large numbers of works in which this recurrence takes place,—we must recognize the necessity that the causes of unhappiness and the changing society in which the unhappiness takes place, be *probed,* and not merely scratched at. We ask that writers—student writers, particularly—who deal with this kind of content, *probe,* in their future works, into the causes of what, to date, they have merely described. Since literature is by no means merely an examining force, but may be, at its best, a force of reform, we ask, at the risk of sounding pompous, that these writers imply, in their future works, a code and framework suitable to the new sexual freedoms. Rather than becoming mere documents, their works will become a directing force in the lives of their readers, much, as in a rather different way, Gide's *Les Nourritures Terrestres* became for the French youth of the last generation.

William S. Bayer
Registration, 1959

EDITORIAL: THE VANISHING CAMBRIDGE STORY

Two YEARS ago, even a year ago, when one of our editors came across a story that began, "There was a dead fly in my coffee. It was two o'clock in the morning and the Bick was almost deserted," he would probably shudder and try to get through it as quickly as he could. There had been so many of them, so many imitation *Winter Terms,* and all of them had the same, familiar set of circumstances and emotions. The editors were then pretty well tired of reading about wretched people they had never met and affairs that at a distance seemed far more tedious than tragic. Widener, the Waldorf, the banks of the Charles, a fifth floor in Lowell, the hasty click of slim heels on Claverly's back stairs . . . all elements in a form story that could no longer be read with any interest. The authors were too sincere to make their work properly salacious and too inept to make it dramatic: The unhappy middle-ground was a tale of such self-pity and unconscionable mush that it was all one could do to get through it.

When William Bayer wrote *SEX: The Literary Breakthrough at Harvard Square,* he very well summed up the tired amusement most of us felt at the tide of purience and sentimental bunkum that had been washing over us for three or four years. As far as we were concerned, the Cambridge tale of surreptitious love and college law was the ultimate literary dead-end.

But we haven't seen one of the classic types for half a year and more now, and we must admit that we miss them. Like soap operas and westerns, they were a restfully predictable part of our reading life. The names changed, but never the characters, never the locale, and never the melancholy ending. It is hard to say what has become of them. They may be going outside, but then we can hardly believe that they will get a better reception anywhere else than they got from us. Or their authors may have turned to greater things. There have been rumours that a Cambridge novel, a compendium of all the best in the genre, is coming, but on the other hand, that is not only just a rumour but even if it is true, it doesn't explain the disappearance of a whole species.

The authors were not often people we knew nor ever heard from again once their work had been sent back, but we developed an affection for them. No one could look on the shuddering misery of the Cambridge tale and not feel some kind of sympathy for the soul who wrote it. We suppose that most of them survived . . . horribly scarred but carrying on. Perhaps we even remembered some of the experiences longer than the authors themselves did. Once they had written them, they were probably done with, but what reader, recalling Paul, "who stood staring down into the icy waters of the Charles and longed to sink into their dark oblivion," could ever cross Larz Anderson again with quiet mind. Or who could ever again look up at the windows of Eliot House and not imagine that gazing down there might not be another Linda, "like a small animal, naked and blonde in the caressing sunlight." Perhaps we are getting old and sentimental, but we miss Linda.

For some time the ADVOCATE thought about collecting the Cambridge tales and publishing them in an anthology. But there was always the chance that we might have ourselves sued, and besides that, they were so unprintably bad. How is it then that they are often more memorable than stories that we did publish, stories in every way superior to them? It is hard to say, but none of us who read them will ever forget the descriptions of brick sidewalks in the snow, of hundreds and hundreds of cups of coffee at the Waldorf, of the hours of pleading and declining in the Common, or of the self-destroyers standing on the bridges and looking at themselves in their bathroom mirrors with a last comment that amounted to WHY?

No matter how base the appeal, the appeal was local and therefore less to be resisted than that of other bad stories. And the descriptions of Cambridge often had a lugubrious honesty that none of us could quite deny.

Now that we haven't seen one in so long, we begin to wish that our friends would start writing out their agonies again. (We cannot believe that they have given up having agonies.) We thought we could get along very well without the Cambridge stories a year or so ago, but now that they seem to have gone out of existence—out of the ADVOCATE existence in any case—we begin to feel a little neglected, and we also have begun to miss the rather pleasurable experience of recognition when an author makes a window seat at the Bick or the steps of Memorial Church or the basement of Sever (all places familiar to us and unromantic) the scene of the crucial episode in his life of disorientation and estrangement.

The anthology idea has been given up. It would hardly be fair to present such frank autobiography to the public for the little profit it would give us, but if we can get our Cambridge tales back again, we will be more appreciative. What a tragedy if the springs have all dried up.

Robert P. Fichter
Spring, 1960

Presidents and Pegasi of the *Advocate,* 1866–1966

(* denotes Pegasus, literary editor)